VICIMUS

JOURNALS AND LETTERS OF REGINALD VISCOUNT ESHER

REGINALD, VISCOUNT ESHER, 1907.
From an oil-painting by Edmond Brock.

[Frontispiece

JOURNALS AND LETTERS

OF

Reginald
Viscount Esher

EDITED BY

Maurice V. Brett

"LOYAL JE SERAI"

VOL. 2
1903-1910

IVOR NICHOLSON & WATSON
LIMITED · · · LONDON
MCMXXXIV

FIRST EDITION . . *November* 1934

Printed in Great Britain by
Hazell, Watson & Viney, Ltd., London and Aylesbury.

I DEDICATE THIS BOOK

TO THE DEAR MEMORY OF

REGINALD, VISCOUNT ESHER,

AND TO

ELEANOR ESHER,

WHOSE LOVE AND THOUGHTS WERE WOVEN TOGETHER

DURING A CONSTANT COMPANIONSHIP

OF FIFTY YEARS

Ruskin, discoursing on the Stones of Venice, remarked that restored history is of little more value than restored painting or architecture, and that the only history worth reading was written at the time of which it treats. He excepted such volumes of biography as contained letters, memoranda, and journals which had escaped destruction, declaring them to be unrestored portions of the fabric of a man's life, indispensable to the psychologist and the student. . . .

Cloud-cap't Towers.

REGINALD, VISCOUNT ESHER

1852.   Born June 30th.

1863–65.   Cheam School.

1865–70.   Eton College.

1870–77.   Cambridge University.

1878–85.   Private Secretary to Lord Hartington.

1879.   Married Eleanor, daughter of M. Van de Weyer.

1880–85.   M.P. for Penryn and Falmouth.

1886.   Offered Editorship of *Daily News*.   (Refused.)

1891.   Offered Editorship of *New Review*.   (Refused.)

1895–1902.   Secretary to H.M. Office of Works.

1897.   C.B.

1898.   Asked to write Life of Disraeli.   (Refused.)

1899.   Offered Under-Secretaryship for the Colonies.   (Refused.)

1900.   Offered Under-Secretaryship for War.   (Refused.)
Offered Governorship of Cape Colony.   (Refused.)
K.C.V.O.

1901.   Hon. Secretary to Committee for Queen Victoria's Memorial.
Lieutenant and Deputy-Governor of Windsor Castle.

1902.   K.C.B.
Member of Royal Commission on South African War.

1903.   Director of the Opera.
Co-Editor of *Queen Victoria's Letters*.
Offered Secretaryship of State for War.   (Refused.)
Commissioner of the Exhibition of 1851.

1904.   Chairman of War Office Reconstitution Committee.

1905.   G.C.V.O.
Commander of the Legion of Honour.

1905. Permanent Member of the Committee of Imperial Defence.
Offered G.C.B. (Refused.)

1906. Royal Trustee to the British Museum.
Chairman of Committee to organise Territorial Army.

1907. Governor of the Imperial College of Science.
Trustee of the Wallace Collection.

1908. Offered Viceroyship of India. (Refused.)
G.C.B.

1909. Chairman of the County of London Territorial Force Association.

1910. Chairman of Board of Management of Exhibition of 1851.

1911. Trustee of London Museum.

1912. President of the County of London Territorial Force Association.
Chairman of Executive Committee of the British School at Rome.

1914. LL.D. Cambridge.

1919. D.L. St. Andrews.
Chairman of Committee on Organisation of Indian Army.

1922. Privy Councillor.

1928. Governor of Windsor Castle.

1930. Died January 22nd.

N.B.—He was also offered and refused an Earldom, but as the date is uncertain it has been omitted.

LIST OF ILLUSTRATIONS

JOURNALS AND LETTERS

VOL. II

[*To M. V. B.*]   BROOKS'S CLUB,
                                                     JULY 14TH.

. . . Edith Castlereagh [1] is at the point of death. She had a cold, took a turkish bath on Saturday, and went for a motor drive afterwards. Now she is probably dying of double pneumonia. She is so strong and healthy that her chances are *worse* than those of a weaker and more nervous person would be with this particular illness. They all lean on Millie [Sutherland] who brought her up. Castlereagh is hopelessly broken-down. It will be a tragedy if she dies.

I wrote to the P. of Wales to-day, to tell him how lovely the Ball was, and how far prettier than anything I ever remember in London. This is not flattery. It was in my mind prettier than the Devonshire House Ball in 1897.

[*To M. V. B.*]   ORCHARD LEA,
                                                     JULY 15TH.

. . . I had a busy day. Mowatt,[2] with whom I lunched, told *Cabinet* me that yesterday's cabinet was very stormy, and that the Duke *Split on* of Devonshire plainly indicated his intention to adhere to his old *Tariff* principles of free trade. Ritchie, George Hamilton and London- *Reform.* derry with Balfour of Burleigh, go with him—so this session would break up the Government. Also, he told me, at the Opera, the King had said to Ritchie that he would not consent

[1] Now Lady Londonderry.   [2] Sir Francis Mowatt.

to a tax on the food of the people. It was wrong of Ritchie to repeat this.

I told Knollys that the King should ask Arthur [Balfour]—without mentioning names—to state to his colleagues that it has always been understood that the Sovereign's remarks to a Minister should be most carefully safeguarded—otherwise confidence is impossible. And you can readily imagine the mischief of dragging the Monarch into such a political controversy as this, when feeling runs high.

Chamberlain would have every right to complain, and *might* be exceedingly vindictive.

Queen Victoria's Letters.

I wrote to the Archbishop, and asked him to see me on Friday, to discuss the proposal that the Life of the Queen up to 1861 should be written. I shall tell him that it is not possible to make anything of the subject. The ground has been so often covered. What *can* be done, is to publish "selections" from her papers and letters, up to that date. In such a scheme I would co-operate, but a "Life" would be a failure from the literary and public points of view.

I shall suggest Arthur Benson or R. Prothero as a collaborator with me. Either would do. Georgie Dudley has asked me to Pembroke Lodge for Sunday to meet the King—but I have refused. I cannot be away another Sunday.

The reconstruction of Mr. Balfour's government on account of the Tariff Reform controversy took the following course. The resignations of Mr. Chamberlain (Colonial Sec.), Mr. Ritchie (Chancellor of Exchequer), and Lord George Hamilton (Sec. for India) were announced on Sept. 18th; those of Lord Balfour of Burleigh (Sec. for Scotland) and Mr. Arthur Elliott (Financial Sec. to the Treasury) on Sept. 21st. The speech at Sheffield in which the Prime Minister laid down the fiscal principles on which the Conservative Government would act was delivered on Sept. 30th. On the 6th of October the more important transfers and new ministerial appointments were announced, which were:

Colonial Secretary, Alfred Lyttelton:
Chancellor of Exchequer, Austen Chamberlain:

> Sec. for India, St. John Brodrick:
> Sec. for Scotland, Graham Murray:
> War Office, Mr. Arnold-Forster.

On the same day the additional resignation of the Duke of Devonshire from the office of Lord President of the Council was announced. The letters exchanged between him and the Prime Minister were published on the 7th and are alluded to in these papers on that day. The Duke of Devonshire was replaced by Lord Londonderry, who was in turn replaced as Lord Privy Seal by the young Lord Salisbury.

[*To* M. V. B.]　　　　　　　2, TILNEY ST.,
　　　　　　　　　　　　　　　　JULY 16TH.

. . . I was at Buckingham Palace most of the morning, passing the work to be done for the Queen's memorial this autumn. Also the work within the Palace itself.

Generally mopping up before Scotland. Here (I am writing *Tariff* you from the city) the only topic is the Chamberlain Campaign. *Reform.* No one can possibly foretell how it will go. If there are two or three bad years of trade, I think Joe will win, as everyone will be anxious to try a new scheme. If, on the other hand, the years are prosperous, the feeling will be to let well alone!!

Anyhow, *argument* will never settle the question. There is too much to be said on both sides.

[*To* M. V. B.]　　　　　　　2, TILNEY ST.,
　　　　　　　　　　　　　　　　JULY 17TH.

I have been all the morning at Buckingham Palace discussing the King's arrangements for the Autumn, and endeavouring to see how the deuce he can have his house full of decorators, and live in it—at intervals—during the work.

Monarchs are not easy to provide for, they differ so wholly in their wants and habits from ordinary mortals.

Then, I saw Gladys de Grey, who is very rash—I think—in borrowing motors for the Queen's use on Sunday.

It is all very well, but some day she will get the wrong kind of chauffeur and there will be an accident.

. . . To-night I dine with the Archbishop.

[*To Lord Knollys.*]   ORCHARD LEA,
                                        JULY 17TH.

Editors for the Queen's Letters.

I had a long talk with the Archbishop upon the two points which you discussed with me.

1. He agrees that a "Life" of the Queen, on the usual lines, would not be suitable; that the ground has been covered before; and that except for an instalment of a longer and fuller book, coming down to recent times (which is out of the question) it would not be read; that Memories "pour servir" in the shape of the "Correspondence of Queen Victoria from 1837–1861" is what is required, connected, more or less by notes and introductory passages.

2. As to editorship—that Roland Prothero would not accept the task, as he is engaged in other and lucrative pursuits; that even if he would, Arthur Benson would be superior to him; more capable, more suitable and more trustworthy; and it would be desirable, perhaps necessary, that I should be associated with him in the joint editing of the book.

Arthur Benson leaves Eton at Xmas, and is looking for literary work. He will return to Eton possibly as Head Master later; but he will have a few years probation and rest.

Now what is the next step?

Will you speak to the King, and if H.M. approves, and you will let me know, I will privately ascertain if—*in the event of the suggestion being made*—Arthur Benson would consent to undertake the work.

That is, possibly, the best thing to do. Will you let me know?

[*To M. V. B.*] ORCHARD LEA,
JULY 18TH.

. . . I got home about 1.30 this morning. Lambeth was beautiful. So very impressive. The house occupied by Laud and Cranmer. The robes of Cardinal Pole. The series of portraits unbroken—by the greatest artists.

They are not in very good order, and want thoroughly looking to.

The Primate has to keep up Lambeth at his own expense, so *Lambeth* the necessary work only is done. No extras! This is not right, *Palace.* as the Palace is a National possession. An Archbishop lives, in these days, very simply, in this great house, which was built for a court like Wolsey's. Still, everything was very well done. After dinner he took me to his library, and we sat there and discussed the Queen's papers, and what should be done to prepare certain of them for publication.

. . . I wrote to the King and told him of the gist of our talk. I think he will probably agree to our suggestion. Altogether I had a very pleasant evening, with the most unaffected and one of the shrewdest of men.

[*To the Archbishop of Canterbury.*] 2, TILNEY ST.,
JULY 27TH.

I had a long talk with Arthur Benson yesterday, and he seemed to be captivated by the idea. He is to let me know definitely in a day or two, and if his reply is in the affirmative he is to see Murray, the publisher.

I told him that the King's wish was to publish the "Correspondence of Queen Victoria from 1837–1861," edited by him and by me; a joint Editorship.

We discussed the nature of the book, that I hope may be published on precisely the same lines which you were good enough to lay down and agree to at Lambeth.

The King quite approves of all the details as to method; i.e. not much criticism nor appreciation, but copious extracts tacked together by notes and explanations.

Lockhart's *Life of Scott* remains, I think, the most perfect example of what such a book should be, and we could not do better than take it as a model.

Probably the portion of the Queen's life with which we should deal, would occupy two volumes. I trust that you will approve of the arrangements so far as we have got.

I will let you know when I hear from Arthur Benson.

I hope to call at Lambeth with Haines on Tuesday or Wednesday.

[*To M. V. B.*]   THE ROMAN CAMP,
                                    AUGUST 3RD.

The King
in Ireland.   . . . I have just written to the King and congratulated him on the success of the Irish visit. After centuries of ill-feeling, he has —for the first time—made an impression on both nations—and has drawn them together.

The attitude of the Catholic Bishops and priests is a revelation, and if the King perseveres, he might bring about the pacification of Ireland.

I am reading rather an interesting book about an Italian princess of Mantua. Her letters and correspondence—about the years 1490–1510. It is all modern. The letters to her might have been written last week. She was a very clever woman, and intimate with all sorts of interesting people—Raphael, Michael Angelo, the Borgias, etc. etc.[1]

. . . I feel already the flow of poetic sentiment, which comes so rarely over one in the south. In the hills the spirit hovers like a hawk.

[1] This was probably the first volume of *Isabella d'Este, Marchioness of Mantua, 1473–1539: a Study of the Renaissance*, by Julia Cartwright: 2 Vols. Murray, 1903.

[*To M. V. B.*]　　　　　　　　THE ROMAN CAMP,
　　　　　　　　　　　　　　　　AUGUST 4TH.

. . . Yesterday we went to Strathyre, in the afternoon. There was a slight mist, but we crossed the burn, and went up the hill a short way, and there lay in the heather, and I read Crabbe! He is not really a very bad poet. It is a gentle meandering style, which is not unpleasant. I am taking the new Ruskin—in 30 volumes! I have finished the first two. His early poems, 7 and 9, are queer; and the later ones, 14 to 18, wonderfully good.

[*To M. V. B.*]　　　　　　　　THE ROMAN CAMP,
　　　　　　　　　　　　　　　　AUGUST 5TH.

Yesterday I was for seven hours alone on the Stronetrican. It was a day alternating between high gusts of wind and driving clouds, with flashes of sunshine in between. There were red hinds with some young stags lying on the eastern face of the hill. Young grouse rose with difficulty as they were disturbed by the dogs. I fished occasionally, and got thirteen trout in about a quarter of a mile of burn, all below the little bridge opposite the shepherd's house, where we strike the burn as we walk over from our moor. Then I read.

. . . I have sent the King the Report of the Commission *The King's* privately, and wonder what he will think of it. How well he has *First Year.* done since his accession. There is so much praise of him, that he might almost have an access of "swelled head." If he is not a little affected by all the kudos in the papers, he really is a wonder.

Of course, like all popular favour, it is worth nothing and is blown away by the first breath of adverse breeze. The election of a new Pope is dramatically told this morning. It has always been thus, the selection of an unknown man, at least during the past 3 centuries. From all accounts the choice is a good one.

[*To M. V. B.*]   THE ROMAN CAMP,
                                           AUGUST 5TH AND 6TH.

I brought with me here Macaulay's essays, which I have not
looked at for years. They are so despairingly good, that to read
them makes one marvel that men should be found sufficiently
vain to go on writing books. The same sort of feeling comes
over one after reading Scott and Stevenson. Macaulay covered
such an immense area of ground, and the average man gets all
he wants from these essays, upon every subject touched upon.
And yet, any new driveller who writes about Byron or Cromwell or Frederick the Great, is read by people who never open
Macaulay.

The longer I live the more sure I am, that the best educated
man is he who reads the fewest books, always provided they are
first-rate ones.

[*To M. V. B.*]   THE ROMAN CAMP,
                                                 AUGUST 9TH.

A year ago to-day, we were together from early dawn till eve
at the King's crowning. You probably remember every detail.
I only recollect that it was all very solemn and splendid. . . .

. . . I have just finished *Midshipman Easy*—so fresh and charming, and so absolutely as it used to be when I was a child. It is
full of immortal truths of English boyhood—and so never can
be out of date, so long as England is England.

[*To M. V. B.*]   THE ROMAN CAMP,
                                                AUGUST 23RD.

It is a terrible curse not to possess imagination, not to be
moved by the great works of those who have gone before, and
not to love, intensely, the right people. To be able to clothe

your thoughts with those of others, and your loves with your own, is the greatest of all blessings.

[*To the Duchess of Sutherland.*]   THE ROMAN CAMP,
SEPTEMBER 4TH.

... I have met Arnold-Forster,[1] a pale-eyed determined look-ing fellow, with enough earnestness to carry him far. Different from the usual type of Conservative statesman. If he possesses health he ought to do well. John Morley, with whom I lunched one day at the Carlton, told me that Arnold-Forster is not quite of truly tempered steel, and he may be right—but then his looks belie him. Morley's book is astonishingly good. One would suppose that it would contain, indeed was bound to contain, long interludes of dull matter, but this is not the case, and I hardly skipped any of it. Certainly Mr. Gladstone issues from the press a mightier figure than I ever expected, in spite of his failures. A splendid specimen of the indomitable fighter—whether the cause were good or bad. A man who never doubted but that he was infallible. There is one page, containing an esti-mate of Dizzy, most remarkable coming from Morley, so warmly, so appreciatively fair.

Mr. H. O. Arnold-Forster.

Morley's Gladstone.

We tried to find, among English literary men, a successor to the "Order of Merit" worn by Lecky—but failed. Can you make a suggestion? What a death!

If you have a moment presently, send me a line, just to say that you are well, and happy in the highlands—that beloved land.

Did I tell you that I was building a small chapel over our Loch, as a final resting-place. It stands on a rock command-ing such a view—with a sheer fall—and the great hill of Ben Ledi behind it. Not a bad place in which to await the great mysteries. ...

[1] At this time Secretary to the Admiralty.

[*To M. V. B.*]   THE ROMAN CAMP,
SEPTEMBER 7TH.

*A Board
for the
Army.*

. . . After I wrote to you yesterday, I had a long talk with Amery[1] and we planned out the Army Board scheme. I think the little man was very much amused at the family. He thought us all more or less loony. He went off at 3 via Dunblane.

. . . I had a long letter from Knollys in which he says that the King has returned from Marienbad strongly in favour of a Board for the Army, and has spoken already to Balfour, who assured him that the Cabinet would carefully and seriously take up the question. But of this I hae me doots. Knollys says nothing about the C.-in-C. question, which looks as if the King were not so strong on that point. If they fail to tackle that question, they may just as well leave the W.O. as it is; for the Board would be a farce.

[*To M. V. B.*]   THE ROMAN CAMP,
SEPTEMBER 12TH.

*Chesterton
on
Browning.*

Chat [Williamson] sent me, as a present, Chesterton's essay on Robert Browning. You remember some short essays by him which were clever and amusing, and full of quaint paradox. This study of Browning is also chock full of cleverness, and is often too clever by half; I mean that truth is sacrificed to epigram. Still, there are many things in the book, and I have marked them all, which I think you will enjoy reading. "Our wisdom, whether expressed in private or in public, belongs to the world, but our folly belongs to those we love." "Strafford was something greater than this; if, indeed, when we come to think of it, a man can be anything greater than the friend of another man."

I quote these in order to whet your appetite, as the book awaits you. There are a great many good stories scattered about it,

---

[1] Rt. Hon. L. S. Amery.

many of which will make you laugh. The chapter dealing with Browning's elopement with Elizabeth Barrett is very well written.

Still, the author suffers from his cleverness, and often it is impossible to tell whether he speaks ironically of the poems, or in serious earnest; especially when he is discussing the "dramatic lyrics," which he seems to praise, at the expense of other poets, after a fashion which I think you will agree they scarcely merit.

[*To M. V. B.*]   THE ROMAN CAMP,
                                      SEPTEMBER 16TH.

... I wrote for Barrie's key, on the ground that he was the lineal descendant in Scottish literature to the peasant Burns, and that an exception ought to be made for him. I told Pom [McDonnell] that in making such an exception, he would be showing a finer appreciation than Dunbar ever displayed towards Burns, or Mr. Gladstone towards Stevenson. So perhaps this flattery may have the desired effect. Personally I think it would have been far easier to get the little man a Baronetcy than a key to Kensington Gardens.

Barrie and Kensington Gardens.

... The pathos of Burns's life, the pity of it, is almost more than one can bear. Wonderful talents, much that was noblest in ideas and mind, and everything ruined by interference, and a sort of devilish haunting wrong-headedness. Genius enough to have made him the happiest of men, instead of one of the most miserable. In order to make the balance even, Providence blessed him with immortal gifts, and cursed him with the weakest will ever man had. However, luckily the *man* will be forgotten, long long before his songs cease to be sung by Scottish women to their children, and by lads to their beloved ones.

His Majesty has asked Akers-Douglas to come to Balmoral to meet me. He is very favourable to the "Board" scheme, and the King likes him. I don't know how long I shall be at Balmoral.

It depends upon these discussions. In any case I expect to be in London on Wednesday week—if not sooner.

. . . I observe that Seymour Hicks' name is not in the bills, so I am afraid he must be very unwell still. I shall be glad to hear how he is, if you chance to see him or Ella. I am writing to her, but she is not good at answering letters, although in other respects she is the type of what a woman *can* be, who has been tried in the fire and not found wanting.

How few there are. When I look back on all those whom I have loved, men and women, there are not more than three, two men and one woman, who have never by word or deed proved false. Outside this category are you and Nellie. But in others, there has always been something, some little rift, which is fatal to the music of perfect affection. You may think that the fault lies with me, for putting the standard of friendship too high —but it is worth it, for the sake of those who never, by a hairsbreadth, depart from it.

And yet, one lays a great deal of pain up for oneself, by creating gods of flesh and blood—idealising the imperfect. That is what I suppose the cynic would say; but the world would be a poor place, if it were impossible to fix one's heart upon a friend or a beloved one, and vest them with the noblest qualities, truth, perfect confidence, fidelity, absolute candour, and yet feel certain that under no circumstances would deception follow.

These are the conditions under which I have ever embarked, and only in the three cases I have mentioned has the ideal been realised. But it has been worth it.

[*To M. V. B.*]   THE ROMAN CAMP,
                                                 SEPTEMBER 17TH.

. . . If I get a key of Kensington Gardens for Barrie, I shall send it to him with that quotation from M. Arnold, written in

Kensington Gardens, which ought to appeal to the author of *Peter Pan*.

> Calm soul of all things! make it mine
> To feel, amid the city's jar,
> That there abides a peace of thine
> Man did not make, and cannot mar.

You will enjoy the volume of M. Arnold. It is very well done, and full of lovely lines, picked here and there from his poems.

[*To M. V. B.*]　　　　　THE ROMAN CAMP,
　　　　　　　　　　　　SEPTEMBER 18TH.

. . . On Monday I go to Balmoral, starting early, so if by chance you write to me on Sunday, address your letter there. It may happen that I shall not return here. One never can tell, when once in the King's clutches. It should be interesting there, what with the Army discussions, and the reconstitution of the Government. I hope we shall not have too much deer driving. That is rather a narrow plank. This is the King's first Ministerial crisis since his accession—and I am rather glad of the chance to see how he conducts it; having read private accounts of nearly every crisis of the Queen's reign in her letters and papers. *Ministerial Crisis.*

. . . What news in the papers! I suppose Chamberlain could hardly have done otherwise, but it seems a pity. Of course, if he *can*, by exciting the sympathy of the Colonies, create a Zollverein, he will rank next to Mr. Pitt among British statesmen. As Pitt saved England (the Empire?) from Napoleon, so will he have saved it from a disruption which is inevitable unless fiscal unity is established. However, he will have a hard fight. It looks as if the opportunity might be taken to get rid of Brodrick, and I fervently hope that this may be the case. Perhaps he will go to the India Office, and then Douglas or A. Chamberlain might go to the W.O. I hope the King will use all his influence to bring this about. I suppose A. Balfour will take the Exchequer him- *On Chamberlain's Policy.*

self, and probably Selborne will go from the Admiralty to the Colonies. However, we shall know all this in a few days.

[*To M. V. B.*] BALMORAL CASTLE,
SEPTEMBER 21ST.

Offer of the War Office.

If it is only a few lines, I must write to you to-night. Directly I got here, the King sent for me, and I had no sooner kissed his hand, than he asked me to be one of his Ministers, and spoke of the W.O. Of course I was taken aback, and put several objections, which are obvious, and finally said that I would think it over. Certainly I shall refuse. It is not in my line to go back into politics and become identified with party strife. Just imagine what the tie would be, night and day at the W.O.

I am purely selfish in the matter, and I really do not think that I can bring myself to sacrifice all independence, all liberty of action, all my "intime" life, for a position which adds nothing to that which I now occupy. At least that is how it strikes me at first. Arthur Balfour, I suppose, will speak to me to-morrow. He said nothing to-night, but had no chance.

... 22.9.03. The night has brought no counsel and I can only foresee two or three days of worry. However, "I am a fatalist," as I have often heard you say, so I will put the thing away.

Cabinet Reconstruction.

Brodrick, anyhow, goes to the India Office. None of the other places are filled yet. Arthur Balfour, Lansdowne and A. Douglas are here. I suggested to the King that Balfour himself should become Ch. of the Ex. which is the right thing under the present circumstances. It is so often held with the Premiership. But I fancy that part of the bargain with Joe is that Austen Chamberlain shall go there. Otherwise, *he* would be a first-rate War Minister. I also suggested transferring Selborne from the Admiralty to the W.O. The King talked very freely, and evidently enjoys a "crisis." It is his first political scramash! He has gone down a stone in weight, and looks very well.

[*To M. V. B.*]   BALMORAL CASTLE,
SEPTEMBER 22ND.

We started at 10 very sharp to-day in the King's motor, and drove to Birk Hall. There we met the P. of Wales and walked up into the woods, the King riding his pony. We did not get back until past six this evening. We had four drives altogether, and as usual I had all the luck. I got three stags, and one of them a good one. However, the King got one in the last drive; so all was well. I walked a good deal with the P. of Wales, who asked how you are getting on, and was generally charming as he always is!

When we got home, we had an Army meeting in Knollys' room to prepare notes for the meeting of the King with A. Balfour to-morrow. The King wanted a "brief" and we got one for him. No further progress has been made with the Government—Milner having, I believe, refused to take the Colonial Office. They were waiting for a telegram all day, which has now arrived; and from what I gathered, it is a refusal. There is a very unpleasant row on between Hedworth [Lambton] and Hunter, about something the latter said in his evidence about the naval guns at Ladysmith.[1] Hedworth has written a most violent letter to the Admiralty, to say that if he does not get an apology he will resign his command. It is a very foolish letter, I hear, and it has been concealed from the King.

. . . 23.9.03. The Grand Duke Michael came here last night —and does not add much to the pleasure of anybody. How-

---

[1] Lt.-Gen. Sir Archibald Hunter, before the Elgin Commission, 13th February, 1903: "Our gun laying in the Army, judging by comparison and so on, is infinitely better than the gun laying in the Navy. I know I am treading on delicate ground when I criticise naval gunnery, but I say, and I know that it will not be contradicted by a great many men who were in Ladysmith, that the naval gunnery . . . left everything to be desired. . . . The practice made with the naval 4.7's . . . was such that I offered to take the girls out of the school to come and serve the guns, and make as good practice."

This statement was read to Admiral Lambton at the sitting of the Commission on Mar. 17th; and he had replied to it in full on that date.

ever, the King is in excellent spirits. They get no forrader with their Cabinet. I believe Alfred Milner has refused to join them. I cannot imagine why, as he must be in cordial agreement upon all questions. They *must* settle to-day what they propose to do. The King says that we are to have a *dies non*—i.e. no sport, and are to muddle at Cabinet making and Army reforming all day!

[*To M. V. B.*]   BALMORAL CASTLE,
                                             SEPTEMBER 24TH.

*Refusal of
the War
Office.*

The Prime Minister put the thing very plainly to me yesterday. We had a long talk. I told him that I was sure it would be a mistake, that I was not a politician, that I could not undertake to ally myself to a party, and that although I might go into his Government for a while, in order to reorganise the W.O. I could not undertake to get up other questions, and go to public meetings and support the Government—still less, could I undertake, later on, to work for the party in opposition. I said I would think it over until to-day, and now I propose to tell him that I really *cannot* undertake to be Sec. of State. I propose on the other hand to recommend A. Douglas. (Sent for by A. Balfour.)

The Prime Minister has just shown me a telegram to Chamberlain, in which he proposes definitely that I should be Sec. of State and asked me whether the message should go. So I made my counter proposal, which is that Douglas should be Sec. of State, and that he should appoint Commissioners to carry out the W.O. changes—the Commissioners to be myself, Fisher,[1] and Brackenbury.[2]

*Arguments
about the
War
Office—*

I am sure that this would be the best plan, and would relieve

[1] Sir John Fisher, afterwards Admiral of the Fleet, Lord Fisher of Kilverstone, at this date in command of Portsmouth Harbour.

[2] Gen. the Rt. Hon. Sir Henry Brackenbury, at this date Director-General of Ordnance at the War Office.

the public mind, while not imposing upon me the horrible burdens of the War Department. However, I begin to fear that I may be squeezed into the place, although I shall fight till the last gasp. I don't really think that life would be worth living.

Of course, it is all a horrid worry. I am anxious to do all I can for the country and for the King and for Arthur—but I cannot be sure that I *could* be of any practical use as Sec. of State.

I am too bothered to write at length, and I don't remember ever to have gone through a more unpleasant time.

[*From Lord Rosebery.*] DALMENY,
SEPTEMBER 24TH.

MY DEAR R.

I hope this note is not an impertinence. But there is a rumour in the papers to-day that you are going to the War Office, and I cannot help writing to express my earnest hope that it is not true. Forgive me if I have said too much.

Yours ever,
A. R.

[*To M. V. B.*] BALMORAL CASTLE,
SEPTEMBER 24TH.
EVENING.

I am not having a good time here. The meshes are closing round me, and although I have suggested an opening, as I told you, which Arthur Balfour has partially agreed to, nevertheless I feel that the fates may decide otherwise.

He has telegraphed to his colleagues laying before them two proposals. First, that I shall be Sec. of State, and secondly that Douglas shall be Sec. of State, with myself, Fisher and Brackenbury to reorganise the W.O.

The latter is my proposal. If his colleagues reject this alternative, which I pray will not be the case, I shall be placed in a dreadful difficulty—and hoist with my own petard—my accursed Report! You will see that having made these proposals for W.O. reform, I cannot honourably refuse, if asked by the P.M. and the King—to try and carry them out.

I shall, however, if the worst comes to the worst—make three stipulations. One, that although I shall vote in support of the Government on all other questions, I shall not be expected to speak for them. Secondly, that I shall attend to my Department, and not be expected to speak in the country or elsewhere—or attend banquets! And finally, that if the Government goes out, I may retire into private life, and take no part in opposition.

Perhaps these are stipulations which will choke them off. Anyhow, they are *final* with me. Is it not a piece of bad luck, that I, who loathe "public life" should be dragged into it? I feel ill and depressed, and the glory has gone out even of the hills. I have walked alone all the afternoon in the woods—and meditated on our quiet, happy secluded life.

25.9.03. I wish I could have heard from you this morning, as I want some fresh air—but the night has brought counsel and I am determined to tell Arthur this morning that I cannot take office in his Government and embark again on political life. I will act as Chairman of a Board to reorganise the W.O. Beyond that I will not go. I am *sure* I am right.

In the political office I shall fail to satisfy anyone, quarrel with the King, and find myself in much the same position as Brodrick. We go deer driving to-day, and to-morrow early, I go off home.

[*To the Rt. Hon. A. J. Balfour.*]   BALMORAL CASTLE,
SEPTEMBER 25TH.

—and Final Refusal.   I am sure that it will simplify your task or clear the air if I say at once that I cannot—under any circumstances—be Sec. of State.

We are too intimate for us to depart one iota from perfect frankness, and I *know* that as Sec. of State I should fail in the double capacity as a servant of the King and as your colleague.

Political office is abhorrent to me, and I have not the qualifications for it.

On the other hand, if you think it right to adopt the plan of appointing, under your supervision and that of the Sec. of State, a Board of three, of whom I should be the Chairman, to carry out the W.O. reorganisation—I will do all in my power to help you. This is a very different form of work, and I feel I could do it.

I shall never forget all your confidence and kindness, but perhaps this—after 25 years of friendship—is not worth saying.

[*To H.M. the King.*]   BALMORAL CASTLE,
                                          SEPTEMBER 25TH.

Lord Esher presents his humble duty, and begs to say that, the more he reflects, the more certain he is, that he cannot successfully and to the satisfaction of Your Majesty—become connected with a Political Party, and take even the highest political office.

He is deeply grateful to Your Majesty, but he knows his own limitations, and he feels sure that his abilities and training are not such as to qualify him for high political office, and especially for political controversy. . . .

But it is on public grounds, and especially as a faithful and devoted servant and subject of Your Majesty that Lord Esher, while always ready to devote himself to any task which is within his power and capacity, cannot undertake an office in which he is confident that he would fail to give Your Majesty satisfaction.

Lord Esher writes this, as he thought perhaps Your Majesty would like to speak about it when on the hill to-day.

[*To M. V. B.*]   BALMORAL CASTLE,
                                   SEPTEMBER 25TH.

I wrote this morning to the King and to Arthur [Balfour] after the prolonged talks yesterday—and my letters I have kept for you to see. Then we went for a deer drive—and I walked a long time with the King, who was very charming and friendly. We had a glorious day, but it was too hot for the deer to be in the woods.

This evening I saw Arthur and Douglas again—but had been fortified by your letter and telegram.

Then the King sent for Arthur, and afterwards for me. This was the most trying interview of all, and he was pathetic and entreating. If it had not been for your letter I really think I might have given way. But I was firm, and finally the King admitted that perhaps I might be right.

Arthur was quite sweet to me to-night, so all has ended well. At any rate, I had the offer of one of the supreme offices in the State, at a very critical time, which is more than most people can say! I don't know whether it gives you any satisfaction! It has certainly spoilt my visit here. I am writing to you at 2 a.m. (very late) and leave here early to-morrow.

[*To M. V. B.*]   BALMORAL CASTLE,
                                   SEPTEMBER 26TH.

I am leaving Balmoral, I believe and hope, at peace with the King and with Arthur [Balfour]. That they are both disappointed I am sure, but I am equally sure that they are not so disappointed as they would have been, a few months hence, if I had accepted that offer.

It is impossible to add anything to the argument which you have expounded in your dear letter. There is not a word too much said by you, and I do not regret having put aside the temptation. You may say, for of course there can be no secret about it, that when offered Sec. of State I declined it because I felt sure I could not do any good there. That is the best explanation to give.

If Douglas goes there, which I sincerely hope he will do, and if he appoints that commission or committee of three to *carry out* the reform, I think something effectual may be done.

We "drove" all yesterday—a lovely day. I was all the time with the King; walking by his pony and chatting. He was perfectly charming. It was a delightful day, but no sport. There are no live animals here but deer. Not a bird. Except, however, *eagles*! I saw three to-day, splendid ones, hovering and wheeling. Did I tell you that I had been to Abergeldie, and had a walk with the Princess of Wales, who was very friendly and "intime."

[*To M. V. B.*]   THE ROMAN CAMP,
                                        SEPTEMBER 27TH.

Here I am back safe, and very glad to be among our own sweet and quiet hills.

. . . The King said: "Tell Maurice never to remain long in *one groove*! Tell him that is the mistake all soldiers make."

. . . He laughed a good deal over your journal.

[*To H.M. the King.*]   THE ROMAN CAMP,
                                        SEPTEMBER 27TH.

Lord Esher, with humble duty, cannot refrain from expressing to Your Majesty once more his deep sense of Your Majesty's great kindness to him during the trying days of the past week. Lord Esher hopes never again to be put in a position where he cannot immediately obey any command which Your Majesty deigns to honour him with, and it was only his profound sense of duty to Your Majesty as Sovereign, which forced him, on this occasion, to put aside the high honour which Your Majesty suggested might be conferred upon him.

He feels confident that he acted for the best, and calmer examination of all the circumstances of the case only tends to confirm him that he can best serve Your Majesty's interests, and those of the country, in a position of less honour and dignity, but of greater practical effect, should Your Majesty see fit to entrust him with the duty.

That Your Majesty ever deigned to think him capable of discharging the great responsibilities of a Secretary of State will always be to Lord Esher the proudest and most cherished memory.

[*To Lord Knollys.*] THE ROMAN CAMP,
SEPTEMBER 27TH.

*P.M. on
the War
Office.*

The Prime Minister is going to refer to the War Office on Thursday in his speech, so I have put on paper for him the following notes, in order that he may realise fully what is proposed and why.

1. Ordinary business of the War Office cannot, pending reform, be carried on by a Minister who at the same time is engaged on reconstruction.

2. If a Minister reconstructs the War Office himself, he must neglect ordinary current business.

3. If he sticks to the necessary administrative work, then he must delegate reorganisation.

4. In the ordinary way, and under ordinary circumstances, reorganisation would be undertaken either by the permanent officials of the Department, or by a Departmental Committee of War Office and Treasury officials.

5. In the present case this is out of the question. It never would be stood by the public, nor would any reorganisation so undertaken be of value.

6. The alternative is to appoint a special commission under the supervision of the Prime Minister and the Secretary of State, to carry out the scheme of reorganisation based on the sugges-

tions made by the Royal Commission of 1889 (Hartington's), and 1902–3 (Elgin's).

I think this explains the scheme which the King favoured, and to which the Prime Minister agreed.

If this plan is adopted, and I am chairman of such a body, I shall propose to take the War Office Administration right through, from top to bottom, and endeavour to make it a first-class business machine; and do in short for the War Office as a whole what Treves is doing for the R.A.M.C. *W.O. Re-construction Committee.*

That would be the limit of our duty, and with questions of policy on the one hand, or of the Army as distinct from the War Office on the other, we should have no concern.

In such a capacity I feel sure I shall succeed, whereas in the other, so kindly suggested by the King and A. B., I should have failed.

I go south to-morrow, Monday night; 2, Tilney St., will always find me.

[*To M. V. B.*]   THE ROMAN CAMP,
                                  SEPTEMBER 27TH.
                                       EVENING.

This is our last day here, and the river looked so lovely especially this evening, with silvery lights under the overhanging trees, and the shadows of the Glen getting darker and darker as the sun slowly set.

. . . In leaving Scotland there is always a feeling of yearning, a kind of passion for the hills and the murmuring river (for it is murmuring deliciously over the stones to-day) comes over me, and makes me share your wonder why we cannot live peacefully and happily here, away from all the turmoil of the great hot feverish world. This can never be for me, until I am resting on the rock which overlooks the loch, parted from my beloved ones.

[*To the Rt. Hon. A. J. Balfour.*]   THE ROMAN CAMP,
SEPTEMBER 28TH.

*Position
of the
Govern-
ment.*

What brutes there are in the world! I read in *The Times* this
evening that "the rumours are that the Ministry are so dis-
credited that nobody is willing to join them," etc.

If this is in any way connected with what took place at Balmoral, will you make it clear, if you ever care to do so, as far as I
am concerned, that only a profound settled conviction that I
could better serve the King and you by undertaking the task of
assisting in W.O. Reform, prevented me from becoming more
closely associated with your Administration. And be damned
to them!

. . . I am leaving Scotland with tears to-night. How abominable is the south!

[*To M. V. B.*]   ORCHARD LEA,
OCTOBER 7TH.

*Balfour
and the
Duke of
Devonshire.*

. . . I wonder what you think of the newspapers this morning! The Duke strikes me as very dignified and altogether in the
"grand manner." Poor Arthur [Balfour] very peevish and
petulant. Not the sort of State paper which Dizzy or Mr. Gladstone would have written under similar circumstances. Evidently the whole thing, Chamberlain's resignation, etc., was an
intrigue and it has failed. As for the Government, I am glad not
to be of it, and your judgment was flawless. To be called a "stop
gap" is not pleasant. However, I hear that I am in disgrace at
Balmoral, that I am thought to have shirked my duty, and
to have been actuated by the charming motive of wishing
to reap all the credit and take none of the risk.

Is it not curious that men never allow anyone to be the
guardian of his own reputation and his own honour in politics.
However, this is only a squall, and will blow over; but had I gone

to the W.O. I should soon have been the middle of a most regal gale. It does not seem to be appreciated that I never asked to be on the War Commission. Indeed, I was reluctant to go on it— that having done my best, I was *insulted*! by being offered *political* office!

That is another point of view, which perhaps escapes men who live in political camps, but I am sorry that it should have escaped the King. However, I shall draw attention to these things.

[*To Sir William Harcourt.*]   ORCHARD LEA,
                                            OCTOBER 10TH.

Thank you for your letter, so full of cordial affection. I knew *Lord Esher* you would be interested and guessed you would approve the *and Sir* decision at which I ultimately arrived. It was, I thought then, *William Harcourt.* and still think, an exceedingly unfair position in which to place me. Not a member of their party, with no parliamentary train- ing, or special aptitude for controversial politics, I should not have been called upon to accept one of the highest offices of State, for which I do not feel myself qualified, or be left with a sense of having refused to undertake a great public duty.

Yet, this was my dilemma, and although I finally determined to put aside the offer, and to retain the haunting feeling of failure, I think the decision was justified by consideration of the mani- fold objections which there must be to entering an Administra- tion whose acts one is not ready to defend, and associating one- self with colleagues with whom one is not in agreement or sympathy.

Arthur [Balfour] of course, waved lightly away these scruples, but as I told him, this was easy for a friend of 20 years' standing; but I was bound to consider the feelings of his col- leagues, none of whom—except Douglas—I know well and the majority of whom I hardly know by sight. . . .

[*To M. V. B.*]   2, TILNEY ST.,
                                                 OCTOBER 11TH.

*The King
and Lord
Esher.*

I saw Francis Knollys this evening. He says that the King was vexed at my letter. I understand this. Kings never like opposition or remonstrance—even the best of them. Then we argued the whole question over again, and I explained once more my position. I pointed out that I was in reality the aggrieved person; that I had been put into a dilemma from which there was no satisfactory escape, and that although for the reasons which finally seemed overwhelming, I decided to refuse the W.O., yet I shall always be left with the feeling that I *may* have shirked a public duty. Knollys said that the King was undoubtedly angry at my refusal, but that he would get over it!

I am to see him to-morrow and perhaps the difficulty will be overcome. Meanwhile, I read Mr. Gladstone's life, and realise the solemn way in which Peel and the men of his day took these things. To go into the Cabinet was a kind of sacrament.

12.10.03. Saw the King to-day. He was cold at first. There was a lot of business to transact, and we walked in the garden with Redesdale and McDonnell for an hour or more. Gradually he seemed to thaw, asked me to sit, and then began! He reiterated all his grievances, that I had shirked my duty, that Milner had behaved badly also, that now he had Arnold-Forster "forced on him," etc., etc. I said very little, for it seemed useless to argue when really the whole thing is a question of "feeling."

*Personnel
of the
Esher
Committee.*

Then he came to the practical question of a committee to re-organise the W.O. Upon this he has given way unasked, and sees that A.-Forster had better *not* be upon it—that Fisher, a soldier and I could do the job. We discussed at length Brackenbury and Clarke,[1] and I inclined to the former. Finally he became quite his old self, and I kissed his hand, and everything is made up. Meanwhile he asked me to write his views to Arthur [Balfour].

[1] Sir George Clarke, afterwards Lord Sydenham, and at this date Governor of Victoria.

13.10.03. I saw Jack Sandars,[1] and explained to him the King's views. He will write fully to Arthur. I drafted the reference to the Committee which must state that the *Principles* of my memo. are adopted. Left, to work out the details. This I ought to be able to do by Xmas.

14.10.03. Saw the King again this morning. He had given the seals to A.-Forster. I don't think he disliked him. I said to him, "Sir, one nearly always gets on better with a man whom one is convinced is impossible, than with someone from whom everything is hoped for"—and this is true of all Sovereigns! I did not add the last words! The King was very kind and amiable and frank. He told me that Donoughmore, a young man of 25, had been proposed to him as Under Sec. for the W.O. This is rather a strong order, as this young man will be a member of the Board or Council. However, the method of giving places in this Government is wholly irresponsible. The names might as well be taken out of a hat! I suggested Mansfield, but am pretty sure that it is too late.[2]

As I said before, to men of the Peel and Gladstone type the duties of the State were religious functions of the highest moment. Modern Ministers " pick up " a Government much as an "eleven " would be picked up at school.

I am all the more convinced that I acted wisely in refusing to be Sec. of State.

Now, I think that I shall carry through my scheme, whereas as Sec. of State, I doubt if I should have done so. It is the old story—Power and Place are not often synonymous.

[*From Sir William Harcourt.*]   MALWOOD,
                                                            OCTOBER 12TH.

DEAR REGGY,

I was very glad to receive your letter. You know that for 30 years I have taken a deep interest in all that concerns your wel-

---

[1] Private Secretary to the Prime Minister.
[2] Lord Donoughmore was in fact appointed.

fare, which you have always richly returned by most affectionate kindness.

I think the decision you have arrived at was conclusively justified by the considerations stated in your letter. I think you
ought not to allow your mind to be disturbed by any sense of
failure to undertake a public duty. For this I can see no cause
whatever.

Your affect.,
W. V. HARCOURT.

[*To M. V. B.*]   ORCHARD LEA,
OCTOBER 19TH.

*The King
and the
War
Office.*

Went to Buckingham Palace this morning, and the King sent
for me. He was in the Belgian room, having just held a Council.
He told me that he had written to Arthur Balfour expressing a
desire that the War Office Committee should be nominated at
once, by the P.M. and not by the Sec. of State, that I should be
the Chairman, and Fisher and Brackenbury the other members.
He complained of procrastination on the part of the Ministers.
He was in one of his most business-like moods, and saw the
importance of getting the change in War Office Administration into working shape *before* Parliament meets. In that,
everything lies.

As I left him, I walked through the room where the Alaskan
Commission, headed by Lansdowne, was waiting an audience.
In the afternoon I saw Sandars, who had telephoned asking to
see me. He told me two unpleasant things.

*Difficulties
over the
Committee.*

1. That Fisher is being urged by the Admiralty *not* to go on
the Committee. That comes of talking too much about a thing
not settled, and of procrastination.

2. That there were serious objections to Brackenbury. The
most important of the latter is Fisher's reluctance to serve with
him. I gather that Prince Louis of Battenberg is one of those

influencing Fisher to draw back. Why, it is not easy to guess, but it will anger the King.

I settled that Sandars was to go to Portsmouth to see Fisher, and Arnold-Forster, who is at Southsea. Also, that if Brackenbury is the stumbling-block, Grenfell[1] should be substituted for him. He is not nearly so capable, but Fisher being indispensable, concession must be made.

20.10.03. Knollys saw Sandars with me to-day and we agreed upon yesterday's programme. There were numerous telegrams and letters from Fisher on the one hand and A. Balfour on the other. It is most tiresome.

In the evening we saw Tyrwhitt, who was Fisher's flag captain, and who is to go down and see him to-morrow; to do what he can.

It is impossible to say how it will end. Fisher telegraphed late to say that he will agree not to have his letter submitted to the King until Selborne has been consulted. So time has been gained. I suppose to-morrow the matter will be settled.

[*To M. V. B.*]   ORCHARD LEA,
                              OCTOBER 27TH.

When I got to Buckingham Palace this morning, expecting to find everything about the Committee settled, it was all again in the melting-pot. The A.G.,[2] who knew nothing of what was going on, saw the King yesterday, and heard from H.M. about Grenfell. Upon this he launched out on the subject of Brackenbury, got leave from the King to go to Portsmouth, saw Fisher, whom he brought up to town, and there they all were, arguing and discussing anew. It is unedifying, bad for the Prime Minister, for the Sec. of State and for the King. When I saw Arnold-Forster, immediately afterwards, he showed at once his reading of the situation, i.e. either he or the A.G. will have to go.

Second Dispute on the Membership of the Committee.

[1] At this date in England, in command of the 4th Army Corps.
[2] General Kelly-Kenny.

Arthur Balfour will have to assert his authority in political matters. It is dangerous for the King, and may be dangerous for the monarchy to let the present state of things develop. . . .

I like Arnold-Forster. His knowledge and memory are profound. He has blue eyes, and looks at you very straight. I think he will go far, if his health holds good. Certainly he looks to me a firm, determined, unself-seeking man. He talked very frankly.

This evening I saw Sandars, and we composed together a letter to A. J. B., on all these various points, calculated to inspire him to hold his own, and fight the question. If the matter is not settled soon, some other new points will arise, and the whole thing may break down. Fisher was splendid to-day, so downright. I don't really care whether the military member is Brackenbury or Grenfell, but I *do* care about the three not being exceeded.

[*To M. V. B.*]   ORCHARD LEA,
                                              NOVEMBER 4TH.

The Final   When I saw the King at Windsor two days ago, he talked
Membership.   very intimately and freely about the W.O. and the Army.

But when he spoke to me at luncheon, when I sat next to him, he had not heard of the most recent development, that Grenfell was raising difficulties about serving on the Committee. Now, Arnold-Forster and Arthur Balfour are opposed to pressing Grenfell, so we fall back on Sir George Clarke, no doubt a better man, but 12,000 miles away.

He is to be sent for. Of course the King triumphs quietly over the failure of Grenfell to fulfil expectations! Fisher and I shall begin, and Clarke must pick up after the groundwork has been laid. I liked Arnold-Forster at my second interview with him, but his manners are decidedly against him.

[*To M. V. B.*] 2, TILNEY ST.,
NOVEMBER 26TH.

I meant to keep notes of the King of Italy's visit, and of the galas at Windsor, and of my long talk with the King on the Army, and his expression of willingness to get rid of *all* the W.O. officials, without exception; but somehow the days slipped away, and I wrote down nothing.

. . . I have spent the morning with Sir Percy Girouard— Kitchener's director of railways—such a queer little fellow—a mass of cleverness and knowledge. *Very* small, with a most impressive eyeglass! There is nothing he does not know about railways and transport.

You shall see the notes of our interview. I want you to keep in touch with the enquiry, as we go along. It is an education in Army administration. You must also read Fisher's notes for his Mediterranean Fleet lectures. They are a model. Wonderful fellow!

[*To the Rt. Hon. A. J. Balfour.*] 2, TILNEY ST.,
NOVEMBER 27TH.

. . . In the face of the House of Commons, my dear Arthur, as you well know, you can juggle for ever with figures and with numbers. Past experience teaches us that. But what I have seen of the work of the Defence Committee makes it hard to believe that departmental legerdemain will avail much in that quarter.

My suggestion to you comes to this, do not let Arnold-Forster be in a hurry. Brodrick created six beautiful Army Corps *on paper*. Let his younger colleague beware. No one believes more implicitly than I do in the acute civilian intelligence brought to bear on these Army problems, assuming that the Minister can probe trained and competent professional minds around him. Hitherto, Ministers have been denied this advantage. The soldiers to whom he has been forced to turn may have been brilliant commanders in the field, or men who have risen rapidly, thanks to foreign service, or slowly by seniority, to the highest ranks of the Army. But they have not, as a rule, given time or attention to problems of organisation, which are by no means on all fours with the normal duties of a soldier. Hence, a series of abortive schemes, and a system of patchwork, which it would be lamentable for a man of Arnold-Forster's capacity to perpetuate.

I can imagine the fate of these Memoranda if they come before the Cabinet. They will be riddled with criticism by Brodrick and Lansdowne, whose administration they largely condemn. They will be mangled, and made the subject of inevitable compromise.

And when all is said, we shall not be much nearer the only true solution, to which your Defence Committee Draft Report of the 11th November so powerfully and lucidly points.

This letter is for your eyes only and is written with profound respect for Arnold-Forster, and with a complete understanding of his intense desire to alter and amend the present hopelessly inefficient organisation of the Army, together with a belief in his capacity to do so, always provided that he avoids haste and *begins at the right end.*

[*From Sir John Fisher.*]　　ADMIRALTY HOUSE, PORTSMOUTH,
DECEMBER 4TH.

DEAR LORD ESHER,

. . . "*We strain at the gnat of perfection and swallow the camel of unreadiness,*" and that permeates every Branch of Naval and Military administration forgetting the homely proverb that "half a loaf is better than no bread!" but please God! "*the dauntless three,*" Esher, Clarke, and myself (as I see we are now called!) will change all that. "We'll stagger humanity," as old Kruger said! In violent haste,

Ever yours,
J. A. FISHER.

[*To the Rt. Hon. A. J. Balfour.*]   2, TILNEY ST.,
DECEMBER 15TH.

I have read Arnold-Forster's memoranda with much *Arnold-*
interest. They are very able, but what do they show? To my *Forster's*
mind, that a very clever, hardworking, thoughtful minister, *Scheme.*
Army
when he brings a trained mind to bear on Army questions
fails to produce any more than his predecessors have done,
a scheme which contains the germs of either consistency or
permanence.

. . . Evidently in Arnold-Forster's mind, there is running
some scheme which is the reversal of the principles upon which
our Army has been based since the days of Cromwell. He may
be perfectly right, but does it not prove the necessity for some
body or department, containing elements of permanence and
continuity, whose business should be to deal with these problems?

Brodrick is a very able, hardworking Minister, with years of
official experience behind him. He deliberately adopts certain
principles of "Army Reform." Within a few months we have
Arnold-Forster, equally able, with another scheme, based on
different principles. Probably in (as nations go) a short time
we shall have Asquith or Edward Grey or heaven knows who,
with a third scheme. If Arnold-Forster is wise, he will bury this
memorandum for the present, and will throw all his energy into
the creating of a "Department" for the Defence Committee (we
will call it a General Staff) and a War Office Council, as an
executive authority. To the former you as Prime Minister can
then put the questions:—

What is the minimum regular army we require?
On what terms can it be enlisted?
What will it cost?

It is not a problem of Home Defence. The Navy can deal
with home defence. It is a problem of foreign defence.

[*To the Rt. Hon. A. J. Balfour.*]   10, DOWNING ST.,
DECEMBER 30TH.

Clarke is *excellent*. All on the right lines—very amiable—and *fat* and comfortable! A great thing.

I have just got back with him, from Portsmouth, where we had a most satisfactory meeting with Fisher. These memoranda I want *you* and you only to see. They will give you a clear idea of the lines on which we are working now. Both my colleagues accept them, and what we propose to do is this :—
To formulate,

Esher Committee: First Recommendations.

1. the demand for a Department for the Defence Committee under the Prime Minister;

2. a W.O. } Council with 4 military members, and three an Army } civilians, constituted by Patent, to be set going at once, as a *representative* body, i.e. representative of the great branches of the W.O., leaving the detail to be worked out immediately after the body is constituted with the assistance and co-operation of the new members.

We shall present these demands to you, after the manner in which the Code Napoléon was presented to the Constituent Chamber, in two short documents, leaving the further demands to be made in sections.

I avoid the word "report" as of ill omen! I need not roll this out any flatter, for you understand always *à demi mot*. I am writing in Ramsay's room, and shall be in Tilney St. if you want any further explanation. But I send you these papers, in order that we take no step without your moral support.

I see that Clarke himself will have to be your permanent secretary to the Defence Committee. He is cut out for the place, and should not be allowed to return to Australia.

I have talked all this over with Fisher, but not with Clarke. Of course the *table* I send you is tentative and not final—by any means. It is drawn up by me as a ground-work upon which the Committee would be asked to proceed.

But roughly, both my colleagues approve. I look to the Defence Committee as the coping-stone of the Edifice, and we begin constructing from the top! an inversion of the usual method, necessary in this case for many and vital reasons. I wish to impress on you the vital and urgent importance of getting these two points

(*a*) Defence Committee
(*b*) New Army Council

settled before February 2nd.[1]

[*To Mr. J. S. Sandars.*[2]]　　　　2, TILNEY ST.,
JANUARY 3RD, 1904.

I saw the C.-in-C. to-day, and found him recovered in health; and instinctively I feel that his passing half-formed wish to retire quietly has evaporated with returning health. *The Committee and the Commander-in-Chief.*

I mention this, as you well know the insurmountable obstacle which Lord Roberts' retention of the Command of the Army would place in the way of War Office Reform. His retirement unfortunately is the condition precedent upon which our scheme hinges. It is also an urgent matter, as we propose very shortly to lay before the Prime Minister two recommendations, which we shall urge upon him to carry out at this stage, before any conclusions are arrived at upon the detailed re-arrangement within the office itself of responsibility and business. The reason for this is first that it would be almost essential to work out the details in consultation with the new and unprejudiced (let us hope) occupants of the offices to be created, and secondly, because it is only by compartments—so to speak— that practical Army reforms can be enforced.

Success or failure will largely be determined by the amount of decentralisation which we can accomplish and until the new

---

[1] The date fixed for the opening of Parliament.
[2] Private Secretary to Mr. Balfour.

Army Council is formed, and until the S. of S. is surrounded by a fresh set of men, it is impossible to discuss practically either with him or with them a scheme of decentralisation. You will realise, perhaps, how urgently your presence will be required, when the two first sections of our proposals are ready. In another week this may be the case. Will you therefore give me some idea of your movements, and of those of the Prime Minister, after he leaves Chatsworth.

I hear that the P.M. is in town to-day. If so, could I see him at any hour?

[*To the Rt. Hon. A. J. Balfour.*]   WAR OFFICE,
                                           JANUARY 16TH.

I think it will be simplest to take your observations *seriatim,* and do my best to explain the points about which you are in doubt. I may say that the draft has been amended, and I venture to hope that the passages you note have been made clearer. Of the amended draft I send you a copy. It is in reality the final shape which the first two sections of the Report will assume, and we have instructed our secretary, Colonel Ellison, to forward you a copy officially.

In reference to your remark about "military opinion" I may say that I have indicated generally to Lord Roberts the lines on which we have made our recommendations, and I found him most friendly and sympathetic.

There is every reason to hope that the proposals will receive from him, at any rate, a cordial support.

No one realises more clearly than Lord Roberts the drawback to the existing system, under which the C.-in-C. is an administrative rather than an executive officer; a "clerk in an office rather than a soldier in the saddle."

He realises too the failure of the present system to get the best work out of men who are really capable, but enslaved by bad conditions; and my inference is that from the C.-in-C. you will get assistance and support in starting the new scheme, should you think fit to adopt the proposals we have made.

I turn to your reflections on the "permanent nucleus" of the Defence Committee. The paragraph to which you allude when read with what precedes it in the last paragraph of our introductory letter, and with the words "permanent office" used in the 11th paragraph of the last section of the Report, makes clear our intention that the "permanent nucleus" will stand in precisely similar relation to the Defence Committee as Sir Thomas Sanderson and his staff, who may be said to be a "permanent nucleus" of the Foreign Office, stand to Lord Lansdowne.

Definition of the Defence Committee.

We had certainly no idea of limiting the freedom of action of the Prime Minister. Indeed, we have clearly stated in our letter that he should be free as to the *selection and variation* of its members, and his power must always remain as elastic as possible in this respect. The Secretary would attend the meetings of the D.C., to keep the minutes and to perform other duties associated with the office of secretary, but he would not be a member of the D.C., and would have no right to express an opinion, in council, unless called upon by the Prime Minister.

We do not believe that the "permanent office" for the Defence Committee would lead to reduplication of work, nor that it would clash, nor create friction with the Intelligence branches of the Admiralty and War Office. The one is a collective, the other a collative function. Prince Louis of Battenberg, to whom I spoke yesterday on the point, concurs with this view.

The First Sea Lord and the First Military Member of the Army Council have definitely assigned duties strategic and collative. The work of the Secretary of the D.C. would be to prepare material for the Prime Minister, collected from these sources, *as well as from other departments*, in order that the Defence Committee may lay down principles of action, which would in certain eventualities co-ordinate the efforts of these two high professional offices.

The First Sea Lord and the First Member of the Army Council, together with their subordinates, the D.G.M.I. and the D.N.I., would, I imagine, be summoned, as heretofore, to the Defence Committee, as *members* of that body. But instead of laying their plans before an uninstructed and unprepared Prime Minister, who must now often have to collect beforehand, as best he may, facts upon which to base his judgment, they will find him posted in all the material conditions of the problem under discussion.

The subordinate officers under the Secretary to the D.C. (who might himself be conceivably a civilian) would actually be members of the Naval and Military Intelligence Branches, but temporarily attached to the Prime Minister's Office. They would be "orderlies" who would save the Prime Minister the trouble of personally applying, as now, to the various offices for information.

You ask whether if we had a Moltke available, he should be the Secretary to the Defence Committee. The answer is emphatically NO, for Moltke took, and must always take, the field.

The German H.Q. staff, to which you allude, is not a parallel case, but the Naval and Military *Cabinets* of the Emperor are in a certain sense what we mean you to have, from the point of view of co-ordination, in the "Permanent Office" of the Defence Committee. In Germany it is the Emperor who co-ordinates the action of the German Navy and Army. In Britain it can only be the Prime Minister. That is a constitutional axiom.

I heard yesterday from Prince Louis that quite recently, in France, a co-ordinating committee has been formed very much on the lines which we have been considering.

I think you need have no fears, and that the proposal we make to you will conduce to the higher efficiency of the Defence Committee, as well as to its permanence.

The question you put in reference to the "Inspector-General" we shall endeavour to answer in the 3rd section of our Report, with which we shall speedily furnish you.

[*To the Rt. Hon. A. J. Balfour.*]　　WAR OFFICE,
JANUARY 27TH.

We have considered very carefully what should now be our *The*
course of action, and we think no good purpose can be served by *Esher*
attempting to work out the details of our scheme while first *Committee.*
principles remain undetermined.

You realise that the question raised in regard to the retention
of Sir William Nicholson is not a personal one, but is in our
opinion vital to the successful working of our proposals.

This being so, we feel that we cannot usefully continue our
labour, until the point has been finally settled. I am very sorry,
but no other course seems open to us.

[*To the Rt. Hon. A. J. Balfour.*]　　WINDSOR CASTLE,
JANUARY 30TH.

I was from 11 till 1 and from 2.30 to 4 in the King's room,
going through the Report. There were a good many shoals,
but we steered through them.

I think that there is nothing in H.M.'s letter to you which conflicts with the Report, nor with the spirit of your wish. But I
would recommend settling these as soon as possible, before
intriguers get to work. You may rely on it that strenuous efforts
will be made. French [1] is here till Monday. He will back up
splendidly, as he is enthusiastic.

It is very satisfactory to find all the young officers of the Army
with us. I regret that you sent such peremptory orders by
Fisher to expunge certain laudatory but only too well deserved
expressions.

I thought them most vital to the argument. However, the
inference is pretty plain from the words as they stand.

[1] Lt.-Gen. Sir John French, afterwards F.M. Earl of Ypres.

[*To Lord Roberts.*]   WINDSOR CASTLE,
                                         JANUARY 31ST.

*The
Office of
Inspector-
General.*

As you were so very kind as to speak openly to me about your wishes in regard to the "Inspector-General," I think it right to tell you exactly what has happened.

Our proposal that the I.G. should be the President of the Selection Committee was strongly opposed in the Cabinet. At a Conference with our Committee, last week, the Prime Minister and his colleagues pressed this objection, and we considered it our duty to submit, although we refused to withdraw the recommendation, which, as you see, remains in the Report.

To the best of my belief the matter stands thus. With your consent, I mentioned to the King and the Prime Minister what you said to me, i.e. that were the office of I.G. defined according to the terms of our Report, you would consent to hold it for a short time, but that if the authority of I.G. was circumscribed, you could not, consistently with your sense of responsibility, do so.

I would now venture to suggest that you should see Mr. Arnold-Forster, who is aware of the circumstances, and speak freely to him on the subject in order that he should not feel that, in any degree, his province as Secretary of State has been encroached upon by any of our Committee.

This will obviate all possibility of misunderstandings, and I hope you will forgive me for respectfully making this suggestion.

[*To M. V. B.*]   ORCHARD LEA,
                                         JANUARY 31ST.

I merely wish to record the meeting with the Cabinet this past week, where we had a sharp conflict over the policy of the "clean sweep." As we would not give way, and as the Government could not afford to let us resign, they had to climb down. The

P.M. was all the time on our side, but Selborne [1] was obstinate. When we met at Windsor on Friday he had yielded.

You recollect that at our first meeting with Fisher at Portsmouth, the 30th January at 6 p.m. was fixed upon as the date when the Report was to be settled; and issued. *The Committee's Report.*

Yesterday the 30th at 4 p.m. the King approved of the publication and it was sent off. We had a long day. I was with the King from 11 to 1 working at the Report and Arthur Balfour's letter. The Duke of Connaught was telegraphed for, and arrived at 1.30 (when I met you).

At 2.30 we began again in the King's room, and by 4 I had drafted the King's reply to the P.M. and it was approved. There was a good deal to be got over at one time and another, but by urging postponement of points which were not vital and giving way about the nomenclature of the office, I got the King's approval of the Report as it stands. The Duke behaved very well, the King showed admirable sense. So far, so good. I got back to Windsor this morning, and hope to see French. I shall discuss with him the scheme, and the *names* which cannot yet be published. But I am very anxious to get them settled as soon as possible. Otherwise it will open the door to intrigue of every description. Lord Roberts writes that he has had a long talk with A. J. B. and wants to see me to-morrow urgently. I hope that it is not to press for Nicholson again.

[*To M. V. B.*]   ORCHARD LEA,
                                   FEBRUARY 3RD.

You can imagine all the difficulties of getting our Report launched—but everyone, including the King, played up well, and it was done. The Press has received it with a chorus of approval, and this is the only thing which makes me doubt that we may be right! *Reception of the Report.*

The thing which gratifies me is the enthusiasm of the young

---

[1] At this time First Lord of the Admiralty.

officers of the Army. They are more than friendly. Lord
Roberts alone, among the older men, is full of congratulation.
He says that we have carried out everything that he has for years
wished for, and he is most anxious to be the first to assist in
carrying out the scheme. I have seen all the Ministers and they
said very friendly things, but the warmest congratulations came
from Chamberlain, whom I met at Lansdowne House. He
shook hands very warmly and said, "It very seldom falls to the
lot of any man to be able to do such good service for his
country." This is a phrase I can never forget.

In all questions of this sort the *personal* element is the prime
difficulty. We have got the officers selected who are to hold the
first places on the Army Council, but there are many heart-
burnings. Still, I believe that we have chosen the best available.

[*To M. V. B.*]   WAR OFFICE,
                                                FEBRUARY 9TH.

*Lord
Roberts.*

Only a few lines. A very worrying day again, but we have
got on a step or two. The King was most reasonable yesterday,
and told me exactly what passed between him and Lord
Roberts. He was very kind but very firm in telling Lord
Roberts that he ought not to accept the I.G.[1] place; that it
would be undignified, etc. From what I saw of Lord R., afterwards, I don't think that he made much impression. The little
man is very tenacious. The D. of Connaught called here and I
drove with him to Paddington.

[*To the Rt. Hon. A. J. Balfour.*]   WAR OFFICE,
                                                FEBRUARY 11TH.

*Argument
about the
Inspector-
General.*

Since we presented that section of our report which deals
with the post of Inspector-General several important things
have happened.

                  [1] Inspector-General of the Forces.

First, the Cabinet has demurred to our proposal that the Inspector-General should preside over the Selection Board, on the ground that the position of Inspector-General might thereby assume a greater degree of power and responsibility than is consistent with the principle upon which the Commander-in-Chief was abolished.

Second, the suggestion has been made that the first Inspector-General should be Lord Roberts, who has three times, in India, in Africa and in Great Britain, held the office of Commander-in-Chief, a fact which in itself, were he to be appointed I.G., might lead to the assumption that the post of I.G. exceeds in importance that of Commander-in-Chief of an Army Corps.

It is not within our province to discuss possible holders of the office in question, but we desire to state that in view of the careful definition of the duties of the I.G. which we have drawn, we do not share the fears of the Cabinet that the presidency of the Selection Board will carry with it undue authority. That proposal was made by us, in order to give the Selection Board a member, in its chairman, who, from his independence and wider purview, would be likely to look upon appointments rather from the standpoint of the Army and the Empire as a whole, than from the somewhat narrower point of view of the efficiency of any one Army Corps.

The definition of the duties of the I.G. makes it clear that this officer is not to be the superior, but the equal of officers commanding Army Corps. Our intention was and is, that he should be an inspecting and reporting officer, and not a superior nor a commander entrusted with the power to give orders.

His functions are to Review and to Report, and his Report is to be sent to the Army Council and the Sec. of State, and not to the Army Corps Commander.

It was never intended that the I.G. should be received by the Army Corps Commander with the honours hitherto conceded to the Commander-in-Chief. Whatever power the I.G. may possess cannot be exercised by him, but only through the Army Council, should they approve and agree with his Report.

We are of opinion that these considerations should be made clear beforehand to any officer to whom the post may be offered, in order that there may be no misunderstanding, and we have consequently suggested to the Sec. of State that a draft order in council should be prepared upon the lines indicated, for the information of the Cabinet, and in order to remove any possibility of misconception.

[*To M. V. B.*]   2, TILNEY ST.,
                                          FEBRUARY 11TH.

Such a scurry to-day. No time to write, but I will write fully to-night. Our torpedo has exploded and the little C.-in-C. has left the W.O. for good in a devil of a temper. Of this anon.

You and Ellison are asked to Portsmouth on the 19th. We are all quartered in ships for 3 days (as the King occupies Admiralty House), and after his departure we come together again. I think you will enjoy it. A very original experience.

[*To the Rt. Hon. A. J. Balfour.*]   ST. JAMES'S PALACE,
                                             MARCH 1ST.

*Sir
George
Clarke.*

I spoke to Clarke yesterday, and told him that he obviously had enemies in the Press and in other quarters, a fact which in view of his remarkable ability and *reasonableness* I cannot myself understand. From start to finish he has never once insisted upon his view when it conflicted with those of his colleagues, and he is more open to argument than any man with formed opinions I ever met.

For the Defence Committee "Nucleus crew" he will make a perfect secretary. His knowledge of both services is really profound, and he has thought much on Defence questions.

Neither you nor any of your colleagues will find him obstinate, nor, *I am certain*, is he an intriguer. In former days he had relations with the Press. It was at that time that he incurred the displeasure of Lord Wolseley (who was not himself guiltless of a similar weakness) and of Spencer Wilkinson.[1]

Since then I doubt his having made an enemy in the world, except since he became connected with my committee, the fate of which in that respect he shares.

Believe me, if you take Clarke you will never regret it. I have only one objective in view, which is the strengthening of your really great edifice—the Defence Committee—against attack hereafter, and the good of the country, which is bound up in your achievement.[2]

[*To Mr. J. S. Sandars.*]   2, TILNEY ST.[3]

In reply to your question, as to whether we should have been prepared to discuss and *amend* Part 2 of the Report, I must tell you frankly that we had determined under no circumstances to alter a line.

. . . I fail, I must confess, to comprehend the "soreness" which is said to exist in some quarters. In our Report, there is no reflection upon the individual servants of the Crown. We attacked a system. In speaking with some severity of the Finance Branch, we laid no blame on excellent civil servants who were acting, as they believed, under orders emanating from authorities long since dead and gone. We criticised the *system* under which such orders had become possible. For individuals to feel "sore" shows a total misconception of our Report and its aim.

Misconstructions of the Report.

Similarly, the Prime Minister can hardly have expected our

[1] Military Correspondent.

[2] Sir G. Clarke was Secretary of the Committee for Imperial Defence, 1904–1907.

[3] Dated March 16th, but placed by context.

Committee to recommend and *help carry into effect* a total change of W.O. administration without some attempt to show the defects of the existing system, to which our remedies were applied.

We followed the method adopted by the Sec. of State, who before writing his *Blue* Paper, in which he details his Army Reform scheme, circulated his *White* Paper, in which he blows the existing Army organisation to atoms.

However, I need say no more. We have done our best, and it was obvious—from the beginning—that we should say and do things which former occupants of the W.O. would not like.

The whole point now is this, that you have got a scheme of reform, fairly complete. Half is in *actual operation*.

To throw the machinery out of gear by not adopting the complementary proposals would be such a waste of time and force, that I cannot contemplate it as a possibility.

[*From the Rt. Hon. H. O. Arnold-Forster.*]   WAR OFFICE,
MARCH 1ST.

DEAR LORD ESHER,

Secretary for War on the Report.

I have now received a copy of your Report, and you have informed me that the Committee over which you preside has now closed its labours at the War Office. I think the time has therefore come when I may with somewhat more formality than is possible in a hasty conversation, tender my thanks to yourself and your colleagues for the great work you have performed.

I wish to thank you in the first instance, in my capacity as Head of the War Office. I honestly believe that the changes which you have recommended, and which I hope it will be my privilege to carry into effect, will prove of great and permanent value to the Office over which I at present preside. The good effects of your work will last long after I have left this place, but as I am the first to benefit, it is fitting that I should be the first to acknowledge the debt.

For the Army, I, as a civilian, have no right to speak with authority. I think, however, I know the feeling of the Army well enough to be able to say with confidence that your work has evoked an almost universal sentiment of gratitude and satisfaction among Officers of all ranks. I cannot thank you on behalf of the Army, but that the Army does thank you very sincerely I am confident.

Lastly I wish to thank you on my own behalf as an individual, and to acknowledge in the fullest manner the invariable courtesy, patience and sympathy you and your colleagues have shown on all those occasions when I have been brought into consultation with you. Of the quality of your work I will say little. You know how high an opinion I entertain of it. But I must confess that even with the knowledge I possess of the powers of your two colleagues, and with the knowledge I have lately acquired of your wonderful capacity for dealing with facts, figures and men, I stand astonished at the rapidity, the thoroughness and the correctness of your work. May I add that its intrinsic merits appear to me to be equalled by the excellence of the form in which it is presented. No small matter in my opinion. . . .

. . . Let me say one more word in conclusion. I believe that the work done by your Committee will furnish a useful example to be followed in the administration of the public affairs of this country. Within my recollection it is the only instance of a great problem being attacked by a thoroughly competent body of critics, who have been permitted to deal with it continuously, as a whole and with one clear idea guiding all their deliberations. How many of our great National problems might be solved if a similar treatment were applied to them! One thing of course is needed to complete the process in such a case as this, I mean executive action following quickly on enlightened recommendations. It is my business now to see that such action shall follow. I am taking the liberty of sending a copy of this letter to your two distinguished colleagues, and I beg that you and they will believe me to remain,

Your very devoted colleague and sincere well-wisher,

H. O. ARNOLD-FORSTER.

[*From Lord Knollys.*]   BUCKINGHAM PALACE,
MARCH 5TH.

MY DEAR ESHER,

I have shown the enclosed to the King, who thinks that nothing could be "nicer" than the way A. Forster expresses himself towards you and your colleagues, and the best of it is that what he says is quite true.

Yours ever,
KNOLLYS.

[*From Sir John Fisher.*]   MARCH 10TH.

Fisher on the Manœuvres.   Just back from English Channel and very enthusiastic! Beloved Chairman of the War Office Reconstitution Committee! We really must arrange to get the British Army to sea somehow or other! Yesterday all the mice died in their cages and two of his crew fainted, but the young Lieutenant of the submarine didn't seem to care a d——n whether they all died so long as he bagged the battleship he was after! and he practically got her and then came up to breathe! Depend on it we shall have more "Niles" and "Trafalgars" so long as we continue to propagate such young bloods as this! But see how splendid if we could shove the same "ginger" into the young military "aspirants" and they all come from the same stock, but the whole secret is to catch them very young and mould them while they are then so plastic and receptive to be just what you want them. Another submarine had an explosion which made the interior "*hell*" for some seconds (as he was bottled up and diving to evade a Destroyer who had caught him with an inch and a half grapnel), but he saw them all d——d first before he would come up to be caught! Another fire eater had his periscope smashed but bagged a battleship nevertheless by coming up stealthily to blow and look round. *It really is all lovely!* but what I am writing about is—you *must embark the First Army Corps every year and give them a sea training*.

Yours till death,

J. FISHER.

Keep this letter private. I'm treading on people's toes! Stamping on them!

[*To M. V. B.*]   ADMIRALTY HOUSE, PORTSMOUTH,

MARCH 13TH.

All goes on here very much as it did when you were here with the King. There was a smaller party at dinner, and the Prince of Wales wore ordinary mess kit, and not the "Ball dress" and epaulettes, which the King prefers.

We had church in the morning, as before, and this afternoon *Prince of* we shall go to tea with the officers in barracks. To-morrow *Wales at* there is a fight off the Nab. The Prince of Wales went down in a *Manœuvres.* submarine, and fired off a torpedo himself. His young lieutenant was the boy who nearly stifled his crew, three days ago—a most dashing youth, so the Admiral was jolly glad when he saw the heir to the Throne reappear. Everyone was averse from the Prince's going down, but he *insisted*, and I think he was right. It will give a lift to the submarines—and being a sailor, why should he not take risks?

We had nothing but sailors to dine last night. All splendid fellows. What a profession!

. . . I gave the King yesterday all those curious papers about Lady Flora Hastings, and strongly advised that they shall be burnt. Old world scandals, out of which no one concerned came well, had better be put behind the fire. He too was astonished at the precocious knowledge shown by the Queen (aged 19) and the outspokenness of Lord Melbourne.

[*To M. V. B.*]   ADMIRALTY HOUSE, PORTSMOUTH,
                                        MARCH 14TH.

Manœuvres.   We had a splendid day. So gloriously fine. Not a breath of wind, and warm sun. Starting at 10 on the *Mercury*—a second-class cruiser—we went out to the Nab, and waited for the Fleet. Wilson[1] on the *Revenge*, and seven other battleships, five cruisers and 24 destroyers left Portland at 3.30 this morning. It was pitch dark, and he brought the Fleet out through what is called the "hole in the wall," only a bit wider than a battleship, no lights, and as risky an operation as can be imagined. "Good for the nerves of his captains," he said. They caught one submarine, but lost two battleships in the fight. It was a sight to see him handle his fleet. Then he came on board the *Mercury*, and we had luncheon. Got back this evening.

A tremendous argument between Fisher and Wilson as to whether it was justifiable to fire a torpedo under a destroyer. There is great risk of sinking, as the sides of a destroyer are very thin. There are not two more dashing sailors in Europe than these two men.

. . . You will be pleased to hear that C. B. [Campbell-Bannerman] called us a "damnable dictatorial domineering Trio." The Prince of Wales is delighted with this description.

[*From Sir Douglas Haig.*]   MARCH 23RD.

MY DEAR ESHER,

Haig   . . . You must be overwhelmed with congratulations on the
on the   success of your labours, but I feel sure that no one appreciates
Esher
Committee.   [1] Admiral Sir Arthur Wilson.

what you have done for the Army more than I do. I never believed it possible to get such a thorough reorganisation without undergoing first of all some military disaster! At the time it seemed impossible to get the country and the politicians to interest themselves in the condition of the Army. Now, thanks to your energy, things seem on the right road for efficiency. . . .

Yours very sincerely,
DOUGLAS HAIG.

[*To Mr. J. S. Sandars.*]　　ORCHARD LEA,
MARCH 29TH.

You asked me some little time ago to elaborate our argument for a Secretariat for the Defence Committee. I have attempted to do this, and send you some copies of a memorandum, which you can dispose of to anyone who will treat the document as private.

[*To M. V. B.*]　　PARIS,
APRIL 10TH.

I travelled over with Cambon, and Albert Mensdorff. The French Ambassador is very good company, but his French is almost too academic and perfect; never a word out of place—so that he is very embarrassing as a companion. Makes one feel so slovenly. It is fine weather here—the brilliant sun of Louis XIV. Paris is not what it was! This is due to London having caught up the French, and this much-vaunted hotel is not anything near as good or as comfortable as the Carlton.

I lunched at Voisin, the celebrated restaurant, and then went to the Louvre with Violet. It is gorgeous. So are the streets. I think that I may find you some little *objet d'art*. I hope so. I left my name on the President, and left cards on Delcassé, just to maintain the entente cordiale!

Paris,
1904.

[*To M. V. B.*]   PARIS,
                                            APRIL 13TH.

I cannot, alas, get away to-day. This accursed business [1] is not
finished. I hope to be back for dinner to-morrow night, but
will telegraph in the morning. It is a nuisance, as I am bored to
death here. Luckily there is something to do all day, but then it
is mostly uncongenial work. Such a lot of tiresome detail.

[*To the Rt. Hon. A. J. Balfour.*]   2, TILNEY ST.,
                                            MAY 12TH.

The Esher   Your Committee having now concluded their labours, and
Committee   disposed of the few remaining matters which required to be
Dissolves.   dealt with, after presenting their Report,[2] we beg to thank you
with great sincerity for your unlimited patience and forbearance
during the past few months.

In taking leave of you, we wish also to ask you to be good
enough to express our gratitude to Mr. Sandars for all the
invaluable help he has given us.

[*From the Rt. Hon. A. J. Balfour.*]   10, DOWNING ST.,
                                            MAY 19TH.

MY DEAR ESHER,

The Prime   I cannot permit your Committee to dissolve without express-
Minister's   ing my sense of the debt which the country owes to you and
Thanks.   your colleagues for the service you have performed to the
cause of War Office Reform.

I am well aware that it was at considerable personal inconvenience that the Members of the Committee undertook the
task entrusted to them; and the strenuous and unremitting
labour which has been given to the consideration of the difficult
questions with which you have had to deal has earned, and will

---

[1] For Sir Ernest Cassel.   [2] On the reconstitution of the War Office.

receive, the gratitude of all those who realise how hard is the problem of Army organisation under the conditions which prevail, and must continue to prevail, in this country.

Believe me,
Yours very sincerely,
ARTHUR JAMES BALFOUR.

[*To M. V. B.*]   WINDSOR CASTLE,
                                        MAY 25TH.

Everything has gone off perfectly. Two ceremonies. The King wonderful. Finding a kind word for everybody. I have been walked off my legs, and pulled off them by the children. The youngest is the most riotous. The eldest, a sort of head nurse. It was queer looking through a weekly paper, and coming to a picture of the eldest with the label " our future King." Prince Albert at once drew attention to it—but the elder hastily brushed his brother's finger away and turned the page. Evidently he thought it bad taste.

[*To M. V. B.*]   WINDSOR CASTLE,
                                        JUNE 9TH.

I have just come away from a long rehearsal with the boys. I went down in state with the Head [1] to the Albert Bridge with all the boats, seated in the Royal Barge! It will be a charming sight.

[*To the Rt. Hon. A. J. Balfour.*]   2, TILNEY ST.,
                                        JUNE 17TH.

A. F. [Arnold-Forster] is in bed, and feeble. But I think I *On Arnold-* managed to cheer him up. Encouragement is the only method *Forster.* with him, as he has the weakness of a child.

<hr>

[1] Headmaster of Eton.

Criticism is fatal. This is a hard characteristic for the would-be reformer to wrestle with in the watches of the night. However, I was with him for an hour and a half, talking details, and he said at the end that he thought he saw daylight!

. . . Still, *you* will have to take it in hand.

[*To M. V. B.*]   ORCHARD LEA,
                                                    JUNE 18TH.

Yesterday I called at Downing St., about 11, and saw the Prime Minister in his dressing-room. He was just out of his bath, hurrying on clothes, in order not to be late for his Defence Committee Meeting.

Army Scheme Abandoned.

We talked very rapidly about the abandonment, *sine die*, of Arnold-Forster's Army scheme, and I tried to impress him with the views that I wrote to Knollys on the previous day. He asked me to see Arnold-Forster, whom I found in bed, being dosed every half-hour by his excellent but rather harassed wife. We talked for an hour and a half, going over all the points of his scheme, and I did my best to put a little courage into him.

His weakness is that he has convictions, but not the courage of them. This morning I went to Windsor Castle early.

It is Waterloo Day, and the Duke of Wellington arrived with the Tricolor Flag which it is his duty to present to the King, and by the presentation of which he holds Strathfieldsaye. It was a quaint little ceremonial—the Duke dressed in a frock coat, kneeling and offering this miniature banner to the King.

Balfour on (the late) Lord Salisbury—

After luncheon Arthur Balfour, who is staying at the Castle, came to my room. He looked at some of his predecessor's letters, and we talked about the proposed publication of Dizzy's life, which is to be done in *The Times*. A method which he thinks unsatisfactory and rather degrading. I told him of the correspondence with the Queen from 1874–80 which the King gave me the other day, and he commented upon his uncle's share in those transactions.

He said that the tension between Lord Derby and Lord Salisbury was at one time most acute, and that the two men's characters were exceedingly hostile, Lord Derby being a "glorious philistine" and his uncle a "glorious bohemian."

[*To M. V. B.*]   ORCHARD LEA,
                                    JUNE 20TH.

. . . Arthur Balfour then went on to talk about the Army. I *—and on* told him of my interview with Arnold-Forster, and the two *the Army—* principles which I tried to impress upon him were essential to be considered before any Army Scheme could be satisfactorily framed.

1. That the Prime Minister's memo. on National Defence should be published.

2. That the question of how large a reinforcement for India was to be contemplated should be settled.

Upon these the constitution of the Army hinges, and it is futile to talk about a scheme until these points are clear in people's minds.

At present a man like Arnold-Forster may have convictions, but he has not the courage of them. He thinks of a small and highly efficient Army, but he schemes for a larger force than we have at present. His standard, like Brodrick's, is in reality numerical. He has got to break away from this superstition, or else compulsory service becomes an immediate necessity. Arthur ended by saying that he thought he would have to take the question in hand himself, and work out a plan. Possibly this is how it will end.

He told me that Curzon was very "difficult," and that he quarrels with his old friend Brodrick and is at sixes and sevens with K. [Kitchener]. Arthur hopes that he will not return to

India, and in that case (only this is a profound secret) he will send out Selborne, whom he has sounded, and who would go. It would be a good appointment. We then talked of Jacky Fisher, and I told him of the latter's difficulties and he asked me to let him know that he would himself see him and talk over his naval policy with him.

—and on Procedure at Change of Government—

. . . He then said that in possible view of the fall of his Government, he had had a memo. prepared, showing all the precedents, culled from public sources of information, for the action of the Sovereign, and he asked me whether I could supplement these from the private memoranda and letters of the Queen. This, with the King's leave, I could easily do, as every letter bearing upon the successive changes of Government during the Queen's reign has been carefully kept, and bound up in special volumes.

We discussed the probable action of the King, and he agreed that it was most important that on the first occasion during his reign, when the King was called upon to use his prerogative to form a new administration, his action should be strictly constitutional and according to precedent.

—and his Possible Successors.

Arthur Balfour has no doubt that the King should send for Campbell-Bannerman, and *not* for Lord Spencer; on the ground that the former *is* the recognised leader of the Liberal Party while the latter is only the leader of about 20 Peers; and that the question as to whether C. B. could or would form a Government is not one that in its primary stages need concern the Sovereign.

He said that he had reluctantly come to the conclusion that Rosebery was hopeless, as he would have been glad, for Imperial reasons, to transfer the Government into his hands. But that as circumstances had shaped themselves, he could only aim at leaving the country, at the expiration of his term of office, in such a state (especially in relation to Foreign Affairs) that the new Government would merely have to carry on insured against any dangerous foreign complication. In view of the "unforeseen," this is not easy!

[*To M. V. B.*]   2, TILNEY STREET,
    JUNE 22ND.

I send you two letters, one from your General [French] and one from Fisher. They explain themselves, but you see that the Admiral is very affectionate. I think his talk with the Prime Minister must be of benefit to the country. But the Army Scheme makes me more anxious every day. I am so afraid that something will be done to upset the only good thing Brodrick did, which was to provide a small and highly efficient striking force trained under officers who will command it in war.

I am thinking of publishing my brochure on the Defence Committee after the debate in the House of Lords last night. *Misconceptions about the Defence Committee.* There seems to be so much misunderstanding on the subject.[1] I shall ask leave of Arthur Balfour—but I do not think he will refuse it. I have been elected an Hon. Member of the *Junior* Naval and Military Club, which I appreciate, as it shows the feeling of the *younger* officers of the Army—and it is *their* opinion that I attach most importance to.

[*To M. V. B.*]   2, TILNEY ST.,
    JUNE 30TH.

I wrote to French and thanked him for my visit to your camp at Newbury, and the charming day on the downs yesterday. The most striking thing is the zeal and keenness of all the officers from the General downwards. Nothing in the Navy could be

[1] In this debate the Duke of Bedford elicited a statement of the extent to which the recommendations of the Esher Committee had been carried out. It was found necessary to explain to the House that the responsibility of the Sec. for War was not in any way reduced by his association with the Army Council or the Committee of Imperial Defence.

In this debate also the relations of the military and financial officers of the War Office were discussed, and Lord Lansdowne said the report of the Esher Committee gave a wrong view of the matter. See p. 45 (to J. S. Sandars, March 1904).

better. If the infantry come up to this standard, that force at Aldershot is a real asset, and is the nearest thing we possess to the Japanese model of perfect efficiency.

The more I see of the little General the more I am impressed by his romantic earnestness and his strength of purpose.

[*To M. V. B.*]   2, TILNEY ST.,
                                                          JULY 12TH.

*Trouble
over the
Militia.*

. . . A Cabinet has been sitting all day to try and work out a compromise on A. F.'s [Arnold-Forster's] scheme. The Government are so frightened! It appears that the Tory members are all against the abolition of the Militia, of which they got wind through the newspapers.

I had a talk with Revelstoke to-day about the city which I hate, and which I don't think I shall be able to stand. Still, I want to do so if possible, as I shall like you always to have as much money as possible, both now and hereafter. Still, it is not a nice life!

[*To M. V. B.*]   ORCHARD LEA,
                                                          JULY 12TH, MIDNIGHT.

. . . It is a hot night, with a slow summer rain falling, which brings a bitter sweet smell of flowers through the window. Everyone is in the Gallery, and I am alone in my room, with only the pictures of one or two people I love about me, and old and rather sad memories. Why is it that such a night recalls so many others, full of intense happiness, some of them, and others so full of tender pain? For days one goes on treading the ordinary path of life, and not noting the immense flight of time, and perhaps not realising the changes in face and in heart of those among whom one moves. Then suddenly a lightning flash discovers all the secrets of lapsing time, and very little seems left but the memory of other days.

[*To M. V. B.*]   2, TILNEY ST.,
                                          JULY 22ND.

. . . I went to the H. of L. for the Army debate, but it was so
hopelessly dull, that I came away after an hour, and went to see
George Curzon. He is far from well, but full of wonderful   *Curzon's*
vigour. We talked over all sorts of problems, including   *Opinions.*
Kitchener and his future in India and here. He gets on with him
all right, although both men are self-willed and have inordinate
opinions of themselves. Rather like *Owd Bob* [1] and the Tailless
Tyke. Some day there will be a row. George will not allow K.
to remodel the Army on his own lines. As he very truly says,
K.'s idea of rule is K., and that you cannot rely on a succession of
K.'s. Of course this was the principle at the base of my original
proposal for the Army here. You *must* legislate for the average
man, and not for the exception. Curzon is not impressed by the
way business is carried on here either by the Cabinet or by the
Defence Committee. He is full of admiration for A. J. B. [Bal-
four] but thinks—and he is right—the Cabinet hopelessly unwieldy and that the P.M. has ceased to control. He recalled to
me what I had said on the subject in writing about Sir Robert
Peel which I myself had forgotten!

In the morning I said good-bye to the P. and Princess of
Wales. She was sitting in the garden, lying in a garden chair,
and we had a long and very friendly talk.

[*To M. V. B.*]   THE ROMAN CAMP,
                                          AUGUST 6TH.

. . . I have got a very interesting letter from Jackie Fisher   *Fisher*
about the King, with whom he had 5 hours straight away on   *and the*
the yacht.   *Govern-*
Jackie fusses because he thinks he will have fights with Sel-   *ment.*
borne, and he wishes for the advent of a new Government. But

---

[1] By Alfred Ollivant.

it is always six of one and half a dozen of the other with these people; and although just now he gets sympathy from Spencer and E. Grey, if *they* were in office he would get sympathy from Selborne, and would have to fight the others. Sympathy is a cheap article.

Lord Esher now gave up his connection with Sir Ernest Cassel, as he could not grasp the intricacies of high finance.

[*From Sir John Fisher.*]   ADMIRALTY HOUSE, PORTSMOUTH,
                                                             AUGUST 21ST.

DEAR ESHER,

Fisher on Selborne.

Selborne came here and was so cordial and responsive I made the plunge *and with immense* success! He has swallowed it all whole although I fully explained to him that in accepting it all he was writing himself down an ass for not having done it all sooner! I sat him in an arm-chair in my Office and shook my fist in his face for $2\frac{1}{4}$ hours without a check! then he read 120 pages of foolscap and afterwards collapsed!

"New measures demand new men" (see Esher on the War Office!), see para. 17, Sec. 11, Army Council, p. 16, and he has agreed to all the new blood I want. Of course everyone will say I have "packed" the Admiralty with "my creatures" (very sorry, but I can't help it!).

Yours till death,
J. F.

[*To Sir John Fisher.*]   THE ROMAN CAMP,
                                                     AUGUST 24TH.

You have captured the first position, and of course you will win all along the line.

I never read anything better than the "Preamble."

It is a new *gospel* and *magnificent*! That same principle—of concentrating (1) expenditure upon efficiency, (2) your effective force in the "King of Israel," is what the Army Council should take to heart. I wish you could drill it into them.

Will you read the enclosed and send it back to me. I am pressing the point hard upon A. F. [Forster] and Lyttelton, i.e. to make a beginning at Aldershot.

When we have got thus far, we will take Ireland in hand.

Bless you, my dear Colleague, till Trafalgar eve.

[*To M. V. B.*]   THE ROMAN CAMP,
SEPTEMBER 1ST.

. . . Cassel has replied in very nice terms, saying that when he comes to London, he will arrange the matter to our mutual advantage. This is precisely the line which I hoped he would take.

It is most satisfactory to hear that Seymour [Hicks]'s play is going to be a success;[1] and I hope Ella thinks so too. She is a good judge. Was she enthusiastic? And how did you like Zena Dare? Is she at all attractive?

[*To M. V. B.*]   THE ROMAN CAMP,
SEPTEMBER 6TH.

. . . I am rubbing hard into the Sec. of State that if he wants to do anything, he must back up his friends and ignore his foes.

. . . The Japs do not seem to have found Kuropatkin an easy *Russo-* nut to crack. Still, they have turned him with his back to the sea *Japanese* —so that his line of communication is badly threatened. Should *War.* they have enough troops, and fresh troops, they may destroy part of his army. I am glad that he has made a good fight and that the West is not hopelessly beaten by the East. It would not be a good thing for us, *in the long run*, if that were so.

[1] *The Catch of the Season.*

[*To M. V. B.*]   THE ROMAN CAMP,
                                      SEPTEMBER 7TH.

. . . The Japs have missed their big coup, but they have done very well. The future does not look very bright. A prolonged war, for now it is bound to go on, and a secret and very intimate understanding between Russia and Germany. Of this there is no doubt in the world. It should make the F.O. careful, and accounts for the friendliness of the French towards us, as they never can have much reliance on Russia the moment they suspect a German alliance.

[*To M. V. B.*]   THE ROMAN CAMP,
                                      SEPTEMBER 8TH.

. . . I go to Balmoral on the 26th for two or three days. A. Balfour and J. Fisher are to be there. But there will be no worries like last year, thank heaven.

. . . Did I send you a cutting about Edna [May]'s success in New York? I am glad, for I think she would have hated a failure. Seymour Hicks's excitement just now must be intense. Their first night is to-morrow, is it not?

[*To M. V. B.*]   THE ROMAN CAMP,
                                      SEPTEMBER 9TH.

Foreign Policy of Germany.

. . . The immediate danger is the relations between Germany and Russia. This may land us any day in grave trouble. Always remember that the "Low Countries" were the battle-fields of Europe for centuries, and will be again. It is vital to Germany to absorb Holland. *Kiel* is insufficient for a power that desires Naval supremacy and Colonial Empire.

That Germany is always contemplating the absorption of Holland into the *Empire* is certain. So that there must come a day when France and England will have to fight Germany in order to *neutralise* the Dutch kingdom, and this day may not be very far off.

[*To M. V. B.*]   THE ROMAN CAMP,
SEPTEMBER 15TH.

All the news seems to show that Kuropatkin's retreat was a fine performance—and he stands out, to my mind, among all the generals engaged on both sides.

How the newspaper correspondents loathe the censorship of *both* armies. In similar circumstances would any British Commission dare to muzzle the Press? Criticism of a commander in the field ought to be a *criminal* offence. It disheartens the troops, and is a form of national treachery.

[*To M. V. B.*]   THE ROMAN CAMP,
SEPTEMBER 23RD.

. . . I go this morning to Edinburgh and on to Whittinge-hame. I may go to see George Binning to-morrow at Meller-stain and then return here. It depends on motors and trains and things.

[*To the Rt. Hon. A. J. Balfour.*]   ROMAN CAMP,
SEPTEMBER 25TH.

Requirements for an Expeditionary Force.

I return your volume under another cover. May I have a copy of the *last* memo.? If so, will Mr. Short tell Sir George Clarke to send me a copy?

You gave me, a long time ago, the "National Defence" memo. and two of the Indian ones. All these papers are invaluable. Please remember that you say the "striking force" maintained under A. F.'s [Arnold-Forster's] scheme should not be less than *two divisions*!

This is absolutely sound, and is the minimum. Under A. Forster's scheme it is a Brigade short. This is all wrong. *He* says that the number of men, even so, will be greater than French has now at Aldershot. Granted—but that is the old fallacy of "counting heads."

The real question is the number of "cadres" and not of men. The "striking force" should have two whole Divisions of *long* service infantry, *cadres* complete—and a Division of short service.

Then you have a force which may be of some service. Reduce below this, you have only a toy. On page 3 of this last memo. of yours, paragraph (f) reads inconsistently with the conclusions of your National Defence Memo., don't you think?

. . . I send you a copy of the pamphlet corrected.

[*To M. V. B.*]   ROMAN CAMP,
                                                  SEPTEMBER 26TH.

. . . I shall have to run up and see Cassel when he comes back. He is in Paris now.

Disputes
in Indian
Government.

. . . I may mention that there is a feverish row on in India between K. [Kitchener] and the Military Member of Council. Lord K. has resigned his command.

. . . Of course it will be smoothed over, and Lord K. will get his way—but at present he is determined to come home!

. . . Also I doubt Curzon returning to India whether that poor dear little woman lives or dies. This means great changes. You know who his successor is to be. I told you. Only this is a deadly secret. Selborne—who is anxious to go, and you can

imagine what a difference it will make to the Admiralty. Jackie
Fisher *may* find that the "evils he wot of," etc.

[*To M. V. B.*]   BALMORAL CASTLE,
                                          OCTOBER 2ND.

Here I am, back amid the scenes of last year, when that
momentous decision was taken, which I have never regretted.
We have done well since then! Arnold-Forster is here, and his
enemy old K. K. [Kelly-Kenny]. It will be rather interesting
to see what comes of the meeting.

I should like to see the old man employed for a year, until he
reaches the age limit. He ought to go to Salisbury till then, and
by that time Ian Hamilton will be ready to take over the
command.

Prince Arthur of C. and Francis Teck are here. I sat next the
King at dinner. He was in first-rate spirits, and *most* amiable.
His kilt is not very well cut. The stuff is too light and thin,
and does not hang well.

Lunched at Aberdeen with the P.M. who was on his way to
E. Lothian. He was charming as usual—and talked very intimately about his plans and views.

He would far rather Curzon did not return to India, and *Balfour*
would like to see Selborne established there. K. has withdrawn *on India.*
his resignation and gained his point; but there can be no real
settlement in India until the "dual control" is abolished. Curzon
will never agree to this.

The P.M. is going to make a very important speech to-
morrow, and is in some trepidation, whether he will not finally
split his party. Still, he is going to take the only right and
possible line.[1]

[1] In continuation of the fiscal controversy the Prime Minister made a
speech at Edinburgh on this date which in essence was a firm reannouncement
of the policy of the Sheffield speech a year before, and which dissociated the
Government neatly, clearly, and equally from the Liberals and from Mr.
Chamberlain.

[*To M. V. B.*]   BALMORAL CASTLE,
                                           OCTOBER 3RD.

It is Sunday night. We had church at Crathie this morning,
and this afternoon I walked with old K. K. [Kelly-Kenny] who
was amiability itself.

Then I interviewed Arnold-Forster and tried to get him to
appoint K. K. to the Salisbury command for 1 year, pending
Ian Hamilton's return, but I don't think I made much impression. However, A. F. told Knollys that he could not be sufficiently grateful *to me* for all I had done for him since he came into
office, and that had it not been for *me*, he does not think he
could have held on! So the poor little man has some sense of
gratitude. Of course I have always felt that I owed him a good
turn for having backed me up all through the committee days,
which he might, on the other hand, have resented. The King is
charming. In excellent humour—and very confidential.

. . . To-morrow I *stalk*! Everybody else—except V. Churchill,
who also stalks—goes to a picnic. The King offered me the
choice and I chose stalking! Old Donald—the P. Consort's
stalker, walked back from church with me this morning. He
was beautifully dressed in a kilt *and* plaid, and walked like a
six-year-old hill pony. He is 80 years of age.

. . . Poor old Sir Billy! [William Harcourt]. But what a
happy death. Could anyone wish for a happier? He has had a
most successful and happy life—and died at home—while still
cared for by those whom he loved.

[*To the Rt. Hon. A. J. Balfour.*]   BALMORAL CASTLE,
                                           OCTOBER 5TH.

. . . Much satisfaction at your speech, which was everything
anyone could wish. And there are no traces at present of offence
given anywhere.

After Joe [Chamberlain]'s speech we shall know more. Will you confer a Knighthood on Aston Webb, R.A., on November 9th? He is Pres. of B.I. of Arch. this year, and I think the moment has come to recognise his work on the Queen's memorial, for *his* share is practically completed.

The King will approve, if you propose it. Remember *you* are now the chairman of the Q.V. Memorial Committee! I suppose old Jack Sandars will make a row, as he has probably 10,000 candidates for honours!

[*To M. V. B.*]   BALMORAL CASTLE,
                                        OCTOBER 5TH.

... We have been at Invercauld to-day, driving deer, in rain and a wrong wind—so I did not see a beast all day, except an eagle who came about 30 yards over my head. A splendid fellow.

Shooting at Balmoral.

I had old Donald Stewart with me. He is extraordinary. He was stalking before the Queen ever came to Balmoral at all, i.e. before 1848—and was out with Prince Albert on his first stalk. Only two gentlemen had a stalk in his time —the Duke of Roxburgh and Lord Panmure. He called John Brown every name under the sun. He said he was an "abominable mon."

We had tea at his house, a sort of lodge of which he is the caretaker, called Dantzig. The King was wet through when he came in, and said, "Donald, lend me a pair of your shoes and stockings at once," and presently he appeared in them looking very queer.

Many thanks for General [French]'s Lecture to the Army Corps. It looks first-rate. I will read it to-night.

I sat next the King at dinner to-night, and he called me every name under the sun because my writing was so illegible. This was the pot and the kettle!

[*To Sir Douglas Haig.*[1]]   BALMORAL CASTLE,
                                               OCTOBER 7TH.

*Letter
on the
English
Army.*

I have not written to you for ages; but you need not suppose that I have slackened in the interest which I have always taken in the efforts which Lord K. and you are taking to get things into shape in India.

I have seen many of Lord K.'s admirable memoranda, and I think I know fairly well the merits of the case, which I hope he will fight to the finish.

The "dual" system has received a death blow in London, and there is no reason why at Simla it should not meet with a similar fate.

I doubt whether you can realise, so far away, the full import of the changes which have taken place here in military administration.

It is the spirit, as well as the substance, here, which has undergone such a complete revolution.

With you the struggle has been between two conflicting military departments. Here it has been between the military and civil elements of the W.O.

Now the field is clear, and if the soldiers display prudence and tenacity, the government of the Army is in their hands.

As you can imagine, the difficulty has been to find the right type of soldier to inaugurate the new system. As I told you before, no man who was much over 50 years of age, at the conclusion of the war, possessed a mind open to new ideas and novel conditions.

And among the younger men there were none of exceptional ability who could be spared from active command to undertake administrative office work.

Besides, as Lord K. will realise, a system dependant for its successful working upon a succession of Lord K.'s or Douglas Haig's (without flattery) is not a system suitable to the average conditions under which work has got to be done here.

[1] Then Inspector-General of Cavalry in India.

Between ourselves, the Army Council are not "fliers," but they are hard-working average sort of men, who are employed in settling the groundwork of an administrative plan, which, in the hands of a strong Chief of the General Staff, may, one of these days, become a very highly efficient machine.

It has been a difficult piece of work to carry through the necessary changes, and it has been impossible to relax effort for a day since last January.

But I think that the end is now coming into view. I have lived altogether among soldiers for over a year now, and have found the keenest support and enthusiasm among all the younger men, and a really high level of intelligence, and anxiety for reform.

Among them all, French has been the truest and most helpful; the broadest-minded, and the man who has shown most "elasticity and progress" in ideas. *On Gen. Sir John French.*

He has come on day by day, stones at a time; and though he has developed late in life, he has a high imagination, and a real enthusiasm for the art of war.

He has also managed to infuse this spirit into those surrounding him.

Anyway, if you could come back for a flying visit, you would, I am convinced, find a very different spirit prevailing here, to what you left behind.

When you have finished your work in India, and when Lord K. has finished his, you will both find the soil here well tilled and ready for your sowing.

There will be no necessity for Lord K. to accept Rosebery's dangerous blandishments, and convert himself into a General André, for he will find an adequate field for his great gifts prepared for him, outside the province of controversial political life.

In India, you will have great changes, for I doubt George Curzon returning. He is such an uncertain subject for prophecy that one cannot be sure, but as in any case he would not have remained beyond April, it seems hardly worth while to return in December or January.

Anyway, his successor has already been designated. One thing seems clear to everyone here, including the Prime Minister, which is that the days of the Government will not be prolonged beyond the General Election. I suppose this is equally clear to you from your distant standpoint.

We have had a curious party here, including old K. K. [Kelly-Kenny] and Arnold-Forster, but everything passed off most amicably.

I don't suppose you want to hear gossip, as you have endless correspondents who retail to you everything that is most talked about and is most untrustworthy. So I won't add to the number.

[*To the Rt. Hon. A. J. Balfour.*]   2, TILNEY ST.,
                                          OCTOBER 12TH.

Arnold-Forster's Position.

Glance at the enclosed, and you will see what a first-rate man you have in French, as I told you. A. F. [Arnold-Forster] was a great success at Balmoral, and when K. K. had gone, the King said to me, "It is a pity that Kelly-Kenny is so badly informed about the Army." So it was a score all round for our little friend; he has plucked up courage, and got his Army Council by the beard. I was so mortally afraid that his administrative capacity was like his shooting. He knows all about guns, but he can't hit a haystack. To-day I was at the War Office and everything is going better than you could have expected or hoped. I saw Clarke to-day, and told him to ask you to let me have that Memo.

[*To the Rt. Hon. A. J. Balfour.*]   2, TILNEY ST.,
                                          NOVEMBER 4TH.

I think this will interest you. I have also a most graphic letter from French, describing his journey. He is the best soldier we have got. More "character" and imagination than any other I have met, although a man recently educated and developed late in life.

[*To Mr. J. S. Sandars.*]   BUCKINGHAM PALACE,
                              JANUARY 13TH, 1905.

I have rushed in here because I am so mortally afraid of missing the post. A. F. has read me his letter, and it goes to the P.M. to-night.

He asks for a committee for the purpose of seeing whether the Army can be run for £25,000,000. That is the upshot of his request. He suggests eight names, from which the P.M. might select four. He says that the committee should report to the P.M., and mentions that he has talked over the matter with me. He does *not* suggest that the committee should be a sub-committee of Imperial Defence. *Enquiry into Army Organisation.*

This, however, is in my opinion essential for the reasons I gave you. Please rub this in. A. F. would like it, but did not venture to make it part of his proposal. He realises that in that case Clarke would be Sec. of the Committee and he would welcome that. I am sure that *four* members are sufficient, and I am sure that Roberts, French, G. Murray and myself could do better than a large number. His names are over the page.

. . . Roberts, Esher, G. Murray, L. of Battenberg, J. Fisher, Butler, Brackenbury.[1]

[*To Mr. J. S. Sandars.*]   2, TILNEY ST.,
                              JANUARY 14TH.

I have just telegraphed as follows to the Chief:—[Begins] I saw Fisher last night. I did not suggest topic, but he expressed *Fisher's Proposal for the Enquiry.*

[1] At this date Lord Roberts, Sir William Butler, and Sir Henry Brackenbury were in retirement. Sir George Murray was Perm. Under-Secretary to the Treasury.

strong opinion that best solution of problem would be the old Triumvirate. He would very much like to serve himself. I think you should know his opinion, though I do not share it. Curiously enough, I think A. F. would agree with Fisher from what he said to me. Esher [Ends].

The meaning of this is that I saw Jackie [Fisher] last night, and without telling him what was going on I discussed with him the general position of Army matters. He said that in his opinion the only way to deal with the whole question was to revive our committee. He said that there was nothing he should like better than to serve, and there is no reason why he should not do so.

He said one thing which is perfectly true, which is that a committee, if it is to be of any practical use, must be unanimous before it begins to sit, and that, except ours, he knows of no committee of which this can be predicted.

As I told you the other day, curiously enough, I don't think A. F. would object. In fact I think he would trust us far more readily than he would any other body. I still, however, maintain my view that unless you could hitch such a committee on to the Defence Committee there are grave objections to appointing it.

[*To the Rt. Hon. A. J. Balfour.*]   2, TILNEY ST.,
                                          JANUARY 17TH.

I send you back your draft, A. F.'s letter, and my reply to your note to me.

I have talked over the whole matter at great length with Jack Sandars and Sir George [Clarke]. They approve my reply to the points you raised. I am very hopeful that if you see your way to this *secret* committee (for that is what it should be in its initial stage) very good work can be done.

Believe me, there are lots of 3rd class cruisers and old iron embedded in Army Estimates. As A. F. truly says, *he* is obliged to cut away at the sound links of the Army and has to leave unpruned the rotten branches.

[*To M. V. B.*]　　　　　　　　　　JANUARY 30TH.

I have sent your letter to Pittsburg, U.S., where I hope the fair Edna [May] is getting thousands out of the iron-masters, including old Carnegie.

If he has any decent romance in him, he will found an Edna May free library at once.

We had a long meeting with A. J. B. [Balfour]. He does *Army* not really understand A. F.'s [Arnold-Forster's] scheme. I am *Schemes.* not sure that anybody does.

To-morrow we are going to try and discover what is the total force of *regular* troops that are produceable in peace under A. F.'s plan, and to what extent they can be expanded in war.

I think a prolonged catechism is the best way of approaching the subject. *Then*, we can ask A. J. B. whether he desires to increase or limit numbers. We shall, after that, have some basis upon which to frame a scheme. Clarke expounded *his* scheme. But it is a *paper* affair, like A. F.'s, and would not stand a puff of criticism.

[*To Lord Roberts.*]　　　　　　　2, TILNEY ST.,
　　　　　　　　　　　　　　　　　FEBRUARY 18TH.

I hear that Arnold-Forster—after the Selection Board yester- *Intrigue* day—told the Officers present something of Mr. Balfour's pro- *about the* posals. He put various points to them—in a fashion which did *Army* not convey the real scheme—and then tried to elicit from them *Schemes.* a hostile opinion.

This is hardly fair.

I explained to Lord Grenfell—who told me of this—that he must not take everything which Arnold-Forster says to represent accurately Mr. Balfour's views. We have tried hard to keep the committee secret; so that it is going rather far for Arnold-Forster to refer to our work.

I am just about to see the King—and if he says anything of it to me (as he saw Lord Grenfell this morning, who may have mentioned it to H.M.), I shall ask him to see you, and ask *your* view.

I hope that nothing has been told him, as these half-truths are very misleading.

[*To Mr. J. S. Sandars.*]   2, TILNEY ST.,
FEBRUARY 19TH.

*A Check
to Intrigue.*   Your letter, and the action of Arnold-Forster in trying to get an opinion upon Mr. Balfour's scheme from the officers composing the selection board, confirm my opinion mentioned to you some time back, that Mr. Balfour would do well to ask these same officers, i.e. French, Grenfell, Methuen and Tucker, together with the four military members of the A.C., to a meeting of the committee. He could also ask A. F. to be present.

I would then suggest that Mr. Balfour should deliver a short but exceedingly trenchant address, to the following effect,

1. He could tell them "what the Army is for."

2. Roughly what the numbers of the Army should be.

3. The conditions under which an army has to be maintained :
   a. voluntary service,
   b. retention of the militia,
   c. due regard to economy.

4. In general terms, his idea of how the Army should be constituted.

5. Appeal to them to *help* to solve the problems; *not* to go about outside criticising and finding fault; but to place before him difficulties which strike them; and solutions which occur to them.

6. Conclude with an appeal to be loyal to Arnold-Forster and to *him*, and to all those who, like themselves, desire that the Army should be as well organised and efficient as it can be made, subject to the conditions aforesaid!!

I am confident that no step which the P.M. could take would

be better calculated to smooth over difficulties. *But* it should be a *sine qua non* that *no one else* says a word!

[*To Sir John Fisher.*]   2, TILNEY ST.,
FEBRUARY 21ST.

I want you to read this exordium to a paper which we drew *Military* up to-day, and which I wrote feeling that somehow it was *Policy.* "Fisheresque."

"It must be assumed that the Army is maintained for offensive-defensive purposes of the Empire. It is *not* to be organised for the defence of these shores, but is intended to take the field, at any threatened point, where the interests of the Empire are imperilled, and especially on the N.W. frontier of India.

"All questions of what hitherto has been called Home Defence have been excluded from consideration as outside the purposes for which the British Army is required."

Do you agree?

[*To M. V. B.*]   ORCHARD LEA,
FEBRUARY 21ST AND 22ND.

. . . Tullibardine lunched with me, and was as clever as possible. I took him off to the Defence Committee afterwards, as he had plenty to say about Yeomanry.

We had a long day. From 11 until 5.30, but I drew up a paper, stating first the principles upon which the new Army ought to be based, and then the suggested numbers and constitution. I want the P.M. to have it to-morrow before the debate.

It was agreed to by Bobs and the others. Directly it is printed, I will send you a copy to show the General [French]. Tell him this. Here is my exordium:—

"The Army is maintained for offensive-defensive purposes of the Empire. It is not to be organised for the defence of these shores, but it is intended to take the field, at any threatened point, where the interests of the Empire are at stake, and especially on the N.W. frontier of India."

Position of the Govern- ment—

Ask Johnny [French] if he approves. There was great anxiety to-day about the Division to-night. Certainly the Government got the worst of the debate yesterday, and George Wyndham was very feeble and downhearted to-day.

[*Journals.*]   ORCHARD LEA,
                                                  MARCH 7TH.

The position of the Government has been very insecure from day to day and it is contrary to their anticipations that they are still in office. The MacDonnell incident was the great difficulty,

—the MacDonnell Incident,

for the feeling in the party was that owing to the imprudence of George Wyndham the Unionist position was given away. So strongly did Londonderry and Carson feel about the matter that they were quite prepared to leave the Government if Wyndham remained a Minister, and such was the temper of the whole Conservative Party that the Whips were forced to rely upon and press the feelings of personal loyalty to Arthur Balfour in order to prevent the whole Unionist Party from walking out of the House on the night of the Division.

Wyndham spoke amid dead silence, and altogether the position has been very painful and a great trial to the P.M. He was very reluctant to part with George Wyndham and only consented to do so when he found that to keep him was not only to invite defeat but to destroy the party organisation. The crisis is not yet over, because if MacDonnell remains the whole party will feel that they still have a mortal enemy within the citadel. On the other hand, it is very difficult to get rid of him, as he is an eminent public servant and there is no immediate place to put him into.

There has been great difficulty in filling Selborne's place and there are yet two vacancies in the Cabinet. So altogether the position of the Government is full of difficulty and danger. They will probably always survive a direct attack, but their flanks are very much exposed from day to day.

The Afghan crisis is not so acute as it was a week ago. Arthur Balfour has been very firm and has refused to allow the Indian Government to withdraw our envoy, which they were anxious to do. George Curzon has put a pistol to the Amir's head and wished to tell him that he must either sign the Treaty which we offered him, or our Envoy would be withdrawn. The Cabinet, on the other hand, decided that the Treaty proposed by the Amir, although not satisfactory, was sufficient, and that in any case it was the lesser of two evils that Dane should come away with an unsatisfactory Treaty in his pocket than with no treaty at all. That the "forward party" in India headed by Curzon, believed that a war with Afghanistan and the occupation of Kandahar by us while Russia is in difficulties is the right policy, there can be very little doubt, and that some pretext will be found in a comparatively short time to bring on a war is more than probable. *—The Afghan Treaty.*

Selborne was very anxious to go to India and it was practically arranged that he was to do so, but as Curzon has given no indication of an intention of leaving India within a measurable distance of time, Selborne, with some doubts of the prudence of the step, has elected to go to Africa instead. He will probably live to regret his decision.

It is pretty certain now that Campbell-Bannerman will form the new Government, and it is not at all impossible that he will go as Prime Minister to the House of Lords and leave Asquith to lead the House of Commons as Chancellor of the Exchequer. There seems to be grounds to believe that Rosebery will not be averse to serving as Foreign Secretary under Spencer, and some think that this will affect the situation, but I personally do not share this view. Great pressure is being put upon the King to send for Spencer and Campbell-Bannerman together and to ask their advice. I trust that he will not give way to this temptation, as it would be to give away the most important prerogative of *Probable Liberal Prime Minister.*

the Sovereign. Although many people think otherwise, there is no precedent for such a step. I have looked through all the precedents for the King in the private archives at Windsor and there is not a single example in the Queen's reign of her asking advice of anyone except the outgoing Minister as to the person upon whom her choice should fall. The obvious duty of the King is to make up his own mind, and the wisest thing he can do is to adhere rigidly to precedent.

Work of the Defence Committee.

I have been sitting for a month on a Sub-Committee of the Defence Committee, presided over by the Prime Minister, in order to try and frame a scheme for the re-organisation of the Army, and in his absence I have been presiding.

My companions have been Lord Roberts and Sir George Murray, with Sir George Clarke acting as Secretary. This is a very secret matter, but we have done a lot of work and have drawn up what I think is a very good scheme. One thing at any rate we have done, and it is to lay down quite clearly the principles upon which an Army should be maintained, and what the size of that Army should be.

This has never been done before, and as it is placed on record in a very solemn document signed by the Prime Minister and left behind with the Defence Committee, there is very little doubt that the new Government will accept our conclusions and act upon them should the present Government quit office.

Notes on the preceding entry:—

The period from February 21st, and earlier, until March 7th was occupied in the House by the amendments to the Address and by discussion of the MacDonnell incident.

A scheme for devolution in Ireland, put forward by a body styled the Irish Reform Association, had been prepared with the assistance of Sir A. MacDonnell, Under-Secretary for Ireland, who had supplied much information for the purpose. This excited the anger of the Unionists, particularly of Carson and Londonderry. The subject was discussed at length on a motion of Mr. Redmond condemning the Irish government as unpopular, ineffective, extravagant, and productive of universal unrest. The motion was defeated by 50. Seven or more Irish Unionists and some English Unionists, sympathising with them, abstained from voting. Two days later Mr. Redmond obtained leave to raise the matter again on a motion for the adjournment, and on this occasion the Government majority fell to 42.

Mr. George Wyndham was the Secretary for Ireland at this date, but was soon afterwards compelled to resign by the conviction that the MacDonnell incident had deprived him of the power to do any good in Ireland.

Lord Selborne went to South Africa on March 2nd, and the Earl Cawdor, formerly Chairman of the Great Western Railway, was appointed to the Admiralty on the 6th.

Sir Louis Dane was in Afghanistan from the end of 1904 until April 1905 before he could negotiate the renewal of the treaty that the English had made with the Amir's father; and it was then renewed only at the cost of an increased subsidy.

During the month of March, and onward to October, the Russian revolution usually called "of 1904" was at a height which left the country almost devoid of effective government.

[*To the Rt. Hon. A. J. Balfour.*]   ORCHARD LEA,
MARCH 11TH.

Do you not think that it would be well, at this stage, for you to write to A. F. [Arnold-Forster] a letter which might be of use hereafter, stating the two main purposes of your Memorandum? *On the Army.*

That you wished, before approaching any question of Army Reform, to lay down in clear and unmistakable terms the uses for which the Army has to be maintained, and what the strength of the Army should be in time of peace, and to what size it should be capable of expansion during the first year of a great war.

Since, according to the gospel of Jackie [Fisher], "repetition is the essence of conviction," you might explain that the first part of your Memorandum is based upon a prolonged correspondence with Kitchener, and is the result of a careful enquiry and discussion by the Defence Committee; that upon this portion of your Memorandum you do not wish at the present stage any comment to be made, and you must ask him to accept it as defining the conditions precedent to the consideration of any scheme of Army reform.

With regard to the second part of your Memorandum, you invite criticism and discussion. I think it would be well to tell him that you would be glad to hear the views of the Army Council upon the suggestions you have made, which are an attempt to combine the principles of his scheme with the retention of the militia as a substitute for his Home Service Army.

Forgive me for bothering you, and do not answer this.

[*To M. V. B.*]   ORCHARD LEA,
                                                     MARCH 15TH.

. . . There is not much news. Not a word from India, and the Treaty with the Amir is not signed yet.

On Russia. . . . The Russians appear to be throwing up the sponge, and no one believes that with the affairs of the Empire in their present state it will be possible to raise new levies. Was there ever so great an object lesson in the value of careful and scientific preparation, or so heavy a blow dealt to the policy of "muddling through"? A similar series of disasters to us would destroy the Empire, as although we might not have a street revolution, we should inevitably have an overwhelming party in favour of reducing the sacrifice in blood and money on the altar of Imperial rule. It would be a case of "India is not worth a shilling on the income-tax or the lives of 50,000 street-bred people."

[*To M. V. B.*]   2, TILNEY ST.,
                                                     MARCH 17TH.

Government Position Improved. The Government have got through the extreme severity of the Irish crisis, and the Prime Minister said to me yesterday he thought they might survive Easter. There are of course a good many points not yet quite settled. Dudley's position is unsatisfactory and he will have to go, but the most favourable moment for his retirement is difficult to settle.[1] Walter Long behaved beautifully; he was very anxious to be First Lord of the Admiralty and had the strongest objection to going to Ireland. But he waived his personal feelings in the matter. He has not yet settled what he is going to do about MacDonnell.

You will have seen that Rosebery and Edward Grey have been making speeches about Ireland in a contradictory sense, but neither of them in a sense which appeals to the majority of the Liberal Party. This confusion in the ranks of the enemy has strengthened the Government's position.

The King was rather unwell for four days. One of his lungs has been a little affected and he has had a very bad cough. As he cannot eat much or smoke, he is very uncomfortable. I was with him for a long time this morning, and though he was rather drowsy he is slightly better. However, he has got a big dinner-party to-morrow night which he is not going to attend. He remains in London till the end of the month, when he goes to Knowsley for the Grand National.

Foreign Affairs: Portugal—

The Queen went three days ago to Portsmouth to the yacht, but the weather has been too abominable. She has not yet started for Portugal. Princess Victoria, as you know, is not a very good sailor. The idea is that the Queen should go on from Portugal to Gibraltar, but the lateness of her departure will probably prevent this as the German Emperor is expected at Gibraltar shortly and she has no desire to meet him there.

—Russia—

There was a telegram to-day to say that Kuropatkin was relieved of his command, which will be regretted by all the foreign officers who have been attached to him. They all agree that although possibly not a genius he was the best of all the Russians in the field.

[1] Lord Dudley, Lord-Lieutenant in Ireland, had been associated with Sir A. MacDonnell in the incident already mentioned.

For many reasons, strategical and other, his task was hopeless from the beginning.

—Baghdad Railway.

It is a very curious thing that the Defence Committee and the General Staff have been very much exercised of late about the Baghdad Railway. There are some very interesting papers written by them which point to the conclusion that the action of the Government in refusing permission to us to take part in that enterprise was a grave political and strategical mistake. A great deal of information supplied by the Foreign Office to the Defence Committee as to the form of the original negotiations is erroneous and shows that they never fully grasped what the effect of the proposed arrangements would be if they had carried them out.

The view, however, of the Defence Committee is that if they had been constituted as they are now, and working as they do now, when these arrangements were under consideration, we should have participated in the making of the Baghdad Railway.[1]

[*To M. V. B.*]   2, TILNEY ST.,
                                                          MARCH 21ST.

. . . The King is better to-day, and though he is still in his room, he is convalescent. I shall go and see him this afternoon, when I have lunched with Nicholson. Not a sign of Tullibardine, so I don't know whether he expects me to dinner or not. Look at Redmond's speech in *The Times* to-day in answer to Rosebery. He says some very true things in a very trenchant manner. . . .[2]

. . . Millie [Duchess of Sutherland] dined with some of the "souls" last night, and when she arrived there was a dead

---

[1] See ante, Vol. I, pp. 386, 396, 397, 410.

[2] Lord Rosebery, speaking in the City a few days before, gave as a ground for postponing the consideration of Home Rule that the demands of the Irish Party had changed and they were now advocating a dual control. Mr. Redmond very ably demonstrated that his party had not altered their programme in any particular since the time of Mr. Gladstone.

silence, and she looked round and saw a monk, tonsured, telling his beads. She was told it was Father Gapon, just arrived from Russia. He was very shy and speechless. When they went in to dinner, he remained behind, and then it turned out that he was a "super" from the Garrick. Do you call that funny?

[*To M. V. B.*]　　　　　　　　　　2, TILNEY ST.,
　　　　　　　　　　　　　　　　　　　　APRIL 10TH.

I think that the telephone—although we only get 6 minutes —is a substitute for letters.

. . . There is no news at all to-day. I have been in the City and have seen no one of importance. Barrie was very small and sweet to-day, very like one of the lost boys in Peter Pan. He is the most quaint personality that ever found its way into literature.

The Russian Fleet seems to be making a very loud demonstra- *The* tion, but what account they will give of the Japs, is another *Russian* matter. Still, if it comes to a fight, they ought to be able to *Fleet.* injure some of the Japanese ships. Togo is not likely to risk a pitched battle, but I should think would fight them with Destroyers and Cruisers. He is very strong in both.[1]

[*To M. V. B.*]　　　　　　　　　　2, TILNEY ST.,
　　　　　　　　　　　　　　　　　　　　APRIL 18TH.

. . . The P.M. thinks there are three rocks ahead of the *Balfour's* Government :— *Forecasts.*

1. The Kitchener business in India. The P.M. does not agree with Lansdowne, and if either of them hold out, I think the

[1] Admiral Rozhdestvensky, on his way to the Far East, was sighted off Singapore on the 8th, after his movements had been unknown for some time. In his final meeting with the Japanese fleet he lost nearly the whole of his fighting ships.

P.M. will let the Government go. George Curzon writes that if he is overruled, both he and his Council resign, but that he is sure K. does not mean resignation. K. writes that if *he* is overruled he resigns, but that there is no fear of George Curzon quitting India under any circumstances.

2. The Arnold-Forster scheme. If A. F. commences to recruit for his short service army, the P.M. thinks it would be better to let the Government go, than to have an internecine struggle.

3. A most difficult Church question which looms ahead.

[*To Mr. J. S. Sandars.*]   ST. JAMES' PALACE,
MAY 4TH.

The Indian Government Dispute.

. . . Everything that I hear from India and about India leads to the conclusion that if Kitchener is overruled he will throw up his command. But there again there is room for compromise. As the party hostile to Kitchener have sent an emissary, General de Brathe, over here, it might be a good thing to ask him to send over someone to represent his views; it is quite possible that Marker, A. F.'s [Arnold-Forster's] Private Secretary, who was with Kitchener a long time and is a shrewd fellow, would be capable of answering questions which arise upon Kitchener's Memoranda.

Perhaps Kitchener might be asked whether Marker is sufficiently familiar with his views. To every unprejudiced mind it should be clear that two Military Members of Council, which is the present regime, are a source of inconvenience and confusion. The only weak point in Kitchener's case is the possible situation which may arise in the event of a great war, when the Commander-in-Chief would be with troops in the field and the Viceroy left with no Military adviser at all. This might be remedied by appointing an Assistant Commander-in-Chief, or Chief of the General Staff, or call him whatever name you please, who would, as a matter of course, take the Commander-in-Chief's place upon the Viceroy's council in the absence of the Commander-in-Chief.

By some such method as this you ought to be able to ensure continuity in the military advice given to the Viceroy without friction and without resort to extraordinary measures. One obvious fact stands out with absolute clearness amid all this controversy, and it is, that the P.M. cannot possibly allow Lord K. to leave India at this moment when great military changes are in progress, only half completed, as the result of differences of opinion upon the question of military administration. Even if Kitchener were wrong, which I don't think he is, to allow him now to throw up his task would be to choose the greater evil. The broad fact remains that the Military Members of Council have had an opportunity for the last ten years to carry out the reforms, which Kitchener has initiated, and they have shown themselves unequal to the task. The inference is obvious.

MEMORANDUM ON INDIAN ARMY ADMINISTRATION

MAY 11TH.

The *Terms of Reference* contain the pith of the whole question. *The Indian Army.* In 1879 a Commission presided over by Sir Ashley Eden reported in strong terms against the continuance of the dual system of Army Administration in India.

Their solution was to remove the C.-in-C. from the Council of the Viceroy, and make him merely "executive commander" of the Army.

Lord Lytton, in a memorandum, written with remarkable lucidity of thought and style, strongly endorsed the arguments of the commission, but differed from their conclusion.

Lord Lytton's reasoning was on all fours with Lord Kitchener's, and his solution of the problem precisely that which Lord Kitchener proposes.

Lord Lytton's memorandum has never been answered, and is not susceptible of being satisfactorily controverted.

Lord Dufferin arrived at other conclusions, and was satisfied with the system as he found it, but in this respect he differed from the Eden Commission (of which Lord Roberts was a member) and his argument is a poor one, mainly drawn from analogy with English institutions, which in fact cannot be compared with those by which India is governed.

The Secretary of State's despatch to India dated 2nd December 1904 is very moderate and sensible; and clearly shows how much he is impressed with the seriousness of the situation, and how little confidence he feels in the existing system.

In the reply of the Government of India dated 23rd March, there is nothing of importance. It is a colourless document, merely intended to enclose the real "pièces justificatives," which are—

(a) Lord Kitchener's Memorandum.

(b) Sir E. Elles' rejoinder.

(c) The Viceroy's summing up.

In addition (but not included in these papers) Lord Kitchener wrote an elaborate criticism of Sir E. Elles' paper, in the form of a letter to a member of the Indian Council at home. It is of great length, but of admirable clearness.

It does not add materially to the weight of Lord Kitchener's original Memorandum dated 1st January 1905, but the case is argued in greater detail.

When all has been said, the case resolves itself into the following facts:—

(a) Lord Kitchener's far-reaching reforms of the Indian Army, accepted by the Government of India, prove that the Army was *not organised nor prepared* for war on a great scale under modern conditions. There is nothing to show that if Lord Kitchener had not gone to India these reforms would have been initiated.

The state of things, condemned by the adoption of these reforms, had been tolerated for years under the existing system of Administration.

(b) Lord Kitchener's argument, showing the unfitness of the present organisation to cope with the conditions incidental to a war of the first magnitude, is unanswered.

(*c*) The Viceroy and the Military Member of Council argue their case from the point of view of Peace and not of War conditions.

(*d*) Lord Kitchener, whose talents are generally admitted to be primarily *administrative,* condemns as thoroughly unsound the present system of administration.

Under these circumstances, an unprejudiced observer would be likely to draw the inference that in this controversy Lord Kitchener is likely to be right and the Government of India wrong.

[*To the Rt. Hon. A. J. Balfour.*]   2, TILNEY ST.,
MAY 12TH.

After reading your wonderful speech, I am intensely proud of two things:— *Balfour on the Defence Committee.*

1. That I was the first to suggest to you a "permanent nucleus" for the committee which *you* founded: and that I insisted in putting this in the forefront of the Report.

2. Much more proud of the fact, that for 25 years I have been honoured with your friendship. *That* is a solid fact, which leaves everything else rather in shadow.[1]

[*From the Rt. Hon. A. J. Balfour.*]   MAY 16TH.

MY DEAR REGGIE,

One line to say how grateful I am for your letter. There can be no doubt that you and your Committee were right in pressing for a larger and more important Staff for the Defence Committee. I hope that public opinion will not allow the machine

[1] Mr. Balfour's speech was on the constitution and scope of the Committee for Imperial Defence; and also on its opinions with regard to the possibility of invasion at home and in India. It was in respect of the Committee's opinions that the speech was particularly notable, being the simplest and most direct statement on such problems that had been heard in the House for many years.

that we have so laboriously constructed and set going to be
"scrapped!"   Yours ever,

                              ARTHUR JAMES BALFOUR.

[*To M. V. B.*]   ORCHARD LEA,
                                      MAY 15TH.

Roberts on   . . . This morning I saw Bobs [Lord Roberts] at his house,
Kitchener.   where he was receiving some Gurkhas. We talked about the
C.G.S., and about Rawly.[1] He takes strongly our view. Then
he told me his idea of a compromise with Kitchener. Like all
compromises where a principle is involved, it is defective and
would never work. But we have got to keep K. in harness, and
if the whole of what he asks for cannot be granted, then I suppose some "transaction" will become imperative.

Then I saw the King for about an hour. He was in undress
uniform—and in a charming mood. He approved of all the
Red Cross resolutions, as I had drafted them, and also of the
names of the Council.

Treves came in, and the King told him that he had read his
book with absorbing interest. Derek Keppel was operated on
for appendicitis this morning. All well.

Lady Sarah Wilson's little boy died, because it was too late
to operate. Yet there were no signs that it *was* too late.

[*To M. V. B.*]   ORCHARD LEA,
                                      MAY 23RD.

. . . When at B. Palace to-day the King sent down word
that he wanted to walk in the garden with me, so we walked
two miles, i.e. twice round. He was in one of his best moods,
and even the pursuit of a brood of ducks by his dog, whom *he*
pursued in turn for about five minutes with a stick, did not
ruffle him. He talked a great deal about Nicholson and Lyttelton

_____
[1] General Sir Henry Rawlinson.

and Lord K. I will tell you about it when we meet. He is looking forward to to-morrow. Two of his motors go down.

He knows about our red motor and says it may be useful if one of his breaks down. But he himself must not go in an open motor, as he invariably catches cold. He wears a serge, and service belts. Great coats if cold, and in any case motoring.

The weather looks all right. He asked after you. Mind you get off your horse if you are anywhere near him riding. He is bored by fidgety horses.

[*To M. V. B.*]　　　　　　　　2, TILNEY ST.,
　　　　　　　　　　　　　　　MAY 24TH.

Although I told it all to you on the telephone, it may as well *The* go among your records that the King was *delighted* with his *King at* Aldershot visit. He said it all went without a hitch, and that the *Aldershot.* plan was so simple that he understood it all "much better than last year."

I asked him if *you* had disgraced yourself, and he said you "did not put yourself forward; kept in the background, but were always there when you were wanted, a model A.D.C." He is pretty observant, as you see.

[*To M. V. B.*]　　　　　　　　ORCHARD LEA,
　　　　　　　　　　　　　　　MAY 28TH.

. . . I have been writing some notes on the Draft Treaty which the Japanese Minister handed yesterday to Lansdowne. It is an offensive and defensive alliance for 10 years in the Far East and India. It will not quite do as it stands.

[*To M. V. B.*]　　　　　　　　2, TILNEY ST.,
　　　　　　　　　　　　　　　JUNE 6TH.

. . . The only excitement to-day has been Delcassé's fall, *France and* which is a triumph for the German Emperor. Of course the *Germany.*

crushing defeat of Russia redresses the balance in favour of Germany. Still, it is weak of the French to sacrifice their most successful Foreign Minister. I suppose that he was too successful!

The Republican spirit devours the ablest man—unless the man is strong enough—like Napoleon—to kick over the Republic.[1]

[To M. V. B.]   2, TILNEY ST.,
JUNE 7TH.

. . . The party last night at Buckingham Palace was very well done. Melba and Caruso first rate. The Queen had on her Russian tiara with the Imperial crown behind it, and looked a fitting leader of about 12 Duchesses, one smarter than the other.

Millie [Duchess of Sutherland], of course, looked far the best. The King of Spain is not a bad anæmic sort of boy. One of his courtiers sleeps in his room every night to guard him, like the early Valois French kings. That is pretty mediæval.

[To M. V. B.]   BATSFORD PARK (LORD REDESDALE'S),
JULY 9TH.

This is a very wonderful place considering that it is the creation of a man, who started to make a garden out of a barren hill when he was not young, and has lived to see it a paradise. I wish you could be here.

Chamberlain's Opinions.

Chamberlain has aged. He was 69 yesterday. But he is *in*

[1] At the conclusion of the various Moroccan discussions M. Delcassé found himself attacked by the Left for having made an Anglo-French agreement without consulting Germany, and thus creating a risk of war. At the same time he found himself without support on the Right because he had afterwards given in to the German demands and arranged a second Moroccan conference.

talk as vigorous as ever. He is dead keen for the Government to go out. He thinks that once in opposition Arthur [Balfour] cannot fail to take up the line along which Chamberlain desires to see him move. Mrs. Chamberlain is quite as much *au courant* of politics as her husband.

Only George Dudley, Mensdorf, and the Keppels are here. The rest of the party is family—including Lady Airlie.

. . . I am perfectly certain that if the Government stay in over August, there will come a W.O. crisis and that A. F. [Arnold-Forster] will retire. Then the question will arise whether I shall take his place or not.

NOTE:—Mr. Balfour's Government was defeated on July 20th on an amendment of Mr. Redmond regarding the Irish Land Act, which was carried by 200 to 196. A Cabinet Council was held on the 23rd and on the 24th Mr. Balfour announced that he would neither resign nor dissolve. Campbell-Bannerman denounced this as unconstitutional, Redmond as contemptible, Lloyd George and Winston Churchill spoke in language of unusual violence. Edward Grey said there could no longer be that mutual respect which ought to exist between the House and its leader. After these speeches the Opposition nevertheless allowed the Government's motion for adjournment to pass *nem. con.*

[*To Mr. J. S. Sandars.*]   BATSFORD PARK,
                                                              JULY 23RD.

All the defeats of 1872 are recorded in Mr. Gladstone's letters to the Queen, but there is no hint of a resignation. Two defeats in one week in April were followed by a motion of Mr. Leatham's upon which the Government were defeated by a majority of *one*. This amendment, in Mr. Gladstone's opinion, very gravely affected the efficiency of the Ballot Act. He attempted to get the H. of C. to rescind their previous vote, and was beaten by 28. Yet, there is no sign of resignation.

Precedents for the Prime Minister.

The Queen drew attention to this series of serious blows. Yet, as you know, Mr. Gladstone survived nearly two years.

Perhaps the most absurd case is the defeat of Rosebery's Government in 1894 upon Labouchere's motion to get rid of the House of Lords. This, as you recollect, was a motion on the address. It was carried, and the Cabinet were obliged to adopt a declaration drawn up by Sir William Harcourt, substituting a new address for the amended address. The H. of C. were satisfied with their previous victory, and allowed their expression of pious opinion to be rescinded *nem. con.*

Yet, after this slap in the face, there was no talk of resigning, and in point of fact Rosebery continued just a year longer in office. Please remember that after his defeat on April 16th, 1872, Mr. G. was beaten again on the 18th. So take care!! History so often repeats itself. *Sign the Japanese treaty.*

[*To M. V. B.*]   2, TILNEY STREET,
                                              JULY 24TH.

I don't think I told you about the long talk I had with the Prime Minister on Saturday, and how firmly he put aside all temptation to resign office while the Japanese Treaty remained unsigned. This should be accomplished in a few days.

. . . The General [French] was very well and most amiable. He did not leave town very early. Winston [Churchill], I am told, made to-night one of the most insolent speeches ever heard in Parliament.

[*To Lord Knollys*, at his request.]   2, TILNEY STREET,
                                              JULY 26TH.

On the Office of Secretary of State.

I doubt whether full consideration has been given to the proposal to create new Secretaries of State, which the Government have embodied in a Bill.

One obvious effect of this addition to the number of persons holding high position, will be to lower its relative importance.

At present, when Cabinets are large and inclined to grow larger, what may be called the inner circle of the Government is usually composed of the five Secretaries of State plus the Chancellor of the Exchequer. When Cabinets are in process of formation, these are the offices to which the most prominent men are commonly appointed. The position of First Lord of the Admiralty has in recent times been raised, financially speaking, to the level of a Secretaryship of State, although the rank of a politician holding that office still stands on a lower level. Is it proposed that the two new Secretaries of State shall receive emoluments equal to those of the older offices? If not, these posts will fall at once into two categories, which would be a misfortune.

It is also well, perhaps, to consider that the time is not far distant when the Viceroyship of Ireland will disappear and in that case the eighth Secretaryship of State (for Ireland) will have to be created, which must, of necessity, be followed by the creation of a ninth (for Scotland). It would be hopeless to expect to obtain men of nearly equal calibre to fill these nine high offices, and, in event of failure, the position of Secretary of State must inevitably suffer.

It would not surprise me if the real object of this Bill, which is somewhat obscure, may not be to exercise pressure upon the Treasury to grant a higher scale of salary to all those serving in these two hard-worked departments. That is a laudable object, and if it can only be obtained in this way, the sacrifice (for there *is* a sacrifice) may be worth making, in view of the great importance of the offices of Trade and Local Government in these days.

But I think that the King might perhaps urge these considerations upon Mr. Balfour in order to see what the Prime Minister has to say but I do not suppose that His Majesty would care to press any objection he might entertain to this Bill, should the Prime Minister furnish strong administrative reasons, which do not at present appear either in Sandars' letter or within the folds of the Bill itself.

[*To Lord Kitchener.*]   2, TILNEY STREET,
JULY 26TH.

*Lord
Kitchener's
Position
in India.*

You seem to be getting into smoother waters, and although the final settlement may not be exactly what you wished, I suppose you feel that the future holds possibilities which were entirely absent when the old arrangement was in force.

You have broken down a perfectly hopeless system, although you may not be able at once to rear upon its ruins precisely the structure you wished.

For my part, I wish you could be prevailed upon, now that you have inaugurated this great change in India, to shift your sphere of energy to this country.

I know that you will not agree with me at this moment, but I venture to think that this is because you do not quite realise what has happened during the past year; but I should think the future

*On the
Office of
Chief of
Staff.*

full of hope for the Army, if you would accept the office of Chief of the Staff to the King, and establish yourself here to undertake the great work of reorganisation which would grow rapidly under your hand.

The position—if you were to accept it—would have to be enhanced in importance—and this could best be done by marking your advent

(*a*) By an increase in the emoluments of the post.

(*b*) By giving you at once a Field-Marshal's baton.

Nothing could mark more clearly the intention that you should have as free a hand as is consistent with our parliamentary institutions, to mould the Army into shape.

If I were Secretary of State, I would make an appeal to your patriotism, which I hope you would find it difficult to resist; and I have very little doubt that Mr. Balfour would anticipate the action of any Secretary of State, if he had any idea that you could be prevailed upon to take the British Army in hand.

Perhaps you do not altogether perceive, at a distance from home, the immense power which, under the existing system, a Chief of the General Staff potentially exercises.

No Commander-in-Chief, under the old limitations, enjoyed such authority.

The Statutory powers of the Secretary of State rendered all real power in a Commander-in-Chief nugatory, whereas under the present system a strong and determined Chief of the General Staff, could *administer* the Army practically unchallenged.

Moreover, the Defence Committee increases in power and authority every day, and upon that body a Chief of the General Staff, whose mind is clear, and whose determination was obvious, must wield an authority, which has never been exercised in this country to the same degree since the death of the Duke of Wellington.

These remarks might strike you as exaggerated when you contemplate the very excellent and worthy occupant of the post in question, but, as no one knows better than yourself, it is the man who makes the post, and not the converse, in every system of Administration.

You would, without difficulty, think of several predecessors of your own in India, whose tenure of the high office which you now hold did not enhance its authority.

The mischief here is moral, and lies deep down in the habits of Army officers.

Needs of Army Administration.

What is wanted is an electrifying agency, applied with your special vigour, without a relaxation of effort for six or seven years.

There is no one but yourself who can apply it, with any hope of success.

That is my excuse for a private and personal appeal to you to consider, whether you would not make the sacrifice, should it ever be demanded of you.

For sacrifice it might possibly be, not in the sense of possible failure, for that is out of the question, but sacrifice of moral and material ease.

I have written this unknown to anyone, and it is for your eyes alone, but I have the welfare of the Army so at heart, that I cannot refrain from suggesting to you the method by which that welfare can be most certainly achieved.[1]

N.B.—You realise that the defeat of Russia by Japan and the new treaty between Japan and Britain very much alter the character of the Indian problem.

[To M. V. B.]   ORCHARD LEA,
                                          JULY 28TH.

. . . You see that Fisher is sending the Fleet to the Baltic. He never loses a chance of irritating the Emperor.

[To Mr. J. S. Sandars.]   ROMAN CAMP,
                                        AUGUST 3RD.

Sorry about Tokio. Let us try Simla. I have telegraphed to you a suggestion. Our hopes are not yet wrecked. Perhaps it will be well for you to give a hint to A. F. [Arnold-Forster] that D. Haig ought to be retained as Director of Staff duties, and that the problem is to find a place for Hutchinson.[2]

Will you read the enclosed from the Duke of Bedford, which entirely endorses the chief's[3] views on Army Reform ? When the chief has seen it, give it to Clarke.

[1] For the reply see August 14th.

[2] Sir Douglas Haig was still in India as Inspector-General of the Cavalry. Lt.-Gen. H. D. Hutchinson was assistant Military Secretary at the India Office. The post of Director of Staff Duties ultimately went to Gen. Hutchinson.

[3] Rt. Hon. A. J. Balfour.

VISCOUNT ESHER.

Lord R. [Roberts] was rather inconsequential at the   *Lord*
Mansion House. If we want 500,000 and 7,000 officers, which   *Roberts'*
I do not question, for a great war with a European power,   *Policy.*
rifle clubs are a "ridiculus mus." There is great force in
Spender's article,[1] *West. Gaz.*, 2nd August.

The Defence Committee must not speak with two and uncertain voices. Why cannot these great men walk in Indian file?

[*To M. V. B.*]   ROMAN CAMP,
                                               AUGUST 9TH.

. . . I have received very unsatisfactory letters from everyone,
including the General [French], about the Haig-Hutchinson
affair. It is impossible to push through a thing like that *by letter*.
The General says one comic thing, i.e. that Hutchinson *being an
Indian* could not be posted to an English command. Yet, he *can*
be made Director of Staff Duties, where he has under him the
raising, education, training, etc., of *all* British Officers, and is
supposed to be a fine judge of the idiosyncrasies of British youth.
We are odd people. So wonderfully consistent and practical.

. . . I have been finishing off the years 1853–1856 of the   *The*
Queen's letters. It is wonderfully good reading; and the work   *Queen's*
done by her and by the P. Consort was amazing. Certainly her   *Letters.*
influence over events was most remarkable.

They were the real Ministers of the Crown, and even Palmerston, now and then, had to take a back seat. It was in the hey-day
of their youth and prosperity. In five years he was dead, and her
life was entirely changed. Yet reading these letters they seemed
to stand only on the threshold.

---

[1] The article began by complaining that Lord Roberts ought not to speak
in a sense contrary to Mr. Balfour unless, like Mr. Chamberlain, he were prepared to resign his post under the Government. It then analysed his speech,
arriving at the conclusion that a compulsory army for Home Defence was
only a trick by which to obtain an army for foreign service.

[*From Lord Kitchener.*]   COMMANDER-IN-CHIEF IN INDIA,
SIMLA, AUGUST 14TH.

*Lord
Kitchener
on
Himself.*

Patriotic convictions, my dear Lord Esher, have led many
men to commit great follies and will, I presume, continue to do
so in the future.

You must pardon me for this opening in answer to your letter,
rather in the style of Marmaduke to Lady Betty, but what I want
to impress upon you is that it would take a great deal to convince
me now that it was my patriotic duty to accept the post of C. of
G.S. Why? Because I should fail! I think I know what I can do
as well as my limitations. I can I believe impress to a certain
extent my personality on men working under me, I am vain
enough to think that I can lead them, but I have no silver tongue
to persuade. . . .

Yours very truly,
KITCHENER.

[*To M. V. B.*]   ROMAN CAMP,
AUGUST 18TH.

*Lord
Roberts
and the
Army.*

. . . Lord Roberts has written a letter to Clarke which Clarke
thinks full of exaggeration. But if someone does not fuss about
the Army we shall sink again into quiescence, and inertia will
have full sway as before. After the Crimea, this is what happened. After the Boer War, temporary fury; now the cold fit is
on. Directly the Liberal Government comes in, nothing will be
done for the Army. So, I must say, that whether his remedy is
good or bad, Lord Roberts is more than justified in fuming.

The Army Council have had two years to settle General Staff,
reserve of officers, recruiting, etc., etc. They have done practically nothing. They are not alive to their responsibilities, and
are quite oblivious of the prospective hanging, which they ought
to get if they are caught once more napping.

So, don't let Lord Roberts be too heartily sat on by the

General [French]. It is just as well that all those who want the same thing should sink personal details. It is enough to do to hold one's own against the enemy.

Zena [Dare] ought to think of the stage as a profession apart from musical comedy; she might do very well. Pity a man like Du Maurier does not keep a school for young actresses.

[*To M. V. B.*] Roman Camp,
August 18th.
Evening.

. . . I am getting on with the Queen's letters, and am in the middle of the Italian campaign in 1859. The Prince Consort was taking a stronger hold than ever of the helm of the State and there were constant battles between him and the Ministers. He, acting in the Queen's name. Although he was nearly always in the right, that there was friction is beyond a doubt. Had he lived, his tenacity might have hardened into obstinacy, and the relations between him and a Government founded—like ours—on democratic institutions, would have become very strained.

The Prince Consort, 1859.

Also, there were signs of incipient trouble between him and the P. of Wales, young as the Prince was. So that perhaps his early death was no great misfortune. Probably his mission was fulfilled, and his work done, in the training which he gave the Queen. He lived long enough to sow the seed but not to see the ear ripen. Perhaps it was as well.

[*To M. V. B.*] Roman Camp,
August 21st.

Curzon Resigns the Vice-royalty.

. . . To-day you will see Curzon's resignation in the paper, and Minto's appointment. I should think that he would do very well. He has plenty of sound sense, and will make himself

exceedingly pleasant. But what a confusion, a new Viceroy on the eve of the Prince of Wales' visit.

Of course it is bound to take the gilt off that, as Curzon would have done the whole thing magnificently. Perhaps, in one sense, from the P. of Wales' point of view it has this advantage, that he would have played *almost* second fiddle to Curzon, whereas he will be a bigger man than Minto. All this must be very bitter to Curzon—and he will come home on the worst of terms with all his old colleagues and friends. Not on *speaking* terms with Brodrick and very angry with A. J. B.

Lord K. [Kitchener], on the other hand, will be enchanted. It is a victory for him all along the line, and he can now do pretty well what he likes. Luckily he has shown himself to be a canny sort of customer, otherwise there might be fears for the future. A Liberal Government will accept Minto, and take him on, so any Liberal aspirant to that high office will have to wait five years.

Princess Henry has just sent me a book full of letters from George IV's Ministers to him, about 1822–1827—found by her among some of the Queen's things. It has always been a mystery where the letters of George III and George IV and William IV disappeared to; but it is possible that as these have turned up, others may follow.

[*To M. V. B.*]   ROMAN CAMP,
                                                    AUGUST 24TH.

It is one of those lovely days which you know so well, with only a slight ripple on the loch, and white clouds which throw a shadow over the birches of Ellen's Isle and the brilliant purple heather beyond. We have landed on the slopes of Ben Venue, not quite at the usual place, and after lunch everyone has gone his or her way. I don't suppose that if one wandered thousands of miles south, it would be possible to find a more beautiful spot or a more beautiful sky. We might be on the slopes of Hymettus, or under the shadow of Etna.

. . . *Our* home, too, is full of romance other than that which we may weave about it; and of other poetic dreams—which all the world have loved—this particular spot is the heart and soul. All the Scottish lore, which generations past and to come breathe in with their childhood, seem to gather round and have its origin in the hills and lochs and burns of the home which is ours.

All the happiest days of our very happy life have been lived in the shadow of these hills.

[*To Mr. A. C. Benson.*] ROMAN CAMP,
AUGUST 25TH.

I quite realise the difficulties, but I am sure that we shall do wisely to stick to three volumes.

The great thing is to get clearly in our minds what we want to do. The main object, almost the sole object, is to exhibit the true relation between the character of the Queen and the government of her people:

The Queen's Letters; Mode of Treatment.

(*a*) The formation of her character.

(*b*) The early experiences of power.

(*c*) Her schooling in the art of government :

(1) Melbourne.

(2) King Leopold.

(3) Prince Consort.

(*d*) Her method of government.

(*e*) Her sense of "Kingship."

(*f*) Her motherly view of her people.

(*g*) Her guiding principles.

(*h*) The controlling power of the Sovereign.

It is impossible for us to give full accounts of political and historical episodes and personages.

They come partly as:

(*a*) Illustrations.

(*b*) Scenery and *dramatis personæ*.

The central figure through it all is that of the Queen herself.

All the work of these volumes is preparatory to the other volumes which some day will follow—WHEN THE QUEEN IS ALONE.

The book must be dramatic, or rather possess a dramatic note. If we keep these main ideas in view (and if you agree with them), all cutting must be subordinate to them.

I am roughly working upon these lines.

Of course I am making many mistakes, but we can correct them together.

[*To H.M. the King.*]　　　　　　　　　ROMAN CAMP,
　　　　　　　　　　　　　　　　　　　　AUGUST 28TH.

The Queen's Letters; Form of Publication.

Lord Esher presents his humble duty to Your Majesty and with great deference begs to recur to the question of whether the *Selection from Queen Victoria's Correspondence* should be in the form of 3 or 4 volumes.

Lord Esher can assure Your Majesty that the difference between the two forms of publication will not materially affect the interest nor the historical value of the book.

It will be quite possible to get into three volumes everything which is material towards exhibiting in its fullness the development of the Queen's character between 1837–1861, as well as the working of the Monarchical system under the Queen and the Prince Consort during that period.

It will allow of short introductory statements, and notes to the various letters where explanations are necessary. It will *not*, on the other hand, admit of "character sketches" by the Editors, nor of historical disquisitions, and Lord Esher ventures humbly to hope that Your Majesty will not think these necessary or desirable.

Lord Esher is sure that if Your Majesty could see the enormous mass of correspondence, Your Majesty would realise at once that there is no alternative between printing the *whole*, as is done by the Historical MSS. Commission in their publications, and making a real "Selection" upon definite principles, in a comparatively short and readable form.

Lord Esher, therefore, with profound respect, is venturing again to ask whether Your Majesty will sanction the original idea of a publication in 3 volumes being adhered to.[1]

[*To Lord Knollys.*]　　　　　　　　　　ROMAN CAMP,
　　　　　　　　　　　　　　　　　　　　　AUGUST 28TH.

I agree with every word you say about the Curzon-Kitchener correspondence.[2]

I cannot imagine how the Government permitted this correspondence, and also the Curzon-Brodrick correspondence, to be printed. Especially without the leave of the Sovereign, for I do not understand that it was asked. I can only tell you, after studying now, with great completeness, the history of the relation of

Publication of Official Correspondence on India

---

[1] [*From Lord Knollys.*]　　　　　　　　CRAIG GOWAN,
　　　　　　　　　　　　　　　　　　　　　SEPTEMBER 7TH.

MY DEAR ESHER,

I heard from the King to-day who says that he approves of the work being confined to 3 volumes.

Your arguments have therefore prevailed and you can go ahead as soon as you like.

　　　　　　　　　　　　　　　　　　Yours ever,
　　　　　　　　　　　　　　　　　　　　KNOLLYS.

[2] The correspondence between Curzon and Brodrick consisted of a series of telegrams concerning the appointment of a certain officer as Military Supply Member of the Viceroy's Council. Lord Curzon interpreted the refusal of the Home Government to sanction this appointment as a failure to abide by the compromise previously arranged between himself and Lord Kitchener. These telegrams were published as a White Paper.

The telegrams between Lord Kitchener and Lord Curzon were given out through the press, and were of a less official nature. The first was a detailed rebuttal by Lord Kitchener of the charge that certain administrative acts of his were contrary to the agreed compromise. The second was a detailed reply by the Viceroy to each of Lord Kitchener's arguments, and concluded by maintaining the charge.

the Crown to different Administrations, extending over sixty years, that such a thing would have been impossible even under Ministers as headstrong as Palmerston, or as truculent as Lord John Russell. Two things strike me very much, when contrasting the present procedure of Ministers and that of their predecessors:

Relations of the Crown and Ministers.

(*a*) The remissness of the King's present advisers in not keeping His Majesty informed, and in not sending their written reasons or seeking the King's authority BEFORE action is taken.

(*b*) Their carelessness (almost amounting to making it a dead letter) about the sanctity of the privy councillor's oath.

Even you, and I am sure the King also, will be surprised when you come to read the letters of former Prime Ministers, of all shades of politics, of Foreign Secretaries like Lord Clarendon and Lord Malmesbury, and of Ministers (Secs. of State) like Sidney Herbert and Sir G. Cornwall Lewis, written to the Sovereign, and the immense care which these men took not only to keep the Sovereign informed, but to ask the Sovereign's advice upon almost every question of importance within the spheres of their different Departments. Take for instance the treaty with Russia after the Crimean War, or the long negotiations with Italy and Austria in 1859. Every move, and every despatch were discussed with the Sovereign line by line. Take again the serious questions affecting the reorganisation of the Indian Army, containing a mass of detail, after the Mutiny in 1857–9. There was not a single proposition which was not laid before the Sovereign, and discussed, before any decision was arrived at by Sir Charles Wood and by Lord Palmerston. Lord Derby was even more punctilious inasmuch as Lord Stanley (then Sec. of State for India) was inexperienced and occasionally lax in his correspondence with the Queen, which she strongly resented. As for the Army in those days, no promotion to the rank of Major-General, nor reward nor appointment of any kind of an officer over the rank of Colonel, was made without a long written explanation to the Sovereign, a considerable time before there was any question of a Gazette and always in the

handwriting of the Minister, asking the Sovereign's approval
or advice.

Perhaps you would ask what is the conclusion which any dis-
passionate reader would draw from the correspondence of
Queen Victoria and her Ministers. I think I can honestly answer
this question. It is that the Monarchical system as understood by
Sir Robert Peel, Lord Aberdeen, Lord Palmerston and Lord
Derby, and as worked by them in conjunction with the Queen,
was of immense value to the State and to the people of this
country. These Ministers recognised that the Sovereign and the
people immediately about her were unbiased by party considerations, that she was more free from party prejudice than
they were themselves, and that her position among European
Sovereigns and her personal relations with them gave her
opinions weight, which they acknowledged to be of great value
to them, the responsible Ministers of a first-class European
Power. Finally, their experience taught them that the Sovereign's interferences and tenacity, both of which were very
remarkable, had on several very vital occasions stayed the action
of a Minister, when such action involved risks and perils which
reflection convinced him and his colleagues they were not
justified in incurring.

The Rôle of the Crown under Queen Victoria.

There is one very notable example, which is the action of the
Sovereign in restraining Lord John Russell in 1859, when, but
for the tenacity of the Crown, England would have been mixed
up in the Austro-Italian war. The historian of the future, if he
gets to know the truth, will also find that it was due to the direct
action of the Sovereign that reinforcements were poured into
India during the early months of the Mutiny, when Ministers
showed an optimism not justified by the facts; and that it was
due to Queen Victoria that the Indian Army is an imperial
force, and not a local militia.

It would only waste your time if I were to amplify examples,
but the newspapers of the past fortnight, containing these un-
seemly wrangles between men who seem to forget that they are
servants of the King, and that their individuality should be

merged in that honourable capacity, are object lessons which, if the dignity of high office under the Crown is to be maintained, the present Prime Minister and his successor ought to take seriously to heart.

[*To Lord Knollys.*]   ROMAN CAMP,
                                        SEPTEMBER 2ND.

The Prince Consort and the Monarchy.

. . . There is no doubt that the Monarchical system changed materially under the influence of the Prince Consort. I have got here some most interesting letters sent me by Princess Henry from George IV's Ministers to that Sovereign. I am writing to the King about them, a letter which I will forward through you. The change was a gradual one. I have read enough of the correspondence after the death of the Prince Consort to realise that for a long time the old habits prevailed. Lord Palmerston wrote as fully to the Queen *after* the Prince's death as before. For a time at any rate the change that had occurred was not appreciated.

If ever volumes of the Queen's correspondence subsequent to 1861 are published, it will be seen that the Queen's character underwent a fresh development after that date, and it was from that moment that she began to exhibit qualities of independence and self-reliance which before 1861 were wholly foreign to her nature.

Her Ministers who had served her during the P. Consort's lifetime continued in their old ways, but the new and younger men never acquired the habits of their predecessors. Lord Beaconsfield and Mr. Gladstone belonged to the older school. Lord Salisbury to the younger. The death of Sir Henry Ponsonby again made a great difference in the relations between the Queen and her Ministers. He was personally well known to them all, and his successors were not.

The Monarchy under King Edward.

If I may say so, *your* relations with the Ministers of to-day, are those of Sir Henry Ponsonby to their predecessors. I was not thinking, when I wrote, of the King's *authority*, as compared with that of the Queen in later years. If anything the King's is greater and more openly acknowledged. I was thinking of the want of painstaking care on the part of the Ministers to take full advantage of the admirable monarchical system as it was worked by Peel and Aberdeen. No one will understand better than you how great the difficulty became during the late years of the Prince's life, when the Queen was served by a Prime Minister who never had been and never would be sympathetic to the Prince.

This state of things produced results which were possibly not wholly advantageous to the State. But this was a short phase.

The point of my letter was exactly what you say in yours, that the present ministers, mainly through defective training and carelessness, do not adhere (as part of their duty and not the least important) to the old practice of writing fully to the Sovereign upon important questions *before* Cabinet decisions are finally taken.

In the case of the Berlin despatch which you mention, possibly the Queen may not have seen it. That is a point which I can ascertain. But the usual practice was that the Sovereign should see the draft *before* it was agreed to by the Cabinet.

The Prince Consort always objected to bringing the Queen into conflict with Cabinet decisions, very wisely as you will agree. So that the passage in Mr. Gladstone's life to which you refer is not conclusive.

I would not have written to you at this length except that I know you are always interested in historical questions, especially when they have a bearing upon modern conditions.

These particular questions are specially important at a moment when a change of Ministers is imminent, and when it looks very much as if, with the exception of Lord Spencer, the King's Ministry will be composed of men none of whom has been trained in the system of Government which was brought almost to perfection in the middle of the last century.

[*To the Rt. Hon. A. J. Balfour.*]   ROMAN CAMP,
SEPTEMBER 3RD.

*Lord
Roberts'
Army
Policy.*

After reading Lord Roberts' letter, I am not much clearer than before. What is in his mind? I suppose he is driving at two things :

(*a*) That our Army does not possess a sufficiently large reserve of officers and men to conduct a great war on the N.W. frontier of India.

(*b*) That he sees no remedy for this other than universal service.

And he wants you to add to the already voluminous reports of Commissions and Committees, by appointing another body to "enquire and report" upon these two points.

If these are his objects and his meaning, I do not imagine that you are likely to gratify him. With regard to (*a*), you have already full information before you, in the Reports of the Elgin and Norfolk Commissions.

With regard to (*b*), this is both primarily, and in all its bearings, both a matter for the executive Government, as it involves questions of policy and of political expediency with which a Committee such as that suggested by Lord Roberts is not qualified to deal.

I had, in London, several conversations with him upon this subject. As I signed Goldie's note to the Report of the Elgin Commission, urging military training for boys at school, I told Lord Roberts that if *that* was his object, I wished him all success; and I asked him whether it would not be advantageous to his cause to make his real meaning plain, i.e. whether he advocated the military training of boys, in which case there was practical possibility of his succeeding in attaining his object, or whether he was aiming at universal military training for young men from 19 to 21, which, in other words, is "conscription."

He gave no direct answer, but said that he proposed to send me his printed or written scheme; but this he has not done. I also urged upon him the futility of another "official enquiry," and suggested that any committee should be appointed by himself, as Propaganda, and illustrated this by reference to what Cobden did, and Chamberlain is doing.

I strongly suspect, however, that he is in reality aiming at "conscription," although he does not wish to commit himself at present to that particular dogma.

[*To the Rt. Hon. A. J. Balfour.*]   ROMAN CAMP,
                                      SEPTEMBER 10TH.

K. [Kitchener] has been good enough to send me his note on *Lord* Military Policy with a very characteristic covering letter. *Kitchener's*
The inference which you have probably drawn from reading *Policy.* it is that the "*Peace strategy for the next few years*" on the Indian frontier is a matter which can be more satisfactorily settled by the Imperial Defence Committee than by the Government of India.

Could anything be more clear, as is shown by his historical survey of the past and his synopsis of recent events, than that the Government of India is not qualified to deal with questions of external policy.

Could anything be more disturbing of confidence in the methods of Indian Government than paragraphs 23 and 24 of his note. It is a pity that a soldier who can write and think with such vigour and clearness, whether you agree with his conclusions or not, is separated by half the world from *you*.

What an opportunity Curzon lost by not realising what could be got out of K. (as Cromer, who did not particularly like him, *did* recognise).

Did you ever read a more prolix and less "conclusive" dissertation than Lyall's letter to *The Times*.[1] His brain must have softened. Don't answer this.

---

[1] The reference is Saturday, Sept. 9th, p. 12, col. 2. The letter is a defence of the Government of India and of Lord Curzon against Lord Kitchener. It is very long, and too confused in argument to be capable of effective summary. It ends with the statement that Lord Roberts had been somewhat summarily relieved of his post by a committee presided over by a civilian.

[*To M. V. B.*]   ROMAN CAMP,
SEPTEMBER 15TH.

*On the
Theatre.*

. . . We saw 2 acts of Gillette's play[1] last night. The little girl who acts with him is charming, and he is, of course, first rate. There is so much *style* about that American. However, the girl has a very attractive part, and has been taught by Gillette. I am sure that Zena [Dare] could do it just as well, if someone took her in hand. Frohman manages to pick up some very pretty people, and knows exactly how to place them. I think that in the long run, whatever he may be in the short, he is a better friend to actresses than George Edwardes. The latter is too fond of throwing his squeezed oranges into the street.

. . . I agree with Napoleon's idea about the stage. He loved it, but hated Molière, who was a satirist, and Racine who philosophised. He loved the stirring noble plays of Corneille and was always abusing Talma for not playing them oftener. He liked pageantry too, and I am sure would have liked *a good* musical comedy—but *not* the *Spring Chicken*, which he would have loathed!

So between Napoleon and Mr. Stead there was a link in common, however odd it may appear. I see that the latter has seen the Tsar, and the Empress Dowager. Is he not a marvel? Fancy being able to get access to those most inaccessible people.

I hope that this will find you in London, and that you will have a nice afternoon with Zena.

[*To the Rt. Hon. A. J. Balfour.*]   ROMAN CAMP,
SEPTEMBER 16TH.

*Difficulty
with
Lord
Roberts.*

If I may suggest, I think the simplest way out of the difficulty with Lord Roberts, is to be found in that Sub-Committee of the Defence Committee, which Fisher wanted for certain purposes. My suggestion is, enlarge its scope somewhat. There is no

---

[1] *Sherlock Holmes.*

reason why it should only consider *strategic* questions. "Organisation for Imperial Defence," i.e. what provisions can be made for naval and military expansion in the event of a war, might well come before such a committee, etc., etc.

I need not emphasise, as you always understand. Add to the Committee, Milner, Arthur Wilson, French, and if I may venture to suggest myself, I think I could help you.[1] *Then*, say that of course it must be clearly understood, that no one acting on the Defence Committee can, under any circumstances, take part in any public discussion of matters which come within the purview of that committee.

This may get you out of the unpleasantness with Lord Roberts, and you can avoid thus the *personal* conflict with him.

I am sure that in future all questions of *organisation* both for Army and Navy will have to be the work of the Defence Committee. *Administration* will take all the time of the Admiralty and Army Council. Jack Fisher would kick at this notion at present—but will come round to it. *Rôle of the Defence Committee.*

Two years ago, as C.-in-C. at Portsmouth, he snapped his fingers at the "Board of Admiralty," and urged every C.-in-C. to do likewise. Now he pipes a very different tune, the dear old thing.[2] Don't answer, but send this to Jack Sandars. I don't know where he is.

[*To M. V. B.*]   ROMAN CAMP,
SEPTEMBER 17TH.

. . . There is a devil of a row on with Bobs. He has asked for the King's approval of his propaganda. Of course as an officer on full pay, and a member of the Defence Committee, it is most improper of him to stump the country, on the ground of the *indifference* of the Government to the state of the Army. The *Irregularity of Lord Roberts' Methods.*

---

[1] At this date Lord Milner held no official post; Sir Arthur Wilson commanded the Home and Channel Fleet.

[2] Sir John Fisher had in the meantime become First Sea Lord.

King has written to the Prime Minister, and has asked what the
P.M. advised he should reply. The solution lies in appointing
others (who are not officials) like the General [French] and
Wilson, to work upon certain branches in the Defence Committee.

Then regulations as to reticence would apply to all alike, and
would not appear to be *personal* to Lord Roberts. I don't know
that the P.M. will take this view. He may prefer a row with
Bobs. I am sure that it is now too late to carry out that plan which
the P.M. mentioned to me in July. A new Sec. of State in
October, and a new Government in February, leaves no time
and only tends to confusion. Besides, it would be very bad luck
upon me; for I should sacrifice my independence for ever,
neutralise all good which otherwise I might do under a change
of Government, and yet not be in office long enough to carry
out the reforms which I should like to see carried out.

*On
Henderson's
"Science
of War."*

. . . Keep Henderson's book[1] for yourself, as I have got
another copy. Last night, becolded as I was, I read the notes on
Wellington, and the criticism of modern tactics. What a pity
the man did not live to be Chief of the Staff.

Now, that type is exactly what is required, and yet apparently it does not exist in the Army. The appreciation of the
Duke is very good, and there is one passage especially about the
Duke's *loyalty* to *all* his superiors, and his refusal ever to criticise
or listen to criticism, which ought to be embodied in the Articles of War!! He went along regardless of everything which
was said about him to the end. He was never really appreciated
until he died, and *then* no grave seemed large enough for him.

[*To M. V. B.*]   ROMAN CAMP,
                                   SEPTEMBER 18TH.

. . . I send you, very confidentially for the General [French],
Lord Roberts' letter, and a copy of the letter I wrote to the P.M.

[1] *The Science of War.*

The King says there is no doubt that Lord Roberts is aiming at conscription. If so, he had better say so, but then he ought to retire from the Defence Committee. It is *impossible* to carry out a propaganda as a member of the Defence Committee.

[*To M. V. B.*]   BALMORAL CASTLE,
                                        OCTOBER 4TH.

I must tell you again how much I liked the fortnight with you on manœuvres.

... Of course Medmenham will always be a dream for me, our intimate talks and our drive to Hitchin, and the glimpse of Zena.

... We have a large party here. Lord Roberts, who has at last disclosed his scheme; and after all the fuss he has made, it is nothing. He is in a mess, and does not quite see a way of extricating himself.

The P.M. is charming. The King sent for me directly I arrived, and said I *must* become Sec. of State for War if only for 4 months. I pointed out that the time was too short and that I should render myself powerless to serve him when the Government went out. Still, that I would naturally not refuse. But I am *sure* that the Government cannot stand another resignation or dismissal. So nothing will come of it, which is really fortunate.

Renewed Offer of Secretaryship for War.

The King took me and P. Arthur in his motor to the deer drive to-day, and was charming. He is almost affectionate in his manner!

Tucker was a great success here. He amused the King mightily. The King told me that before he had known him 10 minutes, he told him the story of some officers which began in this way, "You know I am bloody old, and you are bloody young, but I can give you the following advice, etc." His power of quiet repartee amused the King.

We saw an enormous amount of deer to-day. I got two stags.

One a royal! Of course I shall not get the head, for all royals remain here. The other is not bad. It was bitterly cold on the hills, which are covered with snow. To-morrow I get a quiet day, as the King wants me to talk with Arthur Balfour. Just sent for by the King. Must close this.

[*To the Rt. Hon. A. J. Balfour.*]   BALMORAL CASTLE,
OCTOBER 5TH.

Future
of the
Defence
Committee.

(Written after conversation with the King, Mr. Balfour, Mr. Haldane and Lord Knollys.)

In view of a possible change of Government next year, is there not a great risk of the partial or total collapse of the Defence Committee?

The existing safeguards for its continuance under a new administration, are first, the permanent Secretariat, and, second, the one permanent member, Lord Roberts.

The danger consists, however, in the vague definition of the duties of the Committee, and the numerical weakness of the permanent element.

The Committee does not, and cannot (under a representative form of Government), possess executive functions. But as a permanent deliberation committee, with powers of enquiry and recommendation, it could be made to fulfil many duties hitherto delegated to "Commissions" appointed *ad hoc*, and it could also be made to relieve public departments of certain responsibilities which in view of our growing Imperial needs they are not qualified to bear.

Recent events have proved that large questions of reorganisation, dealing with Imperial Defence, cannot adequately and efficiently be dealt with by the War Office in conjunction with the India Office, the Colonial Office and the Admiralty, all of which are vitally concerned with them.

Nor are these questions, in their constructive stages, matter which can be adequately treated by the Cabinet; the departments named are absorbed by laborious and complex administrative detail. They have neither time nor machinery adequate to deal with questions requiring careful enquiry, much common deliberation and mutual forbearance.

The Cabinet, composed of men absorbed in administrative and parliamentary duties, growing heavier year by year, cannot undertake to enquire into, nor to construct elaborate schemes involving much technical consideration. The special function of the Cabinet is to arrive at decisions upon facts or theories carefully presented in concrete form; it is not contended that any violent wrench should be given to the existing constitution, or that the supremacy of the Cabinet should be questioned. The Defence Committee, as conceived by the Prime Minister, is an Evolution and not a Revolution.

The question is whether, in the interests of the stability of the fabric, Mr. Balfour, before quitting office, should, by numerically strengthening the permanent element in that Committee, give fresh assurance of its continuity. The proposal is, that two permanent sub-committees should be formed under the presidency of Mr. Balfour, specially constituted to deal with :

(*a*) Certain scheduled recommendations made by the Elgin Commission.

(*b*) Certain strategical questions raised last summer by Sir John Fisher.

A change of Government, taking place while these sub-committees are engaged upon work of the kind suggested would not threaten (for reasons which appear obvious) their continuance, and consequently the existence of the committee itself.

[*To M. V. B.*]   BALMORAL CASTLE,
                                                         OCTOBER 6TH.

. . . Haldane [1] appeared last night, and I had a very interesting talk with him. He wants to be Chancellor, but the King—who would like it—says he has no chance. Reid will be preferred to

Haldane on the coming Government.

---

[1] Afterwards Viscount Haldane of Cloan.

him. He says C. B. [Campbell-Bannerman] has no *intimates* among politicians, and lives exclusively with his old W.O. officials, Haliburton and Knox. That is a bad look-out for the future. All those Roseberyites want C.B. to go to the House of Lords and Asquith to lead the H. of C. Haldane takes very sensible views about the Defence Committee, which is a good thing. The King again opened the subject of the W.O. to-day, and failing that, wants me and Milner to be made *permanent* members of the Defence Committee. I doubt Arthur approving this plan.

Shooting at Balmoral.

I killed two good stags. One, the best-shaped head I ever got here, but only eight points. A real beauty. I hope to be able to have it at Pinkie. The hills are covered with snow, and I was over my ankles in some places. But there was luckily a bright sun. My first stag was killed just under a rock, down which a fool of a woman (who thought herself an alpine expert) fell last week, and broke her leg, and got concussion of the brain. She had to be carried down and her sister remained on the hill all night. The other I killed within a hundred yards of an eagle's nest, a huge creature *in a tree*. Very curious to look at. I picked up a small eagle's feather under the nest, among a lot of grouse bones. Coming down to tea with the most charming of stalkers—a real genius in his way—I met the King driving alone, and he picked me up, and we drove home *tête-à-tête*.

Did I tell you that he had three volumes of photographs given him: pictures of the war, taken by the *Japanese military photographic staff, in battle*! You see the attacks on the trenches and charges up hill. All the formation perfectly clear, and men actually falling. There are only three copies, it appears, in the world.

[*From Lord Roberts.*]   ENGLEMERE, ASCOT,
OCTOBER 12TH.

MY DEAR ESHER,

I have postponed my trip to Ireland until towards the end of next week. Are you likely to be in London, or better still at your Windsor Forest house, before then? I much want to see you.

Yours sincerely,

ROBERTS.

P.S.—What took place at Balmoral after I left?

[*To the Rt. Hon. A. J. Balfour.*]   ROMAN CAMP,
OCTOBER 13TH.

I told you that Haldane had expressed a strong doubt whether *Liberal* C. B. [Campbell-Bannerman] would take the Chairmanship of *View* the Imperial Defence Committee and had also said that he and *of the Defence* Lord Spencer (peace to his ashes) were both hostile to the com- *Committee.* mittee. Haldane himself favoured making the committee more "technical" and "expert" and less political.

This view is shared, as you know, by Knollys, principally because he fears that when your protecting arm is removed, the committee will sink into insignificance, or worse.

No one appreciates more thoroughly than I do your conception of the committee; and if you had three or four clear years before you, I should have no fears at all for its future. But your enemies and political adversaries will score by anything which diminishes its authority hereafter.

Also, it is lamentable to think of any break in the continuity of work upon which the committee is engaged. Personally I think the sub-committee which you have appointed will fulfil the highest functions of a General Staff, the only sort of General Staff suited to our requirements, i.e. a joint Naval and Military Staff.

But I am sure it would be well to go a step further and to hand over to another sub-committee the suggestive clauses of the Elgin Commission Report in order that the details may be worked out, and all the preliminary steps taken to carry them into effect.

Will you ask Mr. Short to make a précis of the enclosed correspondence for you, and send me back the originals, as I have no copies. If the subject does not appear to you of urgent importance, put it aside till we meet.

[*To Mr. J. S. Sandars.*]   ORCHARD LEA,
NOVEMBER 5TH.

I have just seen Lord Roberts, who wants me to give the P.M. an outline of what he proposes to say to the Defence Committee, on Tuesday, and to ask the P.M. whether it meets his approval.

It is, in a few words, to resign his place on the Imperial Defence Committee and appeal to the public, and endeavour to convert the country to universal military training, with a liability to serve in case of emergency in any part of the world. I will call and see you to-morrow.

[*Journals.*]   ORCHARD LEA,
NOVEMBER 16TH.

Balfour on a Date for Resignation.

While I was waiting to see Sandars in Downing St., Bob Douglas [1] came in. The P.M. was to go to Windsor by the 6.30 train, but he wished to have a discussion first about the date of a resignation of the Government.

He sent Sandars in to say that he would like me to be present, and began by analysing the situation. There were two courses :

(*a*) To resign in the middle of December.

(*b*) To call Parliament together early, i.e. January 16th, and resign after the first division.

The former possesses tactical advantages, as it forces the opposition to show their hand, but it is inconsistent with the attitude adopted by the P.M. all along, and would be unpopular with the Party.

[1] The Rt. Hon. Akers-Douglas, afterwards Lord Chilston.

While the latter is full of unpleasant difficulties, especially the necessity of introducing a Redistribution Bill; Acland Hood [1] and Douglas nevertheless favour the latter course, and Sandars favours the former. The P.M. asked my view, and I said I knew nothing about politics, but of the two courses I preferred the latter, as it left his reputation for consistency and straightness unattacked.

But I could not see why he should not dissolve on January 2nd. The idea that it is necessary to put your opponents in to dissolve is a superstition, unless they have to remain some time in office prior to dissolving.

In the present case an appeal to the country would come constitutionally and properly from a Minister whom the Opposition have been unable to turn out, when the term of the Parliament itself is approaching finality.

This idea, I hope, will germinate, for I feel convinced that it offers the best solution of a very difficult problem.

[*Journals.*]   ORCHARD LEA,
                                                 NOVEMBER 20TH.

These last few days were spent at Windsor. The King met with an accident which might have been very serious. He tripped in a rabbit hole, and fell on his gun, mercifully it did not explode; but the stock was broken into splinters. Treves was sent for to look at the sprained foot, and found the tendon achilles snapped in two. Anyone else would have been laid up, but the King refused to give in, and hobbled about in an iron contrivance made by Treves' orders. . . .

I had several hours with A. J. B. [Balfour]. He went through the "change of Government" papers 1873-4, which the King told me to show him. The King asked me if the P.M. had told me his plans, as he could get nothing out of him. I reported this to A. J. B., who then had a long talk with the King, explaining

The King and the Change of Government.

---

[1] Chief Unionist Whip, afterwards Lord St. Audries.

to him the whole situation, and the difficulties with which he was confronted.

I saw the King off, with the King of Greece, this morning; all the afternoon I have been in Downing St., with Sandars, A. J. B., and Gerald Balfour. I think the P.M. has made up his mind to see the King on the 15th and retire. He will be glad to be free of office.

[*Journals.*]   ORCHARD LEA,
                                                 NOVEMBER 28TH.

Yesterday we returned from Paris. London has caught up Paris. Formerly there was such a gap between the two cities. There is nothing, except the climate, in which Paris is now superior.

The French require a successful war; otherwise they will sink to the level of Spain. This would be a misfortune, for in the future, when the intellectual and moral struggle comes between the European and Asiatic races, the Teutons will be all the better for the leaven of the Gallic.

To-day I saw the P.M. He has decided to resign on Monday. His Cabinet were divided; but Lansdowne, Lyttelton, A. Chamberlain were on his side.

Francis Knollys came up from Sandringham; and was admitted secretly through the garden entrance to a conclave. The King was opposed to resignation, but is now himself resigned to it.

[*Journals.*]   ORCHARD LEA,
                                                 NOVEMBER 29TH.

*Lord
Rosebery
and
Ireland.*

I saw Spender, who had been to the Durdans last night. Rosebery was profoundly depressed. He had received a letter from Grey, telling him that both he and Asquith were aware *beforehand* of the words about Ireland, in C.-Bannerman's speech, to which Rosebery had taken such exception.

Spender pointed out that he had only himself to thank, as he had refused to consult with his old colleagues, and had spoken at Bodmin without reference to anyone beforehand. I wrote this to the King.[1]

[*Journals.*]

ORCHARD LEA,
DECEMBER 1ST.

... The P.M. is in excellent spirits, and determined to hold his own at the Cabinet. Walter Long is the only man that matters who is violently opposed to the resignation. At the last moment the P.M. spoke to me about Lord Roberts' retirement from the Defence Committee and my going on to it. I stuck out for French on the ground that it would strengthen the Committee, and that I, alone, was no substitute for Bobs. The King, who was asked, has agreed. Sandars is to have the notice in the papers to-morrow, if the P.M. agrees to what we subsequently drew up.

Then I lunched with John Morley. I told the P.M. I was going to see him, and he told me of *his* talks with Asquith.

Morley corroborated what Spender had said about Rosebery. He mentioned a good many of the likely Cabinet arrangements.

Morley on the coming Government.

---

[1] Lord Rosebery had been speaking all through Cornwall in support of the Liberal candidates, and creating the impression that he would, contrary to what had been expected, consent to take office in a new Liberal Government. Towards the end of this tour Sir H. Campbell-Bannerman, speaking at Edinburgh, raised the question of Home Rule: he declared that it would not occupy the immediate attention of a Liberal Government, but that nothing would be done which was not compatible with its ultimate realisation. Two days later Lord Rosebery, in the last speech of his tour, regretted this return to an earlier error. Two days later, again, Sir Edward Grey demonstrated in a speech that in so far as the work of the next Parliament was concerned there would be no actual difference between Liberal and Unionist policy. And the same declaration was made by members representing other sections of Liberal opinion. Lord Rosebery, however, spoke no more.

He says that Grey urges that C. B. [Campbell-Bannerman] *must* go to the Lords; and Asquith lead the H. of C. Morley wishes for the Exchequer, but if C. B. *remains in the Commons* he would accept the India Office. In that case Grey would have the F.O., Elgin the Colonies.

If C. B. goes to the House of Lords, then Morley would not serve under Asquith. He was charming as he always is. He quite realises the imminence of the crisis, and he is to try and get C. B. up to London by Monday.

As we parted (after Spender and Maurice had joined us, before whom Morley spoke freely) he asked me if I would accept the W.O.! This is ludicrous. To have an offer by one P.M. and a feeler from the other side is an adventure almost unparalleled. And how silly these politicians are.

[*To Mr. J. S. Sandars.*]   ORCHARD LEA,
                                              DECEMBER 2ND.

It is splendid, and I am so glad. Please thank the beloved P.M., and say that I will hold the fort for him as best I can.[1]

[*Journals.*]   ORCHARD LEA,
                               MONDAY—DECEMBER 4TH.

Balfour's   The King arrived this afternoon and the Prime Minister
Resignation.   drove up to the Palace within a few minutes. He was with the

---

[1] Lord Esher had been made a permanent member of the Committee for Imperial Defence. Sir Charles Ottley, afterwards Secretary to the Committee for Imperial Defence, wrote:—

ADMIRALTY, S.W.,
DECEMBER 4TH.

MY DEAR LORD ESHER,

A line to felicitate the Committee of Imperial Defence and the country at large upon the new appointments to the Committee. I *am* delighted.

Yours sincerely,
C. L. OTTLEY.

King a quarter of an hour, and then came down into Knollys' room. He seemed a little moved, which was not strange, on relinquishing his great office, but his spirits revived almost immediately.

A. J. B. [Balfour] and I then drove in his motor to Downing St. We went in at the garden entrance. Alfred Lyttelton came to his room and Jack Sandars, but no one else. And so he ceases to be Prime Minister. The King sees C. B. (who was immediately informed) to-morrow at 10.45.

He came up to town from Scotland, arriving this morning, and summoned by Morley. He saw Grey this afternoon, and met with difficulties, but he is to see him again to-night at 9, when these may be removed. Asquith was out of town.

[*Journals.*] ORCHARD LEA,
TUESDAY—DECEMBER 5TH.

The King's interview with C. B. [Campbell-Bannerman] was very satisfactory. I gave a memorandum to the King and sent a copy through Morley to C. B., showing the procedure which was followed in 1880 and in 1895. *The King and Campbell-Bannerman.*

Knollys went up, just before the King saw C. B., to emphasise the point that the King should ask whether he was prepared to form a government, or prepared to try, and if the former he should kiss hands.

Anyhow, he is Prime Minister without this formality and has gone away to construct his Administration.

I lunched at the Carlton with Maurice and John Morley. The latter told us of his difficulties with Grey. They are purely personal. He feels that Rosebery gave him his first chance in politics, and he cannot, he thinks, properly desert him. *Grey and the New Government.*

Asquith is, of course, placed in a difficulty, as he, though willing to join the Government, cannot easily separate himself from Grey.

There is a fatal contrariness about the Grey family. This evening at Loulou [Harcourt]'s I was introduced to Captain

Sinclair, who has acted for a long time as C. B.'s private secretary, and who seems a man of good easy manners, and excellent sense. He spoke, with the greatest frankness, of the new Government, and the difficulties, and the allocation (as far as they have got) of the various men available.

I am to take him to see Knollys to-morrow morning. I dined with Jack Sandars and Knollys at the Marlborough, but it was impossible to talk with much freedom. It hardly seemed fair.

[*Journals.*]   ORCHARD LEA,
                                        WEDNESDAY—DEC. 6TH.

I have been offered a G.C.B., by Arthur Balfour, but I have thought it prudent to decline it. It would be a pity to start on the Defence Committee, under these new people, with any feeling on their part that I was a spy left behind by Arthur. Appearing in a Conservative list of honours, purely partisan, could hardly help but create some such impression. It is hardly worth it, and the Defence Committee opens a sphere which is most interesting to me. I took Sinclair to meet Knollys this morning, and the interview was very satisfactory. Afterwards I called in Carlton Terrace on George Curzon, who was asked by the King to talk to me, and to say to me what he began to tell the King about Kitchener. George is just the same unchanged, self-confident, good-humoured, autocrat that he has been since boyhood. He divided his discourse into two portions:

Curzon on Lord Kitchener.

(*a*) An analysis of K.'s character and methods, which he illustrated with anecdotes, showing the unscrupulous use which he makes of any means to an end. To achieve a purpose he is Ignatius Loyola and Juggernaut.

(*b*) The merits of this dispute which, as George says, "caused his downfall."

The case against K. is stronger than the case against his policy. It will not be the latter which brings about another 1857, but the former may do so.

The fact is that K., and K. only, caused the downfall of G. Curzon. That K. himself will have to fall hereafter is certain. That type of man always does. George proposes to obtain a Vote of the H. of C., hostile to K., and for this reason wishes to sit for Oxford.

[*Journals.*]   ORCHARD LEA,
                                    THURSDAY—DECEMBER 7TH.

Last night we were at Bristol to see Seymour [Hicks] and Ella [Terris] for the last time in *The Catch of the Season*. Maurice (whom I introduced to George Curzon in the morning) came with us.

It was *not* a success for me. And to-day I have a headache. I saw Francis Knollys to-night. Cromer has refused, as I knew he would. When Sinclair mentioned Monson—I told him "Polonius"! *Progress of the New Cabinet.*

Fitzmaurice,[1] whom Loulou [Harcourt] and I suggested, is on the tapis, because Edward Grey seems finally to have refused. He bases his refusal on two grounds:

1. Loyalty to Rosebery.
2. That with C. B. [Campbell-Bannerman] in the Commons the Government will be weak.

Asquith accepts the Ch. of the Ex. Haldane, who has been offered the Attorney-General or the Sec. of State, has not replied.[2] To-day, Sinclair told the King that H. Gladstone was

---

[1] Lord Edward Fitzmaurice: he was actually made U.S. for Foreign Affairs.

[2] The Secretaryship referred to was the Home Office. Lord Haldane's autobiography makes it clear that on the 6th he was offered the Attorney-Generalship or the Home Office in a verbal message through Asquith; that on the 7th he received in writing the offer of the Attorney-Generalship only; and that there was no question of the War Office until he asked for it himself. The meaning of the reference to Campbell-Bannerman's "winning all along the line," in the following item, is merely that he had persuaded these reluctant members into the Cabinet: not that he had them where he first wanted them.

proposed for the W.O. This would be a thoroughly bad appointment.

[Journals.]

ORCHARD LEA,
DECEMBER 10TH.

*Grey
Accepts
Office.*

On Thursday night at 8 o'clock Grey wrote 6 pages to C. B., finally declining to join the Government. At 11 he went to Belgrave Square with Haldane, and said he had changed his mind. Haldane to the W.O., Grey to the F.O., C. B. has won all along the line. I saw Haldane and had a long and most satisfactory talk. He professes that he is "willing to be nobbled" by our Committee!

To-day I telephoned to London for Ellison,[1] and asked him if he would like to be Haldane's private secretary. This would be a great stroke.

Ellison came down to O'Lea, had a talk and said yes. There and then I telephoned through to Haldane, who was with Clarke, and he will see Ellison to-morrow. I take him there at 11. This means that we shall arrange it. Of course nothing could indicate more clearly the "nobbling" of Haldane by our Committee!

[*To M. V. B.*]

2, TILNEY STREET,
DECEMBER 11TH.

It has been an awful day here. Absolutely impenetrable fog, and the King's carriage to-night was preceded and followed by a dozen running footmen with flaring torches, a thing perhaps never seen in London before.

The fog does not suit him, and he was very unwell at dinner. It was nothing *except* the fog, as he asked me to luncheon, and I

---

[1] Now Lt.-Gen. Sir Gerald Ellison. He had acted as Secretary to the War Office Reconstruction Committee.

sat next him and he was quite cheerful and well. Still, his staying in London in such weather is really dangerous, for it affects his breathing. I had a long morning with Haldane, and he was more than satisfactory. He liked Ellison, and will, I think, take him.

Haldane's Army Policy.

He told me that he proposed to rely upon Clarke and me, but I take these assurances a little "*cum grano*," as he is a "manager" of men! He told me that C. B. had given him a free hand, and, in regard to the Imperial Defence Committee, that C. B., although he admitted he did not like the institution when it originated, accepts it as a *fait accompli*, and will preside over it and use it!

I think C. B. will remove Plumer and possibly put in Nicholson. This will not matter as Q.M.G. He approves of bringing home D. Haig in Hutchinson's place. Then talked about plans, and I urged him to complete

(*a*) W.O. organisation,

(*b*) 1st Army Corps ;

and next year

(*c*) To begin to think about estimates and the militia. He saw Ward and Lyttelton to-day in that order on my recommendation. He found Lyttelton very flabby. So much for the W.O. In other respects all has gone well, and I hope that the new Government will not disappoint us.

Tell the General [French] that *Morley* took a great fancy to him, thought him very interesting as being unlike his conception of a Cavalry General.

Evidently he expected Murat with feathers in his top hat. I never saw anyone more pleased than Loulou [Harcourt].

[*Journals.*]　　　　　　2, TILNEY STREET,
　　　　　　　　　　WEDNESDAY, DEC. 13TH.

This morning I had an hour and a half with C. B. [Campbell-Bannerman]. He was most amiable. He spoke with great openness in a most friendly tone. I started by saying that I knew of his original objections to the Defence Committee. He replied

Lord Esher and Campbell-Bannerman.

that criticism in opposition was one thing; accomplished fact another; and that he feared he too frequently indulged the weakness of poking fun at people. This was the *amende honorable*. I then had to explain the functions of the Defence Committee; its constitution. He said he proposed to work it on the existing lines, and would make no change until the working had been well tested. I then said that I was most intimate with A. J. B. [Balfour] and had been absolutely loyal to him: but that I would work as loyally with C. B. and his Government.

I explained my relation to the King, and the confidence with which I was honoured. C. B. said he welcomed all the help I could give him; and he had no sort of objection to the confidence with which the King chose to honour me.

He then spoke *most* freely about all his difficulties, about his colleagues, all this with much humour and shrewdness. He said, that at the rate of progress made by Haldane, the latter would probably resign in about 10 days after having exhausted all possible reform of the W.O., and of the Army. He calls J. Morley (whom he likes extremely) *Priscilla*.

Altogether I feel confident there will be no difficulty in working with C.B.

[*To the Rt. Hon. J. Morley.*[1]]   St. James' Palace,
                                                        Dec. 15th.

Would you like my *eldest* boy as a sort of additional secretary? It would be such a pleasure to me if he could serve you. He is *very* intelligent. He has been—since Eton—to Berlin and Paris, and he has worked with Spender on the *Westminster*, and of late has been electioneering with Haddo in E. Berkshire.

I am sure you would like him, and it would be a "chance in a lifetime" if he could be thrown into personal contact with *you* for a while.

[1] Then Sec. of State for India.

You would find him very trustworthy, and a most excellent arranger and compiler of papers, etc., for which he has both taste and talent.

I hope you will forgive me for asking. I believe Loulou [Harcourt] has been trying to get C. B. [Campbell-Bannerman] to take him—but *personally* (only this is private) I would rather he went to you.

[*To the Rt. Hon. R. B. Haldane.*]   ST. JAMES' PALACE,
DEC. 19TH.

Although it was very clear to us at the time, I am afraid that our Memorandum on the General Staff, a copy of which you carried off with you this morning, does not make perfectly clear the principle which I think vital, in organising a General Staff to meet the requirements of our peculiar island race. No foreign system is applicable to the insular peculiarities of our Army, and by these peculiarities I mean that: *On the General Staff—*

1. It is officered on the voluntary system.
2. It is officered by a caste, with caste prejudices.

There is another point which is worth considering: and it is that you cannot in time of peace maintain all the General Staff posts required in time of war, and therefore you must, in organising a General Staff, provide means of expansion.

Without going into a prolonged argument, you will realise that the deduction to be drawn from these preliminary remarks is that although we may plagiarise the German idea of a General Staff, which consists of a highly trained and specialised body of men intended to provide what has been, rather offensively, called the "brains of the army," we cannot on the other hand satisfactorily copy the system of General Staff Organisation which obtains in the German Army.

In a sentence, our system should be a General Staff List appearing in the Army list as a list of names of men qualified to hold

General Staff posts (although some of them may be employed on other duties either Administrative or Executive), and not as a list of posts earmarked by the name of General Staff.

This is what in our Memorandum we tried to explain, but I am not sure, as I have said, that it is put with sufficient clearness.

There is another point upon which I personally feel very strongly. Since June 1905 I have had the opportunity of discussing very fully, in connection with Lord Kitchener's scheme for a Staff College at Quetta, the question of Staff College Education at Camberley; and I am confident that it will be quite impossible, for a good many years to come, to make the qualification for the General Staff what, in paragraph 23 of our Memorandum, we state that it should be.

—and the Staff College.

If the General Staff is to be recruited from officers who have passed a competitive examination into the Staff College, it will not be possible, in the first place, to obtain a satisfactory General Staff under a very great number of years in point of numbers, owing to the inadequate size of the Staff College; and, in the second place, the competitive system will never as at present conceived and devised produce the best type of General Staff Officer.

I am certain that there is one practical way, and one only, by which we can frame and maintain, for the next ten or fifteen years, a useful and capable list of officers qualified to act as General Staff Officers for the Army in time of war, and it is that officers should be selected by the Selection Board as probationers for the term of one year, and at the end of that time, if confirmed in their appointments by the Chief of the General Staff, they should, if they have not already done so, go to the Staff College without previous examination for the term of two years, passing out of the College after examination according to the present practice.

If this system were combined with the stipulation contained in paragraph 28 of our Memorandum, I think you would get a General Staff better suited to the requirements of our Army, than by any other system which could be devised.

[*To Lord Kitchener.*]   WINDSOR CASTLE,
DECEMBER 21ST.

The battle rages between your partisans and those of the late *The*
Viceroy. After the hard fight in India, with the result that *Curzon-*
followed, you could hardly expect anything else. *Kitchener*
Dispute:—

There is no doubt that when Parliament meets, a severe attack
will be made, certainly on the Policy for which you are held
responsible, and possibly upon you personally.

All the patriotic and decent-minded people will endeavour to
limit the controversy to the political issue, but, as you know,
there are so many men both within and without Parliament,
who fall into neither of these categories. Therefore, I would
venture to suggest that you should either send over, or designate
here, someone fully conversant with all the facts, to watch your
interests. These had far better not be in the somewhat tactless
hands of Mr. Brodrick.

I have seen a great deal of Morley, who started with an unbiased mind, but he has been subjected to the fire of many of
those who disagree with you, some of them very influential
persons. Luckily you have a strong supporter in Godley.[1]

I hardly like to venture a word of advice, but as seen from *—Advice*
these islands, whence the perspective is not always a bad one, I *to Lord*
should say that provided you— *Kitchener.*

(*a*) Keep profound silence yourself, whatever be the nature
of the attack ;

(*b*) Keep on intimate and friendly terms with Minto;

your position personally and your policy are proof against
all attack.

That many who supported your views have now swung
round, you are no doubt aware, but the main point in the whole
controversy which cannot fail to strike unprejudiced men (and
they are the ultimate judges) is that the late Viceroy and you
agreed upon a compromise and upon an amendment of the
Brodrick Despatch.

[1] General Sir Alexander Godley, then Commandant, Mounted Infantry.

This is the crucial point, because the worst of all compromise is, that the compromiser cannot go back upon his action, and Lord Curzon and his school will find it impossible to contend that your proposals are essentially fatal to good government in India, since he himself agreed—upon certain conditions—to try them.

The moment that—in a great controversy—a politician finds himself struggling, not for a principle, but for an expedient, his battle is half lost.

Meanwhile, *write to Morley*, full and privately; for this cannot possibly do harm, and may be of much service.

You must remember that I am a very old friend of Lord Curzon's, and I am very sorry for him, although, upon the question which has divided you from him, I agree altogether with you; and he knows it.

The Change at the War Office.

The change of government has produced one great good at least. It has rid us of Arnold-Forster. I hope that now, the scheme for the Army, which I have had much at heart, will have a fair trial. And above all I hope that we shall see Douglas Haig home, and that you will put no difficulty in his way. It will be of no disservice to you, to get him at home here, and at the W.O., for a short spell.[1]

The new Secretary of State [2] cannot fail to do well. Above all, he has determined to walk slowly, and has no preconceived ideas. He is adroit, shrewd and exceedingly clever.

Many thanks for your letters. If you wish to spare yourself, tell Marker to write to me. He knows your views—and you must be overwhelmed just now.

[*To M. V. B.*]   ORCHARD LEA,
                                   JANUARY 3RD, 1906.

All the events of the change of government I am having typed from the notes I kept and you can insert them among your

---

[1] See 15th March, 1906.
[2] Rt. Hon. R. B. Haldane.

letters. As you were so mixed up in the numerous talks we had with John Morley and Loulou [Harcourt], they will be of permanent interest to you.

To-day Princess Henry came down to Windsor, and we opened, for the first time, all the boxes of the Queen's private correspondence which are in the vaults.

I got her to give me the journal of June 1837, which contains *The* the Queen's account of the accession—and of June 1838, which *Queen's* contains the coronation. Now that I have looked at them I want *Journals.* *all* the volumes to that date. There are about 25 of them to 1838. She began her journal in 1832, when she was 13, and wrote voluminously. It is a pity to attempt a biographical notice of those years without having read the most authentic record of them.

We also found—a great find—the Queen's letters to Melbourne in 1837. No one knew what had become of them, although it was believed that Lord Beauvale had returned them after Melbourne's death.

It is a vast pity that I had not got them earlier. The Princess returns at 1, and I brought Fortescue out to luncheon. Nellie liked him very much. He wrote the *Red Deer* to amuse his nephew, and the *Drummer's Coat* because he was told he could not write another child's story. He now wants to do a play, but he has never seen *Peter Pan*.

[*From Lord Kitchener, Commander-in-Chief in India.*]

CALCUTTA,

JANUARY 11TH.

MY DEAR LORD ESHER,

I am very grateful to you for your last letter and support. I have acted and am acting exactly as you suggest—except as regards writing to Mr. Morley, as I do not wish to follow the lead of those who are attempting to directly influence him in the decision he will have to come to. I have, however, written letters to the Viceroy which will I believe reach Mr. Morley through him.

Hamilton has gone home and ought to be able to give any information that may be required.

Lord Kitchener and the New Viceroy.

My relations with the Viceroy are most amiable. I have not pushed matters at all, but he has himself after full investigation come to the conclusion that the changes were necessary and that I only did my duty in bringing them forward.

He is much astonished at the lies that have been and are being circulated about me at home. As regards the points now under discussion here, I have placed myself entirely in his hands. Of course it is impossible to predict how the case will go. When I read all the lies that are being so actively spread I can hardly believe that any Sec. of State or any parliament will be able to elucidate the truth. Lord Ripon's opposition in the Cabinet will have a great effect, and the opinions of other deluded ex-Indian officials doubtless will be taken as a guide by many. On the whole, therefore, I can hardly expect a favourable verdict. All will I think depend on the way the Government take up the case in Parliament. If by then, as I hope, Mr. Morley is satisfied to at least give the changes a trial, all will be well. If, on the other hand, owing to conviction or political influences, he is unable to do this, we must expect the worst. As regards Haig, no difficulty will be made by me.

Yours very sincerely,

KITCHENER.

[*To M. V. B.*]   WINDSOR CASTLE,
                                   JANUARY 14TH.

Sir John Fisher and the Defence Committee.

. . . I have been here all the afternoon, up to 7 o'clock, doing partly the Queen's Life and partly writing to Clarke and Repington, who are furious with Jackie [Fisher]. Of course he is a creature of moods, and also he is very reticent about naval plans, and rightly so. For them, no preparation is required.

The Navy is always on a war footing, and a telegram can send a fleet to the other end of the earth. So why disclose ideas, if there are any!

However, I must show the General [French] all the correspondence, but he would not understand it until he has seen the *résumé* of the French negotiations.

. . . I am writing a line to Arthur Balfour to say what beasts politicians are!

[*From H.M. the King.*]   SANDRINGHAM, NORFOLK,
JAN. 16TH.

MY DEAR ESHER,

As you are doubtless aware, I have as Sovereign the right to appoint a Trustee for the British Museum.

Trusteeship at the British Museum.

Through the death of the lamented Sir Mountstuart Grant Duff—who was my first nomination after my succession—there is now a vacancy. My great wish is to offer it to you—and hope that you will accept a post which I am convinced you will fill admirably—and it likewise will be one of great interest to yourself to try and promote the welfare of our great National Museum.

Should you accept, I trust you will be able to attend the meetings of the Trustees as frequently as your busy life permits you to do so.

Believe me,
Yours sincerely,
EDWARD R.

[*From the Rt. Hon. A. J. Balfour.*]   WHITTINGHAME,
Private.   JANUARY 17TH.

MY DEAR ESHER,

Your charming letter has just reached me; a thousand thanks for it.

I am almost ashamed of the way in which sheer interest in what is now going on has absorbed the feelings of distress which, according to all the rules of propriety, I ought now to be enduring. But, in truth, something more than the ordinary Party change is going on before our eyes, and I do not think the full significance of the drama can be understood without reference to the Labour and Socialistic movements on the Continent. It is somewhat early, however, to form conclusions on this point, though it is impossible to avoid speculating on it. In spite of my defeat, they insisted on my speaking at Nottingham, and I have got to speak at Glasgow to-night. But Inverness on the day following will, I hope, finish my labours for the moment.

Yours ever,
ARTHUR JAMES BALFOUR.

[*Memorandum sent to H.M. the King.*]   WINDSOR CASTLE,
JANUARY 18TH.

The Kaiser on International Relations— By request, I called yesterday on Mr. Beit, whom I know very slightly. He wished to speak to me about his Audience at Potsdam.

Last year Mr. Beit presented to the Berlin Gallery a very fine picture by Vandyck, as a mark of gratitude for the kindness which had been shown him by the Director of the Berlin Museum. Matters in connection with this presentation were the primary object of the Audience with the German Emperor.

After these matters had been disposed of the Emperor spoke very freely to Mr. Beit on the political situation. He complained bitterly of the Press. He said that the French and Belgian, and even American, Press were bribed. . . .

He wanted to come to a friendly understanding with France about Morocco, and he said that this would be done and that all points were agreed upon. He added that there would be no war with France unless England should continue to incite and upset France's good judgment, but he repeated that there would be no war. At the same time he knew that England wished for war—not the King—not the Ministry—but some very influential people like Sir John Fisher.

He said that Sir John Fisher thought that because the fleet was in perfect order and more powerful than the German Fleet, it was the moment to provoke war. *—On Sir John Fisher—*

Mr. Beit told the Emperor that he had seen Sir John Fisher in Carlsbad and that although Sir John did not conceal that the Fleet was ready for an emergency, he had not used language like that imputed to him. The Emperor replied, "He thinks it is time for an attack, and I don't blame him. It is quite human, I can quite understand it, but we are also prepared, and if it comes to a war, it depends on the weight you carry into action, namely, a good conscience, and I have that."

He was annoyed at Lord Lansdowne's offer of assistance to France while he was trying to come to friendly terms. Mr. Beit remarked that surely the landing of a hundred thousand men in Schleswig-Holstein was ridiculous and that no Government could have made that suggestion. He replied that a hundred thousand men could easily be landed and he said that the English Navy reconnoitred the coast of Denmark with this object during the cruises of the English Fleet. Of course it would be for him to deal with the hundred thousand men when they landed. He said that he had no objection to the *entente cordiale*, but England should not object to his having his *entente* too.

Whilst the Russian-French Alliance was in existence he had the best *entente* with Russia. He could not object to the Morocco Treaty, that was a matter for England and France, and he added "they certainly might have communicated it to me, but I cannot prevent people being rude. I waited for a year, but when France acted as though the treaty bound other nations also, I too was forced to act. I have no doubt that everything will be arranged if England does not incite France." *—On the Moroccan Question—*

He said that by the Morocco Treaty England got Egypt and

Newfoundland, and France a nest of international difficulties in return. Mr. Beit told him that the bad feeling dated back to the Boer War. He said "that is ten years ago," meaning no doubt the time of the Raid, and that France was then very much more bitter. At that time he was approached twice by France and Russia to invade England, but he declined and wired to the Queen and was thanked for his efforts. Mr. Beit made it clear to him that if the Morocco Conference did not turn out satisfactorily England was bound to assist France, and this the Emperor quite understood, but he again repeated that everything would be settled amicably with France about Morocco if England would not interfere.

—On Feeling in England.   Mr. Beit told the Emperor that whilst in Germany it was general talk that England wished for war, the English thought it was the Emperor who wished for war; he quickly replied that for eighteen years he had done his best to preserve peace, and it was ridiculous that he should now be thought to want war and especially on account of a matter like Morocco.

When talking of the attacks by the English Press the Emperor remarked that when Mr. Roosevelt tried to arrange peace between Russia and Japan, the whole of the English Press accused him (the Emperor) of inciting the Tsar not to make peace; but that when Roosevelt cabled him, thanking the Emperor for his assistance, not a paper had the decency to withdraw its former attacks.

Speaking of the English Ambassador (Sir F. L. Bertie) he contended that he was most rude to the German Ambassador.[1] Meeting him in July at a private party, before other people, he began to talk about the Morocco business and said to him, "You won't and shan't have this conference." The Emperor said it was so bad that Prince Radolin would have been justified in challenging him to a duel, but he restrained himself, and prevented a rupture at that time.

Mr. Beit asked the Emperor whether an exceptional position would not be granted to France, especially as to police. He

[1] These were the Ambassadors of the two countries at Paris.

replied, "Yes, on the Algerian frontier, but nowhere else. I will not have a second Tunis."

[*To the Rt. Hon. J. Morley.*]　　　WINDSOR CASTLE,
　　　　　　　　　　　　　　　　　　JANUARY 23RD.

If you have not seen him, will you send for Colonel Hubert Hamilton, who has just returned from India. He has been military secretary to Lord Kitchener, and is much in his confidence. It is worth your while to cross-examine him.

[*To M. V. B.*]　　　WINDSOR CASTLE,
　　　　　　　　　　　　　　JANUARY 23RD.

We had a very lively tea last night. The kids were in high spirits, and Prince Edward as composed and clever as ever. He had thought of a riddle in bed, and it really was quite witty for a child. He grows more like the *old* family every day. He has the mouth and expression of old Queen Charlotte. At half-past five I met the King by appointment in the corridor. He had sent me a note sealed up with a charming head of Edward VI which he had recently bought. He asked me if I had noticed it. He is so queer about those little *minutiæ*.

The Prince Edward.

He came out of his room with a pot hat on, and his stick and his dog, and we wandered about the castle for two hours, as if we were out for a walk. We went to the library and ransacked every kind of bookcase and picture cupboard. He got rid of an enormous number of rubbishy old coloured photographs and things, which will delight his relatives, to whom he has given them.

He told me a lot of interesting stories about Stockmar and the men he remembered in his youth, as we happened across their portraits. Stockmar would never say good-bye to anyone. He hated it—nor would he wear knee-breeches nor decorations.

He used to wear his dressing-gown and slippers till luncheon time. The King went to say good-bye to him on the occasion of his visit ; he broke down and never came to Windsor again.

[*Journals.*]
WINDSOR CASTLE,
JANUARY 24TH.

This evening, before dinner, the King sent for me to show me a final letter about the trouble at Osborne.

The King's letter, in which he appointed me the Royal Trustee of the British Museum, is charming. I got the Royal Warrant under the Sign-manual to-day. He delivered to me a little homily of my duties, showing great knowledge of the working of the place.

Hardinge's last visit to Petersburg was a very hurried one. The Emperor of Russia has positively not a nerve in his body. He is a profound fatalist.

. . . This evening Maurice came to tea, the two Princes and Princess Mary had tea (as they do every night) in my room. Prince Edward develops every day fresh qualities, and is a most charming boy; very direct, dignified and clever. His memory is remarkable—a family tradition; but the look of Weltschmerz in his eyes I cannot trace to any ancestor of the House of Hanover.

[*To M. V. B.*]
2, TILNEY ST.,
JANUARY 30TH.

Death of the King of Denmark.

The poor old King [1] was quite well till luncheon. He had a pain in his chest, and lay down and died quite quietly. The Queen of course feels the break up of her Danish home, which she cared for much more than anything else. I don't think she is very intimate with the brother who succeeds. The new King is

[1] King of Denmark.

very conservative and insists on dining at 6 o'clock. That is the key to his attitude on all subjects. I suppose the Queen will go to Denmark for the funeral, and will then shut herself up for a long time. Adieu the season.

[*To M. V. B.*]　　　　　　　　　ORCHARD LEA,
　　　　　　　　　　　　　　　　　FEBRUARY 4TH.

. . . Lord Rothschild told me that Arthur [Balfour] is *sure* to remain leader. I hope you did not miss Walter Long's telegram in the papers to-night. He is a first-rate sort. Bobs [Lord Roberts] and Lady Bobs were at the meeting; he seemed a little low, I thought—poor little chap. I fear his propaganda is not doing very well. I am sorry, as a great deal of what he is aiming at is excellent. . . .

[*From Lord Roberts.*]　　　　47, PORTLAND PLACE,
　　　　　　　　　　　　　　　　FEBRUARY 5TH.

MY DEAR ESHER,

Herewith the revised programme of the National Service League. Please let me know what you think of it. My object has been, while insisting on universal adult training, and on the likelihood of a citizen Army being eventually formed, to do what is possible in the meanwhile to increase the efficiency of the Auxiliary Forces.

　　　　　　　　　　　　　　Yours,
　　　　　　　　　　　　　　　ROBERTS.

[*To M. V. B.*]　　　H.M. YACHT "VICTORIA AND ALBERT,"
　　　　　　　　　　　　　FEBRUARY 11TH.

The yacht waited for me at Portsmouth, but the train was late, so when I arrived down, the gangway was gone, and she was just pushing off, leaving the *Alberta* behind for me. But she was stopped, and after all the fuss of getting the gangway set again, I got on board and then we waited for Harman![1]

Eager eyes watching, and all the officers and bluejackets at their quarters. Then his goggle eye rolled into view, and we got off. No one wanted to leave Portsmouth, but the King insisted, and he was right, as there is no motion here at Cowes, and there is no drearier quarter than being berthed up against a dock. The King is not very well, as he has a slight cold, but he is in a very good mood, and talked to me about the Army for hours last night.

At Cowes.

When he went to his game of bridge, *I* went to the ward-room, and played for an hour with the Commodore and Fritz [Ponsonby]. You will be happy to hear that I was thought a most superior player!

This morning it is finer, and I think we shall be able to get ashore. The difficulty being that the King cannot easily climb up and down a companion ladder in a choppy sea. I hope he won't stand on deck without his hat for church.

Haldane goes back, I understand, to-night, to receive Edward Grey to-morrow morning, who arrives from Northumberland, poor fellow. He and Haldane are going to live together for the present. It is an excellent arrangement. . . .

Osborne.

I must put in a postscript to say that we had Prince Louis of Battenberg's cadet and a small Cunninghame-Graham, both 12 years old, at luncheon. They sat on each side of the King, and without any sort of shyness talked quite glibly about Osborne and their work—exactly as they might have done in their homes. Absolutely perfect self-possession.

We went to the college this afternoon. Four hundred boys looking splendid. The gym is much improved. There is a portrait of Nelson hung in the gallery—with a motto under it in enormous letters: "There is nothing the Navy cannot do."

There were three boys in bed in the sick ward, and the King

[1] His servant.

talked to all of them. Then we went on to Osborne and saw the convalescent officers; some very bad, poor devils. The place is good and a God-send to those impecunious "liners," as you can imagine.

The sea was very rough and only bluejackets could have got the King into the launch without an accident. We bumped three times on a shoal coming off just now. The King took it quite calmly. There is only one yacht on the "roads" besides ourselves. I shall be in London at 5 to-morrow.

[*To H.M. the King.*]   2, TILNEY ST.,
                                            FEBRUARY 17TH.

Viscount Esher presents his humble duty and begs to return *The Forces in* the Duke of Connaught's letter, which Your Majesty was *S. Africa.* graciously pleased to lend him. It is most interesting and contains some very important statements in regard to the condition of Your Majesty's Forces in S. Africa.

It seems clear that in spite of General Gordon's warnings many years ago that the only way to maintain tranquillity in S. Africa was by a "mobile force, mounted like the Boers," and in spite of the experience of the three years' war, immobility and the scattering of armed forces still remain the rule in S. Africa, instead of mobility and concentration. It is true that there are about 3,000 Mounted Infantry in the Colony, apparently ill-mounted, as are also the Horse Artillery.

This is undoubtedly an advance on the old system—but Viscount Esher feels sure that any experienced officer, such as General French or General Smith-Dorrien, would far sooner undertake to maintain peace in S. Africa with 10,000 well-mounted men, than with 19,000 men as now distributed and equipped.

Two points occur to Viscount Esher, which he would humbly venture to suggest to Your Majesty. The Inspector-General is supposed to send in to the Army Council an Annual

Report, but hesitates to send in "interim" reports. Does not Your Majesty think that in such a very special matter as this H.R.H. should report specially to the Army Council? What would probably be an even more efficacious course would be if Your Majesty were to speak to the Prime Minister on the point.

The second suggestion which Viscount Esher ventures to make is that Your Majesty should point out to the Prime Minister that in such a matter the Defence Committee would probably be held responsible should things go wrong and that the facts ought to be laid before them for consideration.

Viscount Esher hopes that Your Majesty will forgive him for venturing to offer these observations.

[*To Sir George Clarke.*[1]]   2, TILNEY ST.,
           FEBRUARY 18TH.

Of course I may be altogether wrong, but after long talks with J. F. [Fisher] on the yacht and elsewhere, I am perfectly sure that no detail has been left unthought out. I always told you that there was never any question as to the "command" and control of naval operations.

The strategic control will remain always with J. F. The tactical command with the senior naval officer of the Fleet at sea. There is no chance of the German Emperor being beforehand with us. There is far more risk of J. F. taking the initiative and precipitating war.

I don't think he will do so, but the chances are more likely that we shall take the fatal step too soon, than too late. . . .

. . . Please think over the S. African organisation and distribution of troops. I have suggested to the King that he should speak to C. B. on the subject.

On the
General Staff. If there is a catastrophe there, the Defence Committee would probably be to blame. It is *not* a purely G.S. question. As we have created it, the G.S. is going to be our Franken-

---

[1] Secretary to the Committee for Imperial Defence.

stein. I can see that clearly. The Defence Committee should
have been the G.S. for our Empire, with merely an "Intelligence
Branch" for the W.O., developed through the commands. The
German model is going to be our curse. However, we cannot
now go back.

[*To Sir John Fisher.*]   2, TILNEY ST.,
                                          FEBRUARY 18TH.

I send you the enclosed because I have no secrets from you. *Naval*
You see how my dear Clarke fusses. Still, it is a good trait: *Organisation.*
"zeal for the Service," as Midshipman Easy would say. I have
told him that he need not worry. That the strategic control
rests, and always will, with you; the tactical command with the
senior Fleet officer. That there is no chance of the Germans
getting first run, and that the risk is that *we* shall bounce too
soon, if there is any risk at all.

The more I see of the working of the Admiralty the more I
like it. The more I see of the working of the G.S. the less I like
it. The French have not disclosed to us their plans ashore, and I
don't blame them. I say that nothing will induce you to disclose
your plans to *anyone*, and you are right. In war, you must take
chances, and it is better to risk much than lose the enormous
advantage of surprise. . . .

[*From Lord Kitchener, Commander-in-Chief in India.*]

                                          CALCUTTA,
                    Private.   MARCH 1ST.
MY DEAR LORD ESHER,

I have to thank you very sincerely for the support and assist- *The Indian*
ance you have given me throughout this critical period. I fully *Army.*
realise that a large proportion of the Cabinet would have
viewed with composure my overthrow 'twixt cup and lip;

and possibly some of the Government, such, for instance, as Winston Churchill, might have rejoiced at my discomfiture.

I do not know quite why this should be the case, as economy and efficiency in the Army, which it has been my object to obtain, is often quoted as also one of the aims of the present Government. However, I have been so completely misrepresented at home that I daresay this view of the case has been entirely lost sight of or become hidden under the mass of lies that now surround and envelop my personality.

I do not see any great difficulty in working the system as it is now laid down; and under Lord Minto, who takes a real interest in the Army, I have confident hopes of making the new system a success, so that when my time is over everyone will say: "Why did not we do this before?" I suppose some of the old Indian Army officials who have opposed the change foresaw this possibility and thought that any such criticism might be considered as a reflexion on their administration of the Army. I sincerely hope nothing more may now be heard of us and our work out here for at least a year and nine months. It has been a trying time, but thank God it is now over. If I have discovered bitter enemies I have also found staunch friends and the end has justified my action; but it is a lesson to me to have nothing further to do with Army reforms.

Again thanking you as one of the best friends I have found,

Yours very sincerely,

KITCHENER.

[*To the Rt. Hon. Sir H. Campbell-Bannerman.*[1]]

2, TILNEY ST.,

MARCH 1ST.

Mr. Balfour's Interrupted Policy on Imperial Defence.

Your attention has no doubt been drawn to three papers written for the Defence Committee by Mr. Balfour. The object of these papers, which are upon Invasion, Indian Defence,

[1] Prime Minister.

and the Army respectively, was to endeavour to place naval and military organisation upon a rational basis.

This object, which has been vaguely talked about at various times, has never yet been attained, and the result has been a spasmodic increase and decrease of our armaments, accompanied by a steady growth of expenditure.

Unfortunately Mr. Balfour did not ask the Defence Committee to pronounce an opinion upon these papers with the exception of the paper on Invasion, to which he obtained their consent, together with the approval of the Cabinet; nor did he proceed to carry through his original idea, which was to obtain a formal settlement of the principles upon which our national armaments should be based.

Several reasons contributed to this failure of purpose, but the primary cause was the production of a large scheme for Army organisation, by the Secretary of State for War, which that Minister had evolved before he assumed office, and which he determined to press upon his colleagues. Unhappily, no resistance was made to this fresh attempt to follow the idiosyncrasy of a Minister rather than the lines of a rational and comprehensive plan; and although the particular scheme was ultimately defeated by the resistance of the Cabinet and the House of Commons, the mischief was done, and Mr. Balfour's intentions were nullified.

I venture now respectfully to suggest to you that the Defence Committee should take up the work where it was left by Mr. Balfour.

The precise point at which an enquiry might commence is somewhere between the Invasion paper, which was warmly approved by the Defence Committee of the day, and the principles of which have always been advocated by the present First Sea Lord, and the Indian Defence paper, which was never thrashed out by the Defence Committee, and upon which no agreement was come to by the Departments principally concerned.

Recent Admiralty reforms, which are generally admitted to *Recent Naval Reforms—*

have led to a great increase of naval efficiency and unquestionably have resulted in large economies, were based upon a careful reconsideration of the naval requirements of the Empire, subject to those modern conditions of science which govern naval warfare in these days. No similar enquiry has ever been made into our joint naval and military requirements, or into the military requirements of the Empire for offensive-defensive purposes.

The Board of Admiralty found a system of Fleet distribution dating back to 1805. They have redistributed the Fleet, in a manner suitable to the conditions of 1905. The lesson that evolution in mechanical science generally leads to economy of time and labour had filtered very slowly into the minds of those responsible for naval administration. Now the lesson has been driven home, and the present Board of Admiralty can justly claim that they are abreast of modern requirements, and at the same time have lightened very considerably the annual burden upon the taxpayer. Can any similar claim be made by those responsible for military organisation and military expenditure? Yet no great stretch of imagination is wanted to apply those principles which have guided the Board of Admiralty in Naval *—As a Model* affairs to the sister service. It is, at any rate, worth while to *for Army* enquire whether the distribution of the military forces of the *Reform.* Crown is not as antiquated, under modern conditions, as was that of the Navy. And upon the distribution of the Army its organisation mainly rests.

In India, as Lord Kitchener has recently pointed out, the plan of military distribution is much what it was in 1857, notwithstanding the enormous development of the railway system in India.

Is it not equally true that in spite of the expansion of the Empire, of the marvellous increased rapidity of transit, of the great sub-oceanic telegraph lines, and finally of the invention and development of wireless telegraphy, the Imperial distribution of our military forces is much upon the same plan as it was at the close of the Napoleonic wars?

It may be possible that no drastic change is necessary or possible, but this question, since it has never been put to any authority so constituted as to be able to reply to it, cannot be answered.

Possibly, results as great as those achieved by the Board of Admiralty might be obtained. Possibly not. But who can maintain that it is not worth the enquiry?

[*From the Rt. Hon. J. Morley.*]

INDIA OFFICE,
MARCH 2ND.

MY DEAR ESHER,

. . . Very sorry I missed you. You are about the only man I know whom I am never sorry to see. There's for you!!

Yours,

J. M.

[*To M. V. B.*]

2, TILNEY ST.,
MARCH 5TH.

. . . I told you that on parting the King said to me, "Although you are not exactly a public servant, yet I always think you are the most valuable public servant I have," and then I kissed his hand, as I sometimes do.

. . . If you get this before you see the General [French] to-night, tell him that I have seen Haldane to-day, and he gave me a précis of his speech which he delivers on Wednesday in the H. of C. He has adopted the general plan of my memo.; and he will enunciate the doctrine in his speech, and bring up the points at the Defence Committee. So he has done well. There was nothing else of much importance. Only tiresome small questions.

Mr. Haldane's Policy.

[*To H.M. the King.*]   2, TILNEY ST.,
                                                MARCH 8TH.

Viscount Esher presents his humble duty and begs to report, for Your Majesty's information, that the Defence Committee were occupied yesterday almost exclusively with the consideration of six questions raised by the Secretary of State for War, which appear on the additional agenda paper enclosed herewith.

Viscount Esher believes that Lord Knollys has forwarded to Your Majesty a Memorandum which he wrote for the Prime Minister, dealing with certain definite conditions, which he ventured to think should be laid down by the Defence Committee, before Mr. Haldane would be in a position to proceed to consider the organisation of the Army.

Viscount Esher did not think that it was altogether within his province to raise these questions himself at the Defence Committee meeting, provided that Mr. Haldane would consent to do so.

This Mr. Haldane, with the full approval of the Prime Minister, undertook to do.

[*To the Rt. Hon. J. Morley.*]   2, TILNEY ST.,
                                                MARCH 13TH.

Reorganisa- May I venture to suggest that in writing to India you should
tion in India. explain that the questions which you are putting to the Viceroy contain no insidious intention, but are an honest attempt to look once in a way at the strategic and political necessities of the *whole* Empire; and to obtain a rational *modus operandi* in dealing with naval and military organisation, for a period of years. There has been hitherto far too much parochialism in dealing with these matters, tempered by the temporary whim of the proconsular autocrat. It has been quite sufficient for the W.O. to plead General so and so, or Governor this and that, as a complete armour to all criticism. I never need amplify in writing or speaking to you.

Possibly more troops may be wanted in India, possibly fewer. In any case you have a fine field for compromise with K. over *his* big scheme!! There must be some give and take.

[*From Sir Douglas Haig, Inspector-General of Cavalry in India.*]

MEERUT,
MARCH 15TH.

MY DEAR ESHER,

Many thanks indeed for your kind letter of February 15th, received by the last mail. I have wired to thank you for it, and added, "Will accept if offered the appointment."

I need scarcely say how gratified I feel that the King should think *my* presence is necessary at home, especially so as the reason is a military one.

I am very glad also to hear the good account which you give of Haldane, and am sincerely grateful to you for the good opinion which *you* have *made* him form regarding myself.

Yours most sincerely,
DOUGLAS HAIG.

[*To H.M. the King.*]   2, TILNEY ST.,
MARCH 22ND.

Viscount Esher presents his humble duty, and begs to enclose two letters, one from Lord Kitchener,[1] and the other from General Smith-Dorrien, which he thinks may interest Your Majesty.

Viscount Esher has seen Mr. Morley frequently during the past week, in reference to Lord Kitchener's Army Reorganisation scheme in India, which is under discussion at the India Office.

Mr. Morley and Lord Kitchener.

[1] The letter given here under March 1st.

As Your Majesty remembers, it deals with the redistribution of troops in India. Viscount Esher hopes that Mr. Morley will show the same spirit of conciliation and fairness, to these proposals, as to those with which he has already dealt, and Viscount Esher thinks that this will be the case, as Mr. Morley has consented to write privately to both Lord Kitchener and Lord Minto, before he arrives at any decision.

[*To the Rev. C. D. Williamson.*]   ORCHARD LEA,
MARCH 25TH.

You knew we had a fire here. It spoilt Nellie's room and the gallery—but we got it under without serious damage. I have half covered the gallery walls with green *silk*—and I hate it. It is too *nouveau riche* for me, so I am stopping the work to-morrow morning, and reverting to the old stuff. Rather tragic is it not?

Somehow all the harmony of the room has gone. I don't know what to do precisely. I wish you were here. The oak things look so incongruous somehow. You probably know the feeling one has, when a room has been a great success, and there is a radical change in *tone*.

I am so busy with the Defence Committee and the new Government (all of whom I like) that I have hardly a moment for myself.

I sincerely hope that you are having nicer spring weather than we are having here. It has been blowing from the East and snowing for more than 10 days.

[*To M. V. B.*]   HOUSE OF LORDS,
MARCH 26TH.

It is a queer thing to be writing to you from the Library of the H. of L. It is not a place that I affect much, but I am waiting to see Lansdowne, and seize this opportunity.

C. B. [Campbell-Bannerman], with whom I had a gossip this morning, has been corresponding with Lansdowne about the motion expressing confidence in Milner. They both think it is a mistake to bring the two Houses into collision upon a question of that kind. Conflict is bound to come soon enough upon big questions of policy. Of course, some people may say that you cannot have a larger question than this; and I am not sure that I do not agree.

The only person who can effectively interfere would be Milner himself. I hope he will. *I* should, were I in his place, and should ask Halifax not to move the resolution.[1] C. B. was very pleasant, and talked very freely about the Army. He does not at all like the idea of large reductions of the *Regular* Army.

I lunched with Jackie [Fisher] and the Fiskin girls. They love *The Beauty of Bath,* and think Ella [Terris] divine. Pamela has got two books full of photographs of Cupid [2] in *The Little Cherub*. She bought up two shops full! They were full of the Velasquez picture, and last night the girls alternately adopted the attitude of the Velasquez lady, to see whether the drawing of the hips was correct!

[*To H.M. the King.*]   HOUSE OF LORDS,
MARCH 28TH.

Viscount Esher with humble duty begs to thank Your Majesty for Your Majesty's most interesting letter, and he will

[1] A resolution had been put to the House of Commons on March 24th censuring Lord Milner for permitting flogging in the Chinese Labour Camps in the Transvaal. It was rejected in favour of an alternative Government resolution omitting any mention of persons, which was passed by a majority of 220. On March 29th Lord Halifax moved in the Lords: That this House desires to place on record its high appreciation of the services rendered by Lord Milner in South Africa to the Crown and the Empire. This was also passed.

[2] Miss Gabrielle Ray.

endeavour, in all respects, to the best of his ability to carry out Your Majesty's commands.

*Army Redis-
tribution
Abroad.*

Whatever Your Majesty may hear to the contrary, it is certain that there is no intention at present to weaken the garrison in South Africa. Nothing will be settled before the Duke of Connaught's return, after which a proposal may be made to substitute *Cavalry* for Infantry to some small degree, on the ground that the former are more suitable for that country.

On the other hand, it is proposed *at once* to strengthen the garrison in Egypt, in consequence of the Mahommedan unrest all over northern Africa, and probably two or three Battalions will be sent from Malta for that purpose.

Mr. Haldane is heavily engaged in considering the necessary economies for next year. Many of his military advisers are pressing for reduction in the Battalions of Guards.

Lord Milner.

After writing to Your Majesty Viscount Esher met Lord Lansdowne, who wished Your Majesty to know that the resolve to support Lord Halifax's motion was taken at a meeting at Lansdowne House, at which Mr. Balfour was present, and at which Lord Milner strongly urged, in order to give support to the Loyalists in South Africa, and not upon any ground personal to himself, that there should be a division in the House of Lords. His [Lord Lansdowne's] reluctance was based upon disinclination to bring the two Houses into conflict just at present.

Your Majesty will doubtless have heard all about the "Guards ragging" case at Aldershot. Mr. Haldane has appointed a strong Board of Enquiry, presided over by General Morton (late Div. Gen. in Ireland) and four other General Officers, who are to report to the Army Council on the case. The Officers under arrest may employ Counsel, and great care will be taken to arrive at the truth, and to avoid hardship upon anyone.

Great sympathy is felt for General Cuthbert, but there is very little doubt that he was imprudent in not taking the case of the young officer (who was very unsatisfactory) into his own hands. . . .

... These "scandals," taken up by the halfpenny press, do a great deal of harm, as Your Majesty well knows.

Viscount Esher ventures again to thank Your Majesty most affectionately and sincerely for Your Majesty's kind letter.

[*To the Rt. Hon. J. Morley.*]

COMMITTEE OF IMPERIAL DEFENCE,
MARCH 30TH.

Clarke has told me very generally some of the ideas which are running in your mind about Indian expenditure on the Army. *Indian Army Finance.*

May I venture to suggest some such phrase as "most reluctant to sanction any increase in military expenditure until the facts are much fuller before you than at present," rather than a definite closing of the door.

My argument is that although it is plain that K. [Kitchener] has advocated a counsel of perfection in his 9 Divisions, *it is not clear* that he has even 4 Divisions fully equipped. He may have, but it is not certain. I am confident that there are all the elements of a "deal" with K., but this will depend upon the tactical approach to that queer personality. You understand.

Entre nous Clarke is rather *too* cock-sure in Indian matters.

[*To H.M. the King.*]   COMMITTEE OF IMPERIAL DEFENCE,
APRIL 1ST.

Viscount Esher presents his humble duty, and begs to state for Your Majesty's information that he asked Mr. Haldane to see Sir John French yesterday about the proposal to reduce the Guards by two battalions, the effect of which would be to destroy the Brigade at Aldershot. *Proposed Reduction of the Guards.*

Mr. Haldane saw the General and, after a preliminary talk, confronted him with the A.G.

The matter was then fully discussed, and so strong was the impression made upon the mind of Mr. Haldane by the arguments used by Sir John French, that Viscount Esher feels satisfied the proposal will not be proceeded with. As Your Majesty knows full well, under a purely *voluntary* system, Your Majesty's Army can never be a very numerous one, compared with the great armies of the Continent.

It is possible, however, under a voluntary system, to have a comparatively small and *very highly efficient* regular army, and a large half-trained militia.

In regard to the Regular Army, based upon these principles of the highest possible efficiency, no efforts should be spared to maintain the highest possible standard in men, training, and equipment.

There is no difference of opinion upon the admirable *quality* of the Guards. They are the pick of the Army, and it would seem little short of folly, from the point of view of Your Majesty, who is anxious to see the highest standard in the Regular Army, to reduce the best troops Your Majesty possesses.

To reduce the Guards Brigade at Aldershot is to knock the point off the spear; and to blunt the weapon which (as it is a light one) should be as sharp as possible.

Your Majesty will realise that if two battalions of the Guards are reduced, and the Aldershot Brigade is destroyed, the argument that, for the sake of economy, the Guards might *still further be reduced* by another two battalions would become irresistible.

It would be said, that the Guards should no longer be taken into account as a portion of the Army to be used abroad, but should be placed on the footing of a Body Guard *pur et simple* for Your Majesty, and if used at all in war, that a "composite battalion" might be organised on the lines of the Household Cavalry. Those who, merely because Aldershot is unpopular with some officers of the Guards, advocate the reduction of the Brigade, can hardly realise the danger to this splendid Infantry force, of the measure they propose.

In the course of the discussion which took place yesterday Sir John French told Mr. Haldane that if reductions are absolutely necessary, much as he would dislike it, he would far rather see 4 batteries of Artillery reduced than lose the Brigade of Guards, from a force of 3 Divisions, which he would have to command in the Field.

Viscount Esher can only repeat to Your Majesty, that Mr. Haldane was so vividly impressed that there is every hope of this project being once more dropped.

The Adjutant-General was also impressed, and has now gone back to the contemplation of effecting savings in other directions, and to see how they can best be accomplished. Viscount Esher begs that Your Majesty will not be anxious about the matter, for should the proposal again be put forward, Your Majesty will hear of it at once.

Viscount Esher encloses a letter from General Douglas Haig, for Your Majesty's information.

[*To Lord Kitchener.*]   2, TILNEY ST.,
                                  APRIL 6TH.

I have seen a very great deal of John Morley, and have done all that is possible to get him to understand two points : *Mr. Morley and Lord Kitchener.*

(*a*) That you are always ready to discuss frankly any scheme of yours, provided that you know that a serious attempt is being made to arrive at a just and fair decision.

(*b*) That he will always find you amenable to reason and open to conviction, provided that discussion is above board, and that there is no attempt at intrigue.

I strongly urge him to tell you *frankly* what is in his mind, and what he wishes, and I think he realises that you would be always willing to tell him in return what *you* think essential, and to find a common denominator between you.

I hope you will approve this language. I lent him your Note on Military Policy. This was essential if he was to understand your big Redistribution scheme. I took this responsibility, knowing Mr. Morley so intimately and feeling sure that I could do so without prejudicing his mind in any way against you or your opinions. It has had a very salutary effect. If you could only meet the Secretary of State for an hour's talk (a Utopian aspiration) every subject in dispute would be removed easily. The difficulty is to argue persuasively by letter. Luckily both you and he have unusual capacity in that way. Many here are hostile to

(*a*) Your plan of concentration.

(*b*) Your railway schemes.

(*c*) Expenditure on transport, stores, etc.

I am sure that a "transaction" is possible on the following lines:

You to sanction a temporary diminution for 3 years in the number of drafts for India, thus relieving the military tension here, which you understand.

The Secretary of State, on the other hand, to give you what you think most urgent under the above heads, (*a*), (*b*) and (*c*). Will you think over this rough-and-ready proposal? And pray believe me anxious to assist you.

[*To H.M. the King.*]   2, TILNEY ST.,
                                                  APRIL 6TH.

Viscount Esher presents his humble duty and begs to thank Your Majesty for the gracious letter which he has received safely. He ventures to hope that Your Majesty is not bored by the innumerable things which he reports to Your Majesty.

The Amir.   . . . Viscount Esher, to illustrate this point for Your Majesty's information, may mention that he saw this week one of Your Majesty's subjects, who lived for over 5 months in the past year at Cabul, and saw a great deal of the Ameer.

This prince wears European clothes, and dresses by day in a frock coat, and wears an English dress suit at dinner. He sees all the English papers, and on one occasion when Viscount Esher's informant's mail was delayed, he begged the Ameer for the loan of the latest English papers. A copy of *The Times* was sent down to him by the Ameer, and every passage referring to Afghanistan or Indian and Russian affairs was scored through with blue pencil. . . .

. . . Viscount Esher must end with an expression of grateful thanks to Your Majesty for the kind letters he has received and he will bear in mind Your Majesty's warning not to be deluded by his "new glasses." They are rather strange to him, but he reflects often, that it is his duty to wear them, however inconvenient, in obedience to Your Majesty and, he ventures to hope, in the interests of Your Majesty and of the State.

[*From H.M. the King.*]   H.M. YACHT "VICTORIA AND ALBERT,"
[*Private and Confidential.*]   CORFU, APRIL 14TH.

MY DEAR ESHER,

Many thanks for your interesting letter of 6th. Pray write to me fully and confidentially about anything that you think will interest me—and I think you know of old that I take interest in most things. . . .

    Believe me, Yours very sincerely,

       EDWARD R.

[*To H.M. the King.*]   2, TILNEY ST.,
       APRIL 20TH.

Viscount Esher presents his humble duty and begs to thank Your Majesty most sincerely for the very gracious letter he received yesterday.

Owing to Easter, and the absence of all Your Majesty's Ministers, there is very little news.

On Curzon.   Viscount Esher, although, as Your Majesty knows, he has always been on Lord Kitchener's side in the controversy with Lord Curzon, thought it right to attend the dinner given by the Pilgrims to the latter.

It was an interesting evening, and all the speeches were excellent, notably Lord George Hamilton's, which was beautifully delivered.

The Pilgrims' dinners are very well arranged—at round tables holding about ten people, every Englishman being placed next an American—and most excellently served. Lord Curzon spoke in his usual style: eloquently and floridly, but showing himself to be, what he is, one of the very ablest of Your Majesty's subjects.

He remains, of course, vindictive, and anxious to overthrow those whom he believes to be his personal enemies; a not unnatural feeling. Some of his supporters, especially Mr. Chirol of *The Times*, who wrote a bitter attack on Lord Kitchener a few days ago, show an indiscretion which unfortunately is bound to do harm in India.

Mr. Morley is trying hard to examine Lord Kitchener's great scheme for the Indian Army without bias or *parti pris*, but the *personal* element which has been introduced into the controversy renders this exceedingly difficult.

Viscount Esher ventures to suggest that Your Majesty should ask to see the draft of any despatch that goes to India on this *On the Prime* subject, before it is dispatched finally to the Viceroy. Your *Minister.* Majesty has noticed that the communications from the Prime Minister are few and somewhat trivial. From what he has seen of the way the Government business is managed, Viscount Esher believes the reason of this to be that the Prime Minister has aged a good deal lately, and finds it even more difficult than hitherto to fix his attention upon details.

Never a laborious man, his disinclination to master troublesome subjects has now given place to impossibility, and

Viscount Esher believes that the main reason why he writes so meagrely to Your Majesty is that he has very little to tell.

The work of the Government, even on large questions of policy like the Education Bill, is carried on in the various Departments, practically without reference to the Prime Minister, and the result is apparent in the indecisive manner in which questions are dealt with when they come before Parliament, and when the Government is subjected to Parliamentary pressure.

The Labour Bill, for instance, brought about a complete change of policy between a Monday and a Friday, and this change was hastily agreed to at an extempore Cabinet held behind the Speaker's chair.

Liberal Governments, as Your Majesty knows, are peculiarly liable to the complaint of indecision, due to the warring elements within the Cabinet, and even so strong a personality as Mr. Gladstone was unable to ensure unity or consistency of action. Viscount Esher feels sure that the present régime will not last very long, and that the P.M.'s health will not stand even the modest strain which he places upon it; so that Your Majesty will, before long, have the very onerous burden of choosing a successor thrown upon Your Majesty.

[*To Lord Knollys.*]   2, TILNEY ST.,
                                                  APRIL 23RD.

I have had a long talk with Morley. He does not at all relish Curzon's attitude, and dislikes the tone of his appeal. *Morley on Curzon.*

But, so far as he is concerned, he will not put any obstacles in the way, if it is the King's strong wish that Curzon should have a Peerage.

He thinks, however, that C. B. [Campbell-Bannerman] will not consult him. Should he do so, then he will tell C. B.:—

(*a*) That, in his opinion, Curzon has no claim whatever.

(*b*) But that he would not oppose a Peerage for Curzon if C. B. desires to meet the King's wishes in the matter.

I return you Curzon's letter, and the copy of yours to Curzon.

[*To M. V. B.*]   2, TILNEY ST.,
                                                MAY 9TH.

Charles   It was great fun talking to Frohman.[1] He sat curled up in a
Frohman. big arm-chair in Seymour [Hick]'s dressing-room, looking like a Chinese idol, and talked about Edna [May] by the yard.

He evidently thinks himself a sort of providence to her and Ella [Hicks] and others whom he likes. I only hope that he will behave as such in days of stress, should they ever come.

. . . Frohman thinks that all public characters, especially actors and actresses, should be kept locked up in cupboards and inaccessible, so as to perpetuate the illusion and prevent their audiences from ever finding out that they are ordinary men and women. He thinks there is no harm at all in an actress losing her reputation—that it never does her harm, provided that it is untrue; but that if she really has lovers, she is lost as an actress. A curious theory.

I am sure that he is a kind-hearted and affectionate little man.

[*To M. V. B.*]   2, TILNEY ST.,
                                                MAY 9TH.

Relations   . . . We had a hard day yesterday. I lunched with Haldane,
with Turkey. Repington, Ellison, and Lucas, and we talked about Egypt, and then the Army as usual. The difficulty, now as ever, is to get steps taken in good time. Grey is the only man who possesses the power of anticipation.

You realise, that *if* the Sultan does not give in, he gets at least 14 days' start on us all round, and probably a great deal more. No British Government ever takes precautionary measures. Our intelligence of Turkish preparations is very deficient.

[1] Charles Frohman, the theatrical producer.

We ought to have spies all over Syria, and to mobilise *to-day*, and not wait for May 15th.

. . . I asked the King to settle a day for the Aldershot visit. He does not much fancy the 24th.

[*To M. V. B.*]   2, TILNEY ST.,
                                                   MAY 15TH.

You will enjoy *Raffles*! I really think that poor Chudleigh has got a success this time. The audience was enthusiastic. It is an excellent melodrama, and beautifully acted. All sorts of hair-raising escapes; and all the characters are sympathetic. Dot Boucicault is excellent.

. . . To-day I have a long morning at the W.O. My "agenda" for the Committee [1] has been printed. They will be an odious team to drive. . . .

W.O. Committee on Territorial Organisation.

[*To M. V. B.*]   2, TILNEY ST.,
                                                   MAY 22ND.

I was engaged with the Douma [2] yesterday from morn till eve. It went off very well. I will send you to-day the minutes

[1] To work out details of the Territorial Army. The Committee was published before referring it to the King, and Mr. Haldane wrote:—

HOUSE OF COMMONS,
MAY 10TH.

MY DEAR ESHER,

Alas—it is too late. Bron has sent the list to the Press. But I have written one of the most beautiful letters I ever penned to Knollys. I have put the whole blame on you! I have said that having detained H.M. long over other topics, I fled, never doubting that you had mentioned the topic in conversation. The less so that the King had referred to you. I am greatly tickled to-night to find how Clarke has laid hold of the P.M. over the Press Restriction in time of War bill. Never did the Committee for Imperial Defence bulk more largely than to-day. You must set things right with the K. "An inexperienced and raw S. of S." etc.!

[2] Name for W.O. Committee.

of proceedings up to date, which you can give to the General
[French]. It will keep him *au courant* of what is going on. They
still behave well, but I expect an outburst any day. The difficulty is to keep Clarke from making a flank attack. The difficulty of finding a successor for Grierson is very great. Clarke
favours Lawson. The General did not seem to think much of
him. Lyttelton wants Robertson. How would *Rawlinson* do?
I am sure that Murray is too junior, and I think the same remark
applies to Rawlinson and Gleichen under him.

The opera was lovely last night, and Donalda looked the
part perfectly and sang very well. The opera was crammed.
. . . Last night Princess Ena was at the opera, and I said good-
bye to her. She looked very nice.

[*To M. V. B.*]   2, TILNEY ST.,
                                        MAY 24TH.

A very laborious day. We started at 8 sharp in the motor,
and got to Grosvenor Gardens at 8.20. No obstruction along
the road. The Douma was exceptionally well behaved this
morning, and we did a lot of work. Passed 15 resolutions. I
could not get to the tournament as I had to go back to the W.O.
this afternoon. I think we are doing very well; Clarke wrote to
me a silly letter, but I have seen him this afternoon and tried to
soothe him.

C. B. [Campbell-Bannerman] is very much broken. He
gets no sleep, and is up 3 or 4 times every night. He won't allow
anyone but himself to nurse Lady C. B. It cannot possibly go on.

I thought all the arrangements yesterday perfect, and I am
going to see the King in a quarter of an hour, to hear what he
thought of it.

[*To Lord Knollys.*]   2, TILNEY ST.,
                                        MAY 27TH.

I have told Haldane that I think he ought to lay his reduction
schemes before the King *in writing*. As you know, I cannot

sympathise with proposals which are based, not upon the real needs of the country, but upon simple opportunism.

Expense, and high expenditure, are *necessary* for the military purpose of the nation that has determined to abide by a voluntary system of enlistment. They are inseparable from the cost of maintaining an Empire which has not to be defended from within a ring fence, but all over the globe. *On Military Extravagance.*

On the other hand, *extravagance* can be avoided, although it is inherent in the military mind. For instance,

(*a*) South African so-called experience (i.e. generalising from one particular instance) suggests Mounted Infantry as the prime necessity of modern armies in the field. M.I. schools are established accordingly at immense expense. Two years later the Japanese war suggests other lessons. These schools are abolished. Cost? Money *wasted*?

(*b*) Mr. Brodrick "thinks out" six Army Corps. Barracks are built at Salisbury, etc. at great cost. Three years later they are standing empty. Cost? Money wasted?

(*c*) Coast defence.

Defence of London.

Coaling stations.

Certain schemes are adopted, involving creation of Garrison Regiments, Garrison Artillery, purchase of stores, of depots for stores, guns, etc. Four years later schemes are vanished, all are abolished. Cost? Money wasted?

(*d*) The House of Commons presses for increase of pay for the soldiers, and a million is added to the estimates. Three years later, a new House of Commons presses for economy, and the pay is cut down. No one is a penny the better off. Cost? Money wasted?

And so on, *ad infinitum*.

Meanwhile, are we on the track of that "clear thinking" for which Mr. Haldane made so eloquent an appeal? *Requirements for a General Staff.*

The causes of all this lie deep down in our Military System, which has not trained up a body of *trained soldiers* to consider the problems of war.

Our staff system is old-fashioned and unsuited to modern conditions. Picking men out of the Army to act as Staff Officers, and sending them back at intervals to their regiments was all very well when "staff duties" meant merely Adjutant-General or Q.-Master-General duties of a subordinate kind.

Men employed for these purposes are all the better for being dipped again into regimental routine. But for Staff work, which is now designated as "General Staff," a special training is required, and officers who are qualified for the work ought to "specialise" for it, and be subjected to a long and continuous training.

There is not one man on the Army Council, and very few among the Directors at the War Office, who has ever attempted to think about the work they have to do, before they were appointed to their present posts.

Imagine how such a system would work if it were applied to the Treasury, and if George Murray and E. Hamilton had been casually picked out of a bank, or an accountant's office. What would be the value of the advice they could give Asquith? And yet, that is precisely the system which Haldane is called upon to make a success. It is very hard upon him; and if he were to triumph over it, his statesmanship would rank very high indeed.

The public do not realise the real issues and the true nature of the problem with which he has to deal.

Parliamentary Ignorance of the Army.

The House of Commons believes instinctively that the Army is administered extravagantly. That is true. But they also think there is a short cut to economy. That is false.

My hope is that Haldane will present to the House of Commons and to the public the whole case, in full detail, and prove to them that arbitrary reductions do not tend to economy but are a premium upon extravagance, and that the new War Office system which was inaugurated two years ago must be given time to develop; and that the General Staff has got to be *trained* specially to deal with large questions of preparation for war, and to determine how, most efficiently and economically, to meet the complicated requirements of the Empire.

1. The continuous work of the Defence Committee, laying down the principles of offence and defence.

2. The Reformed War Office working soberly and steadily to create the machine best suited, in view of the modern requirements of war, to give effect to those principles.

3. The creation, and continuous training of General Staff in order to man the W.O. and the Commands with the right type of Officer.

These are the only methods by which any large saving can be effected of public money, if in addition to what is called "economy" the King is to be provided with an efficient Army, under the extraordinarily complicated conditions pertaining to the Empire.

I am sorry to have written at such enormous length, but you started the subject yesterday, and this is the result.

[*To H. M. the King.*]   2, TILNEY ST.

Viscount Esher presents his humble duty and begs to report, for Your Majesty's information, that the Army Committee of which, at Mr. Haldane's request, he acted as Chairman, suspended its sittings to-day, in order to give the Secretary of State and the Army Council an opportunity of considering and deciding upon the work so far accomplished. *Work of the Territorial Committee.*

Constitution of the Committee

The Committee was composed of a large majority of persons who hold or have held commissions in Your Majesty's *Regular* Army, and whose prejudices may be reasonably assumed to be favourable to the Regular, when brought into accidental conflict of interests with the Auxiliary Forces.

With one exception, the Committee is composed of men who by political conviction, birth, station, and education are opposed to the Government now in office, and whose predilections therefore may be assumed to be strongly in favour of maintaining the authority of the Crown over all armed forces, whether Regular or Auxiliary, and opposed absolutely to anything in the shape of what is generally understood by the term "citizen army."

Functions of the Committee

The Committee are not responsible for the principles upon which Mr. Haldane's scheme is based, that is to say:—

(*a*) The substitution of County Associations for the Commanding Officers of Yeomanry and Volunteer units, and the administering authority of the Yeomanry and Volunteers.

(*b*) The endeavour to mobilise and support certain units of the Regular Army, especially Army Service Corps, Engineer, and Medical units, which cannot under existing circumstances be mobilised at all, by means of half-trained men.

Work of the Committee

The Committee have worked out in detail a plan for forming County Associations. They have allotted to these Associations certain functions of *Administration*.

They have kept Command and Inspection in the hands of the General Officers Commanding-in-Chief. They have defined the Territorial Army to be existing Yeomanry, Volunteer Cadet Corps, and Rifle Clubs. They have *excluded* the Militia from the Territorial Army.

Political Effect of these Proposals

A grave political danger has hitherto been the "trades unionism" of the Volunteer Forces, voiced in Parliament by a few Volunteer spokesmen, informally accepted as representing that force which controls a large number of votes.

The breaking up of that force into groups constituted in County Areas, with conflicting interests and competing aims, is bound to produce a beneficial effect, and to free the War

Minister of the day from an influence which hitherto has proved pernicious and not in the true interests of military efficiency.

The Military Effect of these Proposals

They should, if carefully fostered and judiciously applied, lead to:—

(*a*) A reorganisation of the Militia; making that force more efficient and more useful, by linking it up closer to the Army, giving it a better class of officer, and enlisting it for service oversea. This was the ultimate aim and object which Mr. Cardwell had in view.

(*b*) The organisation of the Yeomanry and Volunteers into large units, which in a great national emergency could expand the very limited number of Regular Troops (150,000 in all), which are at Your Majesty's disposal now for the purposes of a great war.

(*c*) The fostering, by means of Cadet Corps and Rifle Clubs, of the military spirit of the people, which under a Voluntary system (and for the present all forms of compulsion are ruled out) is essential, if Your Majesty's vast Empire is to be properly safeguarded, should an appeal some day have to be made to the manhood of the nation.

Viscount Esher begs Your Majesty to believe that the simple and direct object of this Committee has been, and is, to endeavour to fulfil the need, upon which the Elgin Commission laid much stress, for a carefully thought out scheme for *expanding* the unfortunately small but highly efficient Regular Army under Your Majesty's Command. It is in no way directed towards substituting for a highly trained, perfectly equipped, and adequately staffed Regular Army, which is essential for nine wars out of ten in which the country is engaged, a Force of half-trained men, whose existence and organisation can only be justified by the always impending fear of a great national struggle for which no army which Your Majesty can maintain on a purely voluntary basis, could possibly be sufficient.

[*To the Lord Chancellor.*] 2, TILNEY ST.,
JULY 3RD.

The King and the Law of Copyright.

By the King's desire I have to ask your advice in the following circumstances:

Under His Majesty's directions, I am preparing, with Mr. Arthur Benson, a selection of the correspondence of Queen Victoria for publication.

The selection is made from the vast correspondence which is the property of the King, and is under my charge at Windsor Castle.

The letters are, nearly all, upon official matters, written to the Queen, as Sovereign, by Her Ministers or servants.

The question I have to ask is, whether the King has legal right to publish letters, addressed to the Sovereign, without applying for the consent of those who wrote them, or their heirs and assigns. Would you give the King your valuable assistance in this matter.

[*To M. V. B.*] 2, TILNEY STREET,
JULY 10TH.

Reductions in the Army.

... We had a Douma this morning and a Defence Committee in the afternoon. At the latter Grey insisted that the garrison of Egypt should not be reduced. This throws out Haldane's plan somewhat, as he had counted on withdrawing a line Battalion from there, which must now be supplied from Malta.

... The King is perfectly furious about the reduction. It is a pity he did not boil himself up earlier in the day. The General [French] very nearly lost his temper at the Defence Committee about Egypt. He got inwardly frantic with Lyttelton, who scoffed at the idea of any attack on Egypt *by land*, i.e. through the Sinai Peninsula, which could not be repulsed by ships in the Suez Canal. The General was quite right, but he was too cross to argue. He became scarlet in the face, and speechless!

The opera was lovely last night, and the first act (*Bohème*) better than ever.

I sneaked across to the Aldwych and peeped through the glass door and saw Zena looking very well.

[*To M. V. B.*]   ORCHARD LEA,
                                        JULY 18TH.

... I have only two things to tell you.

1. I heard Maggie Teyte at the Opera to-day. She sang *Maggie* the simple operatic airs very sweetly, but failed in the big *Teyte.* songs from *Hamlet* and *Louise* which she ought, at her age, never to have tried.

All sorts of fashionable women were at the Opera to hear her. Tosti and Messager both thought her voice had lost much of its freshness; that she had not improved it during the past year. They all say that Jean [de Reske] is a bad teacher; and that the girl wants *rest* and very careful treatment. She was as cool as a cucumber. I incline to think that she will be spoilt.

2. I have finished *Coniston*.[1] You were quite right, and it is a charming story with wonderfully drawn characters, and a very deep undercurrent of purpose. Jethro is most pathetic and the mixture of devotion to the girl for his mother's sake, and passion for her own sake, which rung his heart from time to time, is finely touched on. I like Bob, and his courtship is charmingly done. There are some delightful subordinate characters too. *What* a good writer!

[*To M. V. B.*]   2, TILNEY STREET,
                                        JULY 19TH.

... I dined with Douglas Haig to-night to meet Haldane, *Attack on* who was prevented from coming at the last moment by an *Haldane.* adjournment of the House.

---

[1] By Winston Churchill.

They debated his breaches of faith, and other silly political shibboleths, fixing, as politicians always do, upon immaterial points.[1]

[From Sir Charles Hardinge.]   FOREIGN OFFICE,
                              Private.   JULY 26TH.

MY DEAR ESHER,

The Dardanelles: Point of Attack.

I have been reading Cromer's and your memoranda, based on French's. In my humble opinion they start from false premisses.

I quite understand that the Admiralty would object to attempting to force the Dardanelles, which could not be done without incurring serious losses if the Turks know at all how to handle heavy guns. But as I know the Dardanelles forts well both from the sea and from the Asiatic land side, my conviction is that, unless a lot of new forts have recently been created, which is not very probable, the forts could be taken from the rear by a force landed at Basika Bay after the fort commanding the bay had been destroyed by naval gun fire, a process which it would not be difficult to achieve. I do not know what information the Defence Committee have about the defences of the Dardanelles from the land side, but I would recommend that this should be carefully gone into.

If it can be shown that military operations at the Dardanelles can be satisfactorily carried out, they would present the most effective means of defending Egypt from Turkish attack. Please regard these views as confidential.

                              Yours ever,
                              CHARLES HARDINGE.

[1] The adjournment was moved to discuss the immediate carrying out of reductions in the Army "without the authorisation of Parliament." The time was actually occupied mainly in discussing whether Mr. Haldane had ever declared there would be no reductions and whether he had promised more time for discussion than was actually given. The motion was talked out.

[*To the Rt. Hon. J. Morley.*]   2, TILNEY STREET,
AUGUST 4TH.

I shall be in Scotland this week, and you shall then hear from *Extension*
me fully about K.'s [Kitchener's] railways and things. *of Lord*
Meanwhile will *you* consider the question of his extension ? *Kitchener's*
The King, I know, thinks that the matter should be settled one *Term.*
way or the other, as so many subsidiary changes are pending
which will be affected by your decision.

Personally I think you would do very wisely to maintain the
status quo in India for another year, beyond K.'s term. It will
give time for the new state of things to take working shape, and
will stifle the forces of reaction, which would all revive were a
new man appointed. Besides, I think K. might be very tiresome
on Indian questions, were he at home. Out there you have got
your heel poised over his neck, and he is quite aware of the fact.

All I humbly plead for is that you should decide as soon as
you can.

Please forgive me for venturing to remind you of this
matter, which is important from Army standpoints here.

[*To M. V. B.*]   THE ROMAN CAMP,
AUGUST 15TH.

We started about 11 o'clock yesterday and drove 30 miles to *Cloan.*
Cloan. It is quite a nice Scottish house, standing high on the
hillside, with a splendid view. A frightfully steep approach on
which the motor nearly stuck. Haldane has added so much to
the house that it is practically new—only the centre block
was the old original farm.

He has an old mother of 80, and there were a heap of people
there. Nellie enjoyed it, and so did Oliver. After luncheon
I talked with Haldane for nearly 3 hours, and they were left
with those old Scots, but it was no penance.

. . . We discussed *all* the big future appointments.

[*To the Rt. Hon. J. Morley.*] THE ROMAN CAMP,
AUGUST 16TH.

Territorial County Associations.

I went two days ago by motor to Cloan, for the afternoon, and had a long talk with Haldane. He wobbles, just a little, about his County Associations, under pressure from the Cabinet, etc.

This is a mistake, as he has committed himself hopelessly in public speeches, and it is too late to draw back, unless, of course, some new circumstances can be invented, which apparently justify a *volte face*. The Associations *can* do no harm, and may turn out to be a partial solution of the insoluble problem of voluntary service. Anyhow, they are worth the trial. Haldane's weakness lies in his wish to be all things to all men. It is an obsession with him.

Indian Appointments.

I sincerely hope that you will maintain Lord K.'s services for a further year. I am confident that he will be less trouble to you there than here, and that he is a source of strength (in reserve) in India, should any trouble arise there during your administration. His decided character and plain thinking would be most useful, whether the trouble were external or internal.

And trouble in India is always just under the surface.

As for a financial tussle, you will have no difficulty—provided you let K. know exactly what you wish. He will always "transact" with you—I feel sure.

As for Steadman's successor, before deciding I would suggest that you should see Hutchinson, now Director of the Mil. Training at the W.O. He is very pleasant, and an intelligent officer, and was always very highly thought of by Lord Roberts. He has detractors, of course, as all soldiers have; but as the Indian representative at the W.O. (under Brodrick) he was thought to have done very well.

The advantage of selecting him is that you would see him first—whereas a man from India might turn out to be a *persona ingrata*.

I will think over the commercial member! It is a very difficult thing to find a man, who is worth his salt, willing to go to India. What are your plans? I hope that you have had some decent weather in Sutherland. Here it has been variable. We motored up, sleeping at Lincoln, Durham, and Dunbar. It was charming.

You *must* get a closed motor. You would find it a charming adjunct to life. I am going to Edinburgh to-day to meet Knollys, who is on his way to Aberdeenshire.

What think you of the Pope's encyclical? Clemenceau will have a difficult time.

[*To M. V. B.*]　　　　　　THE ROMAN CAMP,
　　　　　　　　　　　　　　　AUGUST 16TH.

. . . I am thinking of going to Edinburgh this evening, to meet Knollys, who stays there the night. If so, I shall sleep at the Caledonian Hotel, and get back here early to-morrow.

This morning looks stormy, but the glass has risen, so we may get a fine day. We shall have a slack one, anyhow. I sent Zena a brace of grouse by post. If she is alone with Doris Stocker [1] it will do for their breakfast. She can have another brace from time to time, if she likes the delicate attention, or the game.

[*To the Rt. Hon. J. Morley.*]　　THE ROMAN CAMP,
　　　　　　　　　　　　　　　　　AUGUST 17TH.

My difficulty in replying is that Sidney Peel is now Cassel's right-hand man, and I am very uncertain how Cassel would like his alienation to another post.

This much I can say. Peel is endowed with unusual "flair" for finance, and especially for "*haute* finance." He is hard-working

---

[1] Afterwards Lady Segrave.

and accurate, too, and a most charming fellow. I would strongly recommend one of two things. Either

(*a*) That you should write to Cassel, or

(*b*) Let me send on your short note to C.

What are your plans? I hope very much that you get abroad for a while. It will do you much good.

Progress of the "Queen's Letters." I have finished Vols. I and II of *Queen Victoria's Correspondence*, the penultimate revise. It has been difficult work, as, since the book is to be issued by the direct authority of the King, much care must be taken not to allow anything to slip in which can give pain or offence.

The latter term in its most catholic sense. Between ourselves, the King wishes you to look through the final proofs. Will you, when asked, consent?

[*To M. V. B.*] THE ROMAN CAMP,
AUGUST 17TH.

I went last evening to Edinburgh and slept at the Caledonian Hotel. *Very* comfortable. It was to meet Knollys, with whom I dined. He told me nothing of a very thrilling character, except that the Queen of Spain is not altered from a girl. Just as simple as ever. She curtseyed low to our Queen and kissed her hand. That was very perfect behaviour.

[*To M. V. B.*] THE ROMAN CAMP,
AUGUST 23RD.

. . . I think that a new post ought to be created. C.-in-C. in the Mediterranean on the lines of the C.-in-C. at Aldershot—to command *in chief* Malta, Gib., and Egypt, with residence at Malta.

[*Photo: Alfred D. Kissack, Eton.*

VISCOUNT ESHER.

[*To H.M. the King.*]   THE ROMAN CAMP,
AUGUST 23RD.

... Certain events have transpired in connection with the defence of Egypt which show the existing state of the commands at Malta and in Egypt to be far from satisfactory, and there is no doubt that some officer of high authority and sound judgment, and especially of high rank, should be in command in the Mediterranean. Each of the *separate* commands under modern conditions appears to be too small to justify any one of them being held in future by such an officer; and perhaps Your Majesty should consider the advisability of calling Mr. Haldane's attention, on Your Majesty's initiative, to the advantage of making the future Governor of Malta Commander-in-Chief of the Forces in the Mediterranean, i.e. at Malta, Gibraltar, and in Egypt, with subordinates of suitable rank under him. *A C.-in-C. for the Mediterranean.*

Viscount Esher will have the honour, at a later date, to send Your Majesty a memorandum upon the whole question, showing how the proposal has been laid before the Defence Committee to have the "taking of such measures in the Sinai Peninsula as might be required to protect the Suez Canal" by Your Majesty's Agent-General in Egypt.

Viscount Esher has ventured to point out that such responsibility should not be imposed upon a *diplomatic* Agent of the Government. It is a *military* question, and should be dealt with by an experienced Military Authority under guidance from Headquarters.

If Your Majesty would think it desirable to discuss the matter with Mr. Haldane, and if the idea appeals to Your Majesty, it occurs to Lord Esher that the first "Commander-in-Chief in the Mediterranean" of the Military Forces might most properly be H.R.H. the Duke of Connaught. It would lend *éclat* and prestige to the appointment, and give proper weight to the authority of that post in the future.

The importance of this question at the present time is two-fold:—

(*a*) Something will have to be done to meet the difficulty which has arisen owing to the redistribution of troops in the Mediterranean.

(*b*) Mr. Haldane is considering all the changes which must inevitably take place in the high commands a year from next September.

As Your Majesty has so often said, such changes cannot be considered too soon beforehand, both in the interest of the Army and of individuals, following the excellent precedent of the Admiralty in such cases.

Viscount Esher hopes Your Majesty will forgive him for the length of this letter.

[*To M. V. B.*]   THE ROMAN CAMP,
                                                    AUGUST 26TH.

. . . I have bought that book about Queen Elizabeth,[1] and kept it here for you. It is a most careful bit of history and one cannot believe that every character is not real. In fact every character *is* real—for they are all types of the men and women who were living in those days. Certainly if all monks wrote as well and as usefully as this author, monasteries ought to be encouraged in the interests of literature.

. . . To-day is one of those quiet Sundays which I enjoy here. Not too many bells—but just enough to remind one that it is Sunday. The quiet river rippling below the window, and the general air of peace. As it happens, there are battalions of misty vapour sweeping over the crags, but they give them an air of mystery, which is peculiar to Scotland, and suits her history and her people so well. There is very little doubt that few mental tonics are more salutary than to come here for a while. All things seem to drop into their proper place, and lose the relative

---

[1] *By What Authority?* By R. H. Benson.

exaggeration which is so characteristic of great cities and also of the south.

The calmness of the north, and its *justesse d'esprit*, are so health-giving. Yet there is no lack of romantic passion in the hills, as you know.

[*To M. V. B.*]   THE ROMAN CAMP,
                                              SEPTEMBER 1ST.

. . . The first two volumes of Queen Victoria's letters, etc. are finished. I sent them off this morning. Only Vol. III remains. It is a comfort to have got rid of them. It has been delicate work, revising the letters.

[*To M. V. B.*]   THE ROMAN CAMP,
                                              SEPTEMBER 3RD.

. . . Tell the General [French] that J. Fisher has promised to be good, and to come back to the Defence Committee. The King took him to task, and for the present he has buried the hatchet—Clarke and he, however, are bound to fall out again, and especially as Clarke is all agog against the "Dreadnoughts." He has there a supporter in Mahan, who criticises the strategic value of those vessels. *Disputes on the Defence Committee.*

Still, it is no affair of Clarke's. *That* question must be left to the Admiralty. The Defence Committee might just as well take up a new type of Field Gun. In point of fact Clarke *did* meddle with that question too!

[*To M. V. B.*]   THE ROMAN CAMP,
                                              SEPTEMBER 4TH.

. . . The General [French]s' speech[1] is telegraphed to *The Times*. It reads very well. *You* are mentioned as being present! I have cut out the extract for my book. The entente is getting *Inevitability of a German War.*

[1] At manœuvres in France.

on. Not before it is required, either. There is no doubt that within measurable distance there looms a titanic struggle between Germany and Europe for mastery. The years 1793–1815 will be repeated, only Germany, not France, will be trying for European domination. She has 70,000,000 of people and is determined to have commercial pre-eminence. To do this *England* has got to be crippled and the Low Countries added to the German Empire. France contains 40,000,000 of people. England about the same. So even combined, the struggle is by no means a certainty. Of course, the occupation of the Low Countries by Germany means the relegation of France to the second rank among European powers.

In 1814 Holland and Belgium were nearly added to Prussia as a defensive measure against the ambition of France. Luckily Castlereagh and the Duke of Wellington held out against this. Fancy if they had been overcome by the fears and arguments of Metternich! Now, a century later, these countries, instead of being a buffer against France, are fulfilling that function against a far more dangerous power. The *great fear* is that war may come before *we* are ready; this is precisely what happened to Prussia in 1806, and the Germans, having had that bitter experience themselves, may well wish to inflict it upon us.

It will take five years yet to get our people screwed up to compulsory service. Perhaps longer. This is rather a long dissertation on politics!

[*To the Rt. Hon. J. Morley.*]   THE ROMAN CAMP,
SEPTEMBER 5TH.

Censoring of the Queen's Letters.

It is very good of you to say you will look through the final proofs.[1] It has been a difficult task, not only because of the mass of material, but because the book is to be published by the authority of the King, and both as Sovereign and Son, his interests must be carefully guarded. I know that my confrère

[1] Of Queen Victoria's letters.

thinks that I have expunged too freely, but it is better to be on the safe side. Palmerston, who was, as you know, such a *bête noire* to both the Queen and the Prince, has been a great difficulty. Then, the sons of all the people are alive, and an unkind reflection on the part of a colleague does not matter much, but coming from Queen Victoria, it leaves a sting, and there seems to be no sense in giving unnecessary pain. You will realise the difficulty and the responsibility.

I can understand that you should be uneasy, under the heavy *Afghanistan.* burden of your mighty Empire. Just now the sky may be blue enough, but with what marvellous rapidity, on that cursed frontier, do clouds roll up. Still, the Ameer's visit is an opportunity. *I* thought the Dane negotiations absolutely fatuous, and not far from degrading. The Oriental Prince (he is now His Majesty) got so much the better of the argument with the Emperor. Curzon and Dane and the Government at home, all pulling different ways.

Do you mean to do what no English statesman has done yet, *The N.W.* and face the *future* north-west of the border? I have always *Frontier.* thought that—assuming the integrity of Afghanistan is to be maintained—there are only two ways of dealing with the Ameer. One, to recognise him as a Feudatory of the Empire, and make it clear that if we are to defend him from attack, it shall be upon our own terms as regards railways, tribal arrangements, etc. The other, to ignore him, to give no pledges, no subsidy, no arms, but to treat *direct* with Russia.

Our present attitude can only lead to disappointment and possibly disaster. Personally, I think Abdur Rahman was sensible when he asked to be allowed to have a representative, not at Calcutta, but in London.

[*To Sir John Fisher.*] THE ROMAN CAMP,
                                    SEPTEMBER 5TH. *Fisher*
                                                    and the
There is not a word in the Dardanelles paper with which I *Defence*
disagree.   *Committee.*

In the Minutes of our last Defence Committee meeting, there are two serious "conclusions" which I do not agree with; and which ought not to be confused. They are closely connected with this subject. I do not like to write to you about them, as this letter will (or may) probably be opened and read.

But you shall have a printed memo. of mine on the subject when you come back.

Your Achillean attitude in regard to the Defence Committee before you left, was most mischievous. When you are not there nothing goes right.

Certainly, it is not worth while to get angry about Clarke. He has never got the better of you yet, and never will. As an *advocatus diaboli* he is useful, and it is good for you to be contradicted. You have things too much your own way.

What is all this about "wireless telegraphy"? I know nothing about the subject, but my instinct is that what William II wants, we ought to want.

I was very anxious that you should help me to get a first-rate "Historical Section" for Navy and Army built up, under the Defence Committee. The cost ought *not* to fall on Admiralty and W.O. votes, but on ours.

I will send you a short paper on the subject presently. Keep well, and your beloved temper. You never have lost that with me, as yet!

[*To M. V. B.*]   THE ROMAN CAMP,
                                                SEPTEMBER 6TH.

*Foreign
Politics.*

... There is a frantic attempt being made in Germany to injure the entente with France. I hope Repington will keep his eye on it. Tell him that I have written a paper for the Defence Committee upon his "Plea of History" chapter, suggesting that the "Historical Section" should be placed under the Defence Committee. I will give him a copy of my remarks one of these days. I suppose he will turn up for the manœuvres. The more *The Times* cracks up the French entente just now the better. I don't think the King's meeting with William, or Haldane's visit to Berlin, were very useful just now. *L'Allemagne c'est l'Ennemi*—and there is no doubt on the subject. They mean to have a powerful fleet, and commercially to beat us out of the field, before ten years are over our heads.

[*To the Duchess of Sutherland.*]　　THE ROMAN CAMP,
SEPTEMBER 7TH.

... I have done a great deal of work these last few weeks one way and another. Nearly all military. I went up for one day to London to see Douglas Haig, and was two nights in the train.

Anachronisms of our Military Tradition.

I do *not* quite agree with you in your diagnosis of the perfect soldier. Nor, I think, will you agree with yourself presently, as ambition supervenes over all other allurements.

You know that I don't despise any form of sport; but sport at best is never the *real* thing, and is only a substitute. Mediæval soldiering was so different from modern; and yet *we* in England are almost mediæval still. We are certainly 18th century—and it is a terrible danger, and the secret of all our difficulties, that the English people have never awakened to the fact that much has happened in the interval between Blenheim and Mukden. Let us pray that the awakening will not come as it did for Prussia in 1806, or Russia in 1904.

There is a very bad time coming for soldiers; for the laws of historical and ethnographical evolution (it sounds rather priggish) require that we shall fight one of the most powerful military empires that has ever existed.

This is *certain*, and we have a very short period of preparation. I fear that proficiency in games, or in the hunting-field, will not help our poor lads much when they have to face the carefully trained and highly educated German officers.

Our difficulty is that our lawyers and physicians are professional men, but until quite lately our soldiers have been amateurs —and soldiering a pastime and not a "business." Even now, it is the exception and not the rule to find a clever and highly educated soldier.

Compare (not Haig or French or that sort of man) the ordinary young soldier, aged 23–25, with the young professional man of the same age (and you know so many); and put aside their charm, and think only of their attainments. What then? Do not think for a moment that I think less of their natural ability. It is quite on a level with that of any other class. I am thinking of their trained knowledge, and of their grounding in the elements of their business. A soldier requires to be quite as carefully trained in military history (for example) as a lawyer in historical jurisprudence, if he is to be of real use in his profession. The other great qualities, physical and moral, he should possess as well. It is this which makes the art the noblest of all arts. But we are a long way yet from realising the ideal. . . .

[*To the Rt. Hon. J. Morley.*]   THE ROMAN CAMP,
                                                          SEPTEMBER 26TH.

Reinforce-
ments for
India.

As I never have concealments from you, and indeed it would be a *lèse Amitié* if I had, I send you K.'s letter. Two things are worthy of your attention:

(*a*) He evidently is prepared to go slowly with his Army changes;

(*b*) He (from the last paragraph) would like a prolongation of his term.

A third point is a matter for the Defence Committee and H.M.G., i.e. that he relies still on Balfour's so-called "pledge" of a reinforcement in times of emergency of *Eight* Divisions.

Haldane has conclusively shown that these 8 Divisions are a pure illusion.

Under no conceivable circumstances, as you know, could *all* the available troops be sent to India in the event of a war with Russia. And even if they could, it will be years before anything like 8 Divisions can be mobilised for the purpose. Whether you will destroy, or only marvel at, K.'s daydreams, is a matter for your consideration and decision.

I hope that you are profiting by Harrogate. I am just back from a fortnight on manœuvres with Sir John French. *His* visit to France was a brilliant success; and far more politic than Haldane's to Berlin.

As a Nation we are certainly perfidious—as the French have always maintained! When do you return personally to Flowermead?

[*To Lord Knollys.*]　　　　　THE ROMAN CAMP,
　　　　　　　　　　　　　　　　SEPTEMBER 30TH.

I agree with every word you say about the Volunteers. They *Compulsory* are a gigantic fraud. If Haldane goes back on his idea of County *Military* Associations (as he is inclined to do) because of the fear inspired *Service.* by Volunteer commanding officers, he will sacrifice a great deal of reputation—and he will have dropped the only *constructive* policy which he has to his credit.

As you know, I am a confirmed believer in *compulsion*; but until a final experiment has been tried to get the *youth* of the Nation, i.e. between 19 and 25 (or 18 and 24), to *volunteer* for what is called Home Defence—the Country properly refusing to pay for training men over that age—and until the experiment has been proved a failure, there is not much hope of getting Parliament or the Country to agree to the compulsory principle. I am strongly in favour of Haldane's "County Associations" scheme because:

(*a*) It is the most striking form in which that experiment can be tried;

(*b*) When compulsion comes, it is by some such method that it will be made acceptable to the English people. (Compulsory

education would never have been agreed to in a centralised
form; like all our great administrative remedies, it has to be
swallowed in "local" doses.)

*The
Army:
Historical
Compari-
sons.*

As I have so often repeated, at the risk of boring you, we are
precisely in the position of Prussia in 1806. Between 1800 and
1806 the Prussians were worrying over "Army Reform."
They possessed a *small*, highly trained, beautifully dressed,
finely drilled Army; but utterly inadequate to their needs.
Their statesmen and soldiers were aware of this. But in the
midst of their endless quarrels over the *form* which expansion
should take Napoleon came down like an avalanche, and Jena
followed.

The foreign policy of E. Grey, or any other Secretary of
State, might land us any day in a similar plight. We have an
Army in excess of our requirements for "small wars"—and
wholly inadequate to the demands of a great war.

It was pathetic on manœuvres to see a "position" five miles in
length occupied by the Aldershot Army Corps, and to think of
an attack upon such a position, made by German or Turkish
troops, when three times the number of troops would be *certain*
to be employed. We are still living under the conditions which
governed British policy in the reign of Queen Anne. We delude
ourselves with the idea that we are an Island State. We are an
Island *Race*, but we have ceased to be an Island State. The King's
Empire has great frontiers co-terminus with the land frontiers of
some of the greatest military Powers on earth. Russia. Turkey.
And the United States. In addition, the commercial and naval
superiority of Great Britain is threatened by (not the Kaiser
nor any man) *natural forces*, which require the expansion of
Germany to sea frontiers. No greater Empire has ever remained
cooped up, without outlets to the sea. Kiel and the Elbe are
utterly inadequate.

Germany *must* stretch out her limbs seawards. This means
perpetual threats to Belgium and Holland. It is only a *question
of time*. Are we to depend upon "alliances" or upon ourselves?
That is the question.

[*From Sir John French.*]   BAWDSEY MANOR, WOODBRIDGE,
                                      SEPTEMBER 29TH.

MY DEAR ESHER,

Thank you indeed for yours of the 26th. As I told you at
Cloan, there is no doubt whatever in my mind who it is to
whom I am truly indebted for the prospect of engaging in
work which is by far the most congenial to me!

It is *you* to whom I feel the greatest gratitude, not alone for
this but for the immense help you give me in my work by your
interest and encouragement. If I may say so, you enter with
such a *keen intelligence* into soldier's business that it is the greatest
possible pleasure to be associated with you. I agree entirely
that it would be far better if possible to postpone the new
arrangements till next autumn. As regards your ideas on the
subject of the Inspector-General and his work, I wish you would
let me have them in the near future. I would like to know your
views before I begin to lay down principles, and for my own
guidance.

Yours, etc.
J. D. P. FRENCH.

[*To the Rt. Hon. J. Morley.*]   THE ROMAN CAMP,
                                            OCTOBER 3RD.

I cannot imagine that Lord K. [Kitchener] can question the
perfect sanity of the decision of the Defence Committee. In
point of fact, there was no *pledge* from Arthur Balfour that
"8 Divisions of Infantry" should be forthcoming in a crisis;
although I admit that Lord K. had certain grounds for assuming
that a force of that size would be available during the first year
of a war. Still, it was folly to base a mobilisation scheme for
India on such an assumption, for he should have realised that
everything would depend upon the circumstances of the
moment.

Defence Committee and Indian Reinforcements.

Also, he should know that these "8 Divisions" in point of
fact do not exist.

I thought the last paragraph of the W.O. letter which you forwarded to India, to the effect that the "Government of India would be supported by every available man," was very good sense, and politically sound.

I wonder whether you amplified your despatch by a private letter to Minto or K. explaining the motives which actuated the Defence Committee ? They were simply the practical ones:

(*a*) Circumstances must decide the case at the moment.

(*b*) It is useless to promise 8 Divisions if you haven't got them; whereas, if we had 16 we should send them as required; so that "numerical fixity" was in any case unnecessary!

[*To the Rt. Hon. A. J. Balfour.*] THE ROMAN CAMP,
OCTOBER 3RD.

Balfour and Indian Reinforcements.

There has been some disturbance, and more is anticipated, by a "decision" of the Defence Committee that no "pledge" can be given to the Indian Government as to the number of troops which could be sent from this country to India in the event of a war with Russia.

This decision was based on two grounds:

(*a*) That circumstances of the moment must decide the case.

(*b*) That 8 Divisions (the number named) of Infantry do not at present exist.

This decision has been communicated to the Government of India, and is supposed to conflict with a "pledge" given by you to Lord K. I maintained that you gave no "pledge."

Certain numbers were mentioned, and you proposed to accept them (after a good deal of discussion) as a basis of Army organisation in this country.

But it seems hardly reasonable to take that as a "pledge" that in all circumstances the number of troops would be forthcoming. If Lord K.'s mobilisation scheme has been based on that assumption, he will have to modify it.

The Government of India have been informed that in the

event of a war with Russia, or any great emergency in India, every available man will be sent from this country who can be spared.

Do you think that it would be prudent to go beyond that in view of the uncertainty of the circumstances in Europe or elsewhere, which might co-exist with a war on the N.W. Frontier, or an Indian rising?

I write to you because I know how much these subjects interest you.

[*From Sir Douglas Haig.*]   WAR OFFICE,
                                                  OCTOBER 3RD.

MY DEAR ESHER,

. . . Forgive this hurried line. I appreciate most sincerely your kindly words of approval. But I really cannot take credit for the scheme, as I have been aided so thoroughly by Gordon and the officers of his Branch. In fact *they* have done all the hard work; I merely launched the proposals based on Haldane's statements and your remarks at the Duma. I was a little nervous when I first came to this Office whether you had done right in putting me to do this work—so naturally I am relieved that at any rate the beginning is satisfactory. A thousand thanks to you for your help.

                                        Yours ever,
                                        DOUGLAS HAIG.

[*To Lord Kitchener.*]   THE ROMAN CAMP,
                                                  OCTOBER 4TH.

Very many thanks for your most interesting letter. I hope you do not mind my showing your letters to the King sometimes, and perhaps you will allow me to use my judgment in doing so. Nothing can be more friendly than Mr. Morley's attitude towards you; and I assure you, from many talks with him, that

Kitchener and the Home Government.

he is more than anxious to meet your views and to work harmoniously, in all matters affecting the Army, with you and Lord Minto.

You will no doubt have received before now information respecting a so-called "decision" of the Defence Committee in regard to the reinforcements which, in the event of a war with Russia, might be sent to India, if the circumstances were favourable.

Probably you personally never attached to your correspondence with Mr. Balfour the importance which some persons here have invested it with, for you must always have clearly appreciated the facts—

(a) That for a great many years to come the Regular Army here could not supply the number of troops mentioned in that correspondence, and that Mr. Balfour obtained from you figures, not with a view to giving a pledge, but with the idea of having an ideal up to which the Army in this country could be organised.

(b) That no Prime Minister could possibly give a "pledge" that, under all circumstances, a force practically absorbing every regular soldier who could be mobilised here would be sent to India, however grave the crisis there. Circumstances, as you must have realised all along, might obtain in Europe which would render such action impossible.

It seems to me that what I understand now is the decision of the Defence Committee is of much greater value; for it amounts to this, that while it would be unsafe for you to rely on any British Government being able to send reinforcements at all, until command of the sea had been clearly established, when that advantage was gained you would be reinforced by the whole available force of the Empire. *What that amounts to remains to be seen!*

Ultimate Necessity of Conscription.

If it interests you at all, I may say that my view of Mr. Haldane's scheme is that it is the last chance which I imagine will ever be given to the voluntary system. It may succeed up to a certain point, and it certainly has chances in its favour. But more likely it will fail, and in that case, behind our "garrison" Army we must have a National Army on the compulsory basis.

I hope the people here are beginning to realise that although we are an island race, we are no longer an island state. The principle of compulsion is the logical sequence to this new state of facts; only it will take time to get the English people to see it. This transition period is your danger and difficulty in India. You will, however, I feel sure, be the first to appreciate the importance of bringing home this great truth to the minds of our people here, not by the ordinary political methods of declamatory opposition—which only postpones results—but by the dry and hard logic of facts.

It has got to be realised here:

(*a*) What the military resources of India really are.

(*b*) What the military resources of this country really are.

(*c*) What are the possible dangers we have to face.

Not one of these three propositions is clearly understood, not only by the public, but by the successive executive Governments. If they were, it is certain that our Foreign policy would be of a far humbler complexion.

There is a fatal trap into which we may fall, which is to depend upon foreign "Alliances." *"Splendid Isolation."*

But my strong opinion is that the good sense of our people will prevail, and I have great hopes in the actual Ministers who govern England just now. These hopes may be falsified, as they have been before, but until this has been made plain, I sincerely hope that you will give your valuable assistance and advice both to Mr. Morley and Mr. Haldane, and endeavour to assist them over the great obstacles which invariably block, in political life, those who are earnestly striving to administer the country honestly.

I am convinced that the most effectual way of doing this, as far as India is concerned, is to get Lord Minto to conduct a difficult argument *first* by private letter with the S. of S., and to endeavour to settle any controversy which may arise, primarily by that method, *before* the usual form of "despatches" is adopted.

If you would like the various stages of Mr. Haldane's schemes to be sent to you, I am certain that he would allow Douglas Haig to give you the fullest information; and that your criticism would be more than welcome.

I have just returned to Scotland from the south, where I have been for a fortnight on a "Staff ride" and Manœuvres with French. I had Hubert Hamilton and Douglas Haig for my companions, both visitors like myself. So I hope that you will think that I was in excellent company. At the end of this month I shall be returning south for good.

While your letters are always welcome, I am ashamed of trespassing upon your time, which is more than valuable to you.

[*To the Rt. Hon. J. Morley.*]   THE ROMAN CAMP,
OCTOBER 10TH.

On Lord Kitchener.   The King wishes me to tell you that he still strongly supports you, should you wish to prolong K.'s term of office in India.

Apropos, Clarke writes:

" Ewart, who was for some time with K. in S.A., says he never seemed to take much interest in strategic questions, and never gave his mind to them. He was therefore vague and indefinite when it was necessary to be clear and precise. On the other hand, in a question like fighting the Natal Government on their railway charges, he would master every detail and arrive at logical conclusions."

This confirms what I always said to you. Treat him as a great administrator, but not as a *soldier*!

I believe him to be a first-class *diplomatist*. Vide Fashoda.

[*From F.M. Lord Roberts.*]   ENGLEMERE,
Private.   OCT. 11TH.

MY DEAR ESHER,

On Henry Wilson.   I entirely agree with you as to the fitness of Henry Wilson for the Commandantship of the Staff College, and I have written to

Mr. Haldane expressing my hope that he will be appointed. I know that Wilson has enemies at the W.O., and that they are trying to make out he is generally unpopular in the Army. So far from this being the case, I should say that Wilson is perhaps the best known and the most popular man in the Army. He is looked up to as a very promising officer, chiefly I believe on account of the excellent manner in which he performed his Staff duties in South Africa, and I know that the Officers now at the Staff College are looking forward with great hopefulness to his being Rawlinson's successor.

The Staff College in the past has suffered from not having had practical men at its head. Hildyard did much to improve matters. It fell off under Miles, Rawlinson has raised it up again. And now a good man—above all a man of character—is needed to keep it up to the mark.

None of the possible men I have heard mentioned can, in my opinion, and I feel sure I am expressing the opinion of the Army generally, be compared to Henry Wilson for the post.

The fact is that Wilson has too much character for some of the men with whom he is associated at the War Office.

Believe me,

Yours sincerely,

ROBERTS.

[*To the Rt. Hon. J. Morley.*]   THE ROMAN CAMP,

OCTOBER 14TH.

By the King's order, I send you Volume I of *Selections from Queen Victoria's Correspondence*. This is the final revise before stereotyping the volume.

The King would be glad if you would make any suggestions which occur to you. H.M. does not wish anything to be published which could directly or indirectly injure the State or the Crown.

He has also specially commanded that all passages which could inflict pain upon the near relatives of persons mentioned should be excised.

I have been many times over these proofs, but you know how treacherous the eye becomes from familiarity with pages of a book.

I am not enamoured of the Preface, which requires largely rewriting. Any suggestions would be very welcome.

[*To the Rt. Hon. J. Morley.*]   THE ROMAN CAMP,
                                        OCTOBER 16TH.

*On
Handling
Lord
Kitchener.*

I have written some notes on Clarke's Afghan paper, to which he has rejoined. I asked him to have them printed and sent to you. They may help to clear the air. As for Lord K. [Kitchener], your instinct is absolutely correct. He *is* "gemeine" and never will shell it off. You have got to take him with this drawback.

I am strongly for his retention in India, because he is essentially an administrator, and, if you put him on his mettle, an economical one.

The simplest way of dealing with him is to ask him privately "for how much can you do the job?"—always "provided you have a free hand." Details of the Indian Army administration are hopeless to understand on this side. The I.O. military advisers are never up to date. It was so in 1880, and has been ever since.

The broad lines you can yourself judge of quite as well as any soldier. For example, that money is far more profitably spent on railways than on stores, equipment, or bricks and mortar. The one is a "permanent improvement," the other, nine times out of ten, is a waste of money.

The Ameer's visit is full of interest. It carries me back 25 years! Just the same problem. Just the same arguments on both sides. Only the men (save Lord Roberts) have changed.

[*From Sir Douglas Haig.*]   WAR OFFICE,
                                                OCTOBER 17TH.

MY DEAR ESHER,

   . . . I have tried to get off a letter to you for the last two days,
but have always been interrupted. So you must not construe
this delay in reply to you as meaning *ingratitude* for your
"corrections."

   I appreciate your kindly advice and words of approval very
very much—for you must know there are many jarring interests
here, and even Haldane seems carried away at times by "theories"
which are impossible in practice, and by political reasonings. . . .

                                        I am yours,
                                        DOUGLAS HAIG.

[*To the Rt. Hon. R. B. Haldane.*]   THE ROMAN CAMP,
                                                OCTOBER 19TH.

   What we "agreed on when we met" was that there was immi-   *Territorials :*
nent danger of the country getting hold of the idea that you had   *Importance*
"gone back" on your original idea. That idea was County   *of the*
Associations, with real powers, based on the elective principle,   *County*
their main functions being to raise and administer the T.A. The   *Associa-*
autumn disclosed strong opposition on the part of the Volun-   *tions—*
teers to come under this new authority. You were searching
for a compromise. There would seem to be only two ways of
meeting the objections of the Volunteers:

   (*a*) To make the Associations practically a nullity, by giving
them no real functions at all.

   (*b*) By minimising the elective element; and making them
representatives mainly of the Volunteers and Yeomanry in a
County—with certain other *nominated* members.

   In my judgment (as you committed yourself to County
Associations for a *definite purpose* but *not* as to their constitution)
you can proceed safely in the direction of (*b*) but not of (*a*).

   You have got to choose between a certain amount of opposi-

tion in the H. of C. and a loss of personal prestige in the Country.
To my mind the position is not doubtful. You can, with your
large majority, risk the former. You cannot risk the latter. The
question you have got to answer is, "How do you mean to
provide a force for expansion?"

If you mean to rely on the existing C.O.s to provide that
force, no one will believe it. Your scheme will be said to be
mere vapour. On the other hand, and this was their great merit,
no one can say whether County Associations would succeed or
fail. It was a new idea and policy.

I go back to Cardwell for an example and an illustration.
Why did he succeed? Because he faced unpopularity and dealt
with Army Reform on great broad lines. On a very much
smaller scale, why did the War Office Reconstruction Committee score? For the same reason. If we had attempted to
please the existing people in high office, the Finance Minister,
etc., we should have failed to get anything done, as so many
committees have failed before and since.

What is wanted is a plan which seizes hold of the imagination
of the public: which induces them to say, we will give this plan
a trial. "Compromises" are fatal to the success of any scheme
which goes down at all to the roots of public life and habits.
And that is what your scheme has got to do, if it is to be of
permanent value.

*—and
Insufficiency
of the
Volunteers.*

It is over-sanguine to suppose that the G.O.C.s of the big
commands and the Volunteer C.O.s (most of them men of no
local influence whatever) are going to produce for you the
Douglas Haig T.A.

He wants to be able, as I understand, at the end of 12 months
to place an Army of 900,000 men in the field, and keep it there
for five years. Is it conceivable that Howard Vincent and Co.
are going to do this?

Competition between Counties, as you originally suggested,
might have a chance. No one can ridicule the idea. It is an unknown quantity. But that Howard Vincent and Co. can do it,
is—if you will pardon me for saying so—quite unthinkable and

absurd. However, this is my swan-song. If you decide to make the Associations "advisory bodies" with no real powers, and to leave the raising and administrating to the Volunteers on the present footing, merely changing their name to T.A., I have no more to say; and I will, as hitherto, do all I can to help you in every manner possible.

[*From the Rt. Hon. J. Morley.*]   INDIA OFFICE,
OCTOBER 20TH.

MY DEAR ESHER,

I have read it all with the utmost interest and gratification. *Morley* Success in biography obviously depends on three things— *on the* subject, material, handling. *Queen's*
Letters

As for the subject, Queen Victoria stands in the first place, for not only was her rank and station illustrious, but her personality was extraordinary—in its vigour, tenacity, integrity, and in the union of all these stubborn qualities with the suppleness and adaptability required from a Sovereign in a Constitutional system.

Second, your material was evidently rich and copious, and I cannot think but that the King was right not to pinch you. I hope the same liberal spirit will help future volumes.

Third, I entirely applaud your *plan*. A biography of the three-decker stamp, filled out with dead history, would have been, I believe, a great mistake. I always thought Theodore Martin went much too far in that direction. What people want to know, and will always want to know, about Queen Victoria, is her character, her ways in public business, her relations with her Ministers and with her times.

You give quite enough in your excellent introductions to the chapters, to let people know where they are; and if they seek more, there are plenty of books already where they can find it.

I have kept a keen look-out, as you wished me to do, for references or quotations that might touch sore places. I find none such. The air of the whole book is good-natured, as it should be, and I see nothing to give pain to anybody. It will doubtless be harder to walk quite safely, as you come nearer to our own day. Meanwhile I feel pretty sure about you. Of course, I do not overlook the responsibility that falls in a special degree upon the King. So far, I do not hesitate to say, if I am any judge, that there is not a line with which from this point of view anybody can quarrel.

The industry and exactitude with which the elucidating notes, etc., have been prepared, command my real admiration. I know well how much pains is meant by these things. I have jotted down on a separate piece of paper one or two most minute and trivial points that struck me.

One word I should like to add, though it is not within my commission: Don't publish one volume by itself. I am sure, and my publishers agree, that one distinct element in the success of my *Gladstone* was that people sat down to the whole meal at once. You may not choose, or may not be able, to do as much as this. But pray try to approach my counsel of perfection, if and in so far as you can.

I congratulate you, dear Esher, on your associations with a book that all the world one day will read, study, admire, and greatly like (which is more than admiring) as now does,

Yours most sincerely,

JOHN MORLEY.

[*To Sir John Fisher.*]   THE ROMAN CAMP,
OCTOBER 21ST.

*Sir John
Fisher's
Lack of
Diplomacy.*

Many thanks for the paper. I am glad you sent it to me. As you know, *I* am a Fisherite, and do not require converting. Besides, if I thought you in the wrong, I would back you for all I was worth, just the same. For just now, it is *you* who are the national asset, not your opinions. Besides, *amitié oblige.*

So much for that side of the question. As it happens, I think your argument disposes of Mahan, and of Custance and Co.

But, I deprecate, if you will allow me to say so, your *method* in dealing with these opponents. Mahan *may* be *passé,* but from his writing this does not appear. Therefore he should be *answered* and argued with. Not by you personally, but by people properly coached to do it. You need not fear "Fleet St. cabals." You will never go *à la lanterne* that way.

In a country like ours, governed by *discussion*, a great man is never hanged. He hangs himself. Therefore pray be Machiavellian, and play upon the delicate instrument of public opinion with your fingers and not with your feet—however tempting the latter may be.

In any case condescend to convert the "six men who count." As for what you say about the Defence Committee, let me suggest this consideration. The best way of preventing that body from meddling with things which do not concern it is *to give it plenty to do*! For this reason support my policy about an Historical Section. *That* function does not infringe the rights of the First Sea Lord! Again, read up the work of your "Aulic Council"!

In War, it played the devil, because *in war* you want a *Man*!

In Peace, you want a *Party* behind the Man.

Napoleon was defeated, not at Leipsic or at Waterloo, but in the Chancelleries of Europe after the Peace of Tilsit.

No Englishman ought to be Sir John Fisher's "enemy." Every Englishman should be his Lieutenant. It depends on the First Sea Lord himself!

[*To the Rt. Hon. J. Morley.*]   THE ROMAN CAMP,
                                        OCTOBER 22ND.

I cannot say how touched I am by your letter. What is particularly grateful to me is your praise of the "form" of the book, for which I feel personally responsible.

Another decision which was entirely mine was the resolve to publish the 3 volumes (i.e. the whole book as at present planned) simultaneously. This will be done. I hope to send you Volume II in a few weeks' time.

But now I must say a word for Arthur Benson, upon whom the great mass of the labour has fallen, and to whom the book, as a whole, owes everything.

Nothing would give me greater pleasure than if you would be good enough to write him a few lines to Magdalene College, Cambridge, and say that, at the request of the King, you had read Volume I, and then add a few words of praise.

Coming from *you*, this will mean a great deal to him! It would be very good and kind of you. I am sending your letter to the King.

[*To the Rt. Hon. J. Morley.*]   ORCHARD LEA,
NOVEMBER 2ND.

Afghan Affairs.
This morning I got the enclosed from Lord Roberts, who asked me to send it on "before he sees you on Saturday." It does not contain anything with which you are not familiar. He is evidently convinced that the Ameer will come down "wanting something" which will—if refused—leave a soreness. Judging from previous experience, nothing is more likely.

From the extracts you send me, I do not quite get the hang of your argument, as propounded by the G. of I. That the tribal difficulty is much greater than the Afghan we shall learn to our cost one of these days.

That is why I believe in *railways*, and their corresponding influence on warlike races. Enervate not subjugate should be the *mot d'ordre* for frontier officers.

[*To Lord Knollys.*]   ORCHARD LEA,
NOVEMBER 7TH.

Soldiers in Parliament.
I have ascertained from Ellison that the warrant making the change to which his memo. alludes was approved and *signed* by

the King on October 5th. It was issued with the November orders accordingly.

I had not heard of it, but certainly it strikes me as quite sound in principle. If a man wishes to be an M.P. I cannot see how he can also serve the King as a soldier. That profession is no longer fit for dilettanti, and seems to me most unsuitable for a " politician."

The rule that a soldier is not to write to the Press or mix himself up with controversial topics, is an excellent one. Military matters are highly controversial, and it is altogether wrong that young or middle-aged soldiers should (under the ægis of Parliament) be permitted to use language about their superiors which renders discipline and proper military relations difficult, when the politician appears in the Regiment.

In these days an M.P. is supposed to give his whole time to his constituents. If he does so, it is impossible for him to keep, for possibly 4 or 5 years or more, up to the proper military level which modern war requires of every officer. If the effect of this new warrant is to force a man to choose between his profession as a soldier and his political ambition, I confess that in the interests of the King's Army, I do not think much harm will have been done.

I can think of no soldier in recent times who has entered the H. of C. who was of any use to the Army, or who would have been brought back to it with advantage to the service.

[*To M. V. B.*]   ORCHARD LEA,
                                          NOVEMBER 17TH.

Yesterday the King sent for me about 11.

We then went to the Library and met the Queen, the K. and Q. of Norway, Princess Henry, and Princess Louise.

There we stayed till a quarter to 2. The King was in excellent spirits and looked at all the new miniatures and enamels. He had carefully gone through the photographs of pictures I had given him, as proposed for the *Correspondence of Queen Victoria*, and annotated it in his own hand.

He talked a good deal about the theatre. He thinks "Peter's Mother" the *best acted* play he has seen for 40 years!

The Coronation Oath.

To-day I had a talk with C. B. [Campbell-Bannerman], after the P. of W. had been down to my room to discuss the coronation oath. He says the King has left the alteration of that oath to *him*. He wanted me to speak to C. B. about it.

I spoke to C. B., who thinks the question cannot be touched. He says that the alteration can only be made in a hurry—and not in cold blood. But he forgets that there would be no chance of getting the law altered in a *hurry*! i.e. after the demise of the Crown.

The Education Bill.

After lunch the Archbishop came to my room. He had had an hour with C. B. on the Education Bill, and had gone carefully over his case. C. B. admitted that he could not discuss the details of the Bill. He knows very little about them. But he held out no hope of compromise. The Archbishop told him frankly that the difficulty in the H. of L. was that there was no Cabinet Minister of sufficient authority to accept amendments.

Had the Chancellor not been ill, the whole situation would have been very different. They had been obliged to defend every position, every ditch. Then he put the case. C. B. said he had never heard the case put in that way before, and he would look into it. But he again said no compromise was possible, and that the H. of C. would pass a resolution refusing to consider the Lords Amendments.[1]

Of course, if they do this, the Bill will be lost. The Arch-

---

[1] The younger readers of these papers may perhaps welcome the reminder that the Education Bill of 1906 opened the contest between the Lords and Commons which culminated in the Parliament Act of 1911. On the ground that the general effect of the Lords' amendments was "to alter completely the character of the measure as it left the Commons and to contradict the principles on which it was framed," the Commons agreed to treat these amendments as a whole: and as a whole they were rejected by 416 to 107. The Lords reaffirmed them by 132 to 52. And the Bill was thereupon dropped.

bishop is prepared to go before the Cabinet, or argue the points with anyone deputed by them.

The P. of W. was to see C. B. again to-night at the Castle. He *must* get the Archbishop, C. B. and Birrell into the same room. I suggested the Duke of Devonshire as another placable person.

Altogether it looks like serious conflict between the two houses. The Queen settled the Irish Church controversy with great skill. It was an easier task, I admit, for the point was narrowed down. Here the differences are scattered through a long Bill. Also there is no Mr. Gladstone to negotiate with.

Possibly the Ministers feel that *all* their legislation will be nullified by the H. of L., and the sooner they have to stand up and fight the better. The *fact* is that the Nonconformists and Dr. Clifford care nothing for education. All they want is to humiliate the Church of England.

[*To H.M. the King.*]   ORCHARD LEA,
NOVEMBER 22ND.

Viscount Esher, with humble duty, begs to thank Your Majesty for the gracious letter which he received yesterday evening. He at once saw Mr. Haldane, who said that he would write to Your Majesty.

Viscount Esher lunched with Mr. Morley yesterday, who had just come from a long and apparently excited meeting of the Cabinet. *Morley on the Dispute with the Lords.*

He gathered from what Mr. Morley said that the discussion had mainly turned upon the steps to be taken in regard to the Peers' amendments to the Education Bill.

A strong section of the Cabinet were in favour of somewhat discourteous and drastic action, but Mr. Morley was strongly opposed to it, and pointed out that it would inevitably lead to the loss of the Bill.

The argument he then used was that the great mass of the

people are not interested in the Education question, which is mainly fought by certain sects of Nonconformists: and that if *two* sessions were taken up by discussions on this question, to the exclusion of other domestic measures in which the masses of the people take more interest, the blame would fall on the Government.

This reasoning seems to have had its effect, for Viscount Esher believes that it was ultimately decided that the Prime Minister should give a fair consideration to any proposals which were made to him by the Archbishop or the Opposition, *before* calling on the House of Commons to consider the Lords amendments.

Precedents for a Deadlock.

This is a course precisely following the precedent of the Irish Church Bill, when Her Late Majesty called upon the Archbishop of Canterbury to formulate a Memorandum, embodying his objections to the Disestablishment Bill, and to submit it to Mr. Gladstone.

Viscount Esher believes that were the present Archbishop to draw up such a memorandum, and were Your Majesty to instruct him to approach the Prime Minister with it, there would be a chance of an amicable settlement.

Viscount Esher thinks Mr. Morley would be glad to give Your Majesty all the information and assistance in his power, if Your Majesty would be graciously pleased to see him.

[*To H.M. the King.*]   2, TILNEY STREET,
                                                    DECEMBER 2ND.

Defence Committee Examines Haldane.

Viscount Esher presents his humble duty, and begs to inform Your Majesty that for ten days he has been presiding over a sub-committee of the Defence Committee to which the Prime Minister has referred Mr. Haldane's Army schemes.

The Committee consists of Viscount Esher (Chairman), Sir John French, Sir Neville Lyttelton, General Ewart, and Sir George Clarke. The reference is, in effect, whether Mr.

Haldane's scheme satisfies reasonable national requirements, and whether any modification of it appears to be desirable.

The Committee are to report to the Defence Committee as a whole, and they have examined Lord Roberts, General Douglas (the A.G.), Sir William Nicholson, Sir James Wolfe Murray, General Haig, Lord Methuen, Sir Ian Hamilton, and Sir Leslie Rundle.

Mr. Haldane himself gave evidence upon his scheme for a whole day. If Your Majesty would graciously look at the enclosed notes, rather hastily written by Viscount Esher, they will give Your Majesty an idea of the problem involved, and the general view taken so far by those who are conducting this enquiry.

To-morrow Mr. Haldane is to come again for further examination, and by Saturday or Monday, Viscount Esher hopes that the Report will be written, and in the hands of the Prime Minister. There is no doubt that very serious troubles lie in the immediate future for Mr. Haldane, owing to the opposition which his scheme will rouse in the Volunteers, and great strength of character will be required to push the scheme through the House of Commons, where the Volunteers command large interests.

[*To Lord Knollys.*]   2 TILNEY STREET,
DECEMBER 10TH.

The statement which has been made, that Mr. Haldane has not consulted with the Military Members of Council about his scheme for the new Army Organisation, is devoid of foundation.

Haldane and the Army Council.

I told you that I had documents in my possession which would prove how unfair to Mr. Haldane this insinuation is, and I now enclose them for you to see.

Mr. Haldane's scheme was not produced ready-made by him out of his own head, like Mr. Arnold-Forster's, but has been evolved very slowly after enquiries which have extended over a year. This examination was started by him in a tentative memorandum, and has been followed by five others. The first one was dated in January last, and the last one is dated the 8th November. Every one of these Memoranda was circulated to the Military Members before it was shown to anybody else.

I enclose:—

1. A note by Sir William Nicholson, dated 30th June last. Please look at the opening words.

2. The proceedings of the Army Council confirmed on the 6th July last. Please look at paragraph 4.

3. A Memorandum by General Douglas, dated 21st September, of which please note the first paragraph.

4. A note by the Master-General of Ordnance, dated 31st July, and a further Note by him dated 9th November.

And finally remarks by the four Military Members on the Secretary of State's sixth Memorandum, which Memorandum contains his Scheme in its latest form, as submitted by him to the Defence Committee.

I also enclose for you a letter from General Ellison, and I should like to draw your attention to the marked passages, especially to that in which he states that the Military Members themselves appointed representatives of their own branches to work out the details of the Scheme for the use of Mr. Haldane.

I dislike very much making statements to you in contradiction to what you have heard on high authority, unless I am able to substantiate what I have said. And I hope you will think I have done this with fair success.

If the King is aware of what has been said, perhaps you would show him this letter.

[*To M. V. B.*]   ORCHARD LEA,
                                     DECEMBER 12TH.

. . . This year, which is coming so soon to a close. There is a great deal that we have gone through together, of which there is no record in your letters. I regret that I kept no journal.

There were summer months, lazy days here, long drives to Aldershot, riding about there with you, and rushing after Zena and Edna for luncheons and dinners. Then your manœuvres in France, and the culminating success of the year, when you got the *Légion d'honneur*, which—as Huguet told you—has *never* been given before to an officer, French or foreign, of your rank; except the King of Spain, I suppose you are the youngest recipient of Napoleon's order in the world.

Then *our* Staff ride and manœuvres.

. . . Finally our happy days among the hills, and one or two divine days up our own Glen, or on the moor. And since then, first the run to Edinburgh, and again to Bristol, with Nellie and me, to see your Zena. *That* friendship has been a very pleasant one, dominating the year.

. . . Your help to me has been beyond belief, not only in all the small troubles which hedge round one's life, but in the greater world of "affairs."

[*To M. V. B.*]   ORCHARD LEA,
                                             DECEMBER 16TH.

I had an hour and a half with the King. I wrote down for him *The* a series of questions to get answered by Haldane, whom he was *King and* to see immediately. He quickly thawed and talked very well. *Haldane.* He told me of the exceeding frank conversation he had held with the French Ministers, especially about Egypt. His idea is that this is a specially favourable moment to get rid of the trammels which still hamper us in that country.

I then explained H. [Haldane]'s new scheme to him: told him that I proposed to get the Defence Committee to sign the Report that afternoon.

[*To M. V. B.*]   ORCHARD LEA,
                                             DECEMBER 18TH. *The*
                                                            Dispute
This morning no one knew what Lansdowne or Crewe would *with the*
say in the H. of L. If the Bill is destroyed, then the Ministers *Lords.*

declare that the Commons will refuse to vote supplies until the H. of L. agrees to reform itself.

No doubt this screw *could* be put upon them, but it is revolution.

I do not imagine that Arthur Balfour will push the fight *à outrance*. Probably there will be some compromise. The Archbishop is so strongly in favour of one, that he is no longer consulted by the Tory chiefs.

The Prime Minister and Haldane's Scheme.

. . . I have finished the Hohenlohe memoirs. It is on the whole a dull book containing a few sensational paragraphs *because* they are personal about big persons! *Voilà tout!* To-morrow I am to see C. B. [Campbell-Bannerman] about the Army—and our Report. He wants to understand the drift of Haldane's scheme, and has not been able to understand Haldane's rhetorical rendering of it. So I must try my hand in dry prose!

[*To M. V. B.*]   ORCHARD LEA,
                                    DECEMBER 19TH.

Yesterday morning I had a long talk, quite an hour, with C. B. He was most genial, and listened to everything I could tell him about Haldane's scheme. He put his finger, in that quiet way he has, upon the weak points. I think that he will back Haldane. If that is so, our fat friend stands a good chance. He told me all the difficulties with A. J. B. [Balfour] about the Education Bill. And also that Roosevelt had asked for a real "man" as ambassador at Washington; on the ground that there are a good many awkward questions which he would like to arrange before he quits office two years hence.

It was pleasant to see Zena's pretty but anxious face at Tilney St. before you started off on your Peter Pan adventures. If she is prudent and keeps her looks, and doesn't marry, certainly until she is 24, she ought to be a great success on the stage. She has the "regard" of an actress, just as the General [French] has that of a soldier, as the French noticed on Manœuvres. I think you must intrigue to bring her back in February at latest.

. . . I wonder what you thought of the House of Lords debate to-night. It was plucky of Lansdowne to disregard all the threats, and to destroy the Education Bill. But the result is most annoying, as that odious question remains with us. A. J. B. has never wavered from his position taken up at the beginning.

I wonder how Zena is getting on in Manchester?[1] Let us hope that through this week Barrie and Dot [Boucicault] will be kind to her.

[*To M. V. B.*]　　　　　　　　　　2 TILNEY STREET,
　　　　　　　　　　　　　　　　　　DECEMBER 21ST.

The Defence Committee yesterday was not altogether a *Haldane* success. J. M. [Morley] was in a captious mood, and raised *and the* questions upon Haldane's scheme which were unnecessary and *Cabinet.* did harm, by giving the soldiers, especially Lyttelton, an idea that the Cabinet were disunited. This is altogether fallacious, as to-day J. M. was all right, and C. B. [Campbell-Bannerman] also told Haldane that he might count upon his thorough support. The fact is that none of the Cabinet understand, or ever will understand, the question. C. B. is impressed by the fact that the Bill is drawn. He thought that Haldane's ideas were nebulous, and had not been put in concrete form.

Haldane talked to me at great length to-day upon the future of the A.C. [Army Council]. His idea is to appoint *young* men for a prolonged period—say 10 years or so—and thus get over the transition period.

This is probably the only way to get over the difficulty that *Fisher's* older men cannot shape their minds to the new order of things. *Position.* I saw Jackie [Fisher] for 1½ hours this afternoon. He expounded for my benefit his strategical plans, especially in view of a hostile Germany. They are too secret to write down. He sits

---

[1] She was playing Peter in *Peter Pan.*

still under calumny, because to reply would necessarily entail revelation of our strength and the main strategical idea. In point of fact, our power is six times that of Germany at the given point of battle. He discussed with me his own position, and the difficulties raised by his enemies, and his danger from their animosity.

I told him that only four members of the Government matter. The rest are negligible. The King has stuck to him wonderfully. It is *so* difficult to stick to anyone through storm as well as sunshine. Even the most fervent affection is not always proof; so, why place reliance upon any man? I often wonder whether it is not best to go one's own way, and take the pleasures of life where they are to be found, and not worry about the joys and pains of others. In the end, we carve out our own lives, and no man helps us, or woman either. And everyone is forgotten after the night has fallen a few hours.

[*To the Rt. Hon. J. Morley.*]   ORCHARD LEA,
                                                DECEMBER 29TH.

Thanks so much for a most charming day. I hope you will come here some time, and see what you think of our garden. I carried off the enclosed! Please apologise to Mrs. Morley.

Military Needs of the Empire.

Will you look at our report para. 2? It runs, "We note that we are asked to state whether Mr. Haldane appears likely to fulfil the 'reasonable requirements' of the Empire. As, however, *these requirements have not yet been laid down by the Cabinet or the Defence Committee, etc.*"

That is the great question which, if you can get the P.M. to appoint a sub-committee of the Defence Committee, with you in the Chair, and the military and naval members plus myself as your assistants, we might try to solve. *India* is the key.' Vide A. J. B. [Balfour]'s paper.

The requirements of India,

(*a*) In peace, govern the normal size of the Army.

(*b*) In war, the largest call likely to be made on us for rein-forcements. Indian requirements and all others.

Another point. Why don't you take Spender as your U.S. and let him get a seat? The "Westminster" is *dull* nowadays.

[*To H.M. the King.*]   ORCHARD LEA,
                                        DECEMBER 30TH.

Viscount Esher with humble duty hopes that it may interest *On John* Your Majesty to hear that he went yesterday to see Mr. John *Morley:—* Morley at Wimbledon.

The house in which Mr. Morley lives is externally a rather commonplace villa, on the edge of the common; but it contains an exceedingly fine room, added by Mr. Morley, entirely filled with books. There are over 11,000 volumes in the room, and the lighting and arrangement are excellent. This room is the feature of the house, and is most comfortable.

Mr. Morley, as Your Majesty is perhaps aware, was 68 about a week ago, and on his birthday he wrote to the Prime Minister and asked to be relieved of his office, urging his age and the probable disagreements with his colleagues in the coming session.

The Prime Minister remonstrated so vigorously, that Mr. Morley has not pressed the point, but a long talk with him convinces Viscount Esher that, in all probability, difficulties will recur before long.

Mr. Morley, as Your Majesty knows, is extremely sensitive, *His* and much inclined to resent any neglect on the part of his *Difficulties* friends. It was unfortunate, considering his close connection *with the* with the Irish question, that he was not consulted by the Prime *P.M.* Minister about Mr. Bryce's appointment. It was certainly only an oversight, but it left a little soreness which has not been mitigated by subsequent events.

The Irish members have naturally approached Mr. Morley, whom they look upon as the repository of the Gladstone tradition, with their views, first as to the vacant Irish Secretaryship, secondly as to the Local Government Bill, which Mr. Redmond has full knowledge of.

The Prime Minister, as Your Majesty is aware, is not a voluble correspondent, and Mr. Morley feels that he cannot get into complete touch upon these matters, which he considers of first-rate importance, with his Chief—hence a little "feeling." Although a confirmed Home Ruler, Mr. Morley upon Imperial questions, and especially upon Indian questions, is so sound and broad-minded, that he would be a great loss to Your Majesty. He is so vastly interested in the greater issues of statesmanship, that Viscount Esher feels sure that he will remain one of Your Majesty's Ministers, in spite of these occasional "tiffs" with his colleagues. At the same time, from what he said, it is clear that the three Irish Bills contemplated for next session are bound to lead to difficulties, to great differences of opinion within the Cabinet, which it will require all the Prime Minister's suavity to accommodate.

Viscount Esher begs humbly to be allowed to wish Your Majesty the happiest and most prosperous New Year.

[*From the Rt. Hon. R. B. Haldane.*]   CLOAN,
DECEMBER 31ST.

MY DEAR ESHER,

Haldane and Morley.

. . . And now best thanks for your work with Morley. I feel pretty sure that I shall see the good results of this on the 8th. I will remember to follow up what you have said about the Indian Army. I feel pretty certain that until he had your explanation, Morley's mind was on the wrong track—put there by Winston and others. I shall be most interested to see the outcome of your five hours' talk with him on our friend's mind.

Yes, the New Year is a very important one. It is a case of sink or swim. You have helped me enormously, and if you give me the same splendid co-operation I am not without hope that we may land our fish. I have done what I can to secure that our affairs are to be the first of the new session. I look forward to the chance of a couple of hours behind the box on the H. of C. table in the beginning of March.

Yours ever,
R. B. HALDANE.

[*To M. V. B.*]   ORCHARD LEA,
DECEMBER 31ST.

If you believe all you said to-night, and doubt the usefulness of knowledge, I cannot imagine why you should care for my poor attempts to tell you what comes in my way in public affairs, or to keep any record of your life and mine. The relative importance of events and knowledge is so obvious, that if we were not tacitly to admit it, nothing would be worth striving for, when Jupiter, with his satellites, is above the horizon, and probably looking down upon our little vapourings from a point of view altogether beyond our conception. *A Philosophy of Life.*

To the ants, their coming and going, however, is of vast importance. I have no wish to be metaphysical. But the delusion that a man should have one foot in the grave before he can be considered full grown and the intellectual equal of Solon or Winston Churchill, is only a comfortable theory invented by men of feeble will-power and self-indulgent tastes.

Just as I have often told you that the test of a man's progress along the right path is that he should look back over a space of time, arbitrary if you please (for twelve months are a purely arbitrary division of illimitable ages), and see within that space a distinct white stone. . . .

. . . Also, I maintain that within another arbitrary time division, i.e. twelve hours, every man who is worth his salt should be able to find a white pebble, and to say to himself that he has made some distinct progress during the day. That is the Napoleonic outlook—from the old Brienne days—upon life. *On Morley— the Source of his Power.*

I found J. M. [John Morley] in that charming library of his, tacked on to a Wimbledon commonplace villa—the ruler of 200,000,000 of people—whose will is law to them—surrounded by 11,000 books, reading a volume of Calvin. Two servant maids, and a plain old wrinkled wife. Memories of some Lancashire village in which he was born, hovering about him still. *This* home, a palace compared with that in which his father lived and died. He has not read all those 11,000 volumes, but he has read so much, that mysteriously their virtue passes into him. That is the instinct of the educated man, and the secret power works, for it helps to give this frail middle-class library student the moral and intellectual fibre which has led him upward from that Lancashire village to Whitehall, and to a position of power almost despotic over millions of human beings.

To this frail human being come the representatives of the Irish race, rebels, haters of the Saxon (of whom he is one), begging for advice and assistance in the choice of some other ruler, who is to control the destinies of 5,000,000 Britons.

All this is not much exaggerated. It is put perhaps rather broadly, but it represents fairly the truth. What, then, is the secret? Why has power been given by his fellow-countrymen to this man, who has inherited neither position nor wealth? He is decidedly no flatterer of the democracy, and no demagogue. So what is the cause? I do not pretend to explain—but it is certainly *not* that he remained content with half-knowledge or low standards.

You say, when you discuss, that you are only "putting other points of view." If you mean that you are trying Socratic methods on me, it is a waste of effort. For you, there should be no point of view but the right one, and no use for discussion except to arrive at the truth. Leave argument to the Sophists, who throughout the world's history have been the failures in art and literature. Their modern anti-type is the newspaper critic, as Dizzy said most truly. *You* must believe in the trained mind. You would not feed a Derby horse on soft food, or let him stand idle in the stable. Yet men allow their minds to stand idle for years and then expect to win a good race.

[*To M. V. B.*]   ORCHARD LEA,
                                                    JANUARY 3RD, 1907.

. . . Now to come to prosaic things. I lunched with Jackie *Fisher's*
[Fisher] to-day and Francis Knollys at the Carlton. Jackie feels *Anxieties.*
that he is standing on the edge of a precipice to which all great
reformers are led, and over which they ultimately fall. But, in
spite of the numerous enemies whose darling wish is to hurl him
down, it is essential that for a while he be kept up. If he survives
another year, the Navy will be safe.

Another question, the King of Spain wants our King to go to
Madrid. No one believes that it would be safe; and is it a risk he
ought to run? Although I am all for Kings and everyone taking
big risks, this particular one seems so useless. Like the Emperor
of Austria, the King is too big a sovereign to have to go round
Europe—and repay conventional visits. His age and position
exempt him. He would not like the idea of the former, but it
is true. Personally, I hope he won't go, or if he does, then only
to Cadiz *with the Fleet*!

[*To M. V. B.*]   2, TILNEY STREET,
                                                        JANUARY 9TH.

I saw Morley again this afternoon, and although the Cabinet
Committee were not hostile to Haldane's scheme, there was no
enthusiasm about it. What really frightens them is the length
of the Bill, and the *bother* which drastic proposals always
entail.

. . . The reconstruction of the Government goes on slowly. *Changes*
Birrell will go to the Irish Office—and McKenna to the Educa- *within*
tion Department. I think Buchanan will move to the India *the*
Office, and Jack Seely will go to the War Office. It will draw his *Govern-*
teeth. He is a clever fellow and "office" will steady him. The *ment.*
P.M. won't hear of Winston being in the Cabinet at present.

He is, like Mr. G. [Gladstone], old fashioned and disapproves of young men in a hurry.[1]

[*To the Rt. Hon. J. Morley.*]   2, TILNEY ST.,
JANUARY 12TH.

I hear that Clarke has had a letter from the P.M. telling him to communicate with you. So I take it that he accepts your plan in all respects. This is most satisfactory. You will have effected a step in advance of anything which your predecessors have done, if you can get a clear definition of Military policy in India, so far as it governs preparations here, clearly and decisively laid down.

I am at your service any day except Tuesday, should you want me.

At any rate *your* style and modes of thought do not require clarifying! Nothing could be more perfect than the document you read me.

[*To M. V. B.*]   ORCHARD LEA,
JANUARY 14TH.

*The
King's
Breakfast.*

As you are interested in the habits, domestic and public, of King Edward VII, I must tell you about my breakfast party. I got a telegram from Francis [Knollys] saying, "The King would like you to breakfast with him at 10 to-morrow." I got to Buckingham Palace at five to 10, and went up to the Indian Room.

---

[1] The reconstruction of the Cabinet was occasioned by the appointment of Mr. Bryce from Secretary for Ireland to be Ambassador at Washington, and by the retirement of Mr. J. E. Ellis on grounds of health from the office of Under-Secretary for India, which in the event was filled by Mr. Charles Hobhouse.

A page asked me if I would take tea or coffee! At 10 precisely, the King's door opened and he came in with his terrier. We went into the room overlooking the Mall. There was a small table. Two places laid. All the breakfast on the table in front of the King. His tea near him. My coffee near me. He served, and the pages and footmen left the room. He asked me if I would have some fish. There were three dishes. Fish, omelette, and bacon. When we had finished fish he rang the bell, and the servants changed the plates. Same ceremony repeated after omelette. Then marmalade—and he asked me if I would smoke. We sat there till just after 11. We talked all the time. Army and Government reconstruction gossip. . . .

. . . At 11, the King said *au revoir* till Windsor! I think all this is worth telling you, because a *tête-à-tête* breakfast with H.M. is quite a new departure. It is not a bad idea, and saves him an hour of the day, if he adopts it as a practice, which I think is not improbable. Unless of course he was bored.

[*To H.M. the King.*]   ORCHARD LEA,
                                   JANUARY 21ST.

Viscount Esher, with humble duty, begs to remind Your Majesty that in the opening paragraphs of the Report of the Defence Committee, over which he presided, attention was drawn to the fact that the standard of Military requirements of the Empire had never been laid down by the Cabinet or the Defence Committee. *Committee on the Military Needs of the Empire.*

The Prime Minister has in consequence appointed a sub-committee, presided over by the Secretary of State for India, to deal with this matter. Viscount Esher begs to enclose, for Your Majesty's information, the preliminary instructions.

The Committee meets to-morrow, when the examination of Sir Beauchamp Duff will commence.

The main idea, underlying the enquiry, is that the peace requirements of India govern and cover the military requirements of the Empire, inasmuch as a war with Russia on the N.W. Frontier, being the gravest military operation which Your Majesty's Army could be called upon to undertake, covers by its magnitude all other conceivable operations. So that to be prepared for that eventuality is to be prepared for all others.

The ratio of white to native troops, in peace time, involving as it does political questions of the first importance, is not within the scope of this enquiry; and the number of troops, British as well as native, to be maintained in peace within Your Majesty's Indian Dominions, is to be taken as fixed as at present.

The enquiry, therefore, is limited to the reinforcements required for India in the event of a war with Russia, and includes,

(*a*) The probable and possible movements of Russian forces in the event of war, on the frontier of Afghanistan.

(*b*) The strategical movements of British forces on the N.W. Frontier, or in Afghanistan, in consequence of Russian action, and possible tribal difficulties.

(*c*) The probable reinforcements required from home, during the first and second years of a war with Russia.

(*d*) The earliest date, after the outbreak of war, at which the Admiralty could advise the transit of troops from Great Britain to India.

It is in view of this enquiry that Lord Kitchener has sent over Sir Beauchamp Duff, his Chief of the General Staff, primed with his views on the questions of strategy and military organisation which such an enquiry raises.

Your Majesty will readily recognise how materially the whole scheme of military operation in this country is affected by the numbers of the reinforcements which may be required for India. Viscount Esher will have the honour of keeping Your Majesty informed, as the Enquiry proceeds.

[*To Sir John Fisher.*]   ORCHARD LEA,
                         FEBRUARY 4TH.

The paper you sent me is admirable in tone and strong in *Fisher's* argument. You are always chaffing me about the excellent *Lack of* "advice" which I now and then diffidently give you. You *Diplomacy—* never take it!

Under a constitutional government like ours, and with a parliamentary and press system like ours, no man, however great, can neglect certain precautions if he wishes to give permanence to his ideas and policy.

St. Vincent may have brought about Trafalgar, but he fell, and all his good work perished for a while. *You* may have achieved wonders, and you know what a convinced Fisherite I am; but the birds of prey are always hovering about, and they are gathering very thick just now.

My "advice" always was—

Take the Committee of Defence into your counsels, and *force —and them to register your decrees.* *Relations*

Then it is not Fisher *contra mundum*, but the Defence Com- *Defence* mittee which has to be pilloried. *Committee.*

1. Haldane referred his *whole scheme* to a sub-committee of the Defence Committee. In spite of Clarke (who signed the report like a lamb) and his numerous detractors, he has carried his *whole scheme*, one of the most controversial on record, right through the Cabinet. He will carry it through Parliament as well.

2. Morley referred the Afghanistan frontier question, and Kitchener's scheme, to a sub-committee of the Defence Committee, over which he presided himself, and (in spite of the hostile Clarke) will carry his views triumphantly.

Now look at the position of these two men, quite unassailable from "fishing enquiries" or anything else. *You* have shown mistrust and dislike of the Defence Committee instead of converting it to your uses. In my humble judgment you have made a mistake. During the past week or so, the forces ranged against each other have been Fisher versus Beresford. They should have been Fisher plus Defence Committee plus Cabinet versus Beresford, and the odds would have been over-whelming.[1] That is my argument. *You* invent a policy and you get the Defence Committee to *stereotype* it.

[*From Lord Knollys.*]   BUCKINGHAM PALACE,
                                        FEBRUARY 4TH, 1907.

MY DEAR ESHER,

Your letter to Jacky has terrified him. He came to me about it this morning, and I sent him to the Prince of Wales who, I believe, has more or less converted him on the question of the distribution of ships.

                                        Yours ever,
                                        KNOLLYS.

[*To the Rt. Hon. J. Morley.*]   2, TILNEY ST.,
                                        FEBRUARY 9TH.

The Afghan Frontier.

I think I could assist you much more effectively if I knew how your mind is working on the main points.

1. Railways.
2. Strategic Line.
3. Tribes.
4. Reinforcements.

For instance,

1. Do you incline to finish the railways?
2. Do you incline to the Cabul-Kandahar strategic line *in war*?

---

[1] The dispute referred to was concerned with the constitution of the Home and Channel Fleets, of which Lord Charles Beresford was about to take command. The details of this dispute, of which it can fairly be said that Lord Charles's contentions were contrary to the whole Fisher strategy and should have precluded his acceptance of the command, are too many to be summarised here in a reasonable space. An admirable account of the matter will be found in Admiral Bacon's *Lord Fisher*, vol. ii, ch. 2.

3. Do you stand out against making any pronouncement *re* Tribes?

4. Do you think the *draft* asked for by Lord K. might be promised, but no promise given as to reinforcements?

If these, or something like these, are your ideas, I would try to pick out the main points in the evidence supporting them.

Such a dull dinner at Haldane's last night to meet the P.M. who was in bed! Eighteen disappointed Generals!

I shall be at Orchard Lea to-morrow, and London on Monday.

[*To H.M. the King.*]　　　　　2, TILNEY STREET,
　　　　　　　　　　　　　　　　FEBRUARY 11TH.

QUEEN VICTORIA MEMORIAL

Viscount Esher, with humble duty, begs to inform Your Majesty that the Queen Victoria Memorial Executive Committee met at St. James's Palace to-day.

Progress of the Queen Victoria Memorial.

The accounts were considered, and out of a total subscription of £330,000 about £220,000 have been authorised and spent. This leaves a balance to be dealt with of a little over £100,000.

It was agreed that plans should be prepared for Your Majesty's consideration showing certain suggestions made by Sir Aston Webb, within these financial limits.

These plans will be ready in about a month or six weeks. Mr. Brock is experiencing some difficulty in getting the marble delivered from Sicily, but he hopes that the base of the monument will be in position next autumn.

He is progressing as rapidly as possible with the work itself. There have been attacks in some of the papers, and Viscount Esher has received complaints, about the use of Italian workmen for the delicate and highly skilled work of marble working by compass.

Unfortunately it is necessary to use Italians for this work, as only a very few Englishmen are qualified to handle artistically the very hard Sicilian marble of which the statues on the memorial are made. The Trades Unions seem to think that this marble can be worked like the soft stone to which they are accustomed.

Viscount Esher thinks that, on the whole, the progress of the work is very satisfactory.

[*To M. V. B.*]   ORCHARD LEA,
                                   FEBRUARY 16TH.

Royal Visit to Paris.

I told you all about the King's visit to Paris, and how well the whole thing was managed. The Queen had not been there for 18 years. She walked about the Rue de la Paix with Lady Gosford, and delighted in all the shops. She thought everything very cheap, and bought up half the town. At the "receptions" she was at her very best, and created the most favourable impression possible. The Parisians had never seen anything like her. Of course the Faubourg St. Germain was in ecstasies and mocked poor Mme. Fallières, dressed in plum-coloured velvet, who trotted and waddled alternately behind her.

Party Intrigue against Balfour.

Yesterday I had a long talk with Arthur Balfour in his room at the H. of C. He is depressed at the dead set made against him in his party. The curious thing is that not a single one of his more intimate colleagues is other than deeply loyal. Walter Long, at the Levée, got scarlet in the face with fury, when speaking to me of the treatment of Arthur. Yet *he* was the man whom the malcontents put forward as a potential leader. They have dropped him since he nearly kicked a deputation of them downstairs. The King told me that he met Duff last night at Marlborough House and liked him very much.

[*To the Rt. Hon. J. Morley.*]   2, TILNEY ST.,
                                        MARCH 1ST.

I had two very interesting talks about your private affairs with the King and with C.-B.

You shall hear all about them when we meet. But this is only for your own secret information!

[*To M. V. B.*]   WEST DEAN PARK,
                                                      MARCH 5TH.

. . . I am immersed in Mason's new book.[1] It is beautifully written and is the proper mixture of romance and drama. The charm of the writer penetrates every page. I am sure that he lives in an atmosphere of adventure. His excursions into Parliament and society form, I suppose, part of a settled plan to get to the bottom of every social mystery. But his heart is evidently in the desert or on the mountain top.

[*To M. V. B.*]   ORCHARD LEA,
                                                      MARCH 7TH.

There is no record of the King's visit to Windsor, and the talks with Arthur Balfour, John Morley and Haldane. The King was pleased, on the whole, with the appointments which Haldane proposed—notably Methuen's in S. Africa. He likes J. M. and is disturbed by the latter's threats to resign office. I am sure what J. M. really wants is freedom from the H. of C. He likes *his* office, but not parliamentary hours. When I suggested the Upper House, he repudiated the notion, but by his manner I felt it was no new idea to him, and that his inclination leans that way, although his past record alarms him. *Il veut se faire prier*—and *then* he will take a peerage, and remain in office. *The King and Morley :*

The King saw his Chancellor for the first time *en intimité* and liked him, as he was sure to do, for no better fellow lives. John Burns, in knee breeches, was a revelation. His manner absolutely perfect. No self-consciousness and no bumptiousness. *—and John Burns.*

[1] *Running Water.*

Quite respectful, absolutely frank, and quick in the uptake without embarrassment. He showed tact and knowledge, and embarked on no topic in which he was likely to get out of his depth. For half an hour after dinner, he talked to the Queen, and for another hour to the Princess of Wales.

I could not, this time, either meet or despatch the King from Windsor, as we had a Defence Committee both days, and the King would not interfere, very properly.

He profited, by getting a record of two most interesting meetings. Especially the latter, when we got Lord Roberts' evidence. However, you know all about that, as you heard the little man last Sunday, in his own house, expound his views on Afghanistan. Your afternoon there will be a pleasant reminiscence some day.

Fisher and the Prince of Wales.

Fisher has been in stormy waters during the past week, owing to the pointed attack by C. Beresford, and the flank attacks from his various enemies, on the redistribution of the Fleet.

The Prince of Wales wrote an excellent Memo. on the "policing of the seas," which the Fisher policy neglects, and making suggestions which the Admiral has now accepted.

We had a dinner given by the Prince of Wales at Marlborough House to discuss it. Only Fisher, Charles Hardinge and Francis Knollys. Fisher was in excellent spirits.

The only other event of importance is that Haldane has got his Army scheme through the Cabinet. Campbell-Bannerman, whose flair is excellent, says "the public neither knows nor cares about the details of an Army scheme, but as Haldane shows £2,000,000 decrease in cost, and has got a definite scheme, they will say ' *give him a chance.*' " This is a true diagnosis.

The King's visit to Paris is a great success. He stays with the Queen at the Embassy. F. Bertie, the Ambassador, has gone to the "Bristol." It was thought he would be fussy.

The King has seen all the Ministers. Clemenceau's definition for our relations with France and Germany respectively is that they should be, with Germany, "*relations normales*": and with France, "*relations intimes.*" That is very sound.

. . . Perhaps of all our many strokes of good fortune, the day we went to the "English Daisy" was one of the most blessed. You owe a great debt to Zena, which is all the more reason for holding fast to that friendship. Few can look on anything so perfectly sweet and fresh in their lives as this unclouded and untainted intimacy.

[*To the Rt. Hon. J. Morley.*]   ORCHARD LEA,
                                        MARCH 8TH.

DON'T ANSWER

Only a line to say that I hope you will give Kitchener his 2 years' extension, and would humbly suggest that you should write privately to the King, when you have settled it, so that he may hear the news *first* from you.

[*To M. V. B.*]   ORCHARD LEA,
                                        MARCH 18TH.

. . . To-day I lunched with John Morley and we talked over the Afghan report. I think he is altogether on the right lines. But I cannot feel sure until I have seen his rough draft. I also saw Haldane, who is having a battle royal with the Yeomanry. Arthur Balfour thinks that H. is over-sanguine about getting his Bill. Of course the forces of reaction are gathering strength as they always do.

Repington has asked me to luncheon to-morrow to tell me *Letter* of the machinations against *me* personally, which found utter- *attacking* ance (preliminary) in the *Standard* letter! Also, I presume, in *Lord* Arnold-Forster's question. It does not intimidate me. *Esher—*

[*To Lord Knollys.*]   ORCHARD LEA,
                                        MARCH 19TH.

I send you the leading article out of to-day's *Standard*, in case *—and a* you did not see it.   *Leading Article.*

I am told that the attack, which has been brewing for some time, is the work of poor Arnold-Forster. Arthur Balfour thinks he is mad. It is an extraordinary thing, but he wrote to Marker (of the Coldstream) who is a clever writer, and asked him to join in the affray; but Marker refused—and did not keep A.-F.'s counsel.

Haldane feared that I might be "upset" by this extremely silly attempt to throw odium upon my work; but I told him that if he and Campbell-Bannerman are not intimidated, I certainly am not.

Lord Esher's Attitude.

I have no complaint to make of the statements in the article, except in regard to my having "promised" promotions! You, who know me, can acquit me of anything of that kind. There are two points which have been taken, and they both appear to me absurd.

Any "influence" which it is assumed I have, is only what we all have, and is every Englishman's right—i.e. to express his opinions to whomsoever he pleases.

Suppose we any of us urge that A is a better man than B, we have all of us a perfect right to do so, and if injustice is done, the fault lies with the responsible Minister, who is the judge, and not with the advocate. My conscience is perfectly calm, as I can safely say that, with the exception of French, there is no one soldier that I prefer to any other; and whenever I have urged the claims of any officer, and I have often done so and shall go on doing so, it has been solely with a view to the service of the King, and the efficiency of the King's army.

The second point is that my "position" is unconstitutional. This point interests me, as you know I am fond of such speculations. But can you imagine anything more absurd than to label as "unconstitutional" the action of a Minister who employs me or any other private person to *assist* him in the work for which the Minister only is responsible. Everything I have done in connection with the Army, is either adopted or rejected by a Minister. In the former case it is *his* responsibility. In the latter, it is also *his*!

The only annoyance I have felt is that I should have been dragged into a temporary notoriety. I have never sought this, as you know, and I dislike it extremely. It seems rather hard that one should not be allowed to work for the King and for his country, without any desire for reward or recognition, and nevertheless be pilloried by newspaper writers.

However, so long as the King and you and a few others do not mind, and neither Haldane nor C.-B. flinches, I shall remain unruffled !

[*To H.M. the King.*]   ORCHARD LEA,
                                     MARCH 19TH.

Viscount Esher, with humble duty, thinks Your Majesty may *On Lord* like to know that he went to Studley last week, for a day, to see *Ripon.* Lord Ripon.

Viscount Esher, for five and twenty years, went every autumn to the Isle of Harris, when Lord Ripon rented the Forest, or to Studley for a month, and Lady Ripon has always been a close friend. He was anxious to see again the Church near which she lies, and also to spend a day with Lord Ripon.

He is wonderfully well, and interested as deeply as ever in politics, although his life at Studley is inexpressibly solitary and dreary.

The old house is as dilapidated as ever, and even the fine park at this time of the year looked desolate. Lord Ripon will, however, return for Easter and resume his duties in the House of Lords, but Viscount Esher doubts whether he will be strong enough to continue to serve Your Majesty after the fall of the year.[1]

There is very little news in London. Mr. Haldane is as *Prospects* optimistic as ever about the passage of his Bill, but Mr. Balfour, *of the* whom Viscount Esher saw to-day, is *not* so sanguine. He seems *Territorial Bill.*

[1] Lord Ripon was at this date Lord Privy Seal.

to think that Mr. Haldane underrates the opposition of the Yeomanry and Volunteers, and their *political* influence. There is no doubt but that the opposition to the Bill is now being organised by the Duke of Bedford, Colonel Howard Vincent, and Mr. Harry Lawson; and it may become more formidable than Mr. Haldane supposes.

Mr. Morley told Viscount Esher that he had written to Your Majesty, to ask Your Majesty's approval of an extension of Lord Kitchener's term, which will probably be very satisfactory to Your Majesty. He is an element of strength in the Councils of Your Majesty's Government *in* India, which in other respects is weak at the present time.

Cabinet and House of Lords.

Viscount Esher hears that the Cabinet Committee which is considering the question of the House of Lords has put aside, in deference to Your Majesty's own wishes, all idea of making proposals which involve touching the hereditary principle upon which that House rests; and have limited their enquiry as to the method by which a serious deadlock between the two Houses is in future to be avoided.

The more extreme Members of the Government will find this solution inadequate from their point of view, but it is the only one which would be approved by the country.

It may take the form of proposals, the effect of which would be to leave the House of Lords untouched *except when a deadlock occurs*; and that then each House of Parliament should nominate representatives to meet and settle the points in dispute, but, while providing for an adequate representation of minorities, that nevertheless the will of the majority of the House of Commons should prevail.

Your Majesty will at once see that everything will depend upon the *details* of the plan proposed. It might be fair and reasonable, or it might be utterly subversive of the Constitution.

Viscount Esher will only add that after seeing the Queen, and later Mr. Haldane, he was fortunate enough to find a settlement, at any rate for the present, of the Nursing difficulty, which was satisfactory to Her Majesty.

[*To M. V. B.*]　　　　　　　　2, TILNEY STREET,
　　　　　　　　　　　　　　　MARCH 19TH.

Did I tell you that Arthur Balfour thinks Haldane unduly optimistic? His view is that the Yeomanry and Volunteers are being carefully organised; and that they are politically formidable you know. Haldane has approved Kitchener's extension. It is a good thing from the point of view of the Government of India, as the Viceroy's council is lamentably weak.

A despatch from Minto is on its way, proposing a *Native* member of council in India, and John Morley is amazed that this proposition should emanate from Minto—who, I may say, is in a minority of two in his council on the subject. Between ourselves, I think J. M. wishes Minto and his proposal to the devil. It places him, as *radical* S. of S., in a most awkward fix.

[*To M. V. B.*]　　　　　　　　ORCHARD LEA,
　　　　　　　　　　　　　　　MARCH 21ST.

I have heard from Repington, who showed my previous letter to Buckle. They think that it disposes completely of the two points taken by the *Standard*, of undue influence and an unconstitutional position on my part. *Sequel to Attacks on Lord Esher.*

But Buckle seems to think that my connection with Cassel is a source of weakness! So I have written again to give a statement of facts! How in 1902 my agreement with Cassel was made, how in 1904 it was determined. Anyhow sometime *before* I was appointed to the Defence Committee. Of course, I could not have become a member of that committee, had my agreement with Cassel remained in force. So that there is no vulnerable point there! To-morrow I shall have to go up to town, as we have a meeting of the Sanatorium Committee, but I shall come back.

. . . Rosebery made no speech on the Channel Tunnel. Only asked the question. Crewe answered for the Government. *Channel Tunnel.*

You know that a month ago they had settled to leave it an open question. Every Member of the Government to vote as he liked. *Now*, they have plucked up their courage and have declared against it. My notion is that they are probably wrong! Unanimity always is, and upon this question the country seems to be as much of one mind as the idiots who stoned St. Stephen and Copernicus.

[*To Colonel Repington.*[1]]   ORCHARD LEA,
                                                 MARCH 22ND.

Further Explanations by Lord Esher—

There is *no* vulnerable point. Please tell Buckle that the day I left the Office of Works I signed an agreement with Cassel, carefully drawn, undertaking certain engagements, with very large profits, in certain financial concerns, for 3 years. That was in 1902. In June 1904, i.e., two years later, I had come to the conclusion that I was unfitted for the City business, and that agreement was *determined in writing*.

Since then I have had no connection of any kind with Cassel or the City.

I, however, am director of :—

    1. The Central London Railway.
    2. The Egyptian Daira Co.
    3. The Agricultural Bank of Egypt.
    4. The Royal Opera.

But I did not become a member of the Defence Committee until October 1905—or nearly *eighteen months after* all connection with the City had ceased.

I am *certain* nothing would have induced me to accept a seat upon the Defence Committee, had that connection continued.

Is this sufficiently clear and unmistakable? Both transactions were known to Mr. Balfour.[2]

---

[1] Military Correspondent to *The Times*.

[2] In spite of the Correspondence, it does not appear that the question was ever mentioned in *The Times*.

[*From Lord Knollys.*]   PAIGNTON,
                                          MARCH 28TH.

MY DEAR ESHER,

Many thanks for your two letters both received to-day. The —*and*
King, I know, was *very* "nice" about you in connection with the *Lord*
attack by the *Standard*, and was very indignant that it should *Knollys'*
have been made. You know how much attached I am to the *View.*
Prince of Wales, whom I have, of course, known ever since he
was born. I am greatly pleased therefore to read what you write
to me about him and at the way in which he came out at your
dinner. It is an excellent thing that he should have an opportunity of showing his knowledge and intelligence to Ministers
and to others occupying important official positions. Who is
this Mr. Bowles who asked two questions about you in the House
of Commons yesterday? Is he the son of the ex-M.P. for Lynn?
C.-B.'s answer was, I thought, very good, and Haldane's excellent, and I hope nothing more will be said. I go to London on
Tuesday.

                              Yours ever,
                                          KNOLLYS.

[*To H.M. the King.*]   ORCHARD LEA,
                                          APRIL 13TH.

Viscount Esher, with humble duty, thinks Your Majesty may *Odd*
be interested to hear that some short while ago a Surgeon- *Bequest to*
Dentist died at Brighton, and left to the British Museum *British*
2 Stradivarius Violins of high quality, one Viola by the same *Museum.*
maker, and a Violoncello also by Stradivarius, quite unique.

They are valued at a very large sum, at least £12,000. As
Your Majesty is aware, these fine instruments are ruined by dis-
use, and require constant attention, and to be played upon.
Great interest has been roused in musical circles, and Sir Hubert
Parry, representing all the most eminent musicians, has pressed

the Trustees not to accept the Bequest. In that case, the instruments would be sold, and would pass into hands where their life would be prolonged; and the proceeds of the sale would—under this strange man's will—go to the University of Manchester.

The Trustees are divided in opinion, and to-day the question was again postponed until next meeting, a month hence. The Prince of Wales, the Archbishop, Lord Crawford and Lord Rosebery, all take what Viscount Esher humbly ventures to think the right view, that these instruments are of very little interest to the Museum—which possesses no collection of musical instruments—and that it is almost criminal to allow them to perish in a glass case, when in good hands they might give pleasure to thousands.

Secret Papers on Milner.

Another curious point arose to-day. A Mr. Jarvis, who was M.P. for King's Lynn, sent a sealed packet, and a letter requesting that it should be placed in the Museum, under a pledge that it should not be opened till 1950. It purports to contain records of his conversations with Lord Milner in 1899–1900 in South Africa, of the most private character, justifying Lord Milner's action at the outset of the war.

The Trustees, after some discussion, decided that they could not accept this supposed record, without the knowledge and the approval of Lord Milner. He is to be asked accordingly if these conversations ever took place, and if he has any objection to the Record being preserved.

Viscount Esher hopes that Your Majesty may be interested in these rather unusual episodes.

On Harcourt's House at Nuneham.

He motored over a few days ago to Nuneham, to see Mr. Harcourt's improvements. The place is almost unrecognisable. Nothing can, of course, make the house very fine, but it is wonderfully comfortable, and Your Majesty, should Your Majesty visit it, will find all the arrangements of the house quite charming. There are some interesting pictures, but nothing first-rate. On the other hand, the garden will be very fine indeed, as it has been laid out with great taste by Mr. Harcourt, in the old setting, which was highly favourable to gardening operations. Every sort of shrub and flower has been planted and the terraces and walks most cleverly and tastefully arranged. The Park Your Majesty probably knows, and it retains all its beauty.

To motor from here, over the Chilterns, by Nettlebed, took exactly 1½ hours. Your Majesty will do it faster, and the drive is quite perfect.

[*To Lord Milner.*]　　　　　　　　2, TILNEY STREET,
　　　　　　　　　　　　　　　　　　APRIL 13TH.

As misrepresentation is rife, I want to tell you myself that I objected to-day, at the meeting of the Standing Committee of the B. Museum, to accepting a sealed packet, not to be opened till 1950, with a covering letter from a Mr. Jarvis saying that it contains "conversations" with you in S. Africa in 1899–1900. *The Milner Question.*

My view was—and is—that before any sort of imprimatur is given by the Trustees to such a Record, and our acceptance might hereafter be thus interpreted, we should know *your wishes in the matter*.

So you will probably be asked by the donor whether you object. If *you* approve, I shall personally vote for the acceptance of the trust. Of course I have no idea what the other Trustees will do, as they at once agreed to the suggestion I made to-day.

P.S.—Personally I should fight shy of being judged by the records of a Boswell, however akin my biographer might be to that heroic Scot.

[*From Lord Milner.*]　　　　　　STURRY COURT, KENT,
　　　　　　　　　　　　　　　　　　APRIL 22ND.

MY DEAR ESHER,

Many thanks for your letter, which I found here on my return from a short trip abroad. I certainly feel some uneasiness at the prospect of my sayings in 1899–1900 being handed down to the world (though it will probably have forgotten all about me) in a version which I have never seen, and which may be absolutely inaccurate.

It matters, of course, a great deal who the donor is, and I shall wait to hear from him before making up my mind. In any case I think your action in the matter was quite right and thank you for taking the course you did.

Yours very sincerely,
MILNER.

[*To M. V. B.*]   WAR OFFICE,
                                                    APRIL 26TH.

I am waiting to see Mr. Haldane, who is at the H. of C. but wants to see me. . . .

I read you those words of Mrs. Browning's in one of her letters about Art. How it requires the whole man, austerely and unreservedly given: how great things must be done greatly, with a great purpose, a great heart, a great courage, a great energy, and a great persistent patience.

The whole secret of life lies in these words, whether it is Love or War or the career of a politician. When a young man starts on the life struggle, a helping hand can be held out. But this rarely can be done twice. After that first start, if he is ever to be of any good, and if the world is to be better because he lived, his own unaided effort must be the underlying cause.

[*To General Botha.*]   WAR OFFICE,
                                                    APRIL 29TH.

*On an
Imperial
General
Staff—*

I should like to add a few words to the interesting talk we had at Stafford House.

One of the most satisfactory features of the Imperial Conference has been the welcome acceptance by you all of the principle of an Imperial General Staff. As a soldier you must have realised that to give effect to this principle, considering that our General Staff is yet in its infancy, must take time.

As a statesman you will have realised also that that aspiration, however ardent, and even exchange of Staff Officers between the mother country and the over-sea Dominions, are not, taken alone, practical steps towards the creation of an Imperial General Staff.

It will be many years before, in this country, we possess a General Staff which can be compared with those of Germany and France.

The reason is, that a General Staff is an educational growth, and cannot be imposed suddenly or quickly upon an Army, however well organised.

We have made a good start, and hope for the future lies in the ability and aptitude of our younger Army officers. At the root, however, of the problem is education at a Staff College. Without serious and patient teaching no General Staff worthy of the name can be created. This is universally recognised by soldiers in all countries.

For our own wants, the Staff College at Camberley is too *—and the* small, and it will take many years to make it adequate for our re- *Staff* quirements. Yet it is primarily to the Staff College that young *College.* officers from over-seas should come, regularly and systematically, if the idea of an Imperial General Staff is to be realised.

You could render, perhaps, no better service to the military needs of the Empire, than by persuading your colleagues of the advantage of increasing the training capacity of the Staff College.

It would mean that the Dominions over-sea should, as a gift, spend a certain sum in enlarging the College with a view to the special training of Dominion officers. Suppose, for instance, that Canada, Australia, New Zealand and South Africa were to add accommodation to the Staff College at Camberley—a Dominion wing—for two officers each, and were to offer two military scholarships every two years to be competed for by the young officers of their States, no more practical step could be taken in the direction of creating a General Staff Imperial not only in name but in fact.

As a Permanent Member of the Committee of Imperial Defence, I venture, but on my own responsibility, to offer this suggestion; and it is for you to judge of its value, and of the likelihood of its finding favour among your colleagues and your people.

Such a proposal can never come from the Mother Country. It must emanate from you. Please make any use of this letter which you may think fit.

[*To M. V. B.*]   2, TILNEY STREET,
                                              MAY 3RD.

. . . The Opera last night was perfectly charming. *Hänsel und Gretel.* It is very pretty and beautifully mounted. I saw it years ago at the Princesses, and thought it lovely then. It was preceded by a one-act opera by Mozart, written when he was 12 years old! . . . Miss Botha was in the H. of L. last night, and I talked to her for a few minutes. She is a very good-looking girl with the manners of a Duchess.

[*To Sir Wilfrid Laurier.*]   2, TILNEY STREET,
                                              MAY 11TH.

Imperial General Staff.

The suggestion contained in the letter of which I enclose a copy is, I venture respectfully to think, not a bad one, but I met with no cordial response from General Botha. Perhaps you will not think it too late for consideration by you. If, in your opinion, the idea is wholly impracticable, the matter shall be dropped as far as I am concerned.

I had hoped to be able to speak to you on the subject, but never got a favourable opportunity.

[*From Lord Kitchener.*]　　　　　　　　　　SIMLA,
　　　　　　　　　　Private.　　　　　　MAY 16TH.
MY DEAR ESHER,

I have unofficially heard something of the decision on Indian defence come to by Mr. Morley's sub-committee of the Committee of Defence. Apparently practically all the points we have so long contended for (sometimes rather hopelessly) have been accepted. It is simply splendid, and an immense step towards the security of this country. We shall now know what we want and what we ought to work for, and at last we shall have laid down a sound policy for the defence of the frontiers of India.

Kitchener on the Defence Committee.

I cannot help at once writing to thank you for all you have done to bring this about, for I know that it is very greatly due to your constant and active support that this most satisfactory result has been achieved. I also feel that Duff's complete knowledge of the subject and capability has had a considerable effect at home and I hope he will get some reward for his excellent work (a K.C.B. is possible).

We are all very fit and well. I regret that it will be some time before I can personally express to you how sincerely grateful I am for all you have so successfully accomplished for this country.

　　　　　　　　　　　Yours very truly,
　　　　　　　　　　　　　KITCHENER.

[*To M. V. B.*]　　　　　　　ORCHARD LEA,
　　　　　　　　　　　　MAY 21ST.

. . . Albert Grey arrived about 12 from Taplow. He is still bubbling with enthusiasm, and talked incessantly about Canada and all his projects. I told him of my proposal to Botha and

Laurier about the training of Colonial officers. In his hands the idea may make some progress. He has found some old letters written by me to him when we were at Cambridge.

[*To the Rt. Hon. J. Morley.*]   2, TILNEY STREET,
                                                          JUNE 7TH.

*Morley's
Budget
Speech.*

It is almost an impertinence to offer congratulations upon the really splendid speech of last night.[1] If it should prove to be your swan song in the *H. of C.* no one chanted a finer. The King is evidently very proud of "his Minister" and the country and your own party ought to more than reciprocate his sentiments.

If your great radical predecessors know anything of it—from the shades—they should feel a cubit taller to-day.

[*To M. V. B.*]   2, TILNEY STREET,
                                      JUNE 25TH.

I have done your commissions. Salisbury is delighted to ask the French Generals, and Knollys has got your résumé of their biographies.

The Ball at the Russian Embassy was ultra smart. It was a squash really, with dancing in one room. Given for the Connaughts, but graced by the presence of the King and Queen and the P. of W. etc.

I had a long talk with Brodrick in the H. of L. and I don't think he will do more than air schemes of his own. Of course he will criticise the Bill, but I doubt there being a division against it. He was wonderfully civil to me!

Rosebery hunted me down one of the lobbies, and asked *why* Francis Knollys and I had voted against a committee to enquire into the H. of L. He was evidently fussed on the point. I cannot imagine *why*. He is chairman of the committee, but it is packed

[1] A long speech introducing the Indian Budget.

with people who agree with him, and not a single opponent of
his view has been put upon it. He is a queer fish.

[*To M. V. B.*] 2, TILNEY STREET,
JUNE 26TH.

The enclosed from Probyn is rather interesting. There were
scores more of mutiny veterans yesterday at the Levée. I
thought the visit to Windsor a great success,[1] and the *Chef de
Mission* is very attractive. They must have enjoyed their change
of motor. *Visit of French Generals.*

Do you know that 600 motors passed through the Mews on
Saturday, and there were probably 400 more at Windsor. That
represents an outlay of nearly a million pounds on motors. Not
bad for about 3 or 4 years' growth.

There is no keenness for doing anything for the French
officers. The absurd line is taken that they are *private* guests of
General French's! Tell Lowther to combat this view. They
were invited through the F.O. and their expenses are paid for by
the State. It is the "fear of Germany" that is the prevailing note
just now, because the Emperor has been invited here this
autumn.

Both the General and Lowther ought to fight hard for a
G.C.M.G. for Michel and a K.C.M.G. for Marion. Tell
Lowther to bring all the family obstinacy into the contest and
to see Hardinge.

[*To H.M. the King.*] 2, TILNEY STREET,
JULY 4TH.

Viscount Esher, with humble duty, thinks Your Majesty may
like to know how the negotiations between the Government
and the Leaders of the Opposition in regard to the Army Bill
in the House of Lords have progressed. *Progress of the Army Bill—*

[1] Of French Generals.

Viscount Esher, at Mr. Haldane's request, saw Lord Salisbury two days ago, and settled with him, in writing, the main military points upon which the Militia Officers lay stress.

The main points are, that

(a) Promotion should be assured to Militia Officers within that Force.

(b) No distinction to be drawn between the 3rd and 4th Battalions, as to their chance of being sent abroad as complete units.

(c) No man to be "ordered or carried" abroad except under one of the Officers of his Corps.

If the Government concede these points, the integrity of the Militia will be preserved.

Viscount Esher saw the Adjutant-General and General Miles and the Parliamentary Draftsman yesterday evening, and this morning he informed Lord Salisbury that there was very little doubt that all these points would be favourably settled.

The question then arose, as to whether certain necessary and consequential Amendments should be moved by the Leaders of the Opposition, or by the Government.

Upon this point, it is absolutely necessary to obtain a decision from Mr. Haldane, who has been asked to come up from Scotland by to-night's mail, as to-morrow is the last day upon which Amendments can be put down.

There is no doubt that he will anticipate his return, which was fixed for Saturday, as his absence at this juncture is extremely inconvenient.

By Mr. Haldane's concession in the House of Commons to Mr. Balfour, and these further improvements, the Bill assumes an entirely new shape, and reverts to the type suggested by that large representative committee over which Viscount Esher had the honour to preside in the winter.

—and its Ultimate Effects. 101 Battalions of Militia, officered partly by regular officers, comprising between 80 and 90 thousand men, will have been added to the Regular Army, *liable for service abroad.*

1 Major, 4 Captains and 2 Subalterns will have been added to

M.V.B. Sir John French. Viscount Esher.

[Photo: *Gale and Polden, Aldershot.*

T.R.H. THE PRINCE AND PRINCESS OF WALES AT GOVERNMENT HOUSE, ALDERSHOT, 1907.

every Regiment of the Line for service by roster, with the 3rd and 4th Battalions, or a total (including deductions) of some 400 officers will have been added to the Regular Army.

So far as the "first line" is concerned this forms no mean achievement, in the teeth of a large majority in the House of Commons.

[*To M. V. B.*]   ORCHARD LEA,
                                JULY 16TH.

. . . I saw Morley to-day. There is a serious hitch in the Russian negotiations. So serious that Nicolson, our Ambassador, is coming home. Apparently the military party or the Germans have upset the treaty for the present. Grey is rather disturbed in his mind about it.

. . . Lord Kitchener has written a long letter about his *successor*, two years hence. He wants Duff. He urges strongly the claims of the Indian Army for the appointment. It lies between Barrow and Duff. The urgency of the thing is that K. says that should Duff be chosen, he should *now* have one of the big Indian commands (vacant) as preparation.

Kitchener on His Successor.

Personally I think Duff is not the best man for that particular place. The "Indian Army" claim is absurd. Indian experience is another thing.

To M. V. B.]   2, TILNEY ST.,
                                JULY 19TH.

. . . As you have seen, I carried my amendment—and the Army Bill goes down to the H. of C. with no amendment which cannot be accepted. Haldane is delighted.[1]

[1] Mr. Haldane's Territorial and Reserve Forces Act went up to the Lords in a form which would have precluded the County Associations from supporting school cadet corps or rifle clubs. The Lords inserted a permissive

[*To M. V. B.*]   ORCHARD LEA,
                                                 JULY 20TH.

On the Opera.   . . . Zena ought to like the opera. All the people who have
heard the rehearsals say that Caruso has never been so fine, and
Destinn is splendid. We came down after the opera last night.
La Bohème is dead for me without Caruso and Melba. I could
not listen to it, and had to leave the box. Bonci looks and acts
like the waiter he is. Of course the voice is pretty; but so small.

I have tried to get on to you this morning to tell you that
Clarke is appointed to Bombay. The King signed the appointment last night. I wanted you to tell the General [French] and ask
him to think of a successor at the Defence Committee! Not an
easy job.[1] Clarke will be a loss in many ways. . . . Give Zena
my love and tell her that the Little Widow [2] has improved
immensely in her dress. She has some very nice *hats*!

[*To M. V. B.*]   2, TILNEY ST.,
                                                 JULY 22ND.

The King wants the German Emperor to "have a show" at
Aldershot some day between Nov. 11th–16th. *Not* a review.
Nothing smart. *Not* cavalry. Preferably artillery—with Horse
and Field etc. etc.

As big a show as we can give. The General [French] is re-
quested to think this over. No hurry. And to talk about it to
Haldane next week.

clause to remedy this lack. There was some question whether the Commons,
in the state of their temper at the time, might not throw this out again on the
ground that it imposed a charge on the taxes and was therefore *ultra vires*.
Lord Esher moved an amendment precluding the expenditure of any Parliamentary grant for this purpose, but retaining the right of the Associations to
support such bodies out of other funds. After some opposition the amendment was passed by the Upper House.

[1] Sir Charles Ottley was ultimately appointed.
[2] Miss Lily Elsie.

[*From Sir Charles Ottley.*]   THE HAGUE,
AUGUST 13TH.

DEAR LORD ESHER,

It is very nice of you to write me such a charming letter, and I
am immensely grateful both to you and to Lord Tweedmouth,
Sir John Fisher, Mr. Haldane and indeed all the kind friends who
have interested themselves in favour of the naval nominee.
Indeed I was only waiting for the appointment to be publicly
announced before writing to thank you. Sir Henry Campbell-
Bannerman wrote to offer me the post about ten days ago. I
look forward with immense delight to the interest of this new
work, and more particularly am happy to think I shall have *you*
to help and advise on knotty points. In a word, "It's me that's
the proud man!"

I do wish we had you here, for many reasons which I shall tell
you when we meet. The work is very heavy, but is of the kind
which no man in England could discharge as well as yourself.
Certainly I will make a point of seeing you as soon as I get back;
I join my wife in Scotland I hope early in September and will
try and motor over. We are 4 miles from Fort William.

Yours very sincerely,

C. L. OTTLEY.

New Secretary for Defence Committee.

[*To M. V. B.*]   2, TILNEY ST.,
JULY 23RD.

. . . Of course, as you say, Zena is a dear. *A qui le dit tu?* No
one has realised that more completely than I have. And you are
very lucky to have such a sweet friend. I wish she would ride
astride and come out on manœuvres. What an excitement
among the 1st Division, who know her by sight, as well as the
others who do not. She would make a charming companion
for me and Douglas Haig!

To-night we go to the opera, and then to the Iveaghs' ball.
I shall not stay there very long.

[*To M. V. B.*]   2, TILNEY ST.,
                                                  JULY 24TH.

. . . *Aïda* was very fine. Caruso splendid. No other voice is
possible in the opera while one is accustomed to hear him sing.

[*To M. V. B.*]   LEICESTER,
                                                  AUGUST 6TH.

On Leicester   You can walk all over the possible part of this town of 200,000
people in ten minutes. Not a public building, not a shop, not a
house of any mark. Anyway the ancient glories of the Middle
Ages at Warwick, the splendour—although in ruins—of the
Tudors at Kenilworth, though perhaps not up to certain doubtful standards of to-day, have left tangible beauties for subsequent
ages to wonder at. Whereas this home of modern industry
contributes nothing but a uniform level of red-brick mediocrity. The people look comfortably off, dull, unintelligent,
fleshy, and although they make boots for mankind, they will
make uncommonly little else.

—Warwick—   Warwick was a melancholy spectacle. The splendid old
castle, in a site worthy of Lancelot and Elaine, the Avon running
below the walls exactly as Tennyson describes Tintagil in the
"Last Tournament." One almost expected to see Guinevere
sitting on the battlements, and the diamond carcanet flashing
into the river. The gardens a vision of beauty, and—the whole
place overrun by the commonest type of tourist. Simply hun-
dreds of them wandering through the yew walks. We could
not face the house. It seemed such a desecration of Home.
—and   Kenilworth stands finely too. A red brick Tudor castle, just as
Kenilworth.   you read of it in Scott. Here two ginger beer stalls round the
gateway, and the American accent everywhere prevailing.

> " The dews of summer night did fall,
>   the moon, sweet regent of the sky,
>   silvered the walls of Cumnor Hall
>   and many an oak that grew there-by."

You remember how those lines haunted Scott. It was fortunate that he lived too soon to see Kenilworth a prey to the "tripper."

[*To M. V. B.*]   YORK,
AUGUST 7TH.

. . . We had rather a rough drive to-day. We came right *On the* through Sherwood Forest, which is only attractive in name. *Dukeries—* There are no vestiges of Robin Hood, and the climate was degrees colder than either north or south. The "Dukeries" left me with no desire to share their splendour. Welbeck must be a terrible incubus. No wonder the late Duke sought happiness as Mr. Druce.[1]

. . . To-morrow we shall perhaps get to Alnwick, and then home on Friday. Now that one is away from it all, it seems impossible that Parliament can still be sitting, and be keeping sane men talking instead of being in the open air. No other nation in the world transacts business in August, and idles in December. The old hunting craze of our forefathers still rules the customs of an assembly not 10 per cent. of which can sit upon a horse.

[*To M. V. B.*]   ALNWICK,
AUGUST 8TH.

We arranged differently to-day. Breakfasted at 7 at York *—and* before starting, and went straight to Durham. We got there *Alnwick.*

---

[1] It may not be remembered that the Duke of Portland was rumoured to have been one with Mr. Thomas Druce, head of a London furnishing business. The rumour began to be of some importance when representatives of the Druce family laid claim to the Portland estates. They asserted that the grave of Mr. Druce was empty. An exhumation being ordered, it was found to contain a body answering so far as could be discovered to that of Mr. Druce. The claimants then maintained that it was not proved to be his body; but this shift of ground damaged their support among the public. The case has passed from memory because it never resulted in a spectacular trial like that of the Tichborne claimant.

about 11.30 and saw the splendid cathedral and had lunch. Then we came on here where we arrived at about half-past four. It is a charming clean town, and the castle is *not* the incubus which most of these big places are. Heaven knows why. Perhaps it is the extreme severity of the surroundings. All battlements and turf. No smart gardens. It looks a real mediæval castle-fortress. Suited quite to these hard faces and rasping voices. The castle has been well cared for, and admirably restored. Dungeons and oubliettes. There are three drawbridges and 3 courts—like at Windsor. We did not see the rooms. I always hate "sightseeing" other people's houses *inside*.

[*To the Rt. Hon. J. Morley.*]   THE ROMAN CAMP,
                                         AUGUST 13TH.

The Indian   I entirely endorse the wisdom of delay. The thing would
Press Laws.   have been hurried and not satisfactory. But I shall come up and see you next week. Perhaps before then you could let me have in half a dozen lines any points which you would like to discuss.

Kitchener is much less cool-headed than he is supposed to be. He seems to have moments of impulse in which he writes one thing to one person and another to another.

It is fortunate in this case, as he has made it easy for you to refuse a Press Law. The *existing law* is quite strong enough, if properly enforced.

The weather is wet here, but there are more grouse than we expected. Is there any country in the world where a H. of C. not 10 per cent. of which can ride would go on sitting through August to please the shades of hunting squires of the XVIIIth century?

Dispute   [*From the Rt. Hon. R. B. Haldane.*]   WAR OFFICE,
between   AUGUST 23RD.
Defence
Committee   MY DEAR ESHER,
and   The Admiralty are opposing the reference of Balfour's Inva-
Admiralty.   sion paper to the Morley sub-committee on the silly ground

that the question is one for the Navy alone. But I have persuaded C.-B., who was gratified by your letter which he
read to me—to say to the sub-committee the paper must go in
November. An Admiralty representative should of course
join the sub-committee.

Yours ever,

HALDANE.

I go north to-night. When shall we meet? It is easy to
motor for either of us.

[*To M. V. B.*]　　　　　　　THE ROMAN CAMP,
　　　　　　　　　　　　　　　　AUGUST 24TH.

. . . I am furious with the Admiralty because they refuse to
refer Arthur Balfour's letter on *Invasion* to the Defence Committee. I have written to Campbell-Bannerman and Haldane
and this morning I hear that C.-B. decided to overrule the
Admiralty. But I do not trust him. He wobbles. I am writing
to Fisher on the subject, and giving him a bit of my mind.

[*To Sir John Fisher.*]　　　　THE ROMAN CAMP,
　　　　　　　　　　　　　　　　AUGUST 29TH.

What on earth do you mean by maintaining that a paper *Rebuke to Sir*
written by Mr. Balfour for the *Defence Committee* is "purely an *John Fisher.*
Admiralty business"? and talking of an "irresponsible sub-
committee"?

(*a*) Mr. Balfour's original memorandum was a Defence
Committee paper, and his speech in the House of Commons
was *based upon* it, and not upon any Admiralty decision.

(*b*) The Committee for Imperial Defence, of which the *Prime
Minister* is the Chief, and its sub-committees, *if appointed by the*

Prime Minister, are every bit as "responsible" as the Board of Admiralty, of which the *First Sea Lord* is the Chief.

There is no such thing in our Constitution as "responsibility" except the responsibility of a Minister to

(*a*) The Crown.

(*b*) The House of Commons and Parliament.

The responsibility of a *Department* is a delegated responsibility, by the executive government of the day; and the Admiralty is a department like any other.

My contention is that upon such a question as that raised by Mr. Balfour, the opinion of the Defence Committee, empowered to call witnesses, *is* the most careful and satisfactory method devised up to the present.

Upon such a sub-committee the Admiralty would, I assume, be represented; and any documents which the Board of Admiralty prepared would of course form part of the evidence.

The Admiralty will have to recognise, as the War Office has recognised, that the Defence Committee is a new factor in our Administrative system, having its origin in the *proved weakness* from 1899–1901 of the older system, now superseded.

The Prime Minister has now got, in the Defence Committee, a "Department" of his own, working *under him and the Cabinet*, and it is pure anachronism to speak of the Committee for Imperial Defence or its sub-committees as "irresponsible." There are my views for you. All this is *entre nous*. I have said nothing to anyone else.

[*From Sir John Fisher.*]   CARLSBAD,
                                                SEPTEMBER 8TH.

MY BELOVED E.,

I quite expected to get "slated" by you and *I've got it*. Also I fully expected you would have your wicked way and *you've got it*!

                                        Yours ever,
                                        J. A. FISHER.

[*To Sir John Fisher.*]   THE ROMAN CAMP,
OCTOBER 1ST.

I have read your letter to Clarke with much interest. With its *On the* main thesis, I agree, as you well know. But there are two points *Danger of* upon which I differ, and upon which I hold the following views. *National Confidence.*

One is that no state of mind in a nation is more dangerous— or as experience shows, more foolish—than over-confidence.

The other, that under democratic forms of government, no question is "laid aside for ever" or *can* be settled by the *Obiter Dicta* of any Statesman, however powerful and capable. *You* may think your time wasted in discussing what to you is the obvious, with Nicholson and Repington. But you are wrong.

It is the discussions which keep alive popular fears and popular interest, upon which alone rest the Navy Estimates. A nation that believes itself secure, all history teaches is doomed. Anxiety, not a sense of security, lies at the root of readiness for war. Prussia lay fallow after the death and victorious career of Frederick the Great. Then came 1806 and Jena.

Our people thought their Army invincible after Waterloo. Then came 1854 and the Crimea.

An invasion Scare is the mill of God which grinds you out a Navy of Dreadnoughts, and keeps the British people war-like in spirit.

So do not be scornful, and sit not with Pharisees!

Your functions are not only to believe that you possess a Navy strong enough to defeat the Germans at all points, but to justify the belief that is in you, wherever and whenever required!

Tiresome perhaps but part of your day's work. So don't be querulous!

[*To M. V. B.*]   BALMORAL CASTLE,
OCTOBER 4TH.

. . . There is no one very exciting here. Haldane is *most* *Chairmanship* anxious for me to take the Chairmanship of the London Ass. *of the London* What shall I do? *Territorial Association.*

. . . Please *wire* on receipt of this, as the King will press me. I am giving up the Control of Class IV of the Civil List to Frederick, if the King will allow me, as it bores me, and I think the Master of the Household should do that kind of work.

[*From Sir John Fisher.*]   MOLVENO,
                                   OCTOBER 7TH.

MY BELOVED E.,

Just got your letter! It's my unalterable conviction that *whatever* you advise, *whatever* you do, *whatever* you say all is dictated by the sole desire of keeping me in the straight and narrow way (however I have a penchant for the other road!) so you can lecture me, blackguard me, revile me to the utmost, I shall always take it "lying down" from you (but I am going to kick other people's shins if they kick mine!) "*Death found him fighting*" what a glorious epitaph!—one of Nelson's Captains!

                                        Yours ever,
                                             J. F.

[*To the Rt. Hon. J. Morley.*]   THE ROMAN CAMP,
                                         OCTOBER 8TH.

I was sorry to miss you, but I had a meeting here last night, at which I had promised to preside, so I was *obliged* to come away.

It is unlucky that the weather has suddenly turned cold. You will have nice rooms on the ground floor, and you will be left at perfect liberty, so you ought not to be unhappy.

I send you a correspondence to read. It may give you a few moments' amusement. You will see what a desperado is Jackie [Fisher].

I do not deny that he may be right, but he hates anyone else having a word. Nothing can be better for him than a little opposition, and the dire necessity of having to argue his case!

[*To Sir John Fisher.*]   THE ROMAN CAMP,
                                              OCTOBER 15TH.

You are unalterably right, and my sole wish, in writing and   *On the Rôle*
speaking, as I always do, in perfect frankness to you, is to give   *of the Defence*
you glimpses of other sides of questions upon which you feel   *Committee.*
strongly.

If I thought that the Defence Committee could become an
Aulic Council, I should willingly see it perish; but analogies are
dangerous forms of argument—they carry us so much further
than the plain truth.

In War the Defence Committee possesses no functions. It is a
machine intended for purposes of preparation and not of action.
It has no *executive functions*—as I always go on repeating. In
War, its doors should be closed: yes, at the very first shot.

Is it likely that I—at any rate—who have for years thought
daily of war—both by sea and land—should not agree with you
that (once the dogs are unchained) it is a *One Man affair*! Do not
drag in Cabinets. They are the worst form of "Aulic Council"
in war.

It was immensely to the credit of Lord Salisbury's Cabinet
that they never interfered in 1899–1901 except on one occasion,
when they appointed Lord Roberts to supersede Buller. That
was a legitimate form of interference.

But *in Peace* all is changed.

You quote Richards to me; but you say nothing about Lord
Walter Kerr. You naturally believe that Sir John Fisher can rule
the Navy, and secure this country against invasion, without
assistance from outside the walls of the Admiralty.

But are you so confident about Sir John Fisher's successors?
i.e. Lord Charles Beresford and C. Bellairs? Invasion may be a
bogey. Granted. But it is a most useful one, and without it Sir
John Fisher (Captain Fisher as he then was) would never have
got "the truth about the Navy" into the heads of his country-
men.

I claim for the Defence Committee that it is at least as useful

an institution as the *Pall Mall Gazette* of 1882–4. Was it the
Board of Admiralty, or the P.M.G. that got Mr. Gladstone's
Cabinet to increase the Navy?

Your pitfall is that you want to carry your *one man rule* from
War into Peace, and all history shows the fatal track along
which *One Man* has walked to disaster. Over and over again I
have said to you that Sir John Fisher requires the support of
about half a dozen men—no more, but these are indispensable.

Newspapers, politicians, mobs, all these are useful enough.
But the support of the half dozen men or so—who *count*—is
vital. Among these are inevitably certain Members of the
Defence Committee. Sir John Fisher—if he were less obstinate
—would fasten on the Defence Committee as his sheet anchor.
(Forgive the antiquated metaphor.)

I hope to transact with you on these lines; you will back the
Defence Committee for all you are worth in *Peace*, on the condition that its doors are locked, and the key in your pocket, in
War. That is sound sense, and sound policy, consistent with the
best historical experience and tradition. What do you say? But
if you strike this bargain *don't go back upon it*.

[*To Sir Henry Campbell-Bannerman.*]

THE ROMAN CAMP,
OCTOBER 17TH.

*Morley and
the Invasion
Committee.*

Morley has told me of his talk with you about the Defence
Committee. It is a matter of infinite regret—if true—that he
will not preside over the Sub-committee to enquire into the
"Invasion Scare." No one can do it so well, so judicially, and
with sureness that the Report would carry the necessary weight.

So strongly do I feel this, that should he finally decide to refuse, it would be very doubtful whether the enquiry would be
desirable at all, on the lines originally suggested.

The Secretary of State for India, quite apart from his person-

ality, is precisely the Minister who could, with a full knowledge of the call which might be made on our resources in the
event of war, best adjudicate between the rival claims of the
Admiralty and War Office to provide wholly, or in part, for
Home Defence.

But it is Morley's admirable conduct of the two enquiries we
have had, his extraordinary skill in handling the materials as well
as the witnesses and the Committee, which makes it so necessary
that he should preside over an enquiry which differs from those
we have held, inasmuch as it has been provoked by the action of
Lord Roberts and Mr. Balfour, and requires therefore even
greater care in handling than those already undertaken.

Morley, in writing to me, gave me leave to write to you on
this subject. He mentioned other names, but I would rather not
refer to them, as I venture so strongly to urge that you should
exert your influence, which would probably be effective, to
induce him to reconsider his decision.

I have myself recently yielded to pressure from the King and
Haldane to undertake a thankless office, which is odious to me,
so I have less scruples in begging you to use your influence to
get us Morley as Chairman of your Sub-Committee.

[*From Sir H. Campbell-Bannerman.*]

BELMONT CASTLE, SCOTLAND,
OCTOBER 19TH.

MY DEAR ESHER,

When Morley was here he told me that, being overworked in
his proper duties, he wished to be relieved from presiding over
the Committee on Invasion. He urged that the new subject had
nothing directly to do with India, as the two previous subjects
had, and asked that he should be allowed to go.

He is very susceptible as to his health, and therefore I did not
press him.

You however urge considerations of great importance in
favour of his continuing. I see the force of them perfectly and I

am appealing to him accordingly. As I cannot imagine an instrument more effective than your letter to me, I am sending
it to him, marked "private" as it is.

Yours very truly,

H. CAMPBELL-BANNERMAN.

[*To the Rt. Hon. J. Morley.*]   ORCHARD LEA,
OCTOBER 31ST.

I don't know whether you mocked at my enthusiastic letter
to the P.M.—about you—or not, but its enthusiasm was
genuine, as you know right well.

Of course I am deeply sorry, and we shall get on but
indifferently without you, but I *understand*.

Will you let me see you again soon, if possible.

Leaving Scotland I called in my motor at Whittingehame,
where I spent the night. A. J. Balfour talked very freely about
all his troubles and difficulties. It is a bad thing for H.M.G. that
the Opposition are not united and stronger.

I caught cold, and have not moved from here since. By
Monday I hope to be all right. The "book"[1] has gone well.
10,000 copies printed, 7,500 sold to date. In spite of old Moberly
Bell!

[*Journals.*]   WINDSOR CASTLE,
NOVEMBER 16TH.

*Banquet for
the German
Emperor.*

The Banquet last night was said by the Germans to be finer
than any spectacular display of the kind they had ever seen—
finer than the Winter Palace Gala feasts.

It is the juxtaposition of mediævalism and the XXth century;
the Castle itself, the lines of "Beefeaters" in their gorgeous

---

[1] *Queen Victoria's Letters.*

dresses, and the luxury of gold plate, flowers, and diamonds, which impresses them.

Our King makes a better show than William II. He has more graciousness and dignity. William is ungraceful, nervous and plain. There is no "atmosphere" about him. He has not impressed Grey or Morley. Grey had two long talks with him. At the first, he declaimed vehemently against Jews: "There are far too many of them in my country. They want stamping out. If I did not restrain my people there would be a Jew-baiting." On the second occasion, he talked of the Bagdad Railway, but showed no real grasp of facts. "The concession is mine. You must come in on my terms or stay out. We have plenty of money." . . . The Empress is a delightful figure, admirable *tournure*, and well dressed. She had read the Queen's letters with pleasure and intelligence. The Princess of Wales complained that she had been omitted from the list of those to whom the King gave the book.[1] She is the most appreciative member of the Royal Family, and the best equipped with historical knowledge. When I told her so, she blushed like a young girl.

The Queen was laughingly full of the consternation caused in Sweden by page 572, vol. iii. "If the King of Sweden reads it he will die of a fit." [2]

The King told me yesterday that we had been careless about the Neapolitan relationships. Rosebery pointed this out to him. It was not friendly of him to speak to the King before telling me.

I gave the King four packets of letters taken from the box of *Beaconsfield Letters.*

[1] *Queen Victoria's Letters.*

[2] "Viscount Palmerston presents his humble duty to your Majesty and hastens to answer the enquiry contained in Your Majesty's note, which was delivered to him at Southampton. He must, in the first place, explain that much of what was said to him by the King of Sweden and by Prince Oscar was not clearly understood by him. They would both speak English—which they spoke with difficulty and in an indistinct utterance of voice—and he did not like to break the conversation into French, because to have done so would have looked like a condemnation of their English, of any imperfection of which they did not seem to be at all conscious."

Lord Beaconsfield's correspondence, sent down by Lord Rothschild at the request of H.M. They were:

(a) Private letters from the Queen about the Royal Family (*very* private).

(b) Letters from the King to Lord B.

(c) Correspondence relating to Princess Frederick's marriage.

(d) Letters from members of the Royal Family.

The King will destroy them all. The Queen's letters on political subjects go back to Lord Rothschild.

Successor to Campbell-Bannerman.　　I told the King of a long talk I had this morning with Morley about the succession to C.-B., who is very unwell. Morley discussed the rival claims of Grey and Asquith. The Cabinet might, if polled, support Asquith, but he, Morley, would not serve under him. He prefers Grey who has "more character," "less intellect," but "fewer drawbacks." He, Morley, would like the F.O. under Grey. "It is hard work, but I think I could do it." I told Morley that the King would consult no one, but would exercise his prerogative unaided.

Morley is strongly in favour of our continuing the Book [1] till 1880. "It is difficult, but we are all of us engaged in surmounting difficulties. It is dangerous to leave the subsequent volumes to be dealt with by other hands, as it may destroy the conception of the Queen's character now fixed in the public's imagination."

The Times in Difficulties.　　Later I saw Cassel, who is staying here. He has been approached by *The Times*. They require £200,000. 50 per cent. of this to buy out shareholders who are giving trouble, 50 per cent. for new working capital. Lord Rothschild, Cassel, the Duke of Devonshire and Lord Derby have been approached. No dividends have been paid for some years.

Pearsons want the paper, and propose to work it in with the *Standard* and the *Daily Express*. Cassel will not find any money unless the *management* is in new and competent hands. He favours a reduction to a penny. Buckle and Walter to retire.

Our party at home last night. Sir John and Lady French, Maurice and the girls.

[1] *Queen Victoria's Letters.*

Fisher refused absolutely to hear any evidence on the Defence Committee prior to Lord Roberts. He was very vehement last night, though loud in professions of friendship.

Lord Roberts came to see me this morning with his list of witnesses: a very long and rather absurd list, including the Prince of Wales!

. . . I gave the Lord Chancellor my Bill, amending the Official *Official* Secrets Act. It was drawn admirably by Kemp, on a Memoran- *Secrets* *(Amendment)* dum furnished by me together with my speech in the H. of L. *Act—* last session. The Chancellor suggested certain amendments, but he approves the Bill. So does C.-B. [Campbell-Bannerman] and Grey was favourable. It will become a government measure, which is quite right; and if the King keeps his Ministers up to the mark, it should get through early in the session.

NOTE.—The history of this Act, to which occasional allusion is made later on, was as follows:—

In the House of Lords on the 30th July, 1907, Lord Esher asked the Lord Chancellor whether written communications on official business of State between the Sovereign and members of the Cabinet, the Viceroy of India, and British Ambassadors to Foreign Courts, were protected under the Official Secrets Act or were in any way safeguarded against unauthorised publication. The tenour of the speech showed that the question had been brought to his mind by his work on the Queen's papers. The Lord Chancellor replied that very scanty and in fact quite inadequate protection was given in the existing state of the law.

No resolution was passed.

The Lord Chancellor's Official Secrets (Amendment) Act was introduced in the House and read a first time on the 17th March, 1908. In his speech the Lord Chancellor asked that particular attention be given to the Bill before second reading, since the measure was a difficult one to frame. Some particulars of its contents were given in *The Times* on the 23rd March (Political Notes, p. 14, col. 2) from which it is clear that the drawing of the Act must have been commended by Lord Esher for exactitude rather than clarity. It is very far from clear. *—and its*

On the 12th May, 1908, in reply to a question in the House as *Fate.*

to the date of the second reading, the Lord Chancellor said: "I propose to postpone the second reading of the Official Secrets Bill. I met a few days ago a deputation representing the metropolitan press on this subject and they informed me of the anxiety lest this Bill should interfere with the legitimate enterprise and freedom of the Press. His Majesty's Government have no such design, I need hardly say, and if I entered upon detail I could show that a great deal of misunderstanding exists as to the clauses of the Bill and their effects. But it should be clear that anyone in the Press conducting his duties honourably should be quite safe. . . . What I should like is, if possible, that those interested should arrive at a common agreement with the Government. I do not know if it is possible. I hope it may be, and I have thought it better to postpone the second reading in that hope, although, of course, this does not mean that the Government have any intention of dropping the subject" (Hear, hear).

No further official word was ever heard of the Bill, but by the 29th July *The Times*, in its Political Notes, was announcing that the withdrawal could confidently be assumed.

[*Journals.*]

WINDSOR,
NOVEMBER 17TH.

The King and Queen of Spain arrived after Chapel this morning. They motored from London. The King would not go in the "lady's motor," but followed. When they got to the outskirts of Windsor, he stopped the motors and got into the first of the two. She is only 20 but has grown to look very matronly.

There were 24 at luncheon in the State Dining Room. The King and Queen, the Emperor and Empress, the King and Queen of Spain, the King and Queen of Norway and the Queen of Portugal. There were 90 at luncheon in the Waterloo Chamber.

The United States. I had some talk with Herman Hatzfeldt, who is in the Embassy now at Washington. He is interested in the similitudes and contrasts between the branches of the Anglo-Saxon race, which he has now had opportunities of comparing! He finds Washington provincial and America quite outside the European and even the world orbit. This in spite of Japan and the Philippines. He thinks that America has great internal problems ahead. "Like a grown man who wears his Eton jacket, and then wonders that it splits—the American Constitution is an anachronism."

... Morley told me that in the passage of C.-B.'s [Campbell-Bannerman's] speech at the Guild Hall which referred to India, and which Morley drafted, he had used the word "stern," qualifying attitude or language. C.-B. altered no word in the draft except that one, for which he substituted "firm." When asked by J. M. for reasons, he said "Firm is a word of principle. Stern is a word of passion." This discrimination and the literary neatness are strange coming from C.-B.

Morley on Campbell-Bannerman—

The doubt which I suggested to J. M. about the Emperor's character has been germinating in his mind. He watched the Emperor last night, noticed the convulsive movements and *wondered*. His energy is a great factor, said J. M., as it was with Napoleon: the "courage of his desires." J. M. did not remember Byron's *aperçu* of Napoleon's character, but he thinks Byron's the supreme historical mind of the XIXth century.

—and the Kaiser.

[*Journals.*]

WINDSOR,
NOVEMBER 18TH.

The King of Spain is charming, good-humoured, and an intelligent boy. He is quite unchanged in the last two years. When I met him in the quadrangle yesterday, he said "I want to give you something!" and took a Malmaison carnation out of his buttonhole and placed it in mine.

This morning, in pouring rain, we said good-bye to the Germans. The King was in excellent humour and spirits—glad to be emancipated. The Emperor was civil, and his people expressed vivid satisfaction at the good results of their visit.

All except Hasler, the Chief of the Military Cabinet, who is a surly Prussian.

I went up in the King's train, and on to Stafford House. M. S. [Millicent Sutherland] lunched with me, and Maurice came at 2, and joined us. She had been anxious about Geordie, who was ill all last week.

I discussed later, at the War Office, the re-arrangement of the General Staff. It is essential to divide the educational establishments between the Directors of Staff Duties and of Military Training. Staff Officers under the former, Regimental Officers under the latter. There were other momentous points discussed.

The Invasion Enquiry.

I then went on to the Committee for Imperial Defence and talked to Ottley about the Invasion Enquiry. Lord Roberts is to be the first witness, Repington to follow. Ottley demurred to calling Bridge and Custance, because they are hostile to Fisher. But I say it is better to call a difficult witness than to lie under the imputation of burking a full enquiry. After all, we are not putting the Admiralty or anyone on their defence.

We are endeavouring to elicit the truth, and to draw sound inferences from ascertained facts.

[*Journals.*]   WINDSOR,
                                          NOVEMBER 19TH.

. . . In the afternoon I had an hour with Sir William Nicholson on the redistribution of work between the Directors of the General Staff. He was very sensible, and my only point was that these Directors are *Staff* Officers, and should not be allowed to exercise independent authority.

On the Education of Army Officers.

I told him how my talk with Haldane on the education of young officers had started, and explained the conclusion at which we arrived. Haldane had said something to him about it. What happened was this.

Politicians and others who are brought into contact with soldiers, notice the comparatively low standard of knowledge between the heads of the military profession and others: *not* in technique, but in general education. Men of fine natural abilities appear stunted. Exceptions there are, of course; but John Morley and Knollys, for example, are both struck by the comparative inferiority of our best Generals to men of equal standing in other professions, including the Navy. What is the reason for this? In most walks of life, the strenuous years are from 20 to 30. It is during these years that at the Bar, in Medicine, in the Church—whether at Universities or under special professional conditions—young men acquire the habit of application. In the Navy an officer's education is not completed at 20, but he works hard during the subsequent years.

In the Army, a subaltern, during the first years of his life, and generally until he reaches middle-age, limits his efforts to acquiring such technical knowledge of his profession as can be absorbed between 9 and 1 daily. There is no inducement for him to educate himself, or to do any more than he is obliged. Hence, during the ten most crucial years of his life, he acquires no habits of application, but devotes himself to sport, or sinks into indifference and idleness. Later on, when the responsibilities of the higher command begin to inspire prospective terror, an officer tries to make up for lost time, and regrets lost opportunities.

No doubt some young officers read books, and improve their minds, but spasmodically, and without real incentive. A lad will think, for a week, that in order to be a General he must "work at" strategy; so he will take real pains to master a campaign of Napoleon. The following week it strikes him that he cannot command armies until he is 40, and he falls asleep in the anteroom. . . .

[*Journals.*]

WINDSOR,
NOVEMBER 21ST.

. . . Mason—the member for Coventry—has written a new novel, following close on *Running Water*. He was in India last *A. E. Mason on India.*

winter, and this last book[1] sums up—in a clever story—the problem of Indian Government. A subject race can be ruled, always providing it remains subject intellectually and morally, as well as physically. But how can 40 millions of white men rule 200 millions of dark-skinned men, when the latter begin to think and feel after the manner of their rulers. A young Prince is educated at Eton and Oxford. He mixes freely and on equal terms with Englishmen, and above all Englishwomen. Then he returns to India, and finds himself a slave in all but in name, i.e. subject not to a Monarch, but to an "Overseer," without the political rights or social privileges of the dominant "caste" of white men.

[*To the Rt. Hon. J. Morley.*]   ORCHARD LEA,
                                        NOVEMBER 22ND.

I send you a novel. Much of the Indian problem is found in its pages. Unsolved!

[*Journals.*]   ORCHARD LEA,
                      NOVEMBER 24TH.

Gen. French on Invasion. The General [French] came to tea. He met C. Beresford at dinner this week, and heard the whole case against Fisher. Beresford is anxious to be called before the Committee for Imperial Defence. Whether Jackie will cross-examine him is the problem. He may refuse to do so.

The General agreed that the hypothesis—the Bolt out of the Blue—upon which Lord Roberts' case is founded, is absurd. For what is to them a decisive engagement, they could have chosen a better position. Can they, at the eleventh hour, shift their ground? . . .

[1] *The Broken Road.*

[*Journals.*]　　　　　　　　　ORCHARD LEA,
　　　　　　　　　　　　　　NOVEMBER 27TH.

The Defence Committee began the enquiry into Invasion *Lord Roberts* to-day. Lord Roberts' peroration, delivered with rhetorical *on Invasion.* emotion, was very well done. Repington put his case, and the mass of information, and carefully compiled detail, were impressive.

Fisher was full of wrath. I said to him that he was fond of quoting Mahan's famous passage about Nelson's storm-tossed ships, upon which the Grand Army had never looked, which stood between it and the dominion of the world; and it should remind him that the Defence Committee, upon which he wished he had never looked, stood between him and a Royal Commission to enquire into the state of the Navy. . . .

[*Journals.*]　　　　　　　　　ORCHARD LEA,
　　　　　　　　　　　　　　NOVEMBER 28TH.

. . . Fisher tried hard to burke any further enquiry. He wants to reply by means of an Admiralty statement in writing, and to leave the matter there. What has he to conceal? He made a great point of the impossibility of divulging a naval plan of campaign. Everyone agrees to that. But there is no necessity for anything of the kind.

Asquith's mind is a perfect instrument, and he takes points *On Asquith as* after the manner of a trained lawyer. But he lacks some element *a Chairman.* of character; perhaps hardiness. I should say he was a soft man; and his chin *recedes* when an attack is possible or imminent.

[*Journals.*]　　　　　　　　　ORCHARD LEA,
　　　　　　　　　　　　　　NOVEMBER 29TH.

A thick fog this morning, and we were very late. Fife had summoned a meeting of representatives of the County of London at 12. Lucas stated very clearly the nature of the

Associations and their functions. A model scheme was then filled in. The whole thing took about an hour and a half.

There is a story of Henry IV being found by the Spanish Ambassador in the Royal Closet on all fours carrying the Dauphin on his back. Henry IV asked him without rising "M. l'Ambassadeur, have you a family?" and being answered in the affirmative, the King replied, "Then I can finish my tour round the room." This story always reminds me of Lord Salisbury (who had nothing in common with Henry IV except a certain XVIth century *tournure*, and a love of his children) and my first visit to Hatfield, when I found Lord S. seated on the fur rug, and being drawn round the great hall by a band of romping boys.

NOTE.—On the 20th November Mr. Haldane, at Sheffield, made a speech resuming the plans for the Army contained in the Territorial and Reserve Forces Act. It contained nothing in fact to justify Lord Roberts' expectations of a rapprochement between the Government's views and his own. Some phrase concerning Home Defence must have been misinterpreted by Lord Roberts.

This is perhaps a convenient place to remind the younger readers of the point in dispute during these years—the point which was responsible for the Sub-committee on Invasion mentioned in these papers. Lord Roberts' school (nicknamed the Bolt-from-the-Blue School) were not convinced of the impossibility of landing 60,000 men on the English coast without the Admiralty having sufficient warning of the attempt to prevent it. Their estimate of the requirements for Home Defence were based on this possibility. The school led by Sir John Fisher, which was nicknamed the "Blue Water School" and to which the Imperial Defence Committee mostly adhered, maintained that the work of embarkation of 60,000 men in ships necessarily withdrawn from commerce for the purpose was a matter which would take weeks to organise and carry out; and that it could not come as a surprise. Their estimate of the requirements for Home Defence was therefore based on the assumption that no landing could be effected on the English coast except after a naval battle in which the fleet should be crippled.

[*Journals.*]   ORCHARD LEA,
                                                      DECEMBER 1ST.

We rode this morning, Maurice and I, to Windsor. Teddy
and Blanchie [Seymour] came to luncheon, and I then went to
see Lord Roberts.

He was well pleased with the progress of the Committee,
coupled with Lord Haldane's speech, in which a decided impetus is given to the *necessity* of preparation for Home Defence.

Lord Roberts keeps a wonderful openness of mind to new *The Crown*
impressions. This is very rare in men after 70. I have had a *and the Prime*
letter from Francis Knollys, dated 29th November, complaining *Minister.*
of the meagre information sent to the King by C.-B. [Campbell-
Bannerman]. He asks what can be done? and says the King is
being made a fool of, in spite of Ministers professing personal
regard and devotion. Yet it is not easy to advise. C.-B. is too old
not to be incurable. The indolence of age is upon him. I don't
for a moment believe that he wishes to keep the King in the
dark, but he cannot bring himself to write. It thoroughly bores
him. His contempt for precedent, the fact that he had no long
apprenticeship in Government, and the fact that the King never
writes to him direct, all tend to make him perfunctory. The
result is sad, both in the interests of tradition and the Monarchy.
In the interests of both, the practice which prevailed under the
Queen should be adhered to, because the position of the
Sovereign should be altogether independent of the personality
of the Monarch, if the Monarchy is to stand. The King's personality is the great factor nowadays, and this is a stumbling
block in the way of his successors. His office should be as sacred
as his person, and C.-B. is lowering the former.

The remedy is far to seek. No one can, in this instance, say
anything to the P.M. The King *himself,* if he would do it, could
write direct and ask whether certain statements are true, and if
so, why he was not informed before any decision was taken.
He could ask for reasons, and then get supplementary information from Elgin and Haldane. It is a matter of extreme delicacy.

According to the ancient usage which has prevailed for 60 years, the fullest statement, supported by reason, should have been placed before the King, anterior to any final Cabinet decision. As it is, the King will know nothing until the decisions of the Cabinet are irrevocable, because to upset them would mean a change of Ministers. The practice which now governs the relations between the King and his Ministers, if allowed to continue, must inevitably end in weakening the authority of the Crown, and in the lowering of the standard of safety in Foreign and Home Affairs, but especially the former, which the necessity of having to explain the reasons to the Sovereign imposes upon a Government and a Minister.

Knollys is looking at the whole question from the point of view of the King himself, and this is natural; while the national aspect, or constitutional aspect, is what comes (from old habit) especially home to me. Yet our conclusions are the same.

The only solution is to get the King to write or dictate regularly and openly to his Prime Minister. . . .

[*Journals.*]   ORCHARD LEA,
                                                         DECEMBER 3RD.

Cassel told me this morning that the crisis in the U.S. is the most interesting financial situation within his experience. He has no belief in an immediate revival. It will, he thinks, take two years for confidence and trade to revive.

He does not now propose to go to America, but he goes to Egypt for two months, and then to Sweden, and he feels obliged to look personally after his interests.

Cassel on the Kaiser. I asked him his impression of the German Emperor, with whom he had three-quarters of an hour. The Emperor did most of the talking. He showed great powers of memory, but his knowledge is superficial. Directly there was a question of any detail of which Cassel could judge, the Emperor's statements were unreliable. He spoke very little of Baghdad. Cassel thought him above the average in ability, and impatient of difference of opinion. . . . Meanwhile the Germans proceed unabashed on their way, and have their objectives clearly in view. The German prestige, rising steadily on the continent of Europe, is more formidable to us than Napoleon at his *apogee*. Germany is going to contest with us the Command of the Sea, and our commercial position. She wants sea-power, and the carrying trade of the world. Her geographical grievance has got to be redressed. She must obtain command of the Ports at the mouths of the great rivers which tap the middle of Europe. She must get a coastline from which she can draw sailors to man her fleets, naval and mercantile. She must have an outlet for her teeming population, and vast acres where Germans can live, and remain Germans. These acres only exist within the confines of our Empire. Therefore, *l'Ennemi c'est l'Allemagne*.

[*Journals.*]   ORCHARD LEA,
                                              DECEMBER 5TH.

Haldane told me yesterday of a somewhat acrimonious *Isolation of* correspondence with the King on the "Guards Enquiry." The *Haldane.* King evidently was very angry, and talked of expunging his name from the Army List.

Haldane resents the presence in the King's Councils of his military enemies. Critics. He has lost the support of the King because he is too "progressive," and has lost the support of the majority of the Cabinet because he is too "moderate." Liberal Cabinets "wear out" quicker than Conservatives. We should have all sorts of difficulties with any successor to Haldane. His weakness is that in wanting to please everybody, he satisfies no one. His strength is that he anxiously desires to create a perfectly equipped military machine, is exceedingly tenacious of main principles, and believes in *force* as the foundation of Empire.

[*To M. V. B.*]   SANDRINGHAM,
                                             DECEMBER 8TH.

It is quite a comfortable party here. All people we know very
well. We have got delightful rooms. A sitting room, bed
room, two dressing rooms and bathroom. I sat between the
Queen and Princess Victoria last night at dinner; and both were
in excellent spirits.

Cinemato-   We had a cinematograph last night. The first scene was a
graph at   review at Aldershot, and you on Lady Madcap most conspic-
Sandringham. uous! I had long talks with the King about the Navy and Army
and his Ministers—but all this will keep till I see you.

[*Journals.*]   SANDRINGHAM,
                                             DECEMBER 8TH.

We arrived here yesterday. The Harcourts travelled down
with us. The Queen was in the hall, and was full of her birthday
presents, and photographs of her new house at Copenhagen.

I sat between her and Princess Victoria at dinner and afterwards between the Princess of Wales and Gladys [de Grey]
at a "Biograph" performance. Prince Charles and his Queen
were there. He is as gay as ever.

The King talked to me after the performance. . . . I said what
Trouble over I could for H. [Haldane]. To-day I told him that Tweedmouth
the Naval   was on the point of resigning the Admiralty. It is only natural
Estimates.   that the Government should resent putting up the Naval
Estimates by £2,000,000. Their *decision* is that the Estimates
are not to exceed last year's figures.

[*Journals.*]   2, TILNEY STREET,
                                             DECEMBER 11TH.

. . . Yesterday the General [French] and I went down to
Cambridge for the Commemoration at Trinity. We stayed at

the Lodge with the Master, and we both spoke at the dinner in the evening. The General was quite excellent. Modest and soldier-like. He is the junior member of the college.

[*Journals.*]   LONDON,
                                                DECEMBER 13TH.

Yesterday was absorbed by the Defence Committee on "Invasion." We examined Lord Roberts and Repington. Both did well, in spite of an acrimonious examination by Tweedmouth. Good fellow as he is, his capacity is unequal to his task as First Lord. It was almost painful to listen to a series of inconsequential and petulant asides, for they could hardly be dignified by the name of questions.

I was not well in the evening, but sat through the "Gay Gordons" with Zena playing Ella's part. She is superior in some scenes, and weaker in others. It is often her temperament that sweeps out of remembrance the art of Ella. She would make a real actress if opportunity were given her, thanks to her intelligence and charm.

. . . To-day has been full of minor worries. Interviews and meetings of Committees. Everyone has left for Orchard Lea, and I am in London alone. I dine with the General [French].

" To live is to change, and to live nobly is to change often." This from Cardinal Newman. It is, alas, true, for to live nobly is to live a life of sorrows. There is too much bitterness in change. Joy lies in the unchanging hills and after all to suffer a sea-change is death, whether of life or love.

[*Journals.*]   ORCHARD LEA,
                                                DECEMBER 26TH.

. . . Last night I translated three of the Anthologia Lyrics, and transcribed them into the book Margaret gave me.

In the morning I went to see Lord Roberts, who looked active and neat in his country clothes, and who in mind is as young as he was at 30. His keenness and openness to new impressions are extraordinary, when it is remembered that he is 76 years old.

He was so anxious to have *Queen Victoria's Letters* from me (although Lady R. had given him a copy) that I sent him the book this afternoon.

On Christmas Eve the General [French] came down for the afternoon, and enjoyed himself, as he always does when he comes here.

[*Journals.*]   ORCHARD LEA,
                                        DECEMBER 28TH.

Symonds speculates about the "mental labyrinth" in which Michael Angelo gives no clue during those years from 1508–43, when he was painting, at intervals, the Sistine, but *writing* about his farms and domestic worries. Was there a "mental labyrinth"? In Millais, perhaps the greatest English artist since Lawrence, there was none. Does the supreme artist make you think? Is, for example, George Eliot to be compared *as an artist* to C. Brontë?

Wellington's Strategy. F. Knollys is reading some book about the Duke of Wellington's campaigns, and writes to ask whether the Duke was really surprised by Napoleon's crossing the Sambre. By his letters written to Henry Wellesley in May, and from his letter to the Emperor of Austria on June 12th, it is certain that he had "appreciated" Napoleon's plan to be a defensive one. He was convinced that Napoleon would not leave Paris. When, on the 10th, he heard rumours of the concentration of troops on the frontier, he put very little reliance upon it, and he had further convinced himself that if the French took the initiative it would be by Mons, so as to drive him back to Antwerp. It was believed at one time that the Duke had been deceived by Fouché, who had promised to keep him informed; but Lord Ellesmere (very intimate with the Duke) always denied that any trust was put in Fouché.

Napoleon left Paris on the 12th, and was at the head of his army on the 14th. In 1842, the Duke wrote a memo on Clausewitz' book, in which he states that he had rejected all ideas of a French attack. Napoleon himself always said that a defensive plan would have given him the month of August for organising his army, but it would have meant abandoning a great portion of French territory to the enemy; and it was altogether contrary to the whole genius of Napoleon to leave the initiative to the enemy.

The strategy of the Waterloo campaign was perfect. Napoleon struck at the weak and the vital spot. Unfortunately for him he had no Berthier as C. of the S. Soult was inexperienced as a Staff Officer. It was a weak Staff that really lost the campaign. We were, as we have often been, exceedingly lucky. Unfortunately we are too apt to trade upon the smiles of Fortune. The Star of a Nation, as of an individual, may set.

[*Journals.*]

ORCHARD LEA,
JANUARY 2ND, 1908.

... Two nights ago we took Chat [Williamson] to see *As you like it*, and he was moved, as everyone must be, to see it interpreted as it is just now (by Oscar Asche, Lily Brayton and Ainley). The fairy spirit of Shakespeare, and his reading of the child nature which is in all men till they die, come floating through every scene of the lovely play. Laughter and tears alternate, and sweep through the audience. It is not only the soul of the Renaissance, but the spirit of eternal joy, which dominates the Forest of Arden.

French as Inspector-General.

I spent one morning at the Horse Guards, at the General

[French]'s request.[1] He read aloud the Memorandum with which he desires to inaugurate his term of office, and asked for criticisms. Henderson and Maurice were present. The document is quite excellent in conception, and is very well expressed. The General's term of office should leave the Army in a different state from that in which it is found to-day.

[*Journals.*]   ORCHARD LEA,
                                                JANUARY 4TH.

" The Merry Widow."

We went again for the *n*th time to see the *Merry Widow* last night, one of the most charming plays with music that has ever been put on the stage. It has captured Europe, and is now conquering the United States. The King first saw it in Vienna, and urged George Edwardes to produce it, which he did with much misgiving, and against the advice of his friends. He is making a fortune out of it. An unknown, untried young girl, Lily Elsie, plays the principal part in most attractive fashion, and an American comedian, Coyne, has made a great and deserved success.

Precedents on the Death of a Prime Minister.

. . . C.-B. [Campbell-Bannerman] had another heart attack in Paris on his way south. A severe one. It brings the succession nearer. Francis [Knollys] is anxious to discover the views of the Cabinet. This is impossible. The King *must* use his own judgment. Also, should C.-B. die (for I do not believe he will resign)

[1] Sir John French had been appointed Inspector-General of the Forces. On this subject Sir William Nicholson had written three months previously:

                                                WAR OFFICE,
                                                OCTOBER 22ND.

DEAR LORD ESHER,

Many thanks for your letter and for your valuable suggestions in regard to the paper about the duties of the Inspector-General. I have inserted a new paragraph (9) accordingly and enclose a fresh proof. I shall be very glad to see you again on your return to London.

                                    Very sincerely yours,
                                    WILLIAM NICHOLSON.

there should be no delay in sending for a successor. When Lord Palmerston died, the Queen heard of it late at night, and next morning she wrote to Lord J. Russell. This should be followed. I propose to get the 1865 papers to-morrow from Windsor, and to send them to F. K.

[*Journals.*]　　　　　　　　　ORCHARD LEA,
　　　　　　　　　　　　　　　　JANUARY 8TH.

I had a letter from Pearson, asking to see me. He wanted two things. First, that I should arrange the dispute between *The Times* and Murray; second, that I should accept a seat on the new Board of *The Times*.

He explained all the financial arrangements of the paper. . . .

I declined the seat on the Board, but I saw Murray, and he is to let me have soon a form of apology which he will accept.[1]

. . . I went with Murray into the finance of the Queen's *Success of the* correspondence. Up to date the cost of the book has been *Queen's* £7,000, and the receipts £15,000 in round figures. This leaves *Letters.* £8,000 for division. Murray gets one-third, and we get two-thirds. Of the latter A. C. B. [Benson] gets the first £1,200, and the balance he and I will divide.

. . . I have had a lot of trouble with the notices for the meeting of the London Association. I want to ask the B. of London, General Booth, and Bourne (the C. Archbishop), possibly the Chief Rabbi, to come on. It would be rather a coup. . . .

. . . Chat [Williamson] thought well of the family. Of all the people he knows, we only seem not to be sitting among the wreckage.

Happiness seems very evanescent in most relations of life. Perhaps this again is part of the hurry. People have no time to be happy. . . .

---

[1] This dispute was an incident in the "book war" between *The Times* and the publishers, and arose out of the publication of details concerning the production of *Queen Victoria's Letters.*

[*To M. V. B.*]   2, TILNEY ST.,
                                                  JANUARY 10TH.

On   . . . But although you may sometimes feel irritated when I
Friendship. attach what sometimes strikes you as unnecessary importance to
small lapses from the high standard of intimate friendship which
is our standard, I can assure you that it is worth while to be ever
watchful, even at the risk of being over-watchful. Decay is such
an insidious thing. Nothing can be maintained intact or even
healthy, except by continuous care.

. . . I am feeling ill to-night, with a splitting headache, so that
you must overlook any weakness of expression.

. . . As you know, introspection is a horrid pursuit and a
terrible curse. But you may perhaps sometimes have wondered
whether the too objective mind which sees molehills as mountains is not equally tiresome. The answer is, and it is a comfort
to think of it, that molehills are sometimes as serious and sometimes as fatal as mountains. I admit to having a terrible eye for
a molehill, but then it has helped me to steer a fairly safe course
along with the one or two people who count anything in the
world at all for me.

. . . I like the notion of your going 500 miles to see Zena. It
is right and worth while. But it is equally worth while to
pick up her handkerchief when she drops it, or to step yourself
upon the stone which might bruise her foot.

The world is stupendous and lies all about us, the universe with
its million worlds is whirling round us. The past and all history
are mighty things, and the future is mightier still. But *joy*,
which is the crown of life, does not lie in these ways, nor among
these gigantic forces. It is not in the storm nor in the tempest,
but joy is the still small voice of love and friendship. If you listen
for it, or wait for it too ardently, you never hear it, but it comes
to those who are the elect.

. . . These are the meditations of an invalid, who for a few
hours has been left on the roadside. They are written for you
to read in the train.

[*To M. V. B.*]　　　　　　　　　　ORCHARD LEA,
　　　　　　　　　　　　　　　　　JANUARY 11TH.

. . . White frost everywhere. They have been skating all the afternoon. I have not moved out. But to-morrow morning I have summoned all the Military Knights to the Armoury and am going to give them a few very strong words. Some of them have been using *Truth* for the purpose of attacking old Courtney. So a little discipline will do them good.

[*Journals.*]　　　　　　　　　　　　　2, TILNEY ST.

. . . To-night dined with John Morley at the Ritz. We were alone. He praised Minto as a *gentleman*. Not *clever*, but the highest type of the old governing class. Lord K.'s [Kitchener's] strength he recognises, but thinks him a most *uninteresting* type. He says Sir George Clarke's letters to him are quite admirable.

Some Judgments by Morley.

We discussed the future C.-in-C., and he recognises Ian Hamilton's Gaelic charm: what an asset it is with Natives and how atmospherically attractive it makes him compared with Duff or Barrow—the ordinary "Linesman."

He told me a good thing of Lord Northcliffe. Someone, Donald of the *Daily Chronicle* I think, was saying how he proposed to run his paper on *sound* lines, no modern journalism, but good solid stuff, etc.

"Yes," said N., "and, my dear fellow, why not print it in Gothic type?"

J. M. told me that he had left *me* his literary executor!

[*Journals.*]　　　　　　　　　　　　　LONDON,
　　　　　　　　　　　　　　　　　JANUARY 17TH.

I have held the first meeting of the London County Association, and a further meeting of the Provisional Cttee. I spoke for

about an hour. Everyone seemed satisfied. Yesterday I saw
Haldane and Fisher, and both told me their version of the
Admiralty troubles. To-day I took Pearson to see Jackie
[Fisher], who talked to him on end for 1¾ hours. It was a lecture
on Naval peace strategy. Quite admirable. It is important that
The Times, under new management, should take the right line
about naval affairs. Why should any patriot wish to upset
Jackie? Only the old-fashioned fogey, the personal foe, or the
political wrecker would want to destroy him.[1]

[*From Sir John Fisher.*]   ADMIRALTY,
                                      JANUARY 18TH, *very early.*

MY BELOVED E.,
  My waking thought is I have not sufficiently expressed my
gratitude to you and *especially for your firm language to Murray*
as thereby I think you have (via him) averted a cataclysm. . . .
                                      Yours till a cinder,
                                                  J. F.

[*Journals.*]   WINDSOR CASTLE,
                                            JANUARY 23RD.

  The King arrived last night. To-day, feeling sure that she
would not be asked here, Nellie went to Birmingham with
Maurice and Syv, to see Phyllis Dare in *Cinderella*. Just after
starting she was asked here to dinner. We caught her by tele-
phone at Birmingham station. Dense fog in London and here.
However, by strenuous exertion she got back. Dressed at the
White Hart, and we dined here. It was an excitement for the
King and Queen and well worth the trouble. Excuses are so ill
received by Sovereigns.
  The French and Russian Ambassadors and the Archbishop
Cantuar were the guests. The King in excellent humour. After

[1] In the event, *The Times* did not pass into Pearson's hands.

dinner I sat and talked old family affairs to the Princess of Wales. She is worried about the bad spelling of her eldest boy David, but he is wonderfully bright otherwise, so it is not very important. The Queen was in one of her frolicsome humours and looked remarkably well. She thinks the Princess of Wales so much improved in looks, which is true. I wore my French Order,[1] by the King's direction, as the Ambassador was present.

Yesterday we dined at Cumberland Lodge. I took in Princess Christian. She told me that her mother, until she came to the Throne, never walked downstairs without somebody holding her hand ; so nervous were they of an accident befalling the Heiress to the Crown.

Prince Christian told Nellie that in the early forties he sat next the Empress Marie Louise at dinner. This carries one back. She died in 1843.

[*To the Rt. Hon. J. Morley.*]   WINDSOR,
JANUARY 25TH.

I must begin by saying that words failed me when you told me of your intention, should I survive you. It was more than any "Order of Merit" to me.

. . . You spoke about a *possible* vacancy on your Council. *On Maj.-Gen.* The only Anglo-Indian who, of late years, has impressed *Sir S.* outsiders as one of the "old breed" is Major-General Sir S. *Beatson.* Beatson.

Of his intellectual force I know little, but of his profound knowledge of India, of Native Princes, of Native troops, I have heard always much. You probably know him because he is in England.

Probyn says that he is in greater sympathy with the Native Officers and soldiers than anyone he knows of just now; for I asked Probyn to confirm what I had always heard of Beatson. He is worth your thought.

[1] The Legion of Honour.

A misfortune has happened here. C.-B.—who was to have come to-day—is laid up with a cold. A pity, as his presence here would have dispersed some clouds which have gathered —not unnaturally—these last few days.

Did you adhere to your intention of sending the P. of Wales occasional Indianpapers? He is so much and so wisely interested in Indian affairs.

[*Journals.*]   ORCHARD LEA,
                                                  JANUARY 27TH.

Progress of the Invasion Enquiry.   . . . This afternoon I went up to the Defence Committee, on "Invasion." Asquith allowed an excess of discursive talk, and the result was 1½ hours of boredom. Repington was very good, but in the last quarter of an hour (which was excellent) he was put into considerable difficulty.

J. Fisher spoke enthusiastically of my letter to the Maritime League. I think he is quite happy now about his position.

[*Journals.*]   ORCHARD LEA,
                                                  JANUARY 28TH.

On Gen. Smith-Dorrien.   The King returned to London this afternoon. I dined with the General [French] at the Carlton, Smith-Dorrien and Maurice. The dinner was given in order to see whether Smith-Dorrien had changed and weakened, as some maintain. He spoke very well on Indian subjects, and seemed a very reasonable, clear-headed man. There are no signs in his manner or appearance of the violent temper he is credited with, and his voice is very pleasant.

I saw L. Harcourt this evening. *He* has no doubt that Asquith, and only Asquith, is a possible successor to C.-B. Grey, according to him, has little influence in the H. of C., and none in the country. Loulou is a reliable judge of public form.

[*Journals.*]
2, TILNEY ST.,
JANUARY 30TH.

Went early to Buckingham Palace this morning. Haldane came to see the King, and I was anxious to get him to be *firm* on the *working* of the T.A. Act. He is pressed on all sides to give away the principles of the Act.

A. Balfour, who had asked me to call on him, was suddenly laid up with influenza.

Spender called. He has been invited to edit the *Tribune*. This had to be communicated to Pearson, for if *The Times* want him they must hurry.

A "Red Cross" meeting at 2.30, and then a long King Edward VII Hospital meeting, both at St. James'.

In the evening we went to the delightful *Merry Widow* for the 20th time!

[*Journals.*]
LONDON,
JANUARY 31ST.

A very long meeting, it lasted 4 hours, of the General Purposes Committee of the London Association. What a tie it is! and makes one marvel that so many people give their time for nothing to such things.

What is the value in cash to the State of unremunerated labour in the public interest? Went home late.

[*Journals.*]
LONDON,
FEBRUARY 2ND.

Heard by telephone from the Castle of the terrible tragedy at Lisbon. The excellent brave King and that nice amiable Duke of Braganza—such a jolly boy—whom I took over the castle a year or so since.

Death of the King of Portugal.

The King had much in common with our King, who will be much distressed. No details yet.

[*Journals.*]   LONDON,
                                                   FEBRUARY 4TH.

. . . Called on Arthur Balfour and was with him ¾ of an hour. He is recovering. We talked almost exclusively of Defence matters. He is strongly in favour of Fisher and against C. Beresford.

Francis Knollys told me that the King found C.-B. [Campbell-Bannerman] very languid and feeble. He could not bring his mind to bear upon any large question of policy.

Asquith meanwhile grows in stature from the mere fact of leading the H. of C. as Deputy.

[*Journals.*]   LONDON,
                                                   FEBRUARY 7TH.

A long Territorial Army Committee, which lasted four hours. Dined this evening with Fisher and Knollys at the Carlton—the "Triumvirate," according to the annexed article from the *National Review*. Some people substitute Soveral for Knollys.

Crisis over the Naval Estimates. The Ministers thought they would be beaten on an amendment to the address moved from the Radical Benches, in favour of reduced estimates.[1] Hence the following:—

I had arranged with Haldane that Fisher was to call on him last Tuesday at 7. There was a little "feeling" between the two men which it was desirable to remove. Here is Fisher's story. At 6 p.m. on Tuesday he received a note from L. Harcourt:

[1] The amendment was postponed by agreement, and taken as a preliminary to the debates on the Army and Navy estimates. On that date the resolution was rejected by 320 to 73.

"My dear Admiral,

"Could you come at once to my room at the H. of C. as I wish to see you on very grave and urgent business. Please come by the Lady's Entrance."

This presumably to avoid observation. When Fisher arrived, Harcourt began by saying that they had known each other a long time, and therefore he proposed to speak very straight. A most curious crisis had arisen, and a special Cabinet had been held that afternoon at 2, to which Whitely, the Chief Whip of the Party, had been summoned. A careful examination of figures had been made, and the conclusion arrived at was that upon Macdonald's motion the Government would find themselves in a minority of 100. Although Arthur Balfour, who had gone to Brighton, had asked his party to vote for the Government, the Unionists had declined, and determined to support the amendment. The Cabinet, therefore, had unanimously determined to reduce the Navy Estimates by £1,340,000, so as to bring them below last year's figures; and a Committee of three—Harcourt, Lloyd George, and McKenna—had been appointed to carry this resolution into effect.

Fisher remarked that the Navy Estimates had already been approved by the Cabinet, and signed. It was by a mere accident that they were not laid now on the table of the House. He added that the Board of Admiralty had gone into them with the greatest care; that they had been reduced by £750,000 and were at their irreducible minimum.

Harcourt then adopted a tone which was arrogant, and almost uncivil, intimating plainly that either five Members of the Cabinet, or the Board of Admiralty, would have to resign.

Fisher replied that under such circumstances the Government might find it difficult to replace the Board of Admiralty, to which Harcourt at once retorted that Beresford was ready to accept the office of First Sea Lord.

Fisher then took up his hat and said, "Well, you seem to have settled it all, and as I can do no good here, I had better return to the Admiralty." And then he left.

—and Lloyd
George—

When he got back to the Admiralty, he found a letter from
Winston Churchill asking him to dine with him and Lloyd
George at the club, as they wished to see him on urgent business.
After dinner, when the servants had left the private room in
which they had dined, Lloyd George began in much the same
strain as Harcourt, only in a more conciliatory style. He urged
Fisher to help them, saying that the Estimates must be reduced,
or some change would be inevitable at the Admiralty or in the
Ministry. Fisher said, "Well, there is a way. Reduce the Estimates by deducting the sum you name, and present them to
Parliament with a note to the effect that the Board of Admiralty
declared the Navy to require the larger sum, but they consented
to accept the smaller on the understanding that the efficiency of
the Fleets should be maintained and that any deficit would be
met by supplementary estimates." Churchill laughed at this,
evidently enjoying the quandary of his colleague.

Lloyd George then said, corroborating Harcourt, that
Beresford was ready to accept the post of Sea Lord, and was
prepared to reduce the estimates by £2,000,000.

Fisher replied that they had better appoint him, but that he
would "sell" them in three months, and he again asserted that
the irreducible minimum had been reached.

—and
Lambert—

Late that night, after he had gone to bed, Fisher was called up
on the telephone from the House of Commons. Lambert
apologised for waking him, but told him that he thought it
necessary to inform him that there was a serious crisis over the
Naval Estimates, that five Cabinet Ministers would resign if the
Estimates were not reduced, and that Beresford was prepared to
succeed Fisher, if the Board of Admiralty retired or were dismissed. To Lambert's astonishment Fisher said he was informed
already of these facts, and he went back to bed.

At 9 next morning, he got a note from Tweedmouth, who
now came on the scene for the first time, saying that a special
Board was called for mid-day.

About 10, Lloyd George's private secretary came over and
told Fisher that the P. of the Bd. of Trade wished to see him

privately, and did not wish to come to the Admiralty. Therefore, refusing to meet in a hole or corner, Fisher went over to
the Board of Trade.

Lloyd George returned to the charge, very civilly, but
firmly, urging Fisher to agree to a reduction *this* year, and
adding that he might have any sum he pleased *next* year.

—and Lloyd George again—

Fisher then asked if he would come over and explain the
situation to the Board of Admiralty, to which Lloyd George
consented.

Fisher then saw Tweedmouth and his colleagues. He urged
upon them the propriety, indeed the necessity, of not appearing
to force the hand of the Government by a threat of resignation,
stating that, in his view, they should inform the Government
that if the Estimates were arbitrarily cut down, it would be contrary to the advice of the Board of Admiralty. He told his
colleagues that, in consequence of the Board having, at his
instance, already agreed to cut down the Estimates by £750,000,
he felt bound to act with them loyally, and to abide by any decision they might now take; but that his advice was as stated.

—and the Admiralty—

Lloyd George attended the meeting of the Board. The votes
were carefully gone through, and the Board decided once more
to maintain their attitude, and to adhere to the figure which
they considered the irreducible minimum.

Fisher believes that he ascertained from Lloyd George that the
five Members of the Cabinet who were prepared to retire if the
Estimates were not cut down were himself, Harcourt, McKenna,
Burns and Crewe. (The last name does not appear likely.)

Fisher never mentioned to Lloyd George or to Churchill his
interview with Harcourt, nor does he believe that these members of the Cabinet Committee took each other into confidence.

The next move in this remarkable game is most curious.

F. asked Robertson (Sec. of the Admiralty), a great friend of
the Prime Minister, to go and see him (P.M.), and to explain
the situation, and, if necessary, to go through every vote showing how impossible it is to cut the Estimates any finer. C.-B.
listened to all he had to say, and then sent for the Ch. of the Ex.

—and the Prime Minister.

He very shortly gave Asquith the gist of what Robertson had said, in Robertson's presence, and added, "I have decided that the Naval Estimates are to stand. Haldane will take £300,000 off his instead. Nothing need be said at present to any other member of the Cabinet." And there the matter rests. The Cabinet Committee are to pursue their labours. Meanwhile the Prime Minister seems to have settled the question, and to be ready to take the responsibility and to stand the shot.

Altogether a most curious episode.

Fisher was in great spirits at dinner, and we did not leave the Carlton, where we dined, till midnight.

Francis told me that the King and the Prince of Wales both thought I was right to agree to the publication of my letter to the Maritime League.

[*Journals.*]   LONDON,
                                        FEBRUARY 11TH.

Morley's Future.

. . . John Morley asked me to luncheon to-day. He made it quite clear to me that he would not accept office under Asquith, and remain in the H. of C. He would *like* to be Prime Minister himself. Failing that he would like to go to the House of Lords. My belief is that he will go to the House of Lords *before* the place of C.-B. is vacant. Now he is embarking on a frontier expedition which, like all those *ignes fatui*, may lead him far afield.

[*Journals.*]   LONDON,
                                        FEBRUARY 14TH.

Rosebery on the Government.

. . . After taking Jack Durham to see Haldane, and Murray, about his County Force, I called on Rosebery. We had a good talk for an hour, the first for many a long day. He said that in Morley's *Life of Gladstone* there was only one good letter, and that was written to Lord Beaconsfield. He never sees Grey! And they were very fast friends. He pities anyone who has to succeed C.-B. and take on a Cabinet which he did not form. It is the worst fate which can befall a Minister. He spoke feelingly from bitter experience.

Saw Miss Ashwell in a very original, fresh kind of play, about the young work-girls of London.[1]

To-day I lunched with A. E. Mason. He wishes to speak on the Navy. His first play is in rehearsal.[2] He thinks it is a harder task to write a book than a play—a bigger theme.

Barrie has made, perhaps, more money than any literary man ever did before. The *Little Minister* has been running four years, and there are four companies still playing it nightly in America. He has made £80,000 by that play alone.

This morning I breakfasted with Alfred Rothschild. This afternoon, a meeting of the '51 Commissioners, to discuss arrangements about the Albert Hall—a ponderous failure.

[*Journals.*]
LONDON,
FEBRUARY 19TH.

At the Levée to-day, Fisher came up in rather an excited manner, and said, "You have had the greatest compliment paid you that was ever paid a man. The German Emperor has written to Tweedmouth nine pages in his own hand, full of abuse of you; all based on your letter to the Maritime League."[3]

The Kaiser's Letter to Lord Tweedmouth

Tweedmouth afterwards told me its contents. There is a good

[1] *Diana of Dobson's,* by Cicely Hamilton.
[2] *Margery Strode*, played by Cyril Maude.
[3] In his letter to Lord Tweedmouth, the Kaiser wrote:—

BERLIN,
FEBRUARY 14TH.

. . . In the letter Lord Esher caused to be published a short time ago he wrote "that every German from the Emperor down to the last man wished for the downfall of Sir John Fisher." Now I am at a loss to tell whether the supervision of the foundations and drains of the Royal Palaces is apt to qualify somebody for the judgment of Naval Affairs in general. As far as regards German affairs Naval the phrase is a piece of unmitigated balderdash, and has created immense merriment in the circles of those "who know" here. But I venture to think that such things ought not to be written by people who are highly placed, as they are liable to hurt public feelings over here. . . .

deal of flattery of the Government, abuse of Fisher and me. "Esher, who was appointed to look after the drains of the Palaces, what does he mean by referring to me, . . ." is the *bonne bouche* of the effusion.

It is a most extraordinary proceeding for the Emperor to write to one of the King's Ministers at all. As the Prince of Wales said to me this evening, "What would *he* say if the King wrote to Von Tirpitz a letter of this kind!"

—Annoys the King.

The King is very much disturbed. He is angry with the German Emperor, and annoyed with Fisher and me! It is very natural. He hates a *fuss*, and like all Monarchs, his perspective is disarranged by trifles which are tiresome. He wrote me a letter of *regret* to-night, that I had used imprudent expressions. This, however, will blow over. The fact will remain that the Emperor has once more intervened in the domestic affairs of another Power. He is trying to treat Fisher as he did Delcassé.

Grey and Tweedmouth were sent for by the King to-night, to compose a reply.

Tweedmouth, at first, seemed rather flattered at getting a letter from so Imperial a source, and was inclined to treat it as a personal compliment. He talked about it everywhere. He has been disabused since.

Francis K. [Knollys] thought the Emperor's letter undignified. There we may leave it. Fisher was enchanted.

[*To H.M. the King.*]   2, TILNEY ST.,
                                          FEBRUARY 19TH.

Viscount Esher, with humble duty, must venture to write to Your Majesty a few lines in reference to certain matters about which Lord Tweedmouth spoke to him at the Levée this morning.

Viscount Esher is sure that Your Majesty will believe that when he gave permission to the Navy League to publish a certain letter, which had been written in reply to a request that he should join a body of persons whose primary object was to remove one of Your Majesty's faithful servants, the First Sea Lord, Viscount Esher was actuated solely by dutiful regard for Your Majesty's service and the country.

The letter was written *not* with a view to publication and for that reason may possibly have contained one expression which might have been differently worded, although Viscount Esher hopes that Your Majesty will believe that the expression in question contains nothing which, directly or by implication, could give any reasonable cause of offence.

When the Navy League asked permission to make use of the letter, Viscount Esher replied in a very few words which Your Majesty has seen, and he had no idea in what form use would be made of it, whether by communication with the Press, or by inclusion in some circular or pamphlet. He was, and is, deeply impressed by the crisis in the affairs of the Navy, owing to the strenuous efforts being made in some quarters to minimise the importance of the German Building programme, and the strong parliamentary pressure being brought to bear upon the House of Commons to insist upon a reduction in naval Estimates.

As a dutiful servant of Your Majesty—and if he may humbly say so—as a member of the Upper House of Parliament, he could not reconcile it with his duty and conscience to refuse permission to make use of an expression of opinion which could, however feebly, strengthen the hands of those who were fighting for the Navy at the present time. Should Your Majesty think that he made a mistake in judgment, he very much regrets the action which he took, and he hopes that Your Majesty will forgive him.

[*From H.M. the King.*]   BUCKINGHAM PALACE,
FEBRUARY 19TH.

The King thanks Lord Esher for his letter of the 19th instant which he received this evening.

He deeply regrets the publication of the letter which Lord

Esher wrote to the Navy League, as the remarks about Sir John Fisher were very unfortunate, and though Lord Esher wished to do Sir John a good turn, the King is afraid the reverse is the result.

The allusion also to the German Emperor was likewise very unfortunate, and has, the King knows, caused him great annoyance. The next time the King sees Lord Esher, he will point out to him how injudicious were the remarks which he made as to Sir John Fisher having told him of the future plans of Sir John when the latter was still Commander-in-Chief at Portsmouth.

EDWARD R. AND I.

[*From Sir John Fisher.*]   ADMIRALTY,
FEBRUARY 20TH.

MY BELOVED FRIEND,

Fisher and the Kaiser's Letter.

I had a good long time with the King. He began in violence against you but I pointed out to him that *I* was the culprit, not *you* because *I* it was who showed you all the plans etc., at Portsmouth, and also it was out of *pure friendship* to *me* that you wrote the letter and the end bit about the German Emperor etc., as true as gospel! so it was rather lovely *and he is a sweet*! He said "Well what right had you to make plans at Portsmouth when you didn't know whether you were going to be First Sea Lord?" I think if you *don't* see him for a few days it will be as ever you were. I said "Well Sir it *was* a good letter wasn't it?" He said "Of course it was because he is a most able man!"

That dear blessed Francis is a real trump in standing by his friends! No time for more. Yours ever, J. F.

I really do feel guilty as I told the King in being the real culprit.

[*Journals.*]   LONDON,
FEBRUARY 20TH.

The King has been very much "fussed," and his Ministers have not helped him much. H.M. was so angry that he wished to write very tartly to the German Emperor. However, he has been calmed down, and will reply shortly and leave the answer to be sent by Tweedmouth and Grey. Of course the King visited his wrath upon me and Jackie [Fisher]. This was only natural. But he will get over it all right.

I saw J. Burns at the "Court" to-night. He is a strong *John Burns on* Fisherite, and would dearly love to be at the Admiralty; for *the Admiralty.* which, by the way, he is quite unfitted. He, however, said truly that he would soon have Beresford under control. " I should send for him, and say 'Look here, Charlie, are you a politician or a sailor? If the latter, then the Quarterdeck and silence. If the former, Westminster and gas.' "

Jackie had a long talk with the King, who was very violent at first, but has calmed down now. Jackie took all the blame upon himself. He *would*! Francis [Knollys] has been like a trump, as he always is.

*

[*To the Secretary of the War Office.*]   2, TILNEY ST.,
                                                FEBRUARY 22ND.

I have the honour to acknowledge the receipt of your letter of the 21st February 1908 a/Ger. num: 419/(T.F.) conveying the invitation of the Army Council and requesting me to serve on the proposed Territorial Force Council.

I beg to state that I shall have much pleasure in placing myself at the disposal of the Council for the purpose of deliberations in regard to the Territorial Force as a whole.

[*Journals.*]   LONDON,
                                                FEBRUARY 26TH.

I called on Arthur Balfour this morning. He was in bed, a *Balfour on* small brass bed, with an electric light over his head. He *Questions of* generally remains there till about mid-day.   *the Day.*

He was rather absorbed by the Education Bill, and, curiously enough, it is a subject which animates him. His own views are not those of Hugh Cecil and the extreme dogmatists, but he is most strongly opposed to the nonconformist bigotry, as he considers it.

We talked a great deal about National Defence, and his sanity is as great as ever. He does not think C.-B. can hold on much longer. A mummified Prime Minister, in these days, he thinks an impossibility. The view was corroborated by Morley, with whom I lunched.

Morley's
Opinions.

He feels sure that before Whitsuntide C.-B. will have retired. For a month he has not seen a colleague or a paper. Asquith he looks upon now as inevitable; but *he* will not remain under him in the H. of C. He will go to the Upper House.

We talked literature and politics for an hour. He told me that Trevelyan, in a speech, once alluded to the "days when I was young and poor." Upon this J. M. remarked, "He never was poor, and he always will be young." What truth about this man of great literary gifts, but unrecognised ability.

Dined with the Goldsmiths. The P. of W. very friendly and affectionate.

[*Journals.*]

LONDON,
MARCH 3RD.

We had a Defence Committee on "Invasion." Asquith has greatly improved, and has got a grasp of the whole question now. Lord Roberts, who was present as a witness, for the first time showed a little failure.

This afternoon I was sent for by the King. He came into his sitting room immediately after luncheon, and made me sit down near the fire. He showed me photographs of the devastation at

The King on
Asquith—

Sandringham, and was quite his old self.[1] He told me of his

---

[1] In consequence of a gale in which many trees were blown down and some damage done to the house, considerable alterations were planned at Sandringham during the spring of this year.

arrangements with Asquith, and, although he respects the P.M. designate, I think he doubts whether his relation with him will be as pleasant as with C.-B.—for whom he has quite a warm feeling.

Then he alluded—but quite kindly—to the German Emperor episode. He told me that the Emperor had spoken very strongly about me to Lascelles, and said my letter was impertinent. The King only laughed at this, and added, "When next the German Emperor comes over, we must hide you away, or send you on a bicycle tour." *—and on the Kaiser's Letter.*

When I said good-bye, I kissed his hand. He was very kind and gracious all through.

This evening I presided over a dinner for the London Orphan Asylum, and talked about "Individualism."

[*Journals.*]　　　　　　　　　　LONDON,
　　　　　　　　　　　　　　　　MARCH 5TH.

I called to-day on Sir Theodore Martin, who has a charming house full of nice, old-fashioned things, in Onslow Gardens. His room on the ground floor is most comfortable. There he was, perfectly hale and hearty, with masses of white hair and beard, a fresh complexion, and not a trace of deafness. 92 years old. We talked for an hour, of the Queen's letters, every word of which he has read. He is particularly pleased with the corroboration which they give to his *Life of the Prince Consort*. He was accused, he said, of having played the courtier and flatterer. The letters give the direct lie to any such imputation. *Sir Theodore Martin on the Queen's Letters.*

He first saw the Queen six years after the death of the Prince. She was full of impulse and keenness, but her judgment and knowledge were much inferior to what they afterwards became. Still, he thinks that publication of correspondence during years subsequent to the death of the Prince is bound to modify the estimate at present current about the Queen's ability, so powerful was the influence and so great were the qualities of mind which the Prince displayed.

The Queen's style, though slovenly, he thinks excellent in one particular, i.e., when she delineated the character of persons whom she met. Then, he does not think it could be improved upon, so graphic and simple was it; and there is truth in this. "She was not a woman of great mental capacity, but full of sound sense and right instincts."

The Prince died of over-work, of that he is convinced. "He put into 40 years the work of 80, and had he lived, would have been an invalid."

In 1870 the Queen said to Martin, "It was merciful the beloved Prince was taken, for had he lived I could never have prevented him from joining the German Armies."

He thought the German Empress—judging from her letters and memoranda—very intelligent in her early youth, but he never knew her well enough in later years to feel sure that she fulfilled her youthful promise. Prince Leopold had no real capacity. The excellent addresses he delivered, in the style of his father's, were written by Dean Stanley. The King, he feels sure, was far the ablest of the family. "Not a reading man, but full of natural ability, and with a sound head and warm heart."

The old man actually *ran* before me upstairs, to show me a fine bust of his wife (Helen Faucet) by Foley R.A. "Not a bit like an actress, was she? She was an *Artist*, and not an actress."

Altogether a very agreeable hour.

The Situation in Portugal. In the afternoon a long meeting of the Committee of the London Association at St. James' Palace. I dined with Francis [Knollys] at Brooks's, Fisher and Soveral and John Fortescue. We had a most pleasant dinner. Soveral is very low about his country, and there is a question of the Fleet going to the Tagus, in order to give support to the Royal House. It would, I think, be a very dangerous proceeding. Nothing in the way of outside support can maintain a dynasty if a nation is determined to change their rulers. How often has the thing been tried—and failed. Not only in our case, but in so many others.

[*Journals.*]　　　　　　　　　　　　　　LONDON,
　　　　　　　　　　　　　　　　　　　MARCH 7TH.

All the papers are vapouring about the Emperor's letter. In *The Kaiser's*
Germany, where they can never have heard of his escapade, *Letter*
they are discreetly amazed. All the Press sleuth hounds are in *Becomes*
full cry. *Public—*

Repington will have ruined his chances of keeping in touch
with Government Officials after this business. From his standpoint he will find that his game was not worth the candle.[1]

Pestered by reporters to-day. I would not see them. Maurice
did the interviewing. Fisher spoke to me on the telephone.
He says the indiscretion was put down by Tweedmouth to *me*!
Kind of him!

The Emperor has, I hear, telegraphed to Bülow, putting the
whole responsibility upon Tweedmouth! This is the best
course he could take, and there is a certain truth in it.

[*To M. V. B.*]　　　　　　　　　　2, TILNEY STREET,
　　　　　　　　　　　　　　　　　　　MARCH 9TH.

The fuss goes on. Did you ever see such headlines as those in *—and*
the *Daily Telegraph*. They are being kept for me by Stanley. *Excites the*
Jackie [Fisher] says that Tweedmouth is frightfully excited *Press.*

---

[1] The letter of the Kaiser to Lord Tweedmouth was a personal letter, and
with the agreement of the Foreign Secretary it was treated as a private letter.
It became to some extent public through a communication to *The Times*
from its military correspondent, who described the letter as "amounting to
an attempt to influence, in German interests, the Minister responsible for our
Navy Estimates." He suggested (and *The Times* leader supported the suggestion) that the letter and its reply should be immediately laid before Parliament. On March 9th, Lord Tweedmouth in the Lords and Mr. Asquith in
the Commons refused the publication of private correspondence. In the
Lords the Marquess of Lansdowne said that the Opposition would not press
for publication, but that the privacy of such correspondence ought to be
better maintained; whereas in this case it had resembled the "private view"
of the Academy.

about it all—and probably will make a fool of himself. If I were he, nothing would induce me to stand in a white sheet. I should defend every step, and insist that I had done exactly what was right, including the gossip!

"What would have been said if I had kept the correspondence secret whereas I never made any secret of the matter" etc. But I feel sure he will not take that line. I am not going to the House of Lords, nor shall I say anything to anybody on the subject. To-night I dine with Jackie *tête-à-tête* at the Carlton. I send you a letter from Francis [Knollys] which gives you *his* idea of the whole thing, from the point of view of the quiet seclusion of S. Devon.

. . . The whole of this bother shows how vital it is that while there is yet time we should put our naval and military forces in perfect order. Nothing can prevent a struggle for life except the certainty that attack would fail. I am sure that the Germans are very patient and very bold. The sort of supremacy which Napoleon dreamed of for France, and nearly achieved—commercial as well as political—they desire as well as the former. And all their efforts are directed to that. The great obstacle is England. They do not want to conquer but to crush.

[*Journals.*]   LONDON,
                                                            MARCH 9TH.

*German
Foreign
Policy.*

. . . Fisher told me of a secret treaty—all the details of which have been sent to him—between Germany and Sweden, for the partition of Denmark. Germany to have the main land; Sweden the islands. Germany would thus control the Belts and Baltic. There would be no appeal, except to deepen the "Sounds" at the cost of a million pounds.

If this were done, it would free the Baltic. But who would spend the money? It is worth our while to find it.

Germany—so the Queen and the Empress of Russia say—is effecting the pacific penetration of Denmark by getting German millionaires to purchase estates across the border, gradually encroaching upon Denmark.

[*Journals.*]   LONDON,
                                                            MARCH 14TH.

... The event of the past few days has been the success of A. J. B. [Balfour] in drawing from Asquith a declaration about the Navy, which never would have been obtained but for the Kaiser's letter. The nett result of that famous epistle has been to force the Government to give a pledge that in the next three years they will lay down ships enough to ensure our superiority. So good has come out of evil, if evil it was.[1]

Government Declaration on Naval Policy.

I drove home with Tweedmouth from the Mansion House luncheon to the Prince of Wales on Thursday, and he was quite friendly and amiable. We were bound for a meeting of the British Museum Trustees in the Chancellor's room, where we elected Lord Collins.

The Scottish Land Bill was thrown out by the H. of L. Nobody cares a farthing.

Jackie [Fisher] told me that Cassel had used rather disagreeable expressions about the German Emperor episode, critical of my action and Jackie's. But I saw him yesterday morning and he spoke very kindly about the whole affair. Of course he takes the German and Semitic point of view of it all. That is only natural. After all, *we* are fighting for our lives, for our Imperial and possibly National existence, which will be at stake ere long. The Cassels are at home in all lands—equally rich, equally composed.

[1] In the House, Mr. Balfour asked if it were not true that on account of the German ship-building year's starting in June, and the British year's starting in December, the German Navy would have the lead of the English in first-class battleships in the autumn of 1911. Mr. Asquith replied that it was doubtful if the German rule of construction could be maintained, but if it was found in 1909 that this position was likely to arise the Government would provide for sufficient extra ships to prevent it.

On Maud Allan's Dancing.

Maurice and I went to see some interesting dancing at the Palace Theatre by a woman called Maud Allan. It is curious and forcible. In Rubenstein's "Capriccio" she dances a Greek dance, with bare legs and feet, and Greek draperies. Then she was Salome, terribly passionate and horror-struck, with the head of the Baptist! All London was there. A curious gathering of politicians, society and the "people."

[*Journals.*]

LONDON,
MARCH 20TH.

On Lord Lloyd.

At the Defence Committee yesterday, there appeared a witness on the Middle East question, whose grave and most engaging smile I thought to recognise. It turned out to be "Skinny" Lloyd [1] who used to steer the Eton eight. He has been six years moving about the Persian Gulf, Mesopotamia, etc. J. M. [Morley] and Grey examined him. He was admirable in clearness, exposition, readiness, without a trace of hasty thought. This is the cleverest of all the contemporaries of Oliver and Maurice. J. M. was captivated. I annex his note, passed over to me, while Lloyd was being questioned by Grey.

[*To H.M. the King.*]

2, TILNEY STREET,
MARCH 24TH.

The Queen's Letters: no more to be Published.

Viscount Esher, having been entrusted by Your Majesty with the duty of examining the correspondence of H.M. Queen Victoria for the years 1861–1881, in order to see whether it would be desirable to add two additional volumes to those already published, with humble duty begs to report as follows:

In order to maintain the continuity of the correspondence, upon the lines hitherto pursued, and to show the development

---

[1] Afterwards Lord Lloyd.

of the Queen's character after the loss of the Prince Consort, it would be necessary to proceed upon the method adopted in the volumes already published.

In these volumes, although care was exercised to eliminate everything calculated to give pain, or create difficulties, there was no concealment of material facts. The whole story of the Queen's conduct of public affairs and of the influence exercised by the Sovereign, with laborious and conscientious care, was truthfully stated.

The excisions consisted of phrases and of comment but not of fact.

After reading the correspondence which covers the period of the wars between Prussia and France, which culminated in the unification of Germany and the foundation of the German Empire, the only conclusion possible is that prudence requires publication to cease at the point already reached.

It is unfortunate that the remarkable development of Queen Victoria's character and its gathering strength, her power of memory and of expression, her tenacity of purpose, her clearness of vision and her ever-growing watchfulness over the welfare of her people, cannot be manifested to the English-speaking people.

But the nature of the correspondence, the exceeding delicacy of the subjects mainly discussed, nearly all relating to Foreign States, and to eminent Personages, some still alive, and some still looming large in shadows which have already sunk below the horizon, render truthful exposition of the period dangerous and impossible.

To eliminate the letters from the Emperor William I, the Empress Augusta, the Crown Princess of Germany, and the Emperor Napoleon, would be to rob any further volumes of their chief interest.

To omit, or tamper with, the letters from H.M.'s Ambassadors abroad, or from Mr. Gladstone or Lord Granville, would be to falsify history.

And yet to publish almost any of these documents would inevitably revive bitter memories and possibly relight the fires of old international quarrels, the embers of which are not yet cold.

The history of the years 1861–1871 is the story of the unification of Germany by blood and iron.

The history of the years 1871–81 is the story of the near Eastern struggle between Russia and Turkey, in which Great Britain played so large and so dominant a part.

In spite of events in the Nation's domestic annals of great interest, and of much that would appeal to the whole English race in the domestic life of the Queen, the lurid background of those Titanic wars throws everything else into deep shadow.

To treat this period with frankness would be impossible, and to treat it with reticence would be dull.

It will be many years before the letters of the greatest interest and importance can be safely published, and Viscount Esher can only therefore advise Your Majesty, with great deference, that any further publication should be abandoned for another generation.

[*To Sir John Fisher.*]   2, TILNEY ST.,
                                            MARCH 25TH.

On the State
of Naval
Policy.

I shall never, and have never, regretted that letter.[1]

It was well worth all this bother (not very much of that) to have done anything however little for the Navy.

I shall always believe that we were then at the parting of the ways.

The Nation was on its trial. The struggle is far from over yet.

You see that Bülow again tries to lull our people to slumber. Next year there will be a bitter fight.

I hope to heaven that Asquith will *make terms* with Lloyd George, before absolutely making him Ch. of the Ex.

Terms, which will fix the total of Naval Estimates for the next 2 years.

[1] To the Maritime League.

[*Journals.*] LONDON,
MARCH 27TH.

. . . My poor old Chief, the Duke of Devonshire, died *Death of the* suddenly at Cannes. The only good phrase and true which I read *Duke of* *Devonshire.* in all the notices of his Life was his "tranquil indifference to praise or blame." Otherwise, no writer in dealing with his character has shown much perspicacity. He had all the old Whig hatred of injustice and irrational *action*. He was *not* an idle man, but he thought slowly. He was one of the most effective speakers I ever heard, when he brought his whole mind to bear on his subject. Massiveness was the word which described his pulverising style of argument. He was not very *human*. He was, in the main, indifferent to men. The only man I ever heard him speak of with affection was Clare Vyner—a curious, romantic, racing man—Lady Ripon's brother.

[*Journals.*] LONDON,
APRIL IST.

J. Morley told me yesterday that he, the first of all his col- *Illness of the* leagues, saw the P.M. for 20 minutes. C.-B. was in bed, but very *Prime* *Minister—* cheerful, and addressed him in broad Scots. They talked philo- sophy and religion. C.-B. said, "You know, I may be dead to-morrow morning, or I may be quite well again." And he finally told J. M. that he had put politics on one side, and never thought about them. As J. M. said, what a curious position for a Prime Minister!

It seems, however, that the doctors have intimated to him that he is going down hill, and that he has settled all his private affairs. Of resignation he said never a word. Asquith saw him in the afternoon.

I went last night on my way back from the H. of L. where we had a most interesting debate on Lady Cathcart's highland property under the "Sinclairism" of the present Government,

with Bron Lucas to see Constance.[1] She lives in a flat in Charles
St., very high up. Her room is full of statuettes of all kinds. A
collection of them. She was dressed—or rather half dressed—as
a boy, and sat on the floor talking to us. The *most* Bohemian
thing out of the Quartier Latin ever seen. She has learnt all
Maud Allan's dancing tricks with her arms and does them
beautifully. The King saw her dance at the Paget's and was
enchanted. He insisted on going to tea with her, and toiled up
all her stairs—a good height—and stayed two hours! He said,
"You know I have always been a bit of a Bohemian myself."
What a curious episode.

[*To M. V. B.*]   ORCHARD LEA,
                                            APRIL 2ND.

I came down here last night after the Defence Committee
meeting.

. . . I sent round a note yesterday asking how (Lily) Elsie
was, and she said she was just off to the sea, and hoped to be
playing next Tuesday or Wednesday.

. . . I am going up to London this morning for another
Defence Committee and shall return this afternoon. Probably
I may remain at O'Lea to-morrow. I hope so. You shall hear
my movements by telegram. The P.M. has seen the Archbishop
of Canterbury four times. He was always supposed to be a sort
of Voltairean, but it appears his talks with the Archbishop have
been very touching, and he has shown himself to be a very
simple Christian, in the very broadest sense of the term.

—His Religion—

[*Journals.*]   ORCHARD LEA,
                                            APRIL 5TH.

—His Resignation.

C.-B. has resigned, and Asquith is to go to Biarritz to-morrow
or Monday. It is a mistake not insisting that the King should

[1] Lady Constance Stuart Richardson.

return. We shall be left without a Sovereign, a P. of W., or a Prime Minister. There is no precedent, so far as I know, for such a state of things; and they are remembered at inconvenient moments. It is not prudent to let the uninitiated into the secret that without a head the government machine works smoothly on.

C.-B. retires amid plaudits of those who vilified him three years ago. An amiable man; possibly below the calibre of his predecessors, with the exception of Perceval, Addington, Goderich and Liverpool.

Asquith is of a very different type. A keen, delving mind, *On Asquith.* with incisive powers of speech. Clear-sighted, and, let us hope, unwavering action.

He has now the cumbrous task before him of putting patches into his Government, after tearing out the frayed pieces. I should imagine that he would lighten the burden of legislative measures.

[*To H.M. the King.*] ORCHARD LEA,
APRIL 8TH.

Viscount Esher, with humble duty, and deep respect, hopes *On the Press* that Your Majesty will not pay undue attention to the *Observer*, *and the Army.* about which Fritz [Ponsonby] has written to him, or what any newspaper says about the Army.[1] How can any of these excellent quill-driving gentlemen know? Your Majesty has had experience of them. The man who writes that kind of article is a clever but half-educated person, who hangs about public offices and writes up anything he can pick up from the Private Secretary of a Minister.

No blame attaches to him for this. It is his daily bread. But

[1] The article was merely another expression of the discontent of the "Bolt-from-the-Blue" school, except that it claimed to represent (without any shred of evidence for the claim) the current opinion of the Army Council and the Regular Officers.

Your Majesty knows well that undue importance cannot be attached to the reflections of any of these gentlemen.

The Army is *not* in the unsatisfactory state described in the *Observer*. Not a single one of the many General Officers *now in active command* would agree with the author of the article.

Sir H. Smith-Dorrien, Sir Arthur Paget, Sir Ian Hamilton etc. etc. would all say that the Army is in quite a different state as regards numbers, efficiency, and preparation for war, from what it was in 1899. Your Majesty can *never*, under the Voluntary system, have an Army on the lines of a Continental Army.

Disadvantages of Voluntary Enlistment.

Your Majesty's House of Commons will not vote more than 27 or 28 millions for the support of an Army.

For this sum, only a *small* Voluntary Regular Army can be maintained. In order that the whole of this small force, at the outside six Divisions of Infantry and a Cavalry Division, can be free to go abroad, 3 millions are spent upon an Army of "Volunteers." Somebody may think of a better system, but so far no one has *worked out in detail* a better plan than Mr. Haldane and his military advisers.

It is a novel plan and a plant of recent growth. If a certain time is not allowed for it to develop, no one can say, not even Mr. Garvin in the *Observer*, whether it will succeed or fail.

Views of Mr. Haldane's Opponents.

Mr. Haldane's critics and possible successors in Office have other views. They do not believe in a Regular Army at all. They think that Your Majesty should depend for defence upon the fleet alone; that India should keep her own army at her own cost, with depots here to be paid by India; that Egypt should do the same; and that a small *expeditionary* force of 10,000 men, and a Brigade of Guards for Your Majesty's personal use, is all the Force required.

It is anticipated that this would save the country at least 10 millions. Their views have got a deep hold upon some influential politicians, newspaper writers, and some of Your Majesty's Ministers.

They are the alternative to Mr. Haldane's plan. Although Viscount Esher differed upon some points of detail with Mr.

Haldane, and does still, he nevertheless is convinced that Mr. Haldane has done more for the Regular Army than any Minister since Cardwell, and that Your Majesty will be very unfortunate when he ceases to be Your Majesty's Secretary of State.

[*Journals.*]   ORCHARD LEA,
                                                                APRIL 10TH.

Cabinet making gives much insight into character. J. M. [Morley] told me yesterday some of the secrets. Lloyd George "put a pistol" to Asquith's head, and *asked* for the Ch. of the Ex. with a threat of resignation. He had previously, however, told Morley that he was about to do this, but *only* if J. M. waived his claim. This he instantly did. Lloyd George spoke deprecatingly of Asquith. His final summary of him was, "He is a man of no initiative, and requires to be briefed." *Reconstruction of the Cabinet.*

J. M. says that in 1892 he proposed *Fowler* to Mr. Gladstone for the Admiralty, in the course of the discussion on the formation of the Cabinet. Mr. G. with great solemnity, and a wave of his hand, "Well, for the Admiralty, I think we require what is called a *gentleman!*"

However, here we are overwhelmed by the middle-classes.

Neither Tweedmouth nor Elgin have yet been told of their fate.[1] Yet the new offices are all in the papers. The leakage is attributed to Ll. George, as the appointments all appear in the paper with which he is connected.

Of Loulou [Harcourt] Asquith said rather coldly, "He must wait his turn." Haldane seems satisfied, and professes to have made his bargain with Asquith as regards estimates for the W.O. in the future. J. M. was remonstrated with by Asquith for leaving the H. of C. and merely said, "I go altogether, or I go to the

[1] Lord Tweedmouth was transferred from First Lord of the Admiralty to President of the Council, and the Earl of Elgin retired. Mr. McKenna became First Lord, and the Earl of Elgin was succeeded as Secretary for the Colonies by the Earl of Crewe.

Upper House." "When," said Asquith. "To-day, this very hour," said J. M.

[*Journals.*]   ORCHARD LEA,
                                                          APRIL 22ND.

On Mrs.
Asquith.
I saw Stead yesterday morning. He told me many indiscreet things Mrs. A. [Asquith] had said about "Henry." When I asked him what he thought the rock ahead of the Government he said "Mrs. Asquith." One thing was rather pretty. Asquith went to see C.-B. when the latter resigned, and C.-B. said to him when he left "You are the most loyal and faithful colleague I ever had." Asquith was much affected and kissed his hand.

Mrs. A. said that, during her illness, her doctor observed the three portraits she had over her bed, Rosebery, A. J. B. [Balfour] and Milner. Asquith, who was there, pointed to them and said, "Three of the most brilliant brains in England—and all dead—finished!" I can imagine similar language being used in 1876 about Mr. G. [Gladstone]. Asquith will not find A. J. B. as dead as he thinks.

Jackie [Fisher] telephoned all the morning to get hold of me, but I only got to him this afternoon. . . .

[*Journals.*]   ORCHARD LEA,
                                                          APRIL 23RD.

Death of
Campbell-
Bannerman.
C.-B. died yesterday. Very peacefully. He told the Archbishop that, though not a dogmatist, his belief was summed up in the words he had placed on the grave where he was to lie (from the Psalms), "My trust is in the tender mercy of God for ever and ever."

The Prince of Wales telephoned to-day asking me to come early, and I went there at one, and remained to luncheon. We had a talk alone for about half an hour. Then the Princess came in.

. . . I sat between the Princess and the eldest boy at luncheon. He is wonderfully improved. Osborne has made him unshy, and given him good manners. He talked just like an Eton boy. All the children tumbled about the floor, with rocking horses and toys, while we had our coffee.

[*To the Rt. Hon. J. Morley.*]   2, TILNEY ST.,
                                           APRIL 25TH.

I am anxious to know your decision, or your doubts about *Morley to the* the name by which you will be called in future, and should *Upper House.* esteem the favour of your confidence.

So perhaps we might lunch at the Carlton next week? I go back to Orchard Lea to-night, but return here on Monday. Poor Winston [Churchill]. The personal inconvenience is a more serious matter than the political blow. Newspapers of course amplify the latter.[1]

I have been shown two letters, very proudly by their recipients, written by you to the King and the Prince of Wales. The Prince keeps his locked away in his desk, and produces it with much solemnity.

I fear that the "frontier" is giving you much anxiety. This, however, was not unanticipated. What do you make of Delane? Of all these things I want to talk to you.

[*To M. V. B.*]   2, TILNEY ST.,
                                           APRIL 29TH.

. . . You are just arriving at Liverpool, and you will not be *The First* much impressed. You may look, however, at the outside of the *Lord Esher.*

---

[1] Mr. Winston Churchill had been defeated in a bye-election at Manchester North-West. Shortly afterwards, however, he was returned for Dundee with a large majority in spite of the opposition of a prohibitionist, a Labour candidate, and the women's suffrage party.

Law Courts, and even at the fine Central Hall. Your grand-father made all his great reputation as an Advocate, especially in shipping cases, in that building. All his early work, and his final forensic triumphs, were served there. He was on what is called the "Northern Circuit." After he became a judge he went to Liverpool as his first Assize. It was during his practice there that he became so intimate with the late Lord Derby. So Liverpool has some family interest for you. I doubt your discovering much other.

[*To M. V. B.*]   2, TILNEY ST.,
                                                  APRIL 30TH.

Our dinner last night was very gay. Millie [Sutherland] resplendent in a colour which matched the Merry Widow's cloak, and in great spirits and looks. Jackie [Fisher], Garvin, McKenna, Winston [Churchill] and F. E. Smith. We created rather a sensation at the Carlton, as you may suppose. After dinner late, they all went to the Palace to see Maud Allan—two boxes thrown into one—and *I* went down to O'Lea!

Garvin was full of enthusiasm about my article, which he had read. Jackie read it at two in the morning, and writes warmly about it to-day.[1] Winston was very "merry and bright." F. E. Smith has a charming face, and is *really* witty. He says that Duddie [Ward]—who lived and read with him at Liverpool— would be making £3,000 a year at the Bar, if he had stuck to it. McKenna is very pleasant. . . . The calibre of Cabinet Ministers all round has been lowered owing to the *large cabinets* of modern days.

On F. E. Smith—

[1] Lord Esher's article, though appearing in the most hysterical of anti-German and pro-conscriptionary papers, was a reasoned explanation of the impossibility of conscription in this country until every voluntary means of recruiting had been tried out: the impossibility of conscription, in fact, unless the sovereign voters of England decided to embody their consciences in an Act of Parliament in order to overcome the weakness of the flesh.

Winston, on the other hand, has very nearly, if not quite, a first-class intellect. Garvin is a sort of inferior Stead. He has much of Stead's wide grasp, but not, I should say, his visual keenness, and certainly not his originality of mind. A prodigious memory, and encyclopædic knowledge, but no divine fire. *—And Garvin.*

[*To M. V. B.*]　　　　　　　　　[IN THE TRAIN],
　　　　　　　　　　　　　　　　　　MAY IST.

The Academy dinner was dull without speeches. The Prince of Wales is bound to have to yield on this subject. Englishmen love getting on their hinders. It is a national craze, and however much H.R.H. may dislike it he will have to give way, or the monarchy will be doomed! I sat next Tadema; and was glad to get away to the opera. The pictures looked second-rate. A fine portrait by Sargent of Arthur B. [Balfour]—very characteristic. On the other hand, his Connaughts, both of them, are very undistinguished. *The Prince of Wales at the Academy.*

Tetrazzini is a first-rate artist. Her acting is really dramatic and is of that quality which forces other people on the stage to act. Her voice is good, but not Melba. The house was crowded, just like a full Caruso night.

[*To M. V. B.*]　　　　　　　　　ORCHARD LEA,
　　　　　　　　　　　　　　　　　　MAY 2ND.

. . . At the Academy dinner Beresford tried not to see Jackie [Fisher], but Jackie *insisted* upon shaking hands with him. Clémenceau, whom I saw, has grown much older of late, but was as friendly and rational as ever. He dined with Asquith to meet most of the Cabinet. There were two bridge tables after dinner, and Asquith played. What a different atmosphere from *The Dignity of Prime Ministers.*

the great Parliamentarians of *my* youth. Dizzy and Mr. G. breathed an altogether different air.

Men and women in their presence felt a sort of moral reserve, which some people feel in church. There was a certain advantage to the state in having at the head of affairs men who necessarily drew the best out of those they met. It kept order in the highest sphere of politics.

Perhaps you will think it altogether priggish, but I am sure that Bridge and Golf should be put aside—except in very "intime" life—by Prime Ministers and Sovereigns.

In these days even the Archbishop has been seen to smoke a cigarette. On the whole there was a good deal to be said for the days when great men were never seen *en pantouffles*.

[*To M. V. B.*]   2, TILNEY ST.,
                                                    MAY 5TH.

I have been sent some Glasgow papers, full of leading articles about *my* articles in the *N. Review.* I don't know whether they were inspired or written by you and your distinguished staff. I see the Prince of Wales quoted last night at his Colonial Institute dinner, my phrase about England. So I am very much to the fore in high circles at present! Think of me too, in cocked hat of gigantic and ludicrous proportions, introducing Viscount Morley of Blackburn this afternoon to the House of Lords. Old Fowler seems to have asked that I should introduce him too, and I said I would see him damned first!

. . . I want you to buy a really *good* edition of Browning with big type. Is there such a thing? Now I am waiting for Maxse, vide enclosed card—to walk down to St. James's Palace! What does he want?

Lloyd George made such an excellent speech last night on the Licensing Bill. He strikes quite a different sort of note from any other speaker. Like Melba in the opera. If you see *The Times*, just glance at the speech. . . .

MY BELOVED E.

Yesterday with all sea Lords present McKenna formally *New* agreed to 4 Dreadnoughts and *if necessary* 6 Dreadnoughts next *Cabinet's* year (perhaps the greatest triumph ever known). *Naval* *Decisions.*

As he says, he has to eat every word he has said at the Treasury and Cabinet, but I am giving him some jam. He tells me Harcourt for certain will resign on it. He, McKenna, funks Lloyd George (*that's why I am writing to you!*) and McKenna is paring down the money with a view to Supplementary Estimates. Of course you'll not breathe a word of this to Lloyd George but this is what I suggest to you to impress on Lloyd George. *Let there be no mistake about the two keels to one in Dreadnoughts. McKenna vacillates on this through funk of Lloyd George,* so let Lloyd George reassure him and tell him to have no fear—it doesn't affect next year as McKenna consents to 4 or even 6 but it does affect the year after and the Admiralty Finance should be arranged accordingly and not deplete next year at expense of year after. I wonder if this is all clear to you that McKenna is going to give us the numbers for next year all right but is wobbling over the money provision to the detriment of the year after. Shove in again the great fact. The Navy and Army Estimates not far different in magnitude and yet the Army can't fight Bulgaria and the Navy can take on the lot. *Ut veniant omnes!* The Army too big for a little War, too little for a big war! You might tell Lloyd George he can rely on my parsimony but he should give McKenna the tip that he is going for 4 or 5 millions on the Army estimates (not all at once of course) to give it to the Navy. Don't let Lloyd George go at the King like a bull at a gate. Francis must pave the way and then let the Celtic eloquence come in! You have a momentous job now in hand. Heaven help you.

Yours, J.F.

Drop me a line if you can how you get on to-day with Lloyd George.

[*To M. V. B.*]   ORCHARD LEA,
                                                      MAY 6TH.

Complaints of   . . . There has been a "food" racket in the house to-day. The
Lord Esher's   servants complained they were not well fed. They are all so fat
Servants.   they cannot waddle, so I told them they could if they liked find
                  homes elsewhere; but they none of them show signs of moving.
                  Just think what they get in their own homes—and what our
                  gardeners, Bromwich and Fred, have for dinner! They want
                  bacon for breakfast every morning. That is the demand—and
                  they resent having sausages and kippers! Are we going up or
                  down hill as a nation!

Introduction   . . . You would have been amused to have seen the ceremony
of Viscount   in the House of Lords yesterday. J. M. did it very nicely. He
Morley.   would not swear the oath of allegiance, but affirmed it. He had
                  to state his "conscientious conviction" and blushed like a girl!

[*To M. V. B.*]   2, TILNEY ST.,
                                                      MAY 7TH.

         I had a *most* interesting dinner last night. Jackie [Fisher],
      Francis [Knollys], Lloyd George and Winston [Churchill]. I
      will tell you all about it if I have no time to write this evening. . . .

[*Journals.*]   LONDON,
                                                      MAY 7TH.

         I saw Lloyd George by invitation this morning at the
      Treasury. . . .
         It was clear that Ll. George does not contemplate a pointed
Asquith and   attack on Haldane. I then went to see Asquith. He received
Lord Esher.   me in the Cabinet room downstairs.
         E. "I came to pay my respects, and to ask you—as I asked Sir
      Henry Campbell-Bannerman—whether you have any special

injunctions for me, as a member of the Committee for Imperial
Defence."

A. "What did he say?"

E. "He said that he hoped I would not vote too often against
the Government in the House of Lords."

A. "I cannot say more, except that I hope you remain on the
Defence Committee, where your knowledge and advice are of
the greatest value to us."

(This was very handsome.)

E. "Thank you Sir; but there is one point I should like to ask
you about. Perhaps you have seen an article of mine in the
National Review. I know that observations have been made. Do
you think it undesirable that I should write in the *Review*?"

A. "Well. I would only suggest that you should stick to
historical subjects. I think the past is more suitable for treatment than the present."

E. "By all means."

This was the essence of the talk.

[*To the Prince of Wales.*]　　　　BRITISH MUSEUM,
　　　　　　　　　　　　　　　　　　MAY 9TH.

I had hoped to be able to thank Your Royal Highness for the
great compliment Your Royal Highness paid me, by quoting a
few poor words of mine, in the admirable speech at the Colonial
Institute. I feel the honour more keenly as I have, in common
with so many of the King's subjects, long looked upon Your
Royal Highness as the first member of the Royal Family who
has ever grasped the meaning, from personal experience, of
Britain oversea. The first speech you made, on returning from
the Colonies, struck a note, the echoes of which vibrate still;
and Your Royal Highness' words at the Colonial Institute have,
I am sure, re-awakened in the minds of all Englishmen, at home
and beyond, the consciousness that they have, in Your Royal
Highness, the strongest link of that chain which is being slowly

forged and which will, at some future time, bring the Empire together.

[*To M. V. B.*]   2, TILNEY ST.,
                                                          MAY 14TH.

Fisher and   I saw Jackie [Fisher] to-day. He was publicly cut by Beresford
Beresford.   at the Levée. In full view of the King and before the Ministers
and C. B.'s naval officers. Jackie tried to shake hands, and
C. B. turned his back. It is all over the fleet.

[*Journals.*]   LONDON,
                                                         MAY 19TH.

. . . Yesterday I attended at the Mansion House, and made a
long speech on the Shakespeare Memorial in favour of an
attempt at arrangements with the "National Theatre" people.
Carried my point, well supported by B. Tree. Maurice went
to Aldershot, with the King.

[*Journals.*]   LONDON,
                                                         MAY 22ND.

Lloyd George   Ll. George asked me to call on him yesterday at his room in
and Lord   the H. of C. He began at once about his financial position.
Esher.   10 millions to find next year, and a nett deficit (after raiding
the sinking fund of 3 millions) of about 6 millions.

He asked me to come before the Committee of the Council
over which he was to preside, on Tuesday next. I said I would
think it over, but that my first impression was adverse to the
idea. My relations with Haldane made it difficult to express
opinions on the Army without his assent, and, finally, his
committee seemed to me about to deal more with questions of

Finance than of Defence. The latter was my legitimate province, and not the former.

[*To the Chancellor of the Exchequer.*]   2, TILNEY ST.,
MAY 22ND.

I have given very careful consideration to your suggestion—
and I am honoured by your making it—that I should be called
before the Cabinet Committee to give evidence upon the question of possible reductions in the cost of the Regular Army.

Lord Esher and the Cabinet Committee.

Your view is that, as a Member of the Defence Committee
and having been a member of the South African War Commission and the Chairman of the War Office Reconstruction Committee, the information necessarily acquired by me might possibly be useful to the Cabinet.

My first impression as expressed to you, was, and it remains
unchanged, that my position as a Member of the Defence Committee, as well as the close relations which have subsisted
between Mr. Haldane and myself during the past two years,
made it difficult for me to appear before the Cabinet Committee,
which is apparently about to deal rather with questions of
Finance than of Defence.

In a discussion by the Defence Committee upon the Military
requirements of the Country, and the strength of the Military
Force wanted to meet them, or in an enquiry by a sub-committee of that body, I should be proud to take part. But I beg
to express my sincere wish that you will leave me outside the
range of a controversy upon matters of policy or finance, from
which for many years I have endeavoured to keep aloof.

I fear enquiry will lead you to conclude that no large reduction of the cost of the Army is possible without large reductions
of personnel, and that to reduce personnel is not practicable
unless the policy of the country in relation to South Africa,
Egypt and India is changed.

Military Policy and Finance.

The Army is not maintained for Home Defence. The

enquiries of the Defence Committee prove, that for such a purpose, an Army however large and well equipped would be useless; for if the command of the sea is maintained, such an Army would not be required, and if the command of the sea is lost, it would be starved into submission.

The Army is maintained for the purpose of re-inforcing British troops in India and Egypt, and for relieving troops wherever they are quartered abroad. Under a purely Voluntary system some such Army as ours, based on a plan like Mr. Cardwell's, appears to be a necessity, if the demands made upon it remain unmodified.

Of course, if the garrisons of our dependencies beyond the sea are *permanently* reduced, the force at home would shrink in proportion, but the power of reinforcement would shrink with it. Large economies, I fear, are dependent upon either restricting our responsibilities oversea, or upon the abandonment of a *purely voluntary* system of service.

I think I have said enough to show how, in my view, questions of military finance are interlocked with questions of policy, and how very little use any evidence of mine would be upon the issues which the Cabinet Committee will have to determine.

[*From the Rt. Hon. A. J. Balfour.*]   4, CARLTON GARDENS,
                     Private.   MAY 23RD.

MY DEAR REGGY,

Balfour and Military Policy.

I think your letter excellent. [A copy of the letter to the Chancellor of the Exchequer had been sent to Mr. Balfour.] The only possible criticisms I have upon it are (*a*) saying that "the Army is not required for Home Defence," though true, as *You* mean it, is, according to my views, rather too absolute. We certainly do not require anything like our present force for Home Defence; but a Home Army is, as we all admit, essential, if only to compel an enemy, if it intends to invade, to invade in force; (*b*) the wording of your last paragraph but two, is of course absolutely correct. But it appears to suggest the view that possibly we might do without the power of re-inforcements referred to.

This, of course, is not my view; and the mere transference of troops from South Africa to England, though it would permit a reduction without destroying the Cardwellian balance, does not lighten the fundamental obligation of keeping adequate re-inforcements for India, which are just as necessary now as they ever were. But these are very trifling comments.

Yours ever,
ARTHUR JAMES BALFOUR.

[*To the Earl of Plymouth.*]   2, TILNEY ST.,
MAY 24TH.

I am sorry that enforced attendance at Windsor will prevent me from being present at the Conference. Because I should have liked to say that in my view we should all of us agree to endeavour to frame a plan for a Theatre to contain a monument of Shakespeare. *On a National Theatre.*

Subject to a "National Theatre" being a practical scheme in its financial aspects, a decision should be come to upon the primary question whether such a theatre should be a subsidised theatre or not, and alternate schemes might be prepared.

This can only, in my opinion, be done by a small committee (not more than six) who would call witnesses and prepare a report *upon evidence* received. Short of this being done, there will be no possibility of approaching any Minister or the Public, with a hope of success.

[*Journals.*]   WINDSOR,
MAY 28TH.

These days have been filled up with the visit of the President of the French Republic. A homely, unimpressive man.

At the City function yesterday, to which I drove with the General [French], Fisher and A. J. B. [Balfour] got the only real "receptions." Both very popular in the City.

The Gala Opera was finer than usual. At the King's Ball two nights ago, Herbert, Minister at Stockholm, told me several things about the German Emperor. His comment on Grey was, "a capable sort of country gentleman." The effrontery of the man, as dear Caryl [Annesley] would say.

I am at Windsor awaiting M. Fallières, whom I receive at the station.

[*To H.M. the King.*]   2, TILNEY ST.,
                                                         MAY 29TH.

Close of the
Invasion
Enquiry

Viscount Esher, with humble duty, begs to inform Your Majesty that Mr. Balfour attended the meeting of the Defence Committee this morning at the request of the Prime Minister.

Your Majesty will remember that the sub-committee on "Invasion" was appointed at the request of Mr. Balfour, in consequence of an appeal made to him by Lord Roberts, Lord Lovat and others, to reconsider, in the light of "new facts" with which they supplied him, and possibly to retract, the main points of his speech in 1905 on the subject of Invasion and Raids. Mr. Balfour forwarded these facts to the Defence Committee, with the request that they should be examined. This enquiry is now closed. It has extended over many months. The Prime Minister, having furnished Mr. Balfour with all the evidence, asked him whether he wished to express any views which he might have formed to the Committee.

The result was the unique meeting which took place this morning, an event quite unique in the history of political administration. Your Majesty knows well that the leaders of two great parties have occasionally, although rarely, settled in their final stages great legislative enactments which were in dispute. But Viscount Esher knows of no case where the Leader of the Opposition has been brought into counsel with the heads of the Government upon the most vital questions of National policy and defence. It is a novel departure full of interest and good omen.

It gave Mr. Balfour the opportunity of making a statement, *Balfour's* lasting about an hour, quite perfect in form and language, and *Speech.* most closely reasoned, of the views which he has formed upon the question of national defence. The general opinion was that no finer exposition of this question has ever been made. Mr. Balfour's grasp of the subject, and his luminous exposition, astonished those of the Committee who were unacquainted with his powers.

Not a question was put to him, and this was perhaps the greatest tribute which the members of the Committee could pay to the masterly performance to which they had listened.

[*To the Rt. Hon. A. J. Balfour.*]   2, TILNEY ST.,
                                                    MAY 29TH.

The occasion was quite unique, for I imagine that although the leaders of the two great Parties have occasionally, but rarely, discussed for the purpose of arranging a final settlement of some great legislative enactment, this is the first time that the leader of a great party met in council his principal opponents.

Considering the place and occasion, it is a happy omen and precedent.

But, and this is a very great motive in writing, I cannot conceive that any reasoned statement upon so grave a matter has ever been made with such masterly knowledge of the subject and so perfect a manner of exposition.

I assure you that everyone was amazed, and those who had not grasped the extent of your powers, were stupefied.

Dear Arthur, I never felt prouder of your friendship. Pray

believe that there is not one word of exaggeration as to the effect you produced. No wonder no question was asked!

[*Journals.*] LONDON,
MAY 29TH.

A. J. B. [Balfour] came before the Committee to-day.

A. J. B. spoke for an hour, with admirable force. The reasoning was of the highest order, and the whole statement was most impressive. Quite the most striking thing I ever heard A. J. B. do. Not a question was put to him, and no higher tribute could be paid to him. Asquith, Grey, Haldane, Crewe, Lloyd George. All were equally dumbfounded.

On President Fallières. Yesterday the President of the Republic came to Windsor. I received him at the station, and drove with him for an hour. He took more interest in the fat cattle and the gardens, than in the castle itself. He has no brilliancy, and nothing of John Burns about him. It is difficult to see what are the qualities that have lifted him from a small provincial town to the headship of the State.

The Foreign Minister, Pichon, is an unattractive sort of person. Quite a mediocrity, I should imagine. Probably a mere creature of Clemenceau, under whom he served as a journalist.

[*From the Rt. Hon. A. J. Balfour.*] 4, CARLTON GARDENS,
MAY 30TH.
MY DEAR REGGY,

I need not tell you what a pleasure it was to receive your letter of yesterday, about my evidence before the Defence Committee. It was more than good of you to write it, and I shall treasure it in my archives.

It also relieved a certain anxiety which I could not help entertaining as to the effect of what I said; for, when one is asked to come before a Committee and be examined, and, after one's statement, not a soul puts any question, one is left in an uncomfortable ignorance as to what effect has been produced. On this point you have reassured me.

With much gratitude.

Yours ever,
ARTHUR JAMES BALFOUR.

[*Journals.*]   LONDON,
                                                     MAY 30TH.

I went to see A. J. B. this morning. He had been rather puzzled by the silence of the Committee, but is now assured of the effect produced by what he said.

I discussed with him the King's Russian visit. He sees the *The King's* constitutional impropriety of the King meeting Isvolsky and *Visit to* Stolypin unaccompanied by Grey. He thought of writing *Russia.* privately to Grey before the debate on Thursday.[1]

I had half an hour with Lloyd George in his room yesterday, and tried to explain to him the impossibility of reducing the Army unless you couple reduction with Compulsion.

[*From Mr. R. McKenna.*]   ADMIRALTY,
                                                     JUNE 2ND.

MY DEAR ESHER,

We had our first meeting of the Estimates Committee to-day but got no further than making a rough forecast of next year's

---

[1] Owing to the internal struggle going on in Russia between the supporters of autocracy and the various democratic and revolutionary parties, the visit of the King to the Tsar was highly unpopular with the left wing of the Government supporters. Mr. Keir Hardie made a violent speech against it at Bristol. Mr. Ramsay MacDonald wrote an astounding article on it in the *Labour Leader*, in which he used such phrases as "hobnobbing with murderers." Memorials were presented to the Foreign Secretary by the Labour Members, with some Liberal support. All these objectors protested against the State visit, and excluded from their scope the question of a personal visit of the King to his relatives. The visit was actually debated on the motion for the Whitsuntide adjournment. When the Tsar was appointed an Admiral of the Fleet, however, no further Parliamentary consequences arose.

deficit. The Army and Navy are to be considered on June 16th. I have not yet seen your Memorandum but I shall ask Lloyd George to show it to me next week on my return from my honeymoon.

We are all indebted to you for helping to clear up our difficulties.

Yours very sincerely,
REGINALD McKENNA.

[*Journals.*]   LONDON,
                                                     JUNE 5TH.

. . . This is Epsom week, but I have not been near the place; it is curious how all interest in and liking for the sport of racing has died within me.

On Hatfield and Aristocracy. Maurice and I motored to Hatfield on Derby day, and spent the afternoon with Salisbury in that most glorious domain. It is a real glimpse of another world, and breath of another atmosphere. Salisbury had camped his Militia Battalion under the trees of the Park, about 400 yards away from the house. Our great country may be on the down-grade, but so long as we have men of his stamp, so simple and strenuous and so aloof from all the temptations which beset men of his class, giving every ounce of his energy which a not very strong frame permits to the service of the country, it is not possible that we can sink very low as a nation. There he was, under the shadow of his perfect Elizabethan place, under trees which may have shadowed *her* before she was Queen, drilling and training seven or eight hundred fine young Englishmen, quite as stalwart as any who fought for the Tudors. It made one reflect whether any simpler spectacle, involving such contrasts and such heart-whole voluntary service to the State, could be seen in any other nation on earth.

The house is beautiful, and indeed there is none more beautiful in England; but the really interesting thing about it is the fact

ORCHARD LEA, 1908.

The Windsor home of Lord and Lady Esher.

that it has an atmosphere which apparently breeds the sound type of aristocrat. Chatsworth and a few other great houses seem able to achieve this miracle, while others can only achieve human drones. It reminded me of Treves' theory of Cancer houses, which, in his view, should be razed to the earth. Perhaps there is a moral microbe of extraordinary vitality, left to be discovered by some Pasteur yet unborn, which clings to the tapestries and crevices of old houses. It would account for many failures, and a few notable successes.

[*Journals.*] LONDON,
JUNE 6TH.

Maurice drove over with me to Nuneham this morning. It took exactly $1\frac{1}{2}$ hours from door to door. We went through Henley and over the Chilterns, and the "position" which was the scene of the autumn manœuvres three years ago.

The Prime Minister was staying with Loulou [Harcourt]. And a large party. We went through the gardens with Loulou. After luncheon they all started to motor up to Huntercombe for the inevitable golf.

Possibly golf and bridge combined may help us to succumb to the Germans when the day of trial comes.

[*Journals.*] LONDON,
JUNE 13TH.

. . . I saw Haldane, who told me that my paper, given to and written for Lloyd George, had been called a "most important State paper" by Asquith, and was ordered to be printed for the Cabinet. I suppose its extreme simplicity appealed to him. It was written for men quite ignorant of military terms. [1]

[1] The paper referred to is not that given here on May 22nd, but a later memorandum on the subject which, having become a Defence Committee Paper, cannot be reprinted.

This morning I went to the British Museum Standing Committee; and the Prince of Wales, as usual, drove me home.

The Prince of Wales on the Navy.

He talked mainly about the Navy and Jackie Fisher. He thinks that the condition of the Navy is so serious, partly its weakness in ships and stores, partly its discipline, that it would be better if Jackie were to cede his place to some other. He was very friendly, as he always is.

The Tsar as Admiral of the Fleet—

There has been a great, almost serious, trouble about the appointment of the Tsar as an Admiral of the Fleet. The King made the appointment without reference to his Ministers. Jackie telegraphed rather peremptorily to McKenna and asked that letters patent should be made out at once. It appears that the King acted beyond his powers; but that is a trifling point. The real grievance is that an act of the kind creates parliamentary complications, and some minor troubles in Japan. Grey is angry. Asquith grieved. Francis [Knollys] saw them both, and very truly rubbed in the point that it was their own fault for not sending a Cabinet Minister of the highest rank with the King. To allow him to go to visit a *Great Power*, unaccompanied by a responsible Minister, is a dangerous innovation, and is trying the constitution too high.

[*Journals.*]
LONDON,
JUNE 16TH.

—Political Consequences.

Francis [Knollys] had an opportunity of speaking to the King about the "Admiral of the Fleet" affair, and the King was most reasonable and friendly about it. He said that he had no idea that he acted unconstitutionally, and was sorry the thing was done in the way it was. He himself afterwards saw Grey, and said the same thing to him. So the matter is ended.

I have been with the King this morning, walking in the garden, and his old *intime* manner has returned. So the German Emperor episode is now forgotten. Time has worked the usual miracle.

[*Journals.*] LONDON,
JUNE 22ND.

The party at Windsor changed on Saturday. The West-
minsters, Londonderrys, Dudleys, etc. left, and were replaced
by Asquiths, Grey, Morley, Mrs. Keppell and the Saviles.
Soveral only stayed on. He is always *persona gratissima*, especially with the Queen.

Margot Asquith sat next to Morley at luncheon. I was the
other side of him, and we talked *à trois*. She absorbed the conversation, and very cleverly too. Her vocabulary is remarkable,
and her ready wit and long memory make her talk vivacious
and arresting. But she flashes too rapidly for prudence, and is
devoid of that instinct called tact. Morley was speaking of a
fine phrase in Carlyle's *Life of Sterling* which had always stuck
in his memory, but before he could quote it, *she* had done so,
and accurately too! "Except in opinion not disagreeing," was
the phrase.

Morley and Mrs. Asquith at Windsor.

Morley I found in a room opening from the corridor,
usually occupied by the Princess of Wales. Someone else had
been put into the Minister's room. He was enchanted, and
revelled in the damask hangings. "At last, at Windsor, I feel
in a palace!"

He spoke laughingly of the strangeness and shrinking which
he feels at the new form in which he is addressed. But he told
me that old Fitz-James Stephen, soon after being made a Judge,
had said to him, "My dear Morley, if any man ever tells you that
he dislikes being met at the station by the High Sheriff and
Javelin men, and also being addressed as 'my lord,' don't you
believe him."

We went through Winston Churchill's Memo. on Army
Estimates (mine has been printed and circulated to the Cabinet
by Asquith); and it looks as if Lloyd George had managed to get
Winston to lead a frontal attack on Haldane, which is bound to
be repulsed with heavy losses. This is not a very auspicious
move for a young Minister. Haldane will remain in posi-

Churchill's Attack on Haldane.

tion. But where will Winston be? Not in such force as before.[1]

The King was to have gone to Lady Paget's on Sunday to dine and see a play with Cavalieri and Maud Allan. This appeared in the papers, and a very excellent letter from a clergyman, couched in touching terms, appealing to the King not to go. He has put off the entertainment, and resolved not to "break the Sabbath" in future.

[*To Lord Knollys.*]   2, TILNEY ST.,
                                       JUNE 26TH.

Haldane's   I saw Haldane yesterday and found him agitated and nervous.
Anxiety.   On reading the statement in *The Times* [2] about the Lord Chancellor, he went straight over to Asquith and told him, that whatever changes occurred in the Chancellorship, he would under no pressure or inducement vacate the W.O.; that he was resolved not to agree to the reduction of another Battalion of Infantry, or Regiment of Cavalry, or Battery of Artillery, and that "his back was against the wall." He told *me* that in the Cabinet he was well supported by Morley, and he relied on Grey, but he did *not* speak with the confidence of a few weeks ago.

Evidently he is impressed by the force of W. Churchill's attack. Of course, his position is *most* difficult. After 25 years of experience of War Ministers, I can truthfully say he is the most popular with senior officers on the Active List, that we have ever had.

[1] It does not appear from the Journals of the Commons that such an attack was ever made in the House: only in the Cabinet.

[2] ". . . In the Category of rumours which are not necessarily idle may be put the rumour that there is a possibility of Lord Loreburn's resigning the Lord Chancellorship. Nothing definite can be said upon the subject except that in the event of such a change it is expected that Mr. Haldane will succeed to the Woolsack. In connection with the post of Secretary of State for War, if thus vacated, Mr. Churchill's name is mentioned."

The Officers of the Army realise that he is their friend; he has not worried them, and he has supported them. But among retired Officers and among politicians of all shades, he has bitter enemies.

Some of these people do not understand the political situation, and that *Haldane alone* stands between us and Churchill.

The others desire the advent of a man who will ruthlessly cut down the Army and the Estimates. It is most unfortunate that poor Haldane, who has worked most loyally for the Army, under terribly difficult circumstances, and in face of an enormous radical majority, should have incurred displeasure in any quarter where support is invaluable at the moment.

He is a courageous man, but no man can stand up for ever, *if he is alone*, and I wish that he could be strengthened by feeling that in this desperate struggle he has the King's good wishes.

Of course, if W. Churchill comes to the War Office I should find it quite impossible to support the Government, or to remain connected with the Territorial Army, even though the Prime Minister were to ask me, under such circumstances, to retire from the Defence Committee.

It would not surprise me if many Chairmen of County Associations and others who, though opposed to the Government, have loyally supported Haldane's scheme, did not follow suit.

However mistaken Haldane may have been in some things (and who does not commit errors?), he really and truly deserves the good will and support of the King—if, for no other reason, that he alone, at the present moment, stands between the King and a political junta that desires to destroy the Regular Army.

[*Journals.*]　　　　　　　　　　　　　LONDON,
　　　　　　　　　　　　　　　　　　JUNE 26TH.

The King's birthday was kept to-day. Among the "Honours" there are few worth noting. Henry Jackson gets the Order of Merit, and his impress upon generations of undergrads is worth it. Francis [Knollys] gets a G.C.B. and, little as he cares for it, the Bath alone remains, among "Honours," fairly untarnished.

I lunched with W. Churchill at the H. of C. to meet the Khedive.

He came to O'Lea three years ago, and since then he has passed through phases of disloyalty, brought on by Cromer's harshness. Asquith, Ll. George, McKenna, Fisher, the Speaker, Haldane. That was the party. Afterwards, on the Terrace, we had some discussion. Ll. George said plainly, "No reduction in Army Estimates next year means no Dreadnoughts." This is bounce. The struggle between Haldane and Churchill accentuates. . . .

Churchill and Haldane. Asquith took me aside and asked me to speak to Churchill and to endeavour to compose this quarrel. . . .

I then went over to the Board of Trade, and had two hours' talk with Churchill. He was clever and ingenious, but wild and unpractical. I think, however, that he realises the difficulty of forcing Haldane's hand, and the undesirability of breaking up the Government. . . .

[*Journals.*]   2, TILNEY ST.,
                                                                            JULY 3RD.

Yesterday I gave a luncheon party at the Carlton. Asquith, A. Balfour, French, F. Knollys and Ottley. There was some very interesting talk. The object was to try and carry a step further the plan of bringing the Leaders of the Government and the Opposition together upon the highest questions of Peace Strategy. I think it had some success.

[*Journals.*]   LONDON,
                                                                            JULY 8TH.

Eddy Stanley resigned the chairmanship of the Lancashire Association directly Shuttleworth was made Lord Lieutenant. He came over to O'Lea and poured out his woes.

I went to see him at Coworth after a talk with Haldane and
Arthur Balfour. Eddy is conscious that he made a mistake and
wants a bridge of retreat. I think we can build it.

Haldane is convinced that Churchill wants to get rid of *him*,   *On Church-*
and that Ll. George backs him. This may be so. My idea is that   *hill's*
Winston wanted to push to the front of the Cabinet. He thinks   *ambition.*
himself Napoleon. But then we are not governed by a
Directoire. Men of the Grey, Crewe and Asquith type (notably
the former) are so unlike the adventurers whom Napoleon
swept out of his path. Our rulers have roots which go deep
down into the political soil.

[*Journals.*]   LONDON,
                                            JULY 11TH.

I called on Northcliffe, who lives in Sam Rogers's house in   *On North-*
St. James' Place. He lives simply, his house is furnished with   *cliffe and*
taste, without display, or ostentation of his enormous wealth.   *The*
                                                              Times.
His talk was mainly of *The Times*, and the method, half skill
and half luck, of its purchase. Since this talk, he has written to
me a curious letter, a confession of his idea in buying the control
of the paper, and his intentions in regard to it, should he die.
Both are creditable to him. His mind is that of an organiser and
speculator, not of the politician. He evidently loves power,
but his education is defective, and he has no idea to what uses
power can be put, except by deputy.

He enjoys the sensation of appointing or dismissing an editor.
But he could never inspire an article and still less could he edit a
paper. Yet I have no doubt that he will convert *The Times*
from a bankrupt into a fine property.

Last night, after listening to Coquelin declaim Cyrano, we
went to M. S. [Sutherland]'s last "Friday" at Stafford House.
Constance did *not* dance, nor was Cavalieri present. The result
was that the evening was rather dull.

[*To Lord Knollys.*] 2, TILNEY ST.,
JULY 12TH.

On Disputes in the Navy : Historical Parallels.

Have you noticed an article in the *Spectator* advocating that both Fisher and Beresford should be dismissed?

McKenna is extolled as the possible "strong man," who may show these sailors that the country is not dependent upon them; such a course is the easy refuge of the weak.

These quarrels in the Navy are no new thing. They wind through all the tangled skein of the Napoleonic wars. You will recollect Nelson's refusal in August 1799 to obey Lord Keith, and to join him before Minorca. He was reprimanded for this gross breach of naval discipline, but not dismissed.

In 1803–4, St. Vincent, who was First Lord, and Nelson were on very bad terms, and the latter was writing and speaking in a highly insubordinate manner. Fortunately Mr. Pitt did not then act on the advice which the *Spectator* offers to McKenna.

" Another good result of the policy we are hypothetically contemplating would be that it would teach naval officers that there are no indispensable men in the Navy, and that the nation can get on without even a Fisher, a Charles Beresford or a Percy Scott."

Substitute St. Vincent, Nelson and Troubridge for these men, and you have the situation of 1803–4. I am not comparing *men*, but circumstances. No one, except the King, can put an end to this stupid feud. I have long believed that the King by sending for Fisher and Beresford, and making them shake hands *in his presence*, and promise *him* that they will have done with this quarrel, both in public and in private, would earn and obtain the fervent applause of the whole country.

It would be a most striking illustration of the King's diplomatic skill, and strength of character. To pacify so dangerous a state of unrest in the Navy as is said to exist, is a task as important to us as international peace. From all I know of the circumstances, I am sure the King would not find the task beyond his powers. Will you think it over?

[*Journals.*]

LONDON,
JULY 23RD.

Dined with Asquith.

I had some talk with George Curzon, who was near me at   *House of*
dinner. He was well satisfied with the proposals of the House   *Lords*
of Lords Reform Committee. I told him I should vote against   *Reform.*
their plan, and every detail of it.[1]

He says that Rosebery makes a very bad chairman, and he
now understands R.'s failure to deal with affairs or with men.
His two great faults are his tendency to treat grave matters
frivolously, and his feminine sensitiveness to criticism. He is
always saying, "The Committee, I observe, will not accept
favourably any suggestion of *mine*," and such like phrases. His
exaggerations are also trying. "I have always felt that the most
important thing in the world next to the sinful Franco-British
Convention, is the necessity for preventing the Indian Viceroys
from sitting in the H. of C." Neither, as George says, being
a subject of first-class importance.

All this is very true observation.

. . . But Lloyd George, with whom I had some very straight
talk indeed, told me that it would not surprise him if the Government broke up in the autumn. He seems determined to get
2 millions off the Army.

The most interesting thing was that he talked with Metter-   *Lloyd George*
                                                                and Metter-
¹ The proposals of the Committee were these. That in future Peers should   *nich.*
be distinguished from "Lords of Parliament." That except in the case of
Peers of the Blood Royal a hereditary title should not give a seat in the house.
That the hereditary peers, including those of Scotland and Ireland, should
elect 200 members to the Upper House in each Parliament. That in addition
any peer should sit in the House who had been a Cabinet Minister, Viceroy
of India, Governor-General of Canada or Australia, High Commissioner
for South Africa, and Lord-Lieutenant of Ireland, or who had been Lt.-
General or Vice-Admiral on the active list, or had sat for a certain period in
the Commons. This recommendation would have added another 130 members. The Crown should be entitled to summon four Life members annually,
the total never to exceed forty. The Lords of Appeal in Ordinary would still
be Lords of Parliament. The result of the report would have been a house of
less than 400 instead of considerably more than 600.

nich. He told him plainly that if he had to borrow 100 millions for the Fleet, he would do so, in order to maintain our relative strength *vis-à-vis* to Germany. I wonder how the Emperor likes this! It is rather splendid of Lloyd George.

[*Journals.*]   LONDON,
JULY 26TH.

On the
Princess of
Wales.

Went over from O'Lea to Frogmore. Found the Princess of Wales in the garden. Sat and talked to her for nearly two hours. Mainly of her children and their upbringing, of her brothers and of the Prince of Wales.

She has more historical instincts and knowledge than any of the Royal Family.

Since we last spoke of her eldest boy, she *has* talked to him, and found him very sensible, and knowing much more of his prospects and responsibilities than she thought. He is treated, however, at Osborne precisely like any other boy, both by teachers and lads.

[*To the Duchess of Sutherland.*]   THE ROMAN CAMP,
AUGUST 4TH.

On the
Spirit of the
Time.

. . . What do you think of the past season? If Strath is a keen patriot, what does he make of the Olympic games, and spirit of "the horde." The Stadium might easily have been the Coliseum in the days of the Decline. And what of the Strand on the day of the performance of *Three Weeks*? Teeming with the carriages of the smart set, all flooding to see a play barred by the Censor?

If the Germans were not making headway against us, these things would be immaterial. As it is, are they not symptomatic? Then you have the Granby pamphlet, and the Cavalieri craze, culminating with the cheering mob at Goodwood, rejoicing over the acquittal of a scoundrel like S——. We only seem to require the Collier de la Reine.

The worst sign, to my mind, is the eclipse of all high literary ideal, and the poverty of writers both in verse and prose. The Victorian age was so prolific, following, as it did, upon those wonderful years at the beginning of the century.

High literature and high endeavour went hand in hand. *Où sont les feuilles d'antan?*

Except for John Morley, the last of the Titans, there is hardly a writer alive (for Meredith is in coma) who is above mediocrity.

There have been times when much the same could be said of England. The period of the restoration for example; but the danger now is that, in Europe, we have a competitor the most formidable in numbers, intellect and education with which we have ever been confronted.

[*To M. V. B.*]   THE ROMAN CAMP,
                             AUGUST 21ST.

. . . Jackie [Fisher] writes me that *Garvin* wants to talk to me about the Army, so I have wired to him if he likes to come down by night mail, stay the day, and return same night, I shall be delighted to see him. I have read an even better book by Wells, *Anticipations*, which I shall make you read when you come up here. Very suggestive.

I miss you dreadfully. It is curious how absorbed you get with Zena's personality. When she is anywhere on the horizon I notice that all other persons and things sink into mental insignificance. Are you conscious of it? I shall tell her some day of the effect she produces. I hope you will think all through the manœuvres (in your quiet moments) of those gentle blue eyes. *I* like them in their softer moments when they do not flash. It is sad that you and Zena should be living a century too soon—while the conventions of the aristocratic and monarchical superstitions still enfold us tightly.

[*Journals.*]   THE ROMAN CAMP,
AUGUST 21ST.

We spent a very happy ten days here in gorgeous summer weather. Bathing in the lochs, and shooting under a burning sun.

I went south with Maurice, and yesterday he went to the Cavalry manœuvres at Salisbury, and I returned here.

Admiral Wilson on Strategy.

I saw Francis [Knollys], who has now gone to the highlands, and a good deal of Jackie [Fisher]. We had one very long talk about Naval strategy and all his worries. J. told me of Arthur Wilson's determination, in the event of war with Germany, *not* to locate his battle-fleet in the North Sea. The rendezvous would be the Orkneys, and there the fleet would lie, ready for battle. Only Cruisers and Destroyers in the North Sea.

[*To M. V. B.*]   THE ROMAN CAMP,
AUGUST 22ND.

. . . I sent some grouse in your name to Zena, and *not* in your name to the Merry Widow.[1]

. . . I am contemplating a drive to Cloan this afternoon.

Lloyd George, France and Germany.

. . . The tone of the French papers shows how much the French resent any philandering with Germany although they have no desire to pick a quarrel. Unless some unforeseen change occurs, in the ambitious designs of Germany, and the feeling of our people, a quarrel cannot long be postponed. The well-meant efforts of the peacemakers in the Press do more harm than good.[2]

[*To M. V. B.*]   THE ROMAN CAMP,
AUGUST 23RD.

. . . Haldane walked with me for an hour. My surmise was correct about Grey, who has taken strong exception to Ll.

[1] Miss Lily Elsie.

[2] The reference is to a very friendly interview given by Lloyd George to the *Neue Freie Presse* a few days earlier.

George's excursion into F. politics. His vehement protest brought Asquith up to town, and a strong prohibitory telegram was sent to L. G. Of course Haldane was delighted, as Grey's action is tantamount to a flank attack upon *his* foe. Haldane himself has lain very low. He is going to-day to Germany, but under a *nom de guerre*. He is going to stay with Manners in the mountains, and return on the 7th.

Tell the General [French] that I discussed the *future* with Haldane, and that he agrees that Lord K. [Kitchener] ought to succeed the D. of Connaught, which *may* be in about ten months' time—and that the General himself should succeed Nick [1] at the expiration of the latter's four years. That will just fit in with the General's term. *Future Army Appointments.*

Haldane wants to settle this with A. J. B. [Balfour] if possible. It is a good notion. He has asked me to speak to Arthur, which I will do.

There is certainly a great advantage in having these points arranged beforehand. Then everybody knows what to work for. Haldane is naturally most anxious about *his* successor should the Government break down, which he thinks might happen in about two years or at any date short of that period. He anticipates Wyndham. I do not agree with him, and I hope that Salisbury will be the Unionist War Minister. He would *undo* nothing, and he is not "on the make"; neither is he so volatile as George Wyndham.

[*To M. V. B.*]   THE ROMAN CAMP,
                                       AUGUST 27TH.

. . . I do not care for any relics of my sojourn on the earth's surface. A few things I hope will be imperishable. Where I have been able to give a slight impetus, which has set bigger stones rolling. I do not value any record of this, but it is pleasant to think of.

[1] Sir William Nicholson.

... Meanwhile, go and steep yourself in your love for Zena. Never miss chances. There are things one regrets. The days which are lost, the galloping hours. If you can only once see the blue of the water reflected in Zena's eyes for half an hour, it is worth a railway journey, and a day of waiting. For these moments come only rarely into human lives, and they are glorious remembrances. You can live for weeks and months in wet tents upon the recollection of an hour spent looking over the sea, with Zena's hand in yours. And keep her *image* in your heart, as well as upon it. This is the safeguard from feeble thoughts, and the stimulus to daring ones.

[*To M. V. B.*]   THE ROMAN CAMP,
                                           AUGUST 28TH.

On Greek Art. ... Last night I looked through my translations from the Anthology. There are some very pretty things, and I think Zena ought to have copies of some of the best. Perhaps it will be a new idea for her that she was glorified in anticipation by Meleager in the first century B.C.

> Zena, dainty darling, slumber
> would that I were with you, dear,
> wingless sleep your eyelids cumber
> may no other soul be near.
> E'en though Zeus himself cajoled you
> let mine arms alone enfold you.

We had a discussion on the true Greek spirit, arising out of the Hellenism of Wordsworth and Keats. In sculpture, according to my ideas, the characteristics of Athenian art in the age of Pericles were simplicity, repose and restraint—in the treatment of every-day matters.

A boy pulling a thorn out of his foot, or scraping himself with a strigil. Wordsworth's treatment of natural subjects—a girl reaping in a field, or a violet under a mossy stone, is much nearer Greek art than the "Ode to a Grecian Urn," or "Psyche." These are Græco-Sicilian of the time of Theocritus or Greek art touched by the fiery spear of the Renaissance. I wonder whether you agree with me.

I could never find in the Greeks any trace of the spirit of Keats, his brilliant imagination, and wonderful depth of word-colouring. I am not speaking of the first century B.C.—when Greece was no more—but of 400 B.C.

Of course, the later Greeks, when they had been influenced by Persians and Egyptians, and the Oriental warmth had touched their lyric muse, were more capable of seeing beauty with the eyes of Keats. The more I read him, the more hard it seems that our literature should have been bereft of his maturer spirit. It is almost impossible to think what he might have given to the world after "Hyperion."

[*To M. V. B.*]　　　　　　　THE ROMAN CAMP,
　　　　　　　　　　　　　　　AUGUST 30TH.

. . . But the man like Napoleon, who chooses the nobler life, *On the Half-* cannot afford to make excursions up bypaths. If he does, he runs *Great Men—* enormous risks. Now and then, as in the General's case, the thing can be done, and a man gets back into his course. But in the vast majority of cases, one slip is fatal.

For years a man goes on straight, aiming at his goal, striving and straining; then, suddenly he "takes a chance" and it is the final, irrevocable end. These are the "mauve" men. Parnell is the saddest of recent examples of really great men. But Dilke comes only a short way behind, and Randolph [Churchill] is another less understood example.

Rosebery's pitfall, too, was self-indulgence, luxury and love of praise, the shrinking from criticism. Yet all these things are inconsistent with the strenuous life.

I have just finished the glorious account of the Peloponnesian war. The lessons it teaches are really precisely the same. Alcibiades—one of the most hopelessly "mauve" of men—and one of the worst influences to which any state was ever subjected. He could urge on a great war, and with a light heart, on the night before the Sicilian expedition, went round with boon companions mutilating the Hermæ, or domestic statues. It is no wonder that he fell and that Athens followed.

Pericles, on the other hand, soldier-like, keen, wise, prudent and brave, splendidly reserved and restrained, spending *his* spare time either consulting Aspasia, or in her arms. There was no "fall." On the contrary it was a vivifying influence, good for Pericles, good for Athens.

—Parnell and Alcibiades.
Parnell failed to see that he could not combine the essential friendship of Mr. Gladstone with his adulterous connection with Kitty O'Shea; Alcibiades, that he could not combine the leadership of Athens with *open* debauch. Pericles saw that his love for Aspasia, courtesan though she was, would give no offence to his fellow-citizens if he kept within the limits of display allowed by Athenian custom, and he immortalized himself and his amours.

[*To M. V. B.*]   THE ROMAN CAMP,
                                       AUGUST 30TH.

On Byron—
It is a wonderful evening, and you know how the western sun strikes in at the windows of this room. Everyone has gone for an after-tea walk. I have been reading Byron's final adventures in Greece. It was the only act of his life that seems to have been creditable—and redeemed much of the rest. What a miserable man he must have been—devoured with unsatisfied ambition and sensitive to every breath of criticism or abuse; and abused (not without justice) as few men have been. Looking at "Hours of Idleness" one is amazed that he ever should have been a poet at all, and it is truly astonishing that at any time, however early in life, the author of *Don Juan* should have written such feeble verse.

No wonder the volume was abused. Not that criticism of the *—and M.* unknown poet counts for much. Perhaps one of the most con- *Arnold.* demnatory things I ever remember to have heard about critics, was Arnold telling my father (who was always very intimate with him) that his first volume of poems fell absolutely flat— only a very few copies were sold. Yet it contained practically everything for which he ultimately was praised, including "Empedocles."

I forget who it was, but I think Browning, who made him republish the volume 15 years later. . . .

I suppose the period, the world phase, has much to do with these things. There is no reason why the force of men's intellects, the beat of the soul of mankind, should not ebb and flow with the Tides.

Those years which we call the end of the 18th century and the beginning of the 19th century—those 5 decades from 1780 to 1830—were marvellously productive of genius in these Islands, and over much of the surface of Europe. For the moment we seem to be in the trough of the sea. However, it is when the night is darkest that the stars pierce out of the infinite.

[*To M. V. B.*]   THE ROMAN CAMP,
                                      SEPTEMBER 2ND.

. . . As I think over the artificial barriers which convention *On Social* has built up, so unnecessarily, between human souls, *mine* rebels. *Conventions.* However, the cost has always to be counted, and experience unfortunately shows that when payment has been made, it is always the woman who pays.

It is easy to see how in the middle ages, and since, men and women have renounced the world. They may have been the weaker spirits, but they are intensely comprehensible. Young men and maids must have suffered when the social barriers were higher than they are to-day, and how vain all this suffering seems to be to us.

To-morrow, when the barriers are lowered once more, then the pain which convention inflicts upon men and maids to-day, will appear equally and tragically vain.

It makes me rebellious to think that you cannot, without sacrificing so much that the sacrifice would itself be vain, make yourself happy by taking yourself and Zena into some obscure and secluded part of this very beautiful world. But under the scheme of things ordained for us by custom, so direct a pursuit of happiness would probably be fatal. It is this which justifies for a moment, the feeling of rebellion against the older Gods. Shams, shams, the worship of shams! So relentlessly tight are these social chains. And then you wonder that, although I serve Kings and wear coronets and things, I care nothing about them, and feel for them only as one feels for anything picturesque and of artistic interest.

> "Beauty is truth, truth beauty" that is all
> Ye know on earth, and all ye need to know.

But alas, that is the ideal world of poets, the world of sacred, intimate things, the world of your thoughts and mine, from which no one can snatch Zena, and where her lips may always be upon yours.

In the world of every-day material work, nothing much counts but the power to leave it the better for your having been born. . . .

[*To M. V. B.*]   THE ROMAN CAMP,
                              SEPTEMBER 3RD.

German Foreign Policy.

. . . I have a long letter from Fritz [Ponsonby] this morning. Most interesting—but it will keep until you come. The German Emperor's speech was received with praise and would have been used as an argument to reduce naval estimates here. Luckily— and we are fortunate people—Bülow and his Master interfere next day in Morocco with such woeful want of tact, that it sets all Europe buzzing again. Of course it may be, and I suspect this, that the intervention in Morocco was determined upon before the speech was made, and that the rhetoric was meant to sweeten the pill. Anyway it will make Grey more keen than ever to resist weakening our armaments and to stick to the entente with France.

[*To M. V. B.*]　　　　　　　　THE ROMAN CAMP,
　　　　　　　　　　　　　　　　　SEPTEMBER 15TH.

. . . The Bishop of London speaking in America at a drawing-room meeting.

Bishop—"You often hear it said that hell is paved with good intentions. I say it is paved with champagne, bridge, fast women and motor cars."

Voice from the Audience (American accent)—"O death where is thy sting."

I wonder what you think of Asquith's intervention in the Catholic spree. It looks as if he was adroitly backing his Scots and Nonconformists against the Catholics, who are always Tories. One can hardly blame him. After all, these open-air religious festivals are silly things. They should stick to their churches, when they have them. The article in *The Times* is so violent against Asquith, that I feel he must have scored.[1]

[*To M. V. B.*]　　　　　　　　THE ROMAN CAMP,
　　　　　　　　　　　　　　　　　SEPTEMBER 19TH.

Here is an adventure. Arrival of the Furry Beast.[2] He wired to say he was coming with Mason.[3] I stumped off to Stirling,

[1] The Government were called upon by Protestant societies to prevent the procession of the Host through the streets of Westminster on the occasion of the visit of the Papal Legate, Vanutelli; and Mr. Asquith did at the last moment intervene—at the last moment because until these societies took action the matter had attracted very little notice.

[2] J. M. Barrie.　　　　　　　　　　[3] A. E. W. Mason.

but Mason did not come. The F.B. is already palpitating to be off fishing.

. . . I was interrupted here by the task of starting away Syv, Barrie and Eve[1] to fish in the burn. Barrie with Nellie's rod— no reel—a bit of line and a box of worms.

Enchanted by the roughness of the life (no servants), having to make his lunch, and borrow an old cap of mine. He has gone to buy garters at Page and Don!

[*To M. V. B.*]   THE ROMAN CAMP,
                                                  SEPTEMBER 20TH.

Barrie on the   . . . I have not talked to the Furry Beast yet about Zena—but
Theatre—   I mean to do so. He says that Du Maurier is the only *man* connected with the stage who is of superior mind. "It is absolutely
a woman's career." Only 3rd rate men have to do with it. Du
Maurier has often determined to throw it up, but then some part
which took his fancy came along. He hates all the detail of stage
life, even to the make-up of his face. His father left about £1,200
p.a. to his widow (who is alive) and all this was made, i.e.
about £40,000, in the last 3 years of his life, and all out of one
book, *Trilby*.

Barrie says, "the most successful book of recent time." He
himself wanted to write a book, but drifted into *What Every
Woman Knows*. I asked why. He says book writing after play
writing appears diffuse. He has got into the habit of compres-
sion. He was doubtful about the success of the play—but saw it
"come right" as the rehearsals went on. He writes elaborate
"explanations" of the part and action to each actor.

These are given to each actor with the script. But none of
them ever read the play as a whole or know what it is about. He
does not believe in "study" of the stage, except voice training.
Either, he thinks, a woman has the power of projecting herself

[1] Miss Eve Brand, afterwards Lady Crerar.

across the footlights or she has not. No teaching will give her
this. He thinks Lily Elsie has it to a great degree.

[*To M. V. B.*] THE ROMAN CAMP,
SEPTEMBER 21ST.

A very quiet Sunday. Barrie sat all day in the River House. *—and on*
. . . He talks without ceasing, when alone like that with us, *Actresses.*
but is rather silent and observant at dinner. He looked at your
room, and sat for some time on your ottoman talking of Zena.
He thinks her "Peter Pan" *as good as it could be.* There is "nothing
wanting" except a taller and better Wendy. He thinks Zena
lovely. He says the difficulty with "these girls" is that they get
spoilt by the high salaries of musical comedy, and want to step
into equally high ones in comedy. They have "not unnaturally"
no patience. So, they look to marriage, but "they generally see
the wrong sort of men. Trivial flashy men. And to many of
them, marriage becomes a light matter, something to do for
the week you have off."

That description ought to amuse Zena. He says that Zena
should deal with Frohman herself—and *not* bargain, but leave
the salary to Frohman. It is the way to deal with him, and far
more successful than any other method. Barrie has not seen
Phyllis for a long while but will go next time he gets a chance.

. . . I cannot remember all the good things he said about politicians, authors etc. on our walk. But this I do remember. Syv
said something about "stupid people" and he rebuked her at
once. "Don't despise stupid people, they are often far better
than the clever ones. It is so *ordinary* to be merely clever and
smart in these days. Every other man you meet is clever."

. . . Barrie thinks we ought never to add to this house, but have
a row of bothies all along the river, each to hold one, with a row
of shops, where would be sold nothing that anybody wants.
There is an armchair on top of the Tump which he thinks a
lovely commanding position. This is the drivel side of his queer

little mind. But what a mind it is really, and how romantic and chivalrous. So wise where real love is concerned, so trenchant and severe where it is not. You should hear him tell of Kirriemuir, and the lives of the factory girls—his sympathy and his admiration. The plumes of his mind are quite unsullied.

. . . He will talk for hours about the psychology of his characters.

[*To M. V. B.*]   THE ROMAN CAMP,
                                                   SEPTEMBER 22ND.

. . . I dropped Barrie at Dunblane on his way to Kirriemuir. He said he had never enjoyed a holiday more, and will come again. He does not know what to do about Wendy—who is wanted for his present piece and Peter Pan. I suggested Pauline to play Wendy and Zena Peter. I think he was rather struck. Here is a story for Zena. Sir John Hare is a *very* disagreeable cross old man at home. He arrived from Blackpool in a towering passion and was unapproachable. At last it comes out. He was leaving his hotel (I think) and saw an enormous crowd, apparently waiting to bid him farewell. But when he came out they took no notice. A man in the crowd pulled him by the coat-tail, and said, "If you stand here a few minutes you will see Miss Zena Dare come out."

[*Journals.*]   BALMORAL,
                                                   SEPTEMBER 26TH.

To-day I left about 9, and drove here through mist and rain. Dunblane and Blairgowrie were decorated in honour of the King's visit on Monday. I got to Braemar at 3.30, having stopped a little over an hour en route.

The King sent for me directly after tea, and kept me about an hour and a half. I kissed his hand and he was most kind, and in one of his most capable moods. His talk ranged over a wide field. . . .

We then talked of the King's interview with the German Emperor. The King said he was "impossible." That when he suggested to his nephew a limitation of armaments, or a discussion on the subject, he at once said that *by law* the Fleet had to be completed up to a certain strength, and there was no power to draw back! As if the law could not be altered by those who made it. Evidently the tone of the refusal made a bad impression. (My breeze with the German Emperor is more than condoned!) " 'Two keels to one' is the only right and safe thing," said the King! *The King and the Kaiser.*

[*To M. V. B.*]   BALMORAL CASTLE,
                                          SEPTEMBER 27TH.

The King told me so many things in his two hours' talk last night that I can remember none of them. There are changes in the Government impending, and they will surprise you when I tell you what they are. Quite satisfactory.

. . . To-day I went for a long walk with Edward Grey. He was most open about all his colleagues, and his policy. His *justesse d'esprit* is remarkable. He is so fair even about the people for whom he has no sympathy.

Villaloba, the Spaniard, arrived at 3 in the morning, having been asked to arrive at tea time. He had lost his luggage and so waited at Aberdeen. His servant and luggage are vital to him, as he has no legs, no teeth, no hair. He is all false except his torso.

. . . Princess Patsy has been my partner to-night in a game of patience. She is very lovely. There is no doubt of that. The Prince and Princess of Wales dined here. A. P. [Paget] is splendid! He played bridge last night with the King, and after they sat down, he bagged (accidentally) the King's cigar. Suddenly the King woke up out of an absent fit and said, "Hullo, you have taken my cigar." "So I have," said A. P., "and a very good cigar it is too"—and threw his own halfpenny smoke into the fire. Not a word of apology. The King had to send for another. Isn't he *impayable*.

[*Journals.*]   BALMORAL CASTLE,
                                                        SEPTEMBER 27TH.

*Edward
Grey's
Opinions.*

To-day, being Sunday, we went to Church at Crathie. A large party, including the Prince of Wales and his family from Abergeldie, and the Connaughts who are here.

After luncheon I had a long walk with Edward Grey up to the Gelder towards Lochnagar. A wide range of subjects. Besides Wordsworth, he reads FitzGerald. Not so much his poems as his correspondence, etc. It is the type of literature he likes.

He thinks the settlement of South Africa the great achievement of the Government, and that, with "trouble in India looming" we should be in great anxiety presently, if South Africa were hostile. . . .

. . . Winston Churchill, on the other hand, he thinks a genius. His fault, that phrases master him, rather than he them. But his faults and mistakes will be forgotten in his achievements. Here he is right. Winston has the real political fire.

Grey is not an admirer of the German Emperor. He thinks him not quite sane, and very superficial. This has always been my opinion. That he is picturesque, and has a certain gift of language, is true, but he is not "a consistent or persistent thinker." Like Winston, he is mastered by phrases. "You should think out a subject before you make phrases about it." "The worst of it is that when most people do think out impartially and drily a subject, the phrases won't come."

He thinks Bülow, Clemenceau and Stolypin would hold their own readily in English public life, but not Isvolsky nor Pichon, etc. Marschall von Bieberstein, he thinks the ablest living German, but he is *too* able for the Emperor, who banished him to Constantinople. This desire to stand alone among second-rate men is the German Emperor's (and Empire's) danger.

What I think of Grey is this. He is a statesman of the old early-Victorian school, honest, dignified, and unselfish. He is thoughtful and laborious, conscientious and scrupulous, with a high sense of duty, and no love of politics. But he is an Englishman to the backbone, and will never abdicate his right to help govern the country. We talked for an hour about fishing and the habits of fish; his *real* delight.

The Author on Grey—

[*To M. V. B.*]   BALMORAL CASTLE,
SEPTEMBER 28TH.

. . . I am tired to death. Such a day on the hill. A very high wind, and rather steep walking. I had two shots. First standing up at a running stag, and got him. He was nearly end-on too, but I hit him in a good place. Just as we approached something put him away.

Then later, I got a good but difficult stalk at a really good big beast with very queer horns, and though I could only see the top of his back I shot him dead! So I am rather proud of myself.

[*Journals.*]   BALMORAL CASTLE,
SEPTEMBER 28TH.

With Mackintosh stalking, I had two shots, and got two good beasts. Both difficult moving shots.

I have written a memo for the King on a long letter of Milner's about South Africa. It is painful to find a man of Milner's ability with such a fixity of mind that he cannot admit facts. He is still moving in the atmosphere of 1898.

—and on Milner.

The Connaughts have gone. The Prince of Wales is not

looking well. His dyspepsia gives him so much trouble. He is now on a rigid diet, and it does not suit him. He is not strong.

[*Journals.*]   BALMORAL CASTLE,
                                                 SEPTEMBER 29TH.

Went fishing with Grey. Any number of red and black fish leaping about, but with a rising river, no sport.

Grey on the Government. We talked a good deal. Grey laid stress on the false perspective of politicians. No one foresaw when the administration was formed the real posts of difficulty and danger. He thinks it was providential, J. M. [Morley]'s going to the India Office—in his opinion, *the* most dangerous post. No one can tell when the gathering storm there will burst, but none of them except J. M., with his unimpeachable record, could have governed India just now, in the face of a sentimental Parliament.

He himself had wished C.-B. to go to the House of Lords, and did not see that the H. of C. would be grasped by the heart, and not by the head (which was too small)—and that C.-B. only could do this.

A man's character, according to him, is formed not by environment, not by action, but by what he thinks when he is alone. This remark is characteristic of him. I gave him Wells's *Anticipations* as a reminder of our talks.

Sat next the King at dinner, who was in high spirits. We talked of Lady Molesworth and Lady Waldegrave, those old rival coryphées. B. Osborne once said of Lady M., who was unusually *fagotée*, "She looks like a State bed." Huddlestone was always alluding to his wife, Lady Diana (whom he was proud of having married) as Di. When he was made a Judge he had to choose a motto. At dinner he asked B. O. across the table, "What motto *can* I choose?" "Never say die," said B. O.

I have looked over a lot of correspondence between Coutts the bankers, and the sons of George III, all borrowing money. The King's leave to publish is asked, and I hope will be refused.

[*To Lord Morley.*]   BALMORAL CASTLE,
                                       SEPTEMBER 30TH.

I have been here nearly a week, and my keen regret is that I
shall not be here when you come. My partial compensation has
been the presence of Grey, who, by the way, is one of your most
fervent friends and admirers. I had two days *tête-à-tête* with him
on the river and he expands strangely with a fishing rod in his
hand.

When we meet, I shall have much to tell you about our talks.
Here is one of those characteristic touches:

"A man's character is not so much influenced by environment
as by his solitary meditations!"

The King is wonderfully well, and in tearing spirits. I think
you will enjoy your visit. It seems always my fate to be here
when Cabinet changes are pending. I wonder what your ideas
and sentiments are upon the subject. The King seems to have
been delighted and most interested by a letter he received from
you. I remain here till Saturday, and then return to my home
in Perthshire.

[*Memorandum.*]   BALMORAL CASTLE,
                                    SEPTEMBER 30TH.

The question raised by the Maharajah of Cooch Behar is not *Precedence of*
simply Indian or social, as Ministers of the Crown and Peers *Indian*
have a political status in this country, which they might *Princes.*
consider affected by the concession of a claim of all Indian
Ruling Princes to have precedence at State functions.

The King's right to give precedence to any subject over
another is unquestioned, and was so stated in 1840 by both Lord
Melbourne and Sir Robert Peel.

Quite recently the King has settled the precedence of the
Prime Minister, in accordance with a constitutional development which has taken place during the past thirty years, with

the result that the holder of that great office is now Primus among his colleagues, and no longer *primus inter pares*.

In the case of the Prince Consort, the Queen's decision that H.R.H. was to have precedence next after Her Majesty, had a decided political complexion, and was clearly understood to mean that had the Queen died during the minority of the Prince of Wales, the Ministers of the Crown and the Leaders of the Opposition were agreed that the Prince Consort should be Regent.

These cases seem clearly to indicate that a question of precedence has not only a social, but may have political significance. Indian ruling Princes fall certainly into two and possibly more classes.

The King may think fit, after all the facts are placed before His Majesty, to differentiate between Princes like the Nizam, Scindiah, Holka, the Maharajahs of Cashmere, Mysore, etc. etc. and rulers over lesser states.

Again, there may be distinctions that would be obvious to Indians, between Rajput Princes of the rank of Jaipur and Sir Pertab Sing. The Maharajah of Cooch Behar himself may come into a different category. The Aga Khan, again, is a unique and somewhat difficult case.

It is also worthy of consideration whether precedence over subjects of British birth might not be accorded to individual Princes, as a mark of the King's favour, rather than as a right. So long as the Church remains established, and a hereditary House of Parliament an integral part of the Constitution, it may be desirable to safeguard the position near the Throne of the Archbishop of Canterbury, who is the "first subject" of His Majesty, after the Princes of the Blood Royal, and that of the Lord Chancellor and the other great hereditary Peers.

Precedence given to Foreign Princes, as a matter of courtesy, or foreigners of distinction, has never been resented by Englishmen. But *Indian* Princes are the King's *subjects*, and in view of the fact that not even the most exalted Indian Prince can exercise authority at present over the meanest European—a system which cannot possibly be for long upheld—the advice given to the King upon the question by the Maharajah of Cooch Behar requires very cautious consideration.

[*Journals.*]   BALMORAL,
                                                    OCTOBER 1ST.

Yesterday I had a quiet day, and wrote two memoranda for the King. One upon the political aspects of a claim for precedence by Indian Princes; the other upon the recent "defence" meeting in Denmark.[1]

Haldane arrived.

To-day we had a deer drive. The King, P. of W., P. Arthur, Horace Farquhar, Pockleffsky, Herschell, and myself. A glorious day in the woods from Alt-na-guisach to Birkhall —but no spoils. The only stag missed by Horace in the last drive, and I shot it—reluctantly, as I was in the next box to the King. But it was not going his way.

Mrs. Keppel and Mrs. Hwfa Williams came to luncheon from Glen Muick. The King in a wonderfully good humour.

[*Journals.*]   BALMORAL CASTLE,
                                                    OCTOBER 2ND.

Haldane suggested this morning that I should explain to the King the great change which has occurred, in the last two years, in the constitution and readiness for war of the Regular Army. *Improved Readiness of the Army.*

It is exceedingly difficult, as I told him, to do this without tabulated figures.

[1] The defence committee in Denmark had been at work for six years, at the end of which each political party, and also the body of military experts, put forward its separate programme. The Premier pronounced in favour of absolute neutrality and expressed the belief that Denmark could defend that neutrality. His National Defence measure, however, could not be brought forward until the following year.

The net result is, no doubt, that the King has *in Great Britain*, a force of 200,000 men which could be ready in 3 weeks, and possibly 18 days, to fight *on the line of the Meuse*.

There is no previous period in the history of this country when such a feat was within measurable distance.

I suggested to Haldane that the simplest way of bringing home these facts to the King, is to send, *every quarter*, a "Field State" of the Army to the King as Commander-in-Chief, such as was presented to Napoleon every morning.

Such a document would not exceed in length half a sheet of notepaper, and would be more eloquent than the longest memorandum.

[*Journals.*]   BALMORAL CASTLE,
                                 OCTOBER 2ND.

Duke of Kent's Correspondence.

This morning the King went through with me the papers which Hartley Coleridge sent: all his grandfather's letters on pecuniary matters to Thomas Coutts. Also endless correspondence of the other royal dukes. It is intolerable that there should be any question of the publication of letters of the kind—whether royal or not. The King has authorised me to see Coutts and remonstrate, and if necessary to say he will withdraw the account.

I went over in my motor to Braemar, where I met Nellie and Maurice and Oliver. They had come over from home.

In the evening we had a servants' ball. The Princess of Wales and Princess Alice danced vigorously all the evening. The Prince of Wales took me into the smoking-room and we had a long talk about the Navy and other things.

[*To Lord Morley.*]   THE ROMAN CAMP,
                                 OCTOBER 5TH.

Morley's Continuing Importance.

. . . As I think my last letter told you, I was struck by Grey's overwhelming sense of an impending storm in your Indian dominions. He seems to feel the gathering thunder-clouds in that region and evidently looks upon your post as that of the greatest danger at the present time. Hence his rejoicing at your presence in the office you hold. "How little," he says, "was the vital importance of Morley's tenure of the I.O. foreseen when the Government was formed." And then he commented on our national good luck.

So you need not think, as you seem to do in some fantastic dream, of a *nunc dimittis.*

Tweedmouth's retirement brings about, I assume, consequential changes, but they cannot be of very great importance. They may, however, add strength in weak places. *No one* remembers 1848. The memories of our modern radicals are as proverbial as those of the Bourbons.[1]

[*To M. V. B.*] THE ROMAN CAMP,
OCTOBER 14TH.

. . . I have a long letter from J. M. [Morley] this morning. *Seizure of* He has been dining *partie carrée* with Grey, Isvolsky and Bencken- *Bosnia and* dorff. It is clear that the crisis—for the present—is on the wane. *Herzegovina.*

England, Russia, and France have agreed upon the terms upon which the two *coups d'état* are to be accepted, and Europe will follow them.

Germany is the power that will suffer most. Austria gets all she wants. But Germany will find herself shut out from Asiatic enterprises, and will have to look for compensation elsewhere.

In fact, Austria has—unwittingly perhaps—slammed the door in the face of her ally.

[1] Lord Tweedmouth, who retired on grounds of health, was replaced by Sir Henry Fowler, Viscount Wolverhampton. In 1848 the Liberal administration of Lord John Russell was very hard pressed, but was re-formed from within. It then became so strong that when it suffered a defeat in the House in 1852 the Opposition was not able to form a government and Lord John Russell returned to office.

[*Journals.*]   THE ROMAN CAMP,
                                        OCTOBER 23RD.

. . . Two days ago left for London to attend the Defence Committee—the final committee on "Invasion," which was held yesterday.

After a meeting at the "Terriers,"[1] I dined with Jackie [Fisher] and we had three hours' talk. All naval and political. . . .

I lunched with J. M. Barrie, Granville Barker, and Archer, to talk about the National Theatre. It was not very illuminating. Barrie was quite silent. The other protagonists of the scheme have faced none of the real difficulties.

[*Journals.*]   LONDON,
                                        OCTOBER 28TH.

Arrived this morning. Yesterday we left home very regretfully. On the previous day, Maurice and I shot over Corriecrombie and Bochastle. A lovely Scottish day, with driving clouds.

The Kaiser's To-day the German Emperor's amazing "interview" appears
Interview. in the *Telegraph*. He thinks himself immortal and omnipotent. It never occurs to him that he may be forced to act against his own inclination. He forgets that Napoleon III and William I were neither of them wishful of war in 1870. It does not strike him that he might be killed in a motor accident. He sets all Europe by the ears—or would if he could—in a rage of egoistic chatter. *He* alone prevented France and Russia from pursuing their design of humiliating England in 1900. *He* alone drafted the plan of campaign against the Boers, sent it to the Queen of England, and saw it victoriously adopted by Lord Roberts. "The majority of his people are anti-English." *He* and a select few are our only friends. He fails to see that he could have furnished us with no more telling argument for "keeping our powder dry." A feckless man.

[1] Territorial Force Association.

I lunched with Morley. We discussed many things. He asked me if I should like to succeed Minto in India! I said decidedly *No*. I should hate it. Besides, the Viceroy to-day is a mere puppet in the hands of the S. of S. I did not say this.

The King seems to have agreed with Morley that I was to preside over the Committee on Indian precedence. But they counted their unhatched chickens. I have not refused, but I have written a memo. which will have the effect of postponing the Committee altogether. . . .

J. M. Barrie gave us a box for *What Every Woman Knows* this evening. What a little masterpiece!

[*To Lord Morley*.]   2, TILNEY ST.,
                                   OCTOBER 29TH.

The enclosed memorandum embodies the views which I ventured to submit to you, after our talk yesterday, upon the question of the Precedence Committee.

I feel sure that if you would explain to Lord Knollys the practical difficulty of examining into the very large number of cases which will have to be considered, without a preliminary enquiry conducted with the assistance of the Viceroy, he will represent the matter very clearly to the King.

No committee can meet profitably here until this has been done, of this I feel sure, after what you have said.

[*Journals*.]   LONDON,
                                   OCTOBER 29TH.

Lunched with Arthur Balfour at the Ritz. An enormous crowd.

. . . Soveral came and sat with us. He is convinced that the so-called "interview" was a carefully prepared project. This he judges by internal evidence. It is corroborated by rumour.

Arthur thinks the Government weak collectively, and with the exception of Grey, Haldane, Morley and Crewe and the P.M., not strong individually. I do not agree with him.

He seems unconscious of the weakness *individually* of his own people. A Unionist Government would really be A. J. B. *et praeterea nihil*. He evidently does not realise this.

[*Journals.*]   LONDON,
                                                 NOVEMBER 2ND.

The G.C.B.   . . . This evening I received a very handsome letter from the P.M. offering me the Grand Cross of the Bath. The terms of his letter were most flattering. It is a "recognition"—but more than this, it is a reply to the German Emperor's impertinences of last year. From that point of view I rather value it. . . .

[*To the Rt. Hon. H. H. Asquith.*]   2, TILNEY ST.,
                                                 NOVEMBER 3RD.

It would be affected on my part, were I to deny that your most kind letter gave me great pleasure. Public recognition is gratifying to everyone, but I cannot conceal from you that even more gratifying to me is the generous language in which you have clothed your offer. "Invaluable" is a strong and I fear unmerited word, but your use of it is invaluable to me.

[*Journals.*]   LONDON,
                                                 NOVEMBER 3RD.

. . . This morning I presided over a Committee on a National Theatre. Bernard Shaw, Pinero, Tree, Barker and S. H. Butcher.[1]

[1] On the following New Year's Day Sir Herbert Tree wrote:

HIS MAJESTY'S THEATRE,
LONDON,
JAN. 1ST, 1909.

. . . I am strongly of opinion that the National Theatre, in order to live, must adopt the method of the modern theatre, and not seek to cater, as I

In the afternoon I had a long talk with the General [French] at the Horse Guards on Imperial Defence, and went through Murray's papers, which are remarkably well done.

This evening Jackie [Fisher] telephoned he was most anxious to see me. He was undecided what to do, having qualms at the idea of leaving the Admiralty next year. I urged him to write to McKenna, telling him that on November 9th, 1909, he would resign. He said that McKenna had expressed to him his strong hope that he would not lose him. I replied, "Very well. If he is sincere, you will have made a wise move." Jackie then said that he was resolved to act upon this advice. *Nous verrons!*

Fisher Considers Resignation.

[*Journals.*]

LONDON,
NOVEMBER 5TH.

We awake to find a European crisis, Germany bullying France.[1] Is it a red herring drawn across the track of the Emperor's "interview"? Is it a diversion in the interests of Austria? Or is it an attempt to detach France from her alliances? Certainly Russia is weak to-day, owing to the Slav explosion, and cannot act with independence in support of France. Austria is

The Franco-German "Casablanca" Crisis.

ventured to say at the last meeting, for "epicures in mediocrity." There have been, and I believe are, managers who have been and are inspired by a genuine desire to give to the public the best Art within their reach, and whose outlook has not been entirely hampered by such commercial considerations as are supposed in some quarters to hamper the activity of managers of to-day.

Some of these managers, indeed, have been able at times to give the public work that a theatre run by a Committee would shrink from risking, from a sense of responsibility as to the funds in their guardianship.

[1] The Crisis provoked at Casablanca in late September by the arrest of five deserters from the Foreign Legion, of whom three were of German nationality, was still unsettled at this date. The Germans were demanding an apology for the seizure of the deserters, who were in the hands of the German consular officers. The French refused, but proposed arbitration. The Germans insisted that apology must precede arbitration, and held to the claim for over a month, until the united opposition of Europe showed that insistence was impossible.

threatened by a Slav revolt and attack. The moment is not inopportune for Germany.

The Emperor, three days ago, flung into Mrs. Cornwallis-West's box at the Opera in Berlin, and gesticulating wildly and shouting loudly, said, "Well, this is the way I am treated in England, when I try to show I am her friend. Just wait a little while, and we shall see how the English will live to regret!" He was in a furious passion.

I have never known a more anxious day. I was at the Defence Committee for many hours. The decision may have been taken by Grey whether he will let the French know that they can count upon us. I am sure that to tell them so would strengthen both the entente and the chances of peace.

[*To Lord Knollys.*]   2, TILNEY ST.,
                                         NOVEMBER 6TH.

The Kaiser's "Interview"

I have had a most charming letter from the King. It was in answer to mine, and I shall value it always, quite as much as the G.C.B. to which it refers. Yesterday was rather an anxious day; but the clouds seem to have lifted slightly this morning. It seems inconceivable that the Germans should have raised this question with no deeper motive than to distract attention from the Emperor's "interview." The more one hears of that document, the stranger the whole thing seems.

Jack Sandars (who must not be quoted) has seen it, and tells me that it was type-written, and corrected in the Emperor's own handwriting. I suppose you have heard of H.I.M.'s incursion into Mrs. Cornwallis-West's opera box in Berlin?

—and the King's Indian Manifesto.

That his "interview" and our King's manifesto to his Indian subjects should have appeared in the papers within a few days of each other, must to all Germany, and to its ruler, have appeared an unpleasant contrast.[1]

[1] The King-Emperor issued a message to the peoples and princes of India on the fiftieth anniversary of the assumption by the Crown of the direct

From all I hear about the violence of Slav feeling in Russia, I cannot believe that the Conference will meet, or that Europe can escape either a rising in Russia or a war in the Balkans after the winter has passed. It will be a great triumph if the danger can be avoided.

You ask why S. Scott was at the luncheon with A. J. B. [Balfour], Lord Roberts, etc. It is because S. Scott supplied all the funds for Lord Roberts' enquiry into the possible preparations which could be made secretly by Germany. It cost him several thousand pounds. Ottley will tell the King—should H.M. want to know—all about the elaborate enquiries made by the Roberts, Repington, Lovat, Scott group.

I am going to-day to Orchard Lea till Monday. I wonder if the King has heard yet from Jackie [Fisher]. Will you let me have Morley's letter back? I thought you would like to see his graceful periods!

[*Journals.*]

LONDON,
NOVEMBER 9TH.

Jackie [Fisher] came into the Defence Committee this even- *Fisher does* ing. He thought better of his resolve to write to McKenna. He *not Resign.* put away his letters, endorsed with the remark that he reserved them for the present. The fact is he cannot bring himself to say good-bye to the Admiralty, even a year hence.

... Huguet—French Military Attaché—came to Orchard Lea yesterday. The French have no hope of support from Russia. The utmost they hope for, in the present state of Russia (the Slav emotion, the weakness of finances, and weakness of western frontier forces in material) is that she would mobilise her

Government of that country. The message, after reviewing the progress of India during that time, regretted the agitation and disorder which had lately occurred and expressed his determination to repress them, but added that he would not be deterred by them from giving effect to those reforms which had been laid before him by the Secretary of State and the Government of India.

Polish forces, and so, possibly, neutralise 3 or 4 German Army Corps.

French Strategy—

The French position is that in Staff and Armament they are at least equal, if not superior, to Germany. Certainly in Artillery they are superior. In numbers they are inferior by about 200,000 men in the first line. Their fortresses are in good order. The chain is from Belfort to Epinal, then a gap, and from Toul to Verdun.

They are manned in peace by men of the first line, who in war are immediately relieved by Territorial reservists. The plan is to hold lightly the frontier—nearly 300 miles—with their reserves in rear, ready to deliver a strong counter-attack.

—and Hopes of England.

They calculate that the Germans can only advance through the "gap," or by violating the neutrality of Luxembourg and Belgium. They propose to wait on the defensive. They want *our* troops to be placed under the French Generalissimo. They would form part of the reserve. The idea that an English contingent is wanted for its "moral effect," which is an idea prevalent here, is scouted by the French. They want the additional force at the decisive point.

I am confident that great difficulties would arise if this proposal was known in certain quarters.

The placing of the whole of our Army under French Generals is such a wholly new departure. There is no precedent for it at all. Certainly alternative plans will have to be prepared.

I was gazetted a G.C.B. to-day.

[*From General Sir John French.*]   HORSE GUARDS,
NOVEMBER 9TH.

MY DEAR ESHER,

One line of hearty congratulations. Although it is H.M.'s Government who are to be congratulated on getting such splendid help with so little reward.

Yours,

J. F.

[*Journals.*]   LONDON,
                                          NOVEMBER 12TH.

The debate in the Reichstag shows how low the Emperor has *The Reichs-*
sunk in the estimation of his own subjects. His inordinate vanity *tag and the*
and the strain of madness which he inherits from George III *Kaiser.*
have ruined him. Bülow was unable to stem the current of
criticism, which almost amounted to abuse.[1]

The "interview" has now been seen by several persons. It is
corrected and signed by the Emperor. On Saturday last it
looked like war. The French were firm and determined. As I
suspected, the Germans drew back. They are bullies, and not
brave (morally, I mean). The French have behaved perfectly, *Anglo-*
and with great distinction. Grey was touched by their self- *French*
restraint. They never asked or attempted to enquire whether *Relations.*
we were going to their assistance. In point of fact, Asquith,
Grey, and Haldane had decided to do so.

Haldane told Asquith that if we failed France, he would not
give ten years' purchase for the British Empire. This was very
straight and courageous. Grey never wavered or doubted. He
proposed to circularise Europe, and to say that so soon after
the Hague Conference, war upon so trivial a pretext was a
crime against humanity; that we proposed Arbitration to
both Powers, and *whichever refused* should be considered to
have outraged the moral sense of the civilised world, to
be the enemy of the human race, and should be treated
accordingly.

This attitude and language make the perfecting of our Navy
and Army more imperative than ever.

---

[1] The discontent in the Reichstag went to the length of a demand for constitutional guarantees against further indiscretions on the part of the Emperor;
and in spite of Prince von Bülow's very apologetic manner in the House,
there was a debate on the 2nd December on the possibility of profound alterations in the Constitution giving responsibility of Ministers to the Reichstag,
with all the limitation of the Imperial power which such responsibility involves—a debate which would never have taken place but for this incident
of the interview.

I remember last year the German Emperor saying of Grey that he was a "good average man of the middle class"! How do they stand in Europe to-day?

[*Journals.*]   WINDSOR CASTLE,
                                         NOVEMBER 21ST.

*The King
and Queen
of Sweden.*
To-day is Saturday. Since Monday the King and Queen of Sweden have been visiting the King in state. They seem good, simple people. No trouble and no anxiety. A great contrast to the German Emperor's visit last year.

The Queen of Sweden is a very unbrilliant person, fond of sport and lawn-tennis. She is very much under the influence of her doctor, a clever, pushing, rather pretentious man.[1] She goes for months annually to the South in his company. Her habits are peculiar. For 29 days out of 30 she retires to bed at 5 p.m., and remains in bed till noon next day. Her manners and appearance are quite prepossessing.

The Banquet was very stately, as usual, and the King, *our* King, spoke excellently. Martin Harvey played *The Corsican Brothers* quite admirably, and the old play did not seem too old-fashioned. We dined that night with Princess Alice in Henry III's Tower, and I took her into supper after the play.

On Wednesday our King and Queen went to Eton to open the new buildings. My Tutor [2] had most of the arrangements in his hands, and I had to see him and the Provost several times about them. It was a great success, and a charming and moving ceremony. The King's speech to the boys was quite admirable in tone, and beautifully delivered. My Tutor came to-day to the Castle, and was decorated with an M.V.O.

*Roberts on
Invasion in
the Lords.*
The Prime Minister was somewhat disturbed by the prospect

[1] Dr. Munthe, author of *The Story of San Michele*.
[2] A. C. Ainger.

of a debate in the H. of L. on Lord Roberts' motion in regard to "Invasion." He asked me to speak to the King, and to see whether Lord Roberts would agree to limit the scope of the debate. The King *did* speak very strongly to Lord Roberts. "As your Sovereign, and with full concurrence of my Ministers and the Leader of the Opposition, I must ask you, as a patriot, not to raise the question of Germany or to refer to the decision of the Committee of Defence."

Lord Roberts, who had announced his intention of burning his boats, and stumping the country, has, I believe, agreed to rewrite his speech. . . .

J. M. [Morley] came two nights ago to Windsor, and I had two very long talks. He showed me his telegram from the Viceroy. . . .

J. M. then talked about Lord K. [Kitchener]'s successor, and we discussed the rival claims at great length. Then he said, "Of course, Minto may go; in any case, he will probably retire in due course before we are out of office. I talked to Asquith about his successor, and I said I had always thought Crewe, who is now out of the question. And after Crewe I should wish to have you as Viceroy. The P.M. quite agreed, but I told him that I had no idea whether you would go or not." *Offer of the Viceroyship of India.*

I said that I was very much honoured, and most grateful, but that I could not give up my work here, both with the King and on the Committee of Imperial Defence.

This is, I believe, a unique experience; within four years to have been offered the S. of S. for War by Mr. Balfour and the Viceroyship of India by his successor in office. I am confident that in going to India I should be throwing away the substance of power for the shadow. For example, I am *certain* that both as regards (*a*) policy, i.e. the form of the coercion to be applied to India, (*b*) personnel, i.e. the new Commander-in-Chief, I carry more weight with J. M. than does Minto. Besides, every day questions arise, of vital importance to our country, when I can have my say, and can sway a decision. India would be for me (it sounds vain, but it isn't) parochial.

[*To Lord Morley.*] WINDSOR CASTLE,
NOVEMBER 22ND.

The King seems to have been charmed by the long talk he
had with you yesterday evening. As usual, you have left
everyone lamenting your departure.

We have just heard that the "interview" between the German
Emperor and Dr. Hale, for the suppression of which the
German Government paid £20,000, is out in some paper in
New York to-day.[1]

The *Daily Mail* had it yesterday, but were dissuaded by the
F.O. from publishing it. It was *sure* to leak out under the
pressure from rich men like Hearst.

I shall never forget *our* talk yesterday, and shall always consider that the highest honour I ever received was that you
should have thought me worthy to serve under you as the
head of your Indian Government.

[*Journals.*] 2, TILNEY ST.,
NOVEMBER 22ND.

. . . I saw the King this day at noon. He sat comfortably in
his arm-chair, and talked for about half an hour. I resigned my
Chairmanship of the Hospital Committee into his hands, and
he told me what to inform the meeting on Wednesday.

He wrote some names of unknown (to me) persons in some
of the Queen's portrait albums. He talked of the General
[French]'s visit to Egypt, and he rather warmly insisted that
there should be no interference with the Duke of Connaught's
prerogative. He asked me to speak to the General, and I have
told the whole story to Maurice. The King is right. "Inspec-

---

[1] The rumour was incorrect. The interview was in the possession of the
Century Magazine, but was suppressed.

tion" of the Mediterranean troops is really a matter for the Duke.

. . . After luncheon, the Bishop of Stepney (designate Arch- *The Bishop* bishop of York) came down to my room, after I had shown him *of Stepney.* round the Castle. He smoked a cigarette, and we discussed the Church problem in its relation to democracy.

The days of the "Cathedral"—in his view—are over. The old buildings are interesting as reminders of the Church of our fathers. But the men to-day want something quite different, and they get it from him and others. He has spoken, since he became Bishop of Stepney, to 40,000 *men* in London and the provinces. Outside his audiences he *never* speaks to women. I should say that his youth and energy and straightness will make of him a great prelate.

. . . At five I went to Frogmore, and had tea with the Prince *The Prince* and Princess of Wales. After tea, we moved into his room—we *of Wales'* three. . . . *Journal.*

The Prince told me that he kept a journal, and had left in-structions that it was to be destroyed at his death. We argued with him, and he fetched a volume, and made me read it. Very simply written, and quite inoffensive, but well worth preserv-ing. . . .

[*From Sir John Fisher.*]　　　　　　　　DECEMBER 23RD.

MY BELOVED E.

Sweet of you to remember me! When Louis the XIVth gave something *very very* trifling as a present to a great friend, he wrote

　　　" *Ceci n'est rien,*
　　　　l'amitié c'est tout " !

with which words I submit enclosed.

Yours till Hell freezes,

J. F.

[*Journals.*]   LONDON,
                                          DECEMBER 28TH.

Balfour and   Asquith and Haldane asked me to see A. J. B. [Balfour] about
Defence.   the Defence schemes. They had offered him all the papers. He
refused these, but said he would gladly hear an explanation of
what was intended. So they asked me to give the explanation.

I was with him four hours in his room at the H. of C. He took
the most profound interest in Murray's [1] paper, which we went
through carefully, with maps. We then discussed the whole
strategical position, and I showed him my marked chart of the
North Sea.

His love of these questions is profound. His superiority to his
contemporaries in grasp and courageous thinking is also marked.

I saw the King for a few moments on the day of the Investi-
ture. He looked pulled down by his illness, but was very
gracious. . . .

[*To the Headmaster of Eton.*]   2, TILNEY ST.,
                                          JANUARY 6TH, 1909.

Eton Boys   From time immemorial, that is, so long as any of us can
at Windsor.   remember, the Eton boys have come up to the Castle on occasions when the Sovereign has received a State visit from a
foreign potentate.

Never, so far as I know, or so far as anybody knows, has any
communication been sent to the Headmaster of Eton except one
year, when there was a question of the route the boys should
take.

It has always been assumed that the boys wish to come and
the Headmaster as an act of courtesy, granted his permission.
This is the footing upon which the whole matter is understood
and approved by the King.

As regards the Officers' Training Corps, the case is different.

[1] General Sir Archibald Murray.

On these occasions they have always been treated as an integral part of the military force under the G.O.C., and they receive their orders from him accordingly.

I hope that this letter answers your questions, and that in the future you will be spared trouble and that no difficulties will arise.

[*Journals.*]   LONDON,
                                                          JANUARY 6TH.

I drove down to Wimbledon and lunched with J. M. [Morley].

. . . J. M. talked a good deal about India. He still would like me to go out as Viceroy to "carry on his policy." But nothing would induce me. . . .

[*Journals.*]   LONDON,
                                                         JANUARY 14TH.

A few days since, Maurice and I dined with the General [French] at the Carlton to meet Huguet, the French Military Attaché. He is an old friend, who was out with us on manœuvres and on the General's Staff. We discussed at immense length, i.e. from 8.30 to 12.30—four mortal hours—many aspects and conditions of a war between France and Germany.

The French View of a German War.

There is a depressing note about all Frenchmen when they discuss the subject.

It is the result of the "defensive" attitude which they have thought it necessary to adopt. This is contrary to the genius of the French people. That the French have a great Army, very sound, and capably commanded, is certain. A war would be no walk-over for Germany. But the real question is the *highest* command. The General would, I feel sure, conduct a campaign on very different lines from those contemplated by the French General Staff.

We discussed very plainly and openly the possible assistance given by England.

Yesterday I drove Francis K. [Knollys] down to luncheon at Wimbledon with J. M. [Morley].

[*Journals.*]
LONDON,
JANUARY 20TH.

Proposed Decoration for Kiamil Pasha.

Asquith and Grey wish the King to give the G.C.B. to Kiamil Pasha. Asquith puts it on the curious ground that this is not to be a recognition of service to Great Britain, but of the Grand Vizier's admirable speech to the First Turkish Parliament.

There is no precedent for anything of the kind. The King very properly objects. It would be an interference in the domestic affairs of another nation. What would be said if the German Emperor decorated Asquith for a speech in the H. of C.? Besides, where is the thing to stop? How about Isvolsky and Clemenceau? It is odd that Asquith should have had this notion. Probably someone suggested it, and J. M. [Morley] says he is the most "casual" P.M. we have ever had. I hope that the King will maintain the sound objection. After all, there must be two parties in Turkey, and we should be taking sides. Finally, the Young Turks are a very young party as yet. Who can foresee the future?

[*Journals.*]
LONDON,
JANUARY 24TH.

The King came down on Wednesday to Windsor, and I met him at the Castle. He was very gracious.

We dine there to-night, and I wore, at his request, my diamond star, given me by Aunt Adèle. No one had ever seen so fine a one. There is only one other real diamond star of the

Bath which anyone had ever heard of, and that belonged to Sir John Moore.

I had a long talk with the Prince of Wales and a short one with Cambon. George Lloyd [1] is staying with us. . . .

[*Journals.*]

LONDON,
JANUARY 26TH.

This morning the P. and Pss. of Wales spent some hours in my room. He wishes all his autographs and letters bound, and brought them to me. Vaughan is to bind them.

I came up late and attended the Defence Committee on Persia. We settled our report. Grey was very humorous. A strange vein for him. Winston [Churchill] made his first appearance, but was quite subdued.

[*Journals.*]

LONDON,
JANUARY 27TH.

Worked all day. First the Castle, where G. Lloyd was introduced to Francis Knollys, and afterwards to Cassel. He created a good impression on both.

In the afternoon—in spite of the thick fog—I presided over the General Purposes Committee of the T.F. In the evening we went by tube, owing to the fog, to see *An Englishman's Home.* A play of "Invasion" most excitingly acted. Barrie has produced it. He was there, and enthusiastic. It is, I think, by a younger Du Maurier.

" An Englishman's Home."

[*Journals.*]

LONDON,
JANUARY 28TH.

Spent the morning with French at the Horse Guards. Numerous questions. Presided over the Defence Committee

---

[1] Afterwards Lord Lloyd.

on aeronautics this afternoon. Examined Hiram Maxim. Then went through our report. Haldane and McKenna both there.

This evening went to the Artists Corps Prize-giving, and spoke for about 25 minutes. Still a thick fog.

Yesterday Francis [Knollys] showed me Asquith's reply on the subject of giving a G.C.B. to Kiamil. He accepts the King's decision in the negative, but he argues the point. . . .

[*Journals.*]   LONDON,
                                                        FEBRUARY 1ST.

The King on His Youth.   The King made me sit down with him to-day, in his room, and went through two volumes of old letters and memoranda covering his early education. He spoke about his Tutors and his boyhood. He *hated* being given a house apart at Oxford, and thinks it injured his education. He detested being made a Lt.-Col. in the Army straight away, and says he should have begun at the bottom of the ladder. He liked old Tarver, his Tutor, but *not* Gibbs. They never "got on."

Then he began to talk about politics and his Ministers, whom he does not view with a favourable eye just now.

[*To the Rt. Hon. R. B. Haldane.*]   2, TILNEY ST.,
                                                        FEBRUARY 2ND.

Baden-Powell and the Territorials.   I have read Baden-Powell's Memorandum, and I can only repeat what I said yesterday, both to you and Murray. The real want is an adequate supply of recruits for the Territorial Force, and subsequently a reserve for the Territorials.

We don't want any more machinery. We want men. Baden-Powell's scheme does not help, and would, I think, interfere with the supply of recruits by driving the minds of young men into other channels. There is only a limited supply of

youth with military instincts. It will inevitably take the line of
the least resistance.

If organisations are created which enable lads to pose as
fulfilling military duties without joining the Territorial Army,
they will do so.

It is not improbable that the Regular Army would also
be affected.

Baden-Powell should confine his efforts to dealing with boys
under the age of seventeen; there he should stop.

[*Journals.*]   LONDON,
                                                  FEBRUARY 3RD.

. . . I was two hours with the Princess of Wales this evening;
the Prince and Princess were cosily at tea when I arrived. We
three talked, mainly about India, for half an hour. Then he left
us. She was most charming and intimate, as she always is. . . .

What with the tremendous Terrier work of the past fortnight,
and preparing my lecture for the Royal Institute, I am worn out.

[*Journals.*]   LONDON,
                                                  FEBRUARY 12TH.

Involved all this week in a campaign to get recruits for the   *Territorial*
Terriers in London. It has made a great stir. The origin of the   *Recruiting.*
whole affair was an "interview" with the *Daily Mail*. I made
some remarks about Du Maurier's play *An Englishman's Home*
and added that we want men not money, and that the *Daily
Mail* might find them.

Next day I had a cheque for £10,000 from Harold Harmsworth, but we have only got 7000 men so far, and we want
11,000 for London. Still, the ferment will do good.

The King's visit to Berlin is a great success. He is charming the middle classes—and the whole result will be favourable to better relations with Germany. I lunched with J. M. [Morley] on Wednesday, who was in good spirits and seemed to have thrown in his lot on naval questions with Winston Churchill and Lloyd George.

Cabinet Dissensions on the Navy.

We met Winston, as we walked back to the I.O., who had been telephoning to me all the morning. He wanted me to tell Jackie [Fisher] that though as fond of him as ever, he [Winston] would quit office rather than agree to 6 Dreadnoughts: that there was no bluff about this, and that the Government would break up.

Next day he hunted me all day, and finally I met him and Ll. George at the Bd. of Trade.

I told them that I had *not* seen Jackie, who was not to be found. I had no wish to deliver the message, in the truth of which I do not believe. Then we discussed the whole position. I am bound to say that they are both attractive personalities.

Character of Churchill and of Lloyd George.

They take difference of opinion so well. Ll. George, in his heart, does not care a bit for economy, and is quite ready to face Parliament with any amount of deficit, and to "go" for a big Navy. He is plucky and an Imperialist at heart, if he is anything. Besides, he despises the "stalwarts" on his own side. Winston is timid and combative. Ll. George—although he takes no trouble—picks up the whole case very adroitly.

Winston works tremendously hard, but gets involved in subtleties. Ll. George realises that in 1912 we shall be in danger of having hardly a *one* power naval standard. Winston cannot see it. I pointed out to them that the great majority of the country is against them. That nobody goes into detail, and that 6 Dreadnoughts—whether rightly or wrongly—stand for sea supremacy. To resign upon the point would ruin them. No one has ever resigned with personal triumph on a negative policy. They really would have betrayed their trust. All this they took admirably. Ll. George, I am sure, agrees; Winston trembles, and would walk over a bridge, but his *amour-propre* demands one. The question is, can it be found ?

[*From Lord Northcliffe.*]   Hôtel Gassion, Pau,
                            February 26th.

My dear Esher,

I was very glad to see your acknowledgement of the *Daily Mail's* work. It is encouraging to the Staff. Their previous experience with the Union Jack Fund disheartened them greatly.

Northcliffe on the Dignity of the Press—

They worked like Trojans, many of them devoting their entire leisure to the task. No other paper mentioned the matter at all. The King in his speech merely referred to the "efforts of the Press."

I had resolved never to allow this paper to be used again in such a way, but when Lord Desborough came to me about the Olympic Games Fund, and assured me credit would be given where it was due, I gave way.

You have shown in this matter of the Territorials that you understand the handling of that most delicate machine, the Press. You may have given rise to temporary newspaper jealousies, but in the end you will find that your proper recognition of the work of a newspaper will be appreciated by journalists in general, who as a body are naturally very sensitive to the way they have been treated by some public men and some public bodies in the past.

I have been here some time making a study of the aeroplane. Our national muddle-headedness has rarely been seen to worse disadvantage than in this particular matter, aviation. Here, some seven hundred and fifty miles from London, is a machine which can fly perfectly at forty miles an hour, at any height up to about a mile. It is stated by the German and French officers here to be practically "unhitable"; provided with wireless telegraphy, the operator can scout an enemy's positions in a way possible by no other means. Despite the fact that this machine is only twenty-two hours distant, nobody has been here from the War Office, although the following countries have made arrangements for procuring Wright aeroplanes: United States, France, Germany, (tentatively) Italy, and (almost certainly) Spain. The English aeroplane arrangements have been put in

—and on Aeronautics.

the hands of an American who, on his own statements, knows nothing about aviation. He got the appointment because he knew something about kites. I see at length that his machine has proceeded seven hundred yards in a direct line, a feat that was accomplished on the Continent long ago by aeroplanists. His machine is unwieldy, a bad copy of many aeroplanes, and contains a feature that has already been discarded. I might as well attempt to produce my newspapers by the aid of a man who confessedly knew nothing of printing, having carefully chosen old-fashioned machines to begin with.

Sincerely yours,
NORTHCLIFFE.

[*Journals.*]

LONDON,
MARCH 3RD.

The "Islanders." ...I had to-day from Mr. Horn, an Australian and real patriot, a "send off," as he nobly calls it, of a large sum for our "Islander" scheme.[1]

This will do more for a big navy than the Government bill and all the Admiralty bounce.

The King sent for Ll. George at my suggestion, and this evening he sent for me. He was in one of his most charming moods. I sat for over an hour. He talked about private family affairs: his sister's financial arrangements and his own. Then about India. He wants me to see J. M. [Morley], which I shall do to-morrow, and urge him to postpone for two years the appointment of a native member of Council.

He had not seen Curzon for some time until to-day, and was

---

[1] A Society founded by Lord Esher for the propagation of the idea that the British Empire floated on the British Navy, and that Two Keels to One was the basis of Naval Supremacy. It was entirely free from any controversial or political bias and aimed at keeping National Defence outside the conflict of parties. About May 1912 Lord Fisher wrote saying that he shook hands "with all the hundred thousand 'Islanders.'"

much impressed by his improvement. "More quiet than he used to be."

He liked Lloyd George, and was not much frightened by what the latter told him of the budget. He also saw the P.M., who was very lucid and clear. "A certain roughness of manner." That is true. The King is evidently very pleased at the success of the Territorial campaign. He said, "You are a wonderful man, everything you touch succeeds." I kissed his hand after this, when he said good-bye.

[*From Lord Knollys.*]   BUCKINGHAM PALACE,
MARCH 6TH.

MY DEAR ESHER,

A line to say how greatly I congratulate you on the success of your lecture. Nothing apparently could have gone off better, and *The Times* has certainly paid you a very great compliment in devoting their first "Leading Article" to it, and in giving the lecture *in extenso*. I hope you will publish it in pamphlet form. We shall meet at Brooks's on Monday at 8.30.

Lord Esher's Lecture on the Territorials.

Yours ever,
KNOLLYS.

[*From Lord Morley.*]   MARCH 9TH.

MY DEAR ESHER,

Your lecture is really a *coup*—its tact, its ease, its delicacy, feel, atmosphere, and deep political suggestion. The P. of W. was holding forth upon it last night, and we all sympathised and applauded. Of course you will at once make an opuscule of it.

Be a friend, and write down "on half a sheet of note-paper" (literally) the excellent points you made for me the other day, for a constitutional letter to H.M. I am swamped in work to-day and the letter must go to-morrow. I shall be very grateful.

Yours,
MORLEY OF B.

[*To M. V. B.*]   2, TILNEY ST.,
                                    MARCH 12TH.

On Prepared-
ness for
War.

The "Islander" Literature is shaping well.

. . . If the thing goes, it will be a very formidable society. Perfectly secret and perfectly democratic. Nothing been seen like it since Ignatius Loyola founded the Jesuits. It wants something like that, if we are not to go down hill as a nation. My talk with the head manager of Vickers before you and the General [French] arrived, only confirmed one's impression of our inferiority in method and in forecast to the Germans. I wonder what you will think of the Admiralty Memorandum when you read it to-morrow morning?

I had a short talk with Haldane yesterday, who is depressed about the Admiralty; and I think he is right in his view that they will do no good until they have re-organised and got a General Staff. It is all right while you have a Fisher there—but they have no training-school for young men. Arthur Balfour will have a fine chance for an attack next Tuesday, and will deliver it bravely, I have no doubt.[1]

. . . This evening I dine at the Carlton with Bernard Shaw and Bron Lucas! Funny couple, and we go on to *The Merry Widow.* I will tell you to-morrow how she behaves!

[1] Mr. Balfour's attack turned upon the fact that the Admiralty had not correctly estimated the rate of construction of German ships of the Dreadnought class, so that the contingency he had pointed out during the previous year (see p. 295) was not prevented. The Unionist attack in general maintained that while the Government had been talking about a Two-Power Standard we had actually fallen below a One-Power Standard.

The Liberal reply to the first charge was that there was still time (by means of the new programme) to prevent German superiority in Dreadnoughts, and that the ships built in '09 and '10 would be better ships than if they had been laid down in '07. To the second charge they replied that the strength of the Navy should not be measured in Dreadnoughts alone, and that in total strength the Two-Power standard was actually maintained.

[*To M. V. B.*]　　　　　　　　　　　2, TILNEY ST.,
　　　　　　　　　　　　　　　　　　　　MARCH 13TH.

. . . I dined with Bron and Bernard Shaw—very pleasantly— *Bernard*
and Bron was delighted with G. B. S., who certainly is an amus- *Shaw.*
ing companion. Then we went to *The Merry Widow*—but no *At " The*
Merry Wid! Can you imagine a greater blow. Shaw, however, *Merry*
was absorbed. He had seen nothing of the kind for 30 years. *Widow."*

He never took his eyes off the stage. In the interval we went
to see Joe Coyne, who was delighted—and Shaw complimented
him very highly. He thought him a charming and whimsical
personality, with a particularly nice look in his eyes. He
thinks he would be excellent in *pathetic* passages.

[*From Sir John Fisher.*]　　　　　MONDAY EARLY,
　　　　　　　　　　　　　　　　　　　MARCH 15TH.
　　　　[Private and secret and *personal.*]

MY DEARLY BELOVED E.,

I have just finished in these early hours a careful study of your *Fisher on*
paper E.5 (which I love) and the criticisms thereon by French *Military and*
and the General Staff. I dismiss French's criticism as being that *Naval*
of a pure, correct cavalry expert, and not dealing with the big *Co-operation.*
question. The General Staff criticism is, on the other hand, the
thin end of the insidious wedge of our taking part in Continental
war as apart absolutely from coastal military expeditions in pure
concert with the Navy. Expeditions involving hell to the
enemy, because backed by an invincible Navy (the citadel of the
military force)—I don't desire to mention these expeditions and
never will as our military organisation is so damnably leaky! But
it so happens that for two solid hours this morning I have been
studying one of them of inestimable value only involving 5000
men and some guns and horses about 500—a mere fleabite! but
a collection of these fleabites would make Wilhelm scratch himself with fury! However, the point of my letter is this—Ain't we
d——d fools to go on wasting our very precious moments in

these abstruse disquisitions on the Grebbe line or the passage of the Dutch German Frontier River and whether the bloody fight is to be at Rheims or Amiens until the Cabinet have decided the great big question raised in your E.5? Are we or are we not going to send a British Army to fight on the Continent as quite distinct and apart from Coastal raids and seizures of Islands etc. which the Navy dominate? Had not the Prime Minister better get this fixed up before we have any more discussions such as foreshadowed to-morrow?

Yours till a cinder,

J. F.

P.S. I shall expect you at 16 Queen Anne's Gate at 6 p.m. this Monday evening unless during the day you send a telephone message to the contrary.

[*To M. V. B.*]   2, TILNEY ST.,
                                                         MARCH 15TH.

*The
Government
and the
Dreadnoughts.*

. . . This evening I spent two hours with Jackie [Fisher]; and I read all Grey's memoranda, and Jackie's, on the long naval controversy.

Certainly no one could have made a more gallant fight and it reflects the greatest credit upon him. It was pleasant reading, as I was doubtful as to the reality of the fight he had made. Now it only remains for Arthur Balfour to *force* the Government to-night to say that all 8 ships are to be commenced this year.

[*To M. V. B.*]   2, TILNEY ST.,
                                                         MARCH 17TH.

I had a long day yesterday. Nearly all Navy. But I had to speak at a meeting in Holborn in the afternoon, which was the only relaxation from *real* fuss, about the Government's intentions. The situation is serious enough, as you know, and as all the country will see from the debate. If we don't build eight ships this year, and eight ships next, we shall be in a parlous state in March 1912. I have never seen Arthur Balfour more upset than he is about the prospect.

Asquith made a good speech, but the question is, not what they *say*, but what they *do*.

. . . There will be no Daly's for us Friday (Barrie and Pinero) as the Merry Wid.[1] is still in bed.

[*To M. V. B.*]　　　　　　　　2, TILNEY ST.,
　　　　　　　　　　　　　　　MARCH 18TH.

. . . Seymour [Hicks] is first rate in the *Dashing Little Duke*. He plays it most seriously, and all his youthfulness and skill have come back to him in the part. You can see that it is a pleasure to him to be *acting* once more, and not fooling.

. . . I wonder what you will think about the Navy? You will *Rosebery's* see that Rosebery, with his usual perverseness, rushes into print *Hare.* to-day, raising the conscription hare. It is so like him not to concentrate on the *eight ships* which everyone (of both parties) who is worth anything, is trying to get—but to raise on his own another deeply controversial issue.

I feel, however, that unless the B. of Admiralty get their 8 ships ordered *at once* they ought to be hanged. I am going to try and put the fear of God into Jackie [Fisher] this morning.

[*To M. V. B.*]　　　　　　　　2, TILNEY ST.,
　　　　　　　　　　　　　　　MARCH 19TH.

The Government are not yielding an inch—so they will have to be smitten hard.

[1] Miss Lily Elsie.

[*Journals.*]   LONDON,
                                                 MARCH 20TH.

The Navy
Splits the   . . . Meanwhile we have been in the throes of a navy scare.
Cabinet.   Well engineered, it will bring us our 8 Dreadnoughts. On
            Friday I lunched at the Mansion House. Sat next McKenna.
            He is very bitter against Lloyd George and Winston Churchill.
            He spoke of Asquith's "weakness." I said that 25 years' experi-
            ence had taught me that P.M.s—even the strongest—Mr. G.
            and Lord Beaconsfield—are called "weak" when they try to
            keep their Cabinet or party together.

            Poor Haldane—for trying to patch up the quarrel—is abused
            by everyone.

            The P. of W. asked me to call on him next morning, which I
            did. We had an hour's talk. Mainly about the Clyde Canal, in
            which he is much interested. Then about the Navy and the
            C.-in-C. in India.

            Yesterday Maurice returned to O'Lea. To-day I have been
            with Kennedy Jones and this evening 2 hours with Northcliffe
            on Navy and then Aeroplanes.

            Meanwhile I have finished my essay for J. W.'s [1] birthday
            book. It is on Adrienne Le Couvreur! What a diversion!

[*Journals.*]   LONDON,
                                                 MARCH 28TH.

" We shall   The Naval controversy has raged all this week. I have seen a
get Our   good deal of A. J. B. [Balfour]. He has been much worried.
Ships."
            One day I asked Jackie [Fisher] and Kennedy Jones [2] to
            luncheon. They had not met before. Kindred spirits. . . .

            We have done well with the Navy. And we shall get our
            ships. Started the "Islanders" this week.

                    [1] J. W. Clarke.   [2] Editor of the *Daily Mail*.

[*Journals.*]

LONDON,
MARCH 30TH.

. . . A defence committee on "espionage" this afternoon. A silly witness from the W.O. Spy catchers get espionage on the brain. Rats are everywhere—behind every arras.

Jackie [Fisher] told me this evening that the General [French] was watched by the Germans, who have invaded his flat! We talked for an hour on the Navy. Battle plans and what the Government propose to do. I urged him with all the force I could muster to insist on commencing the "phantom four" *this* year. .

[*Journals.*]

LONDON,
MARCH 31ST.

Spent all the morning with A. J. B. [Balfour]. He then went to the Mansion House and made the best speech of his "Trilogy." It was admirable. Terse and conclusive.

Dined with Jackie [Fisher] and Sandars. The remarkable *Kennedy* Kennedy Jones joined us. He is truly a man of mark—and pos- *Jones.* sibly may go unnoticed to the grave. He was a compositor once. He is now worth several millions. He sees few people, but wields all the power of Harmsworth's papers.

[*To M. V. B.*]

2, TILNEY ST.,
APRIL 2ND.

. . . I was not home till 1.30 last night. Jackie [Fisher] was in great form. We dined in a private room at the Carlton upstairs, and very cosy. I saw Haldane to-day who, for him, was quite crusty.

I think that either there must be Cabinet dissensions on, or else he did not like the article about Lord K. [Kitchener] this morning. Did you see it? Suggesting his return to put the "organisation" of the Army to rights! What a troublesome time we shall have when he does get back. An idol to be set up, only to be thrown down again later on. Such is democracy.

[*To Lord Knollys.*]   2, TILNEY ST.,
                                                 APRIL 5TH.

Unpopularity   I am sure Jackie [Fisher] will bitterly regret, one of these days,
of Sir John   that he did not send that letter of qualified resignation.
Fisher.   Not that I think the attack of "Critic" in *The Times* very
effective, nor will Armstrong's speech—taken alone—do him
much harm.[1]

But politicians sicken of prolonged conflict and are apt to
blame those who (as they think) have been the protagonists of
the policy which is stiffly contested.

Jackie will, I fear, prove to be the earthen vessel, between the
two iron pots of conflicting parties. *Nous verrons!* Meanwhile,
the "tactics" of Lloyd George and Winston [Churchill] have
been turned against themselves, and the Navy scare—as they
call it—will go further than Tariff Reform to beat them at the
General Election.

[*Journals.*]   LONDON,
                                                 APRIL 6TH.

A meeting of the Shakespeare Theatre Executive Cttee., from
which I shall retire. Also a good talk with A. J. B. [Balfour] on

[1] Unionist candidates like Sir George Armstrong (himself a retired naval officer) were as bitterly opposed to Sir John Fisher as the Liberals, but for the different reason that his reforms were held to have undermined the discipline of the Navy. The text of the speech is in *The Times*, the 3rd April, 1909, p. 10, col. 1.

the Navy and other matters. He is amused at the fuss made about his speeches. All day at Terriers and the "Islanders."

[*To the Earl of Lytton.*]   2, TILNEY ST.,
                                                       APRIL 6TH.

Would you kindly inform the Executive Committee of the *Shakespeare* Shakespeare Memorial that I must respectfully, and with regret, *Theatre* ask that my name should be withdrawn from the list of those *Committee.* who are acting in an executive capacity.

I shall be glad to remain upon the General Body of those who are anxious to have a memorial to Shakespeare; but I am quite convinced that in the hands of an Executive Committee so large and so variable as that which is now transacting the business of the General Committee, there is no reasonable chance of achieving what the Sub-committee believe to be possible.

There are elements upon the Committee unadaptable to the necessities of the case; and with which I could not personally work with any hope of a successful result.

I believe that a National Theatre is not altogether out of reach, provided that those engaged in promoting the scheme can heartily and clearly agree upon the objects they have in view and are prepared to work for.

Further, I have some experience of practical organisation, and of the method by which considerable results are achieved. I am quite certain that such a body as the present Executive Committee is unfitted to bring a National Theatre into being; and, holding this view as strongly as I do, it would be worse than useless if I were to continue any longer a member of that body.

The suggestion I should like to make to you personally, as the success or failure of the thing will rest mainly with you, is that you should endeavour to reduce the Executive Committee to the dimensions of the Sub-committee, of whose meetings I shall always have very pleasant memories.

[*To the Rt. Hon. A. J. Balfour.*]   2, TILNEY ST.,
                                                    APRIL 13TH.

Enquiry
into the
Admiralty.

By all accounts the Government are contemplating some sort of "enquiry" into the Admiralty. It is inconceivable to me that they should be so foolish and so weak.

The Admiralty—unlike the old War Office—has always been homogeneous with the Government of the day. An "enquiry" into the Admiralty is an enquiry into the executive government. At least, so it appears to me.[1]

The "Board" changes with the First Lord. It is not a body of permanent civil servants. However, I send you at Jackie [Fisher]'s request the enclosed.

As you know, I was strongly in favour, some time ago, of Jackie resigning on 21st Oct. (5 years from his taking office) and of his warning the Government of his intention last January.

This he did not do. But *now*, in face of attack, I have strongly urged him to wait till he is *turned out* by a file of marines. It is the only possible course, if he wishes to die a dignified death.

If the Government want to enquire into specific points of Admiralty administration, the P.M. has the machinery which you left him, the Defence Committee, and he should employ no other.

[*Journals.*]   LONDON,
                        APRIL 14TH.

In the evening I came up to town, and had a long talk with Jackie [Fisher]. We agreed that in view of the attacks upon him

---

[1] The necessity for this enquiry arose out of the accusations and criticisms of Lord Charles Beresford, which, though their course is not followed here, had been allowed to continue ever since they were last mentioned. The best account of the enquiry is in Admiral Bacon's *Lord Fisher*, Vol. ii, ch. 2, or in the *Annual Register*, 1909, pp. 192–3.

resignation was impossible. Nothing but a "file of marines" should get him out of the Admiralty. I wrote and told the Prince, and I sent him references to the attacks on St. Vincent in 1804. A good analogy of what is going on here.

[*To the Rt. Hon. A. J. Balfour.*]   2, TILNEY ST.,
APRIL 15TH.

I have asked the Prince of Wales to dine at the Marlborough some night to meet one or two queer people who interest him. Mr. Gribble (your Dutch correspondent, whose most recent communication I enclose) and a Mr. Horn, an Australian, and Harold Harmsworth.

The only other guests will be Bigge and Ottley. I want you, so does the Prince of Wales. He says I must consult you as to dates. Probably the week after next, i.e. from the 26th onwards would suit best. Will you name a day or days?

I send you a letter from Ottley. Asquith has done well in putting Sir Arthur Wilson on the Defence Committee. I have seen Jackie [Fisher], who is full of fight and very indignant at Asquith's reply in the House of Commons to Faber, and his *silence* when asked in a supplementary question whether he was satisfied with the Board of Admiralty.[1]

Fisher and the Admiralty Enquiry.

Directly McKenna returns the Sea Lords are pressing him to ask the P.M. for an explanation. It looks very much to me as if the Government mean to divert attack, and raise a false issue, by granting an "enquiry" into the Admiralty.

It may extricate them from their difficulty in July of having to decide whether they will build 8 Dreadnoughts or not.

[1] In answer to a demand for an enquiry into Naval Administration, Mr. Asquith replied: "I am not sure that I correctly apprehend the scope or object of the proposed enquiry. I have no statement to make on the matter at present." The supplementary question mentioned, though it appears in *The Times*, is not given in *Hansard*.

[*Journals.*]   LONDON,
APRIL 15TH.

Francis [Knollys] came to London. He returns to Paignton
to-night. . . .

Swinburne's death closes the long line of Victorian poets. I
spent four hours with Morley at Wimbledon to-day talking
India and literature. He was charming.

Detail of the
Bosnia-
Herzegovina
Crisis.

I read Nicolson's despatch from Petersburg. Isvolsky told
him that he had a peremptory *mise en demeure* from the German
Ambassador, who presented him with a Note and asked for a
reply in 12 hours. Isvolsky said Russia was hopeless; France
could not be relied upon to fight on such an issue; England had
given warm diplomatic support, but no suggestion of material
aid.[1]

The "hegemony of Germany was established in Europe for
some years." This was his pregnant phrase.

Yet there are people, headed by Winston Churchill, who see
no dangers ahead, and would stint the Navy!

[*To the Rt. Hon. J. S. Sandars.*]   2, TILNEY ST.,
APRIL 20TH.

You shall have a copy of the letter. It was *quite admirable*. I
have written to A. J. B. [Balfour] and told him what Asquith
said to me.

I think Beresford's letter very temperate and well written.
Make A. J. B. remember that he dines with the P. of W. at the
Marlborough Club on Tuesday, May 3rd, at 8.30.

[1] This was the note in consequence of the annexation of Bosnia and
Herzegovina, in which the German Government declared that if the
Russians supported Servia they would be bound by the Triple Alliance to
support Austria.

[*To the Rt. Hon. A. J. Balfour.*]   2, TILNEY ST.,
APRIL 20TH.

Your letter was perfectly admirable. It is decisive upon two *Balfour on the* points—the use of the Defence Committee for the enquiry of *Admiralty* the kind asked for by Beresford, and the relative responsibility *Enquiry.* of the Government and the Board of Admiralty. Asquith sent for me yesterday, and showed me Beresford's letter. He asked me to serve on the Sub-committee of the Defence Committee to be composed as follows:—

> Asquith
> Haldane
> Grey
> Crewe
> Sir A. Wilson
> Myself.

He gave me an idea of what he wished the reference to be, and asked me to talk it over with Ottley.

I drafted some heads yesterday afternoon; not confining the enquiry to one particular point, but covering all the charges in Beresford's letter.

It is useless to shirk anything! Sir Arthur Wilson's permanent appointment to the Defence Committee is quite good and useful. You see that the precedents of the appointments of French and myself have been closely followed in the public notice.

I am off to Edinburgh till Thursday morning. I will call in your rooms at 4 on Thursday afternoon.

The P. of W. wants you to dine at the Marlborough on Tuesday, May 3rd.

[*From Mr. Arthur Pinero.*]   115, HARLEY ST.,
APRIL 24TH.

DEAR LORD ESHER,   *The*
I am sorry to read the contents of your letter to Lord Lytton. *Shakespeare* But I quite understand—and had better say no more. The kind *Memorial*
Theatre.

way in which you speak of the meetings of the late sub-committee is very gratifying. We were a happy family, and our leader endeared himself to us all. For this recollection, if for no other reason, one owes much to the Shakespeare Memorial. When I am further advanced with a task which, I hope only for the moment, unfits me for human society, I am going to beg you to relax your sterner duties and to give me an evening. In the meantime, dear Lord Esher, and always, I am,

Yours most faithfully,
ARTHUR PINERO.

[*From Mr. Bernard Shaw.*]   10, ADELPHI TERRACE,
MAY 4TH.

DEAR LORD ESHER,

Shaw on the Theatre Committee.   Here I am again, I shall be at the Committee on Thursday. As to that body, whenever I try to think of it, my head begins to seethe with the chorus in the *Frogs* of Aristophanes:—

> Brek-ek-ek-ex, Gollancx, Gollancx,
> Brek-ek-ek-ex, Gollancx.

If you leave us with any sort of public emphasis, you will break our backs. If you continue to attend the Committee as it now is, and to preside over its babblings and chatterings, you will lose your reason. We must try to avert both catastrophes, though at this moment, writing in great haste, I don't know how. There is much to be escaped by simply staying away until another phase of real business is reached. As to lunch, yes, with pleasure.

Yours ever,
G. BERNARD SHAW.

[*Journals.*]   LONDON,
MAY 9TH.

The Prince of Wales' Dinner.   The P. of W. dined with me at the Marlborough. I asked A. J. B. [Balfour], H. Harmsworth, Ottley S. H. Butcher, and Bigge.

The P. of W. was quite excellent. Arthur said to me after-wards, "Except the German Emperor, he is the only royal prince to whom I find I can talk as man to man." And he added, "He is really clever."

We sat till 12.30; most rare for the Prince, who wrote next day that he had never had so pleasant a dinner. The talk *was* good.

[*Journals.*]   SANDRINGHAM,
                                                   MAY 14TH.

. . . The King came over from Newmarket this evening in 1 h. 25 m. Arrived about 5. Only Redesdale, Blomfield (the architect), Probyn, Davidson, and George Holford here.

The house is all in curl papers.

I sat next the King at dinner and, although the conversation was general, he managed to talk very freely to me about Fisher, to whom he is perfectly loyal. Redesdale was full of the troubles and scandals of the National Gallery.

[*Journals.*]   SANDRINGHAM,
                                                   MAY 15TH.

. . . In the afternoon walked with the King. We went through the gardens and the stud. Redesdale went up to town and on to Batsford. I sat again next the King at dinner, and he brought down on a slip of paper his errata for my "Journals," of which he said he had "read every word" on the yacht. He has signed the little slip which I shall keep, as the first thing of the kind probably ever produced by a sovereign. The House of Commons telegram arrived at dinner, and the King at once fastened on the P.M.'s statement, in reply to Redmond, on the Catholic Oath Bill. Asquith said "there is no reason in logic or

Asquith and the Catholics.

in policy why the Ld. Chancellor should not be a R. Catholic."
The same might be said of the Sovereign himself.[1]

I expect this statement will lose the Government many votes.
It will offend the Nonconformists and the Evangelical Church-
men. The King told me to write to Francis Knollys on the
subject, which I did at once, and he was to write to the P.M.

[*Journals.*]   ORCHARD LEA,
                                            MAY 16TH.

I left Sandringham early, as I had a meeting at the W.O.
Then came on to O'Lea.

Two sets of proofs looked through to-day, *Adrienne*, and *A
new Imperial Life*. Both quite good.

I am reading Kuropatkin's *Memoirs*, and very full of interest
they are.

[*Journals.*]   ORCHARD LEA,
                                            JUNE 2ND.

Returned from Pinkie yesterday. We had four days there—
in charming weather. I went up specially for a meeting at
Callander to unfurl the Union Jack given by Mrs. Baillie-
Hamilton. Spoke for about half an hour.

Had a glorious Sunday in the Glen with M. Saw Knollys at
the Castle last evening.

Proposals for a   Asquith has recommended Hardy for the O.M. vice Mere-
Literary   dith. I have written a memo. for the King. Hardy's best work
O.M.   is the *Dynasts*, which nobody reads. His realistic novels are not
of the highest calibre. Kipling's service to the Empire entitles
him to a preference.

[1] This remark occurred during the debate on the second reading of the
Roman Catholic Disabilities Removal Bill, which passed the House but was
then shelved by reference to a Committee of the whole House by 124 votes
to 121.

But I suggested James Bryce as a writer much more in the "grand style," if the Order is to be given at all.

[*Journals.*]   ORCHARD LEA,
                                                        JUNE 3RD.

Yesterday the P. of W. telephoned over and asked me to luncheon. We had our usual long yarn about the Navy and Jackie [Fisher]. He gave me a memo. on the Imperial Defence Conference which he had written himself. It is quite well done. He was violent now and then on the indiscipline of the Navy, but altogether very reasonable.

To-day I dined with Francis [Knollys], Soveral, and Jackie [Fisher] at Brooks's. One of our quarterly dinners. Always the same party! It was *very* pleasant. No reticences of any sort. Soveral violently hostile to Germany as usual.

[*Journals.*]   ORCHARD LEA,
                                                        JUNE 5TH.

Lord Roberts has written a charming letter, 8 pages, on my Callander speech—which I have answered to-day. It is another proof of his wonderful vitality.

[*To Lord Roberts.*]   ORCHARD LEA,
                                                        JUNE 6TH.

That you should have taken the trouble to write, and so fully, *On Voluntary* upon my speech at Callander, is very gratifying to me; and I feel *Enlistment.* it more keenly, as you say most kind things, in spite of my use of a word which was certain to be displeasing to you.

Every word that I have written or spoken upon the subject of National Defence, much of which I know you have been good enough to read, must show my firm conviction that the voluntary system is on its trial, and that if it fails compulsion follows.

Although I recognise to the full the force of what you say on the subject, and although I admit to some degree, but not altogether, the analogy between compulsory education and taxation, and compulsory training to arms, I cannot admit that the voluntary system should be abandoned without regret.

After all, the naval and military professions, the profession of arms, at the root of which lies the obligation to die for your country, are the most honourable of all—and that they should be based upon the willingness of a man to come forward, rather than upon compelling him, is an ideal worth contending for, and not to be submerged without reluctance.

You will remember that it was the Roman ideal, in the days of the republic, when she was at the height of her fame. Although as a nation we may be forced to adopt "Compulsory Service," I am afraid that I cannot quite agree with you that this will show an advance upon our part in civilisation.

When, however, I used the word "odious"—which was not well chosen, I admit—I was not thinking of its ethical sense; I had in mind the complete revolution in our national habits—always a hazardous step—and the reconsideration of our national policy, not especially in Europe, but in the Far East, and in India particularly, which is bound necessarily to follow upon the heels of "compulsion."

Consequences of Conscription. The primary danger would be our sea-power; for it is my firm conviction that an armed force at home, able, beyond much doubt, to hold its own against any probable invading enemy, would gradually but surely lead to the weakening of the Fleet.

Successive Governments, whether Unionist or Radical, would be tempted to economise upon naval expenditure, and the standard of our sea-strength, which for Imperial purposes and National Safety should be two to one as against the next strongest European Power, would be inevitably lowered.

What enables the Admiralty to maintain the Fleet is fear of invasion—which every man understands—and not the fear of starvation, which only a few understand, or our subsidence into the position of a fifth-rate power, which no one realises or believes to be possible.

And yet, with a fleet relatively weaker than we have to-day, and in spite of a million of armed men within these islands, we should be sinking into the position of a fifth-rate power, not only in Europe, but all over the world.

The second danger I fear is that while the system of "compulsion" might render us more immune from invasion, it would probably weaken the power of our people to take the offensive in war, upon which hitherto our Imperial position has largely rested.

Particularly, the adoption of compulsion for the Home Army is certain to be followed by a large decrease in the Army which, as you very truly say, is largely maintained for policing the Empire.

As the cost of the Home Army rises, the cost of the policing army is certain to be reduced; the "Cardwell" system will be attacked and destroyed; an "Indian Army" will once more be formed; and although it is possible that we should finally be driven to train a compulsory army, on German lines, for service over-sea in war (though not in peace), the transition period would be full of disturbance and danger, so vivid to my mind, that you can perhaps pardon the use of the phrase "odious," which I should, notwithstanding all I have said, have done better not to use.

Adjectives will occasionally entrap even the most wary. I should be sorry to think that the objects I have at heart are different from the aims you have so nobly advocated. I agree absolutely that we should endeavour to organise, for the defence of our country and our dominions over-sea, every element of our being; and although you have—and perhaps rightly—abandoned all hope of effectively achieving this under a voluntary system, I should—in view of the great awakening during the past few years, so largely due to your efforts—prefer to give that system a little longer trial.

[*To the Rt. Hon. A. J. Balfour.*]   2, TILNEY ST.,
JUNE 9TH.

*Strategical
Position of
the
Dominions.*

A note that wants striking hard is that Great Britain is the heritage of these people [1] as well as ours.

Not only the abbeys and churches and old domains, but the honour of England, and her sea Dominions.

Relatively we grow weaker, and they grow stronger, as their population and wealth increase.

If they agree, as they do, in this ideal, is it not time for them to consider what sacrifices they are ready to make? Sea-power is the base upon which the Empire rests, and it should not be beyond their wit and ours to discover a practical method by which the burden of Empire can be apportioned.

Perhaps you might hint at the permanent representation on the Defence Committee of the Dominions, for Imperial defence questions!

[*To M. V. B.*]   [ORCHARD LEA],
JULY 6TH.

*Meredith's
" The
Egoist."*

. . . I am immersed in *The Egoist*. From the purely literary point of view it is, I should imagine, the best of his books. The character of Clara is very subtle. What a man is Sir Willoughby! Combining nearly everything that one detests in the self-sufficient prigs of everyday life. It is a book of that kind which goes down to the realities of things, possibly combined with the superior outlook upon life which bedridden people invariably have.

[*To M. V. B.*]   ORCHARD LEA,
JULY 7TH.

*The King and
the
Territorials.*

. . . What a good thing it is that the King should have inspected 2 Divisions of Terriers. It will have, I hope, interested

---

[1] The Dominions and Colonies.

him in them—and only good can come of that. He telegraphed very kindly this morning.

[*Journals.*]   ORCHARD LEA,
                                                    JULY 9TH.

During this month I have been unusually hard worked, and the result is that for one week I have been on my back here.

[*From R. B. Haldane.*]   WAR OFFICE,
                                                    JULY 13TH.
MY DEAR ESHER,

To enable you the better to write to Kitchener I enclose a copy of the letter I have written to him.

It was very plucky of you to come to the Defence Committee on Monday.

                                        Ever yours,
                                            R. B. H.

[*To Lord Kitchener.*]   [2, TILNEY ST.],
                                                    JULY 14TH.

I have had the privilege of seeing a copy of Mr. Haldane's letter, and I trust that you will not mind receiving a word from me to say how fervently I hope that the suggested proposals will meet with your acceptance.

Kitchener and the Mediterranean Command.

There are, I am sure, from all the discussions which have taken place on the Defence Committee, great possibilities for the Mediterranean Command.

It requires, however, that you (for there is no one else with the organising and imaginative capacity) should for a year or so take it in hand.

The underlying idea is that the Mediterranean Garrison should form a nucleus of a great Imperial Concentration in time of war—a concentration of Imperial forces, naval and military, drawn from every quarter of the Empire.

I need not elaborate the idea, which you will seize at once; and from that central position you, with your experience and authority, will be able to do more to influence Colonial opinion than you would be able to do, or than *anyone* would be able to do, from here.

Whatever view you may have formed from the newspapers and private letters, I earnestly hope that, in regard to the military developments of the last three years, you will not crystallise your opinions until you have had a chance of seeing the advance which has been made.

And in any case, for the sake of the country, I sincerely hope that Mr. Haldane may be successful in inducing you to accept his proposal.

[*From H.M. the King.*]   WINDSOR CASTLE,
                                              JUNE 15TH.

MY DEAR ESHER,

It is very kind of you to have sent me such an admirable portrait of your kind and excellent father, taken from Sir John Millais' picture.

I am delighted to possess it, as I had such sincere regard and friendship for your father, which you know is retained for his son.

Believe me,
Yours very sincerely,
EDWARD R.

[*To M. V. B.*]   2, TILNEY ST.,
                                              JULY 24TH.

The telegrams to K. [Kitchener] go to-morrow. I think he will accept. Meanwhile there is further complication, because

J. M. [Morley] is inclined to offer him the position of Viceroy. This is between you and me. Haldane, however, has insisted that the question does not arise till next autumn, so that whatever J. M. does is not to interfere with the Mediterranean scheme at present.

. . . The Stafford House party was quite good. Maggie Teyte has a pretty voice, and sings well. I sat next a most interesting Turk at dinner. He was four times imprisoned by *Germany and* the late Sultan. He told me about the papers found in the *Turkey.* Palace showing all the intrigues between Baron Marschall and the Sultan. Each bribed the other's subordinates; and Germany got every concession she wanted.

[*Journals.*]   LONDON,
                                        JULY 24TH.

On Thursday I lunched with the P. and Princess of Wales. We lunched *upstairs* in the little room next to her sitting-room. Only the Prince and Princess and two children. The two younger ones came in later. The household were not there.

It was very homelike, and they talked in the most open way.

. . . The King has telegraphed personally to Lord K. [Kitchener] urging him to accept the Mediterranean command. . . .

. . . Maurice went to Ireland on Thursday night. I dined with Cassel and met the Turks; and sat next a highly intelligent Turkish revolutionary. He contrasted, in a rather striking way, *our* diplomatists with the Germans: the competence and painstaking activities of the latter. Afterwards we went to Stafford House to meet the King and Queen.

Yesterday we dined with Horace Farquhar to meet the King —37 people—and everything beautifully done. I had some interesting talk with A. J. B. [Balfour]. It is not unlikely that the Lords will throw out the Budget.

This morning a Defence Committee. Asquith hurried it

somewhat. Then I lunched at the Savoy and saw little Elsie there. Afterwards to Wimbledon to see J. M. [Morley].

The King has been to see Chamberlain and told J. M. that it was painful because of C.'s inability to *speak* plain, although his brain works easily. J. M. says that his ardent spirit should have gone to heaven in a chariot of fire and not in a bath-chair. . . .

[*To M. V. B.*]　　　　　　　　　ORCHARD LEA,
　　　　　　　　　　　　　　　　JULY 25TH.

Blériot's Flight.　. . . I hear this morning from Windsor Castle that Blériot has flown across the Channel. It is rather splendid. At the same time I have had a very impertinent letter from . . . who asked me to be president of the Aerial League. I mean to give him a snub, and may throw over the whole thing.

[*To M. V. B.*]　　　　　　　　　ORCHARD LEA,
　　　　　　　　　　　　　　　　JULY 26TH.

. . . I was bothered this morning for hours on the telephone to go to luncheon to-day with Blériot. But I stoutly refused. I hate that sort of hysterical thing. Though I admit that the feat is the beginning of a new era.

[*To Lord Morley.*]　　　RANDOLPH HOTEL, OXFORD,
　　　　　　　　　　　　　　　　JULY 28TH.

I enjoyed our talk immensely and hope you were not over-powered by "Adrienne"!

Here we are on our way to Scotland by motor, motoring westwards first, and then turning north.

Kitchener and the Mediterranean Command. I have heard about K.'s [Kitchener's] telegram to you, and seen his answer to the King. If the King wishes, he will accept; and the King *will* wish it. Some of your colleagues, I am told, object to the idea of K. as Viceroy. They think that he would prove too masterful for *you*. I have not seen the man yet who would be that.

Also they think there is an atmosphere about a soldier which conflicts with the air good radicals should breathe. This seems to me, if I may venture to say so, rather *de l'an quarante*.

[*To M. V. B.*]   OXFORD,
                                                   JULY 28TH.

. . . K.'s [Kitchener's] reply to the King was as follows: *The King and* "Your Majesty's wishes are always commands to me. My reply *Lord* to Mr. Haldane was sent off yesterday declining the command *Kitchener.* for certain reasons. I leave the matter entirely in Your Majesty's hands, and will loyally carry out whatever your Majesty will decide."

I strongly urged the King to take him at his word, and to ask him to go to Malta for at least one year. I think he will probably read between the lines that this may lead to the Viceroyalty. In all the circumstances of India, I feel sure that it would be desirable to appoint him Viceroy. It would settle public opinion, both native and European. Morley, I know, in his heart desires it. The Government do not like the idea, but they are wrong. I hope the King will telegraph and clinch the matter.

. . . The only amusing thing I have got to show you is a letter from G. B. S. [Shaw] to me, asking me to give evidence before the Censor Committee. It may just raise a smile if you are in a good temper.

[*To M. V. B.*]   CARLISLE,
                                                   JULY 30TH.

. . . I see Dilke and Bellairs attacked me in the H. of C. *New Attacks* Rather an honour! Haldane answered very becomingly![1] *on Lord*
                                                              Esher.

[1] The debate in Committee of Supply on the 29th of July was an extremely interesting one. It opened with a long speech from the Prime Minister on the

[*To Lord Fisher.*]   THE ROMAN CAMP,
                                        AUGUST 4TH.

On the King's   Hearty congrats on your great success with the Fleet. It all
Loyalty.   seems to have been splendid. It is *very dear* of the King to be nice
about me in regard to the attacks of Dilke, Bellairs, etc. So long
as he sticks to one, nothing much matters. That, as you know,
has always been my view, and I must say that no one that I have
ever met is a more loyal friend.

We have all tried him sometimes, I fear, but it never seems
to detach him from those to whom he has once given his
confidence.

To *you*, H.M. has behaved simply magnificently—for your
enemies were very clamorous in the gate at one moment, and
almost anyone might have been forgiven, had they been shaken.
But H.M. *never was*! For my part, I never have minded the
abuse of those who sin because of their ignorance. All these
silly jealous people come within that category.

And I mind still less, when I feel sure that the one or two
persons for whose good opinion I care, remain uninfluenced.
Bless you, dear Admiral, and I never forget what the Army
and Navy were 8 years ago, and what they are *now*!

functions and utility of the Imperial Defence Committee, together with an
announcement of some of its latest findings. There followed a speech by Mr.
Balfour expressing his entire agreement with the Government, and his attitude on one or two points on which the Committee had altered its opinions
since he left office. The remaining speeches were for the most part improper
to the debate, but intrinsically interesting because they summarised very
clearly the views of the various sections of the community on current
questions of defence.

The attacks made upon Lord Esher were the least important and least
interesting parts of the debate, which should be read for its other aspects.

According to *Hansard* it would appear that Lord Esher was defended by
the Prime Minister, not by Mr. Haldane.

[*To the Archbishop of Westminster.*]   THE ROMAN CAMP,
AUGUST 9TH.

May I venture to send you the enclosed? I acted as Trustee *On the Death*
for the late Mother Superior, whom I saw take the veil 25 years *Duties in*
ago. She had no near relatives, and was connected with some *Convents.*
connections of mine, and Lady Esher and I took much interest
in her.

Her allowance dies with her. It is most unfortunate that this
question of death duties should have arisen.

I have asked the Inland Revenue whether they can absolve
the community from payment of the dues, but had a very
unsatisfactory response.

My first inclination was to place the whole case before the
public, but not feeling sure of the reasons which actuate those
who advise these communities *not* to become "corporate
bodies," I have thought it more prudent to lay the matter
before Your Grace.

I am anxious to help these poor Carmelite Sisters if I can do so.

[*To M. V. B.*]   2, TILNEY ST.,
AUGUST 10TH.

. . . There is a long notice in the *Daily Mail* this morning of
the death of Mrs. . . . She is separated from her husband. She
was staying with us, and left with me this morning. She is perfectly well! Frantic telegrams arrived all the afternoon from
her relations and friends. She felt sure, she said, that it was the
happiest day of her husband's life. She proposed not to unde-
ceive him to-day, but to telegraph to him to-morrow and
condole.

[*To the Rt. Hon. A. J. Balfour.*]   THE ROMAN CAMP,
AUGUST 15TH.

I wonder what you think of Asquith's Report? It is couched *The Report on*
in his usual cold judicial language, and, as you will note, con- *the Admiralty.*

tains no words of appreciation of the value of the naval reforms introduced by Selborne, which lie at the root of the policy which C. B. [Charles Beresford] attacked.

I imagine Jackie [Fisher] will be hurt at the want of direct support given to him, and C. B. will be furious. So I suppose the Report fulfils all "political" requirements.[1]

Territorial Manœuvres.

I have just got back from Salisbury. You have no idea of the wonders of our Territorial Force. It will "initiate" so many important changes in the work of the Regular Army, by reason of the experiments which Terriers do not hesitate to try, but which red tape would forbid to the regular soldiers.

Some of the Motor Transport was really *most* remarkable. All *invented* by Terrier Colonels and their subordinates.[2] I saw the French visitors General Langlois, Rousset, etc. They were enormously impressed—but they think we have made *fausse route* in adopting ordinary F.A. Batteries for a Home Army. They hold that Mountain Guns would be much more useful and practical. What they had to say, and have repeated in the *Gaulois* and other French papers, is worth considering.

I shall have to return to London for a Defence Committee meeting—Imperial Conference—but otherwise do not stir from here till November.

[1] The text is given by Admiral Bacon, *op. cit.*
[2] Lord Esher also wrote on the subject to Mr. Wells, who replied:—

17, Church Row,
Hampstead,
August 23rd.

Dear Lord Esher,

I don't think I know anything at all of military matters, but since warfare is evidently to be waged in the future very largely with novel and untried appliances, I suppose an active and well-trained imagination is sometimes able to produce suggestions—my training has I think served to keep my imagination if anything rather too much alive. Of course I shall be only too delighted and flattered to meet you in London when you return.

Very sincerely yours,
H. G. Wells.

VISCOUNT ESHER, 1909.
From a snapshot by Dorothy Brett.

[*Journals.*] THE ROMAN CAMP,
AUGUST 15TH.

Last week I went south to Salisbury. Stayed with Sir C. Douglas. The Terriers were amazing. The Regulars will learn much from them, because of their initiative and freedom from red tape—especially on the technical side of war. All sorts of new methods will be discovered.

Maurice returned yesterday, and we shot Bochastle. I am reading Fletcher's splendid introduction to English history.

[*To M. V. B.*] THE ROMAN CAMP,
AUGUST 23RD.

There was a huge party at Cloan. All relations and professors. But I was closeted with Pussy [Haldane] all the afternoon.

. . . Haldane says that in *every* profession there are 10 dull years. That may be so. But even then, in many professions *men are free* and can do and say what they please. In the Army men of middle age are *in statu pupillari*.

[*To M. V. B.*] THE ROMAN CAMP,
AUGUST 25TH.

Your postcard from Laon and your telegram arrived simultaneously. It must have been a fine sight, and I am glad you have seen the first show of aeroplanes that has ever taken place. It will be an interesting reminiscence. I see, by the papers, that you were received by old Fallières.

. . . Laon is the place where, if the General [French] ever fights the Germans, I presume he will assemble his forces.

. . . Douglas Haig has sent me his second Cavalry staff ride. He certainly does these things remarkably well. On paper he is hard to beat, although he is so obscure in speech.

. . . I am so glad you had a splendid day with Zena. I wonder what you talked about. If you had not lost the poetic art, I should learn:

> Golden flush on highland skies,
> golden light in dearest eyes,
> golden thoughts on lips divine,
> golden heart in tune with mine.

You see I am still capable of an impromptu.

[*To the Rt. Hon. J. S. Sandars.*]   THE ROMAN CAMP,
AUGUST 26TH.

Of course I see that you have special information. But I have from long experience learnt to mistrust attacks upon men who have risen to the top of their professions.

Everything depends on *standard*. It is incredible that May [1] should have risen so high, if he is as bad as some of his professional colleagues seem to think.

After all, he is *not* an aristocrat, a spoilt child of successive Governments, etc. He is just an ordinary sailor.

The State of the Navy.   My view is that the great thing for the Navy is now:

(*a*) To restore discipline.

(*b*) To create a War staff.

(*a*) In order to do this the Board of A. should interfere as little as possible with personnel for a while, leaving things to settle down; should issue a Fleet Circular warning sailors that all criticism must cease, and the King's Regulations must be observed; give Jackie [Fisher] some honour *at once* and let him alone for a year, after which he could retire!

(*b*) Refer this question—whether McKenna likes it or not—to a sub-committee of the Defence Committee.

If A. J. B. [Balfour] was Prime Minister I should have great hopes of these things being done. As it is, I doubt! I will keep

---

[1] Afterwards Admiral of the Fleet Sir William May.

your letter private. Your first letter, I don't mind admitting, I showed to the King—it was so admirably written and to the point. He thought so too.

[*From Sir John Fisher.*]　　　　　　　August 28th.

My dear E.,

I have just this moment got your letter of Aug. 24 and bless you for it. You use the words I used in describing the Beresford Report to McKenna—that "*5 Cowards signed it*"!

Fisher on the Admiralty Report.

Yours for ever,

J. F.

[*To M. V. B.*]　　　　　The Roman Camp,
　　　　　　　　　　　　August 30th.

... And if I had taken up Art or Literature instead of "affairs" I should have had none of these heart-searchings. Especially as my instincts are very much in those directions. However, *Dieu dispose.*

[*To M. V. B.*]　　　　　The Roman Camp,
　　　　　　　　　　　　September 8th.

It was splendid to hear Caruso sing again. He sang two encores every time; about 9 times in all. *Pagliacci, Bohème, Force of Destiny*, etc.

You should make a great effort to go to the Albert Hall on the 18th. It is not a sensation to miss. *Bohème* will melt you to tears. We have just returned from Alloa. It takes exactly an hour to get there. Nellie and Syv came. Only Charles Hardinge, Lady Mar, Viola, and Willie Erskine. Quite pleasant. A modern comfortable house. Nice old pictures, and relics of James VI, to whom Lady Mar was nurse. The old Tower of Alloa in the garden, date 14th century, is interesting. It was altogether a very pleasant visit, and I had a most interesting talk with Hardinge. He is *delighted* that you are entertaining the French—and takes exactly the opposite view to Haldane. He thinks it most useful *at this moment*, for reasons I will tell you later, but do not think it safe to write. I may say that I started the Channel Tunnel idea, and found him altogether sympathetic. You try your hand on the General [French] when he is in a good mood. I want him as an ally. That question has got to be reopened.

[*Journals.*]   THE ROMAN CAMP,
                           SEPTEMBER 8TH.

Went up with M. on Friday night.

. . . In the evening Maurice, Guy Laking and I went to the Gaiety in Alfred de R.'s box.

Next morning I breakfasted alone with the King. I waited in the little room lined with his Indian armour for a few minutes, then he came in punctually with a dog. He looked wonderfully well. Thinner and younger. We sat down, each with our small silver coffee pot and boiled egg. Fish was handed to me. Then the servants left the room; and he began at once about the Duke. . . .

I told him what Haldane's reply would certainly be, and I asked him if he had read Lord Kitchener's answer to Haldane about the Mediterranean Command. He had not. So he sent for the boxes and we found it. He read there and then all the papers through, and he saw clearly how precipitate the Duke had been.

The King on the Budget. We then passed from that matter to the Budget. He was very much displeased with Winston's speech.

. . . I don't think that the King objects to the Budget, but he dislikes intensely the tone of certain speeches. L. G.'s and Winston's. . . .[1]

. . . He told me a good many things about Marienbad. He enjoyed the place, and was amused. He showed to Clémenceau the extracts from the *Gaulois* which I sent him, about the English army.

Clémenceau said, "Your Fleet is all that is wanted—but your army is not strong enough to be of use to us. It should be as numerous and as powerful as it was *at the end of the Boer War*. If there is any trouble between you and Germany, it is through France that the Germans will strike at you, and *we* shall have to pay." *Clémenceau on the British Army.*

He said Princess Murat had taken a great fancy to . . . and asked her to dinner. "A stiff French woman too. But women abuse her. The fact is they are jealous." I said I thought R., if he had any pluck, would have married her. The King thought so too!

Then I said, "Suppose a young officer in the Guards married an actress, would he have to leave the Army?" "Certainly not," said the King; "the rule is quite clear. If a young officer marries anyone whom his brother officers' wives cannot meet, he must go; but there must be a *real* objection. For instance, if she is a woman of bad character, or has lived with the officer as a mistress." He then quoted an instance. "But if an actress is respectable, he certainly need not leave the Army." Breakfast lasted 1½ hours.

In the afternoon Maurice and I went to O'Lea. Lovely in the garden. I returned to dinner with Redesdale at the Marlborough. The King dined with Haldane. We were 12 altogether. We wore "stars," but no other decorations.

The King was quite charming to me all day. More than friendly. The next day I called on J. M. [Morley]. We were to have lunched together, but I wanted to have my last luncheon

[1] To judge by the dates, this must refer to the famous Limehouse speech and to Mr. Churchill's unauthorised threat of a dissolution in his speech at Edinburgh.

with Maurice and Zena. J. M. had spent the week-end at Mentmore.

Rosebery's Attitude on the Budget.

Rosebery, who is to speak at Glasgow on Friday next, spoke very strongly against the land clauses of the Budget, but he gave no indication of the advice it is assumed he will offer to the H. of L.

Morley told him that if he were leading the Opposition he could throw out the Bill. But even this did not "draw" R. Morley said he could argue that the Budget is not a Budget but a land bill and a licensing bill grafted on to a Budget. He would have no fear of a crisis. First, because the H. of L. is popular. Second, because if the Lords fear to throw out such a bill as this, they abdicate their function, and may as well disappear altogether.

Besides, any General Election at the present time would be bound to bring back the Unionist Party, if not in a majority, in such numbers (say 300 strong) that no vindictive action could be taken against the H. of L.

Rosebery complained that Asquith, in spite of their old relations, has never talked politics to him since he became P.M.

Minto on Kitchener.

Then we talked about India. He showed me a letter from Minto about Lord K. [Kitchener] as a possible Viceroy. It was well written, and not a bad analysis of K.'s character. He says K. is not impulsive and *not* reactionary, but cautious and progressive. On the other hand, that he is idle and tired of India. J. M. is not eager to appoint K. as Viceroy—but he would do so if Indian affairs go badly. . . .

. . . J. M. met Maxime Elliot at Mentmore and admired her immensely. "Beautiful, clever and charming."

[*To the Rt. Hon. J. S. Sandars.*]   THE ROMAN CAMP,
                                        SEPTEMBER 9TH.

On Fisher.

I think you attached rather more importance than I ever intended to my suggestion. My feeling was, that as poor dear

Jackie [Fisher] was sore, and as you like him, a few words (not committing anyone to *policy*) would have been balm. I could show you his letter, and you would then see what I mean. As for rumours or statements about Jackie's proposals *re* estimates, I do not believe a word of them.

I may be wrong, but I shall always believe that he has been actuated for 27 years by the *unique desire* to make the British Navy the strongest in the world.

I do not say that he has not made mistakes. Who has not? But he is a great public servant, and at the end of a long life, devoted to his profession and to the state he is the victim of Asquith's want of moral courage.

I saw Morley, who had a delightful time at Mentmore and Halton; but he knew no more about Rosebery's intentions than we do. Of course they talked a good deal about the Budget, and the land clauses, but Rosebery gave no intimation of the line he was going to take.

It will be uncharacteristic of him, should he offer to lead an attack *right home* on the Bill.

I don't believe a word about a Dissolution. The Government hear that Acland-Hood's estimate is 300 strong at the lowest; they are inclined to believe it. So why should they dissolve?

I had a most charming breakfast—as I told you—with H.M. and there are many interesting things which I cannot write but will tell A. J. B. [Balfour] some day when I see him.

[*To the Rt. Hon. A. J. Balfour.*]   THE ROMAN CAMP,
SEPTEMBER 12TH.

Have you seen a book *England and the English* by Price Collier? If not, glance through it. I think Rosebery must have been reading it. His speech seems to me inconclusive. A stone-mason here, whose forebears have been in Callander for 200 years, said to me, "He [Rosebery] is a spent force." This man is a strong Unionist. *What* does R. want? I cannot understand

On Rosebery's Attitude.

his speech. He says what we all feel about the Bill; that it is a thoroughly bad, dishonest Bill. But the ordinary plain man (tiresome personality if you will, but the pivot of elections) wants to know whether R. thinks the Lords should reject the Bill, with all the dangers and bothers attendant thereon, or let it go through with a firm reliance upon the next Unionist majority to undo the land clauses. As to his views upon that question, I am no wiser than before he spoke.

The latter policy may be unfeasible. But if so, why could Rosebery not say so? After all, frankness is the sole advantage a "cross bench" man has over the leader of a party. Don't answer this.

[*Journals.*]   THE ROMAN CAMP,
                                      SEPTEMBER 12TH.

Rosebery has made his much awaited Budget speech. There is nothing in it which throws any light on the real problem. Everything which could be said for and against the Budget has been said. People's minds have long since been made up on the merits and demerits of the Bill. Nothing will change them.

The vital question is, whether the Lords shall allow the Bill to pass; whether it shall be rejected, with all the accompaniment of disturbance, financial and political; or whether it shall go through, on the understanding that the first Unionist majority shall reverse the land clauses.

Upon that issue R. throws no light at all. Which course does he advocate? The main use of the cross-bench man is to speak out straight to the country. Party leaders have to trim their sails. Once more he has shown fatal irresolution. . . .

Lord Esher on the Conflict of the Houses. When one thinks of the collateral issues involved, the conflict between the two houses, the doubtful constitutional proceeding involved in the Lords touching the Budget, the warnings of Lord Salisbury, the want of precedent, and the certain widening of the area of conflict once begun on such a question, the whole situation too perilously resembles that of 1640 for my taste.

If I were A. J. B. [Balfour] I should solemnly warn the country that I should, when I was given a majority, reverse the policy of the land clauses; and I would then let the Bill pass.

This is the safe and prudent policy. Party leaders are trustees not principals, and have no right to gamble with the fate of those for whom they hold not only the present but the future in trust. This is not cowardice but prudence.

[*To M. V. B.*]   THE ROMAN CAMP,
                                        SEPTEMBER 13TH.

. . . I am writing to Jackie [Fisher] and urging him to carefully *On Fisher's* consider his position. There is no doubt that *if* there was a *Position.* change of Government, he would not be taken on. I am *certain* of this. So it would be so much more dignified for him to make the first move.

[*To M. V. B.*]   THE ROMAN CAMP,
                                        SEPTEMBER 17TH.

. . . I have had a long letter from Sandars, and I gather from it that the Opposition have not made up their minds. They seem haunted by the *knowledge* that the Radicals want a dissolution, and the *fear* that they may be trapped into one. Rosebery's speech, says Stead, is a 20th-century replica of Lord John Russell chalking up "No Popery" on the wall, and then running away. L. G.'s good temper is his strongest card. It attracts people. Rosebery on Dr. Johnson was good, but not up to his highest level. It was too full of laudation. Quite uncritical. This is a great fault in him, his exaggerated praise of his heroes.

I have just finished the *Lady of the Lake*. It was published in *Scott and* the spring of 1810. In September 1809—exactly a century ago *" The Roman* —Scott was staying with Mr. Buchanan at Cambusmore and *Camp."* visited Captain Fairfoul, who was the tenant of the Camp—

which Scott called a "sweet villa," using the Italian word villa then the fashion in society. He perhaps had tea in this room. *Certainly* he sat here and gossiped, and walked about the garden —either before or after walking up to the Bracklin falls.

[*Journals.*]   THE ROMAN CAMP,
                                                  SEPTEMBER 26TH.

Germany and Limitation of Armaments.
We went over one day to Alloa. C. Hardinge was there. He told me that the Germans had been making advances to us on the subject—tabooed at the Hague—of a limitation of armaments.

This is the outcome of our 4 Dreadnoughts and the Imperial Conference. They wish the negotiations or approach kept secret. Grey was rather inclined to submit. But Hardinge *insisted* that the French should be told. . . .

I have just come back from our manœuvres. We were at Faringdon. General Durant, who commands the 6th or frontier Division, was French's guest. Intelligent and capable. Sympathetic too.

The manœuvres were the most successful ever held in this country, it is said. The real feature was the marching and sobriety and cheerfulness of the *men*. The leadership was nothing remarkable. We dined at the French Embassy to meet Asquith, Grey, and Haldane.

Tory Policy.
The P.M. was, I thought, in low spirits. I saw J. S. [Sandars], who told me that it was practically decided to throw out the Budget. The idea is that the General Election will practically destroy the Liberal majority. The whole thing is a political gamble. It may turn out a political blunder. Patience is a cardinal political virtue—as Dizzy's career shows. Time is always on the side of the Opposition. The best way is, as Dizzy said to Lord Wolverton, "Out with this b——y Government."

But I still think that the end will be, not perhaps yet, a complete constitutional change—at the expense of the H. of L.

[*Journals.*]   BALMORAL CASTLE,
                                                 OCTOBER 4TH.

Motored over the pass of Glenshee. A most glorious cloudless
day. I could see Ben Voirlich plain from Stobhall and all the
Grampian range from Meiklour.

I sat next the King at dinner to-night. He is marvellously
well—and in high spirits, as he always is when here.

We talked a good deal about the Budget and the H. of L.
He is strongly opposed to the Lords throwing out the Bill.
Francis Knollys has met with an accident, and is laid up, which
is most unfortunate. At this crisis his sound judgment is badly
wanted.

[*Journals.*]   BALMORAL,
                                                 OCTOBER 5TH.

A terrible day of wind and rain. We went to the Glassalt for
a deer drive. Luckily Mrs. K. [Keppell] and Mrs. Hwfa
Williams came over from Glen Muick; so although we all sat
on the hill and got wet through—the King could remain in the
house. The P. of W. was on the highest point of the mountain.
Of course it was impossible to get the deer to come right. Not a
shot was fired. We joined the King at tea and drove home. I
went to see Francis for a few minutes at Craig Gowan. He was
tired and below par.

[*To M. V. B.*]   BALMORAL CASTLE,
                                                 OCTOBER 6TH.

. . . I have been all day on the hill in the snow and an icy wind.
It has burnt me like anything. I got two stags; one shot dead,
and the other practically so. He only ran a few yards. A very
good rifle borrowed from George Holford. My old rifle is no

use. It is not accurate compared with the modern things. So do not use it. However, I gather that you do not stalk till Monday. Asquith has arrived, but I have not seen him yet.

[*Journals.*]   BALMORAL CASTLE,
                                  OCTOBER 6TH.

I went stalking with McIntosh. He is far the most intelligent of all the stalkers, and an excellent companion. After the storm yesterday there was much snow on the tops. I had two excellent stalks. Got two stags. Then had tea at McIntosh's house.

Sat next the Prime Minister at dinner. He arrived to-day. Very friendly.

[*To M. V. B.*]   BALMORAL CASTLE,
                                  OCTOBER 7TH.

This morning we had a drive. Only one stag was shot. Mine! A Royal one too. Wasn't it tragic? After luncheon another drive. I got a right and left! Then came some more deer, and I stood up, in the hope that they would go up to the King and the Prince of Wales.

They did, but the rain was so blinding that the King could not shoot. The P. of W. had a shot. Pom missed two and slightly wounded a third. Lord Hamilton shot one. Total bag 4 stags, of which 3 were mine. Isn't this awful? It always happens. I have fired six shots altogether in the forest, and got 5 stags. Not a bad average!

Asquith at Balmoral. I have just had a long talk with Asquith about Jackie Fisher— and then about the Defence Committee. He will make Jackie a Peer if he retires, and I am *sure* that if he does not retire either McKenna or some Tory Minister will turn him out. However, he is very obstinate. Then I suggested to A. all our ideas about the Defence Committee becoming the *joint* Imperial General Staff, and with his usual quickness he has grasped the idea.

He was attacked by a suffragette at Aboyne station in the early morning. Asquith has got two detectives with him here. But he is quite nonchalant.

[*Memorandum.*]

In January 1832 Lord Wharncliffe, acting as the representative of a strong section of the House of Lords who were reported to be adverse to the Reform Bill, had an interview with King William IV to discuss the situation, especially with reference to the creation of peers. The King acted with the full knowledge of Lord Grey, then Prime Minister. In 1869, when the two Houses of Parliament were in keen conflict over the Irish Church Bill, Queen Victoria intervened, and corresponded with and saw the Archbishop of Canterbury, who was practically leading the House of Lords against the Bill. Queen Victoria, with the knowledge of Mr. Gladstone, also wrote to Mr. Disraeli, urging him to use his influence with the majority of the House of Lords to pass the Bill. In 1884, when another very sharp and bitter conflict arose over the Reform and Redistribution Bill, the Queen sent for Lord Cairns and the Duke of Richmond, with the knowledge and approval of Mr. Gladstone, and arranged the compromise which was agreed to by both parties.

Precedents for Royal Intervention between Lords and Commons.

Mr. Gladstone admitted on both these occasions that the constitutional intervention of the Queen had prevented the conflict between the two Houses.

[*Journals.*]　　　　　　　　　　　BALMORAL CASTLE,
　　　　　　　　　　　　　　　　　　OCTOBER 8TH.

. . . The King had got several submissions from Haldane. One to make the C.G.S. the C. of the *Imperial* G.S. I wrote some memoranda for the King on this subject and also upon the precedents, 1832, 1869, 1885, for the intervention of the Sovereign in the quarrel of the two Houses. The King proposes on Tuesday to see A. J. B. [Balfour] and Lansdowne, which is creating some fuss among timid people. I have kept a copy of my memo., which reminded the King that in 1885 Mr. Gladstone, who was at Invercauld with Harcourt, approved of the Queen seeing Lord Cairns and the D. of Richmond, who were sent for to Balmoral.

At luncheon I sat next the King, and again at dinner. He was in excellent form. His memory is remarkable for anecdotes, which (unlike most) are always apposite.

Lord James told me that he had once asked Mr. Gladstone who was the most troublesome colleague with whom he had ever served. Mr. G. said that he had had in the course of his Cabinet life 65 colleagues, and that Harcourt was far away the most troublesome.

The King and the Crown Prince. We had a gillies' ball this evening. I danced the quadrille with Princess Maud of Fife. The King looked wonderfully well in his kilt. He told me at dinner that he had asked the Crown Prince of Germany to Sandringham, but had received a letter saying that his father could not spare him. The King wrote back that it was of no use to ask him, as his father obviously never could spare him. It appears that the Crown P. is very English in his dress and sentiments. The Emperor is therefore afraid of English influence. The King says the Emperor has always been jealous of Prince Henry of Prussia's popularity in the Navy. Hence his removal.

[*Journals.*]   THE ROMAN CAMP,
                                                OCTOBER 9TH.

Left Balmoral early and drove over the pass of Glenshee. At the Glenshee Hotel I stopped for a while. The hostess, Mrs. Oswald, comes from Kirriemuir. She was a Miss McKenzie. She and her husband know Barrie intimately. He was married practically from their house. She was terribly shocked to hear of his divorce proceedings.

I met Maurice and Nellie at the Bridge of Cally, and we had a lovely drive through Strathardle to Pitlochry and by Aberfeldy and Loch Tay home.

[*To H.M. the King.*]　　　　　THE ROMAN CAMP,
　　　　　　　　　　　　　　　　　　OCTOBER 11TH.

Viscount Esher cannot refrain from offering his humble and grateful thanks to your Majesty for another delightful visit to Balmoral. To these visits and Your Majesty's unvarying kindness he always looks back as among the happiest days of the year. The whole atmosphere of keen interest in public affairs combined with sport, and the charming surroundings of Balmoral, is one in which he likes to think of Your Majesty, and he cannot therefore be sufficiently grateful for the opportunity which has been so graciously accorded him year after year.

Viscount Esher had a splendid drive home, through Glenshee, Strathardle, and round Loch Tay.

He fears Your Majesty will have some troublesome days and weeks in the near future, but he feels sure that both Ministers and Opposition Leaders will weigh, and will probably yield to, your Majesty's impartial view of the present crisis. Viscount Esher remains Your Majesty's faithful and devoted servant.

[*To the Rt. Hon. J. S. Sandars.*]　　THE ROMAN CAMP,
　　　　　　　　　　　　　　　　　　OCTOBER 11TH.

You will have an interesting week. I gather that you are not quite confident about H.M.'s prudence in seeing A. J. B. [Balfour] and Lansdowne. But there are plenty of precedents. A. J. B. will remember that in 1885, when Mr. G. and Harcourt were at Invercauld, the Queen sent for Lord Cairns and the D. of Richmond to Balmoral.

A. J. B. and I were in the thick of that business. I was looking only a few months ago at the notes I took at the time of all those transactions.

Doubts of the Tory Policy.

I am still unconvinced that it is desirable—i.e. *expedient*—to throw out this rotten Budget. Of course I am not a gambler by instinct. It seems to me that patience leaves all the trumps in A. J. B.'s hand, and that in spite of Dizzy's formula the issue at the General Election, brought about by the rejection of the Bill, would be, not the Budget or the "bloody Government" but the House of Lords.

However, I admit that I am no politician, and still less am I a believer in the "lessons of history." So my opinions are not worth a rap. Asquith was very pleasant and unfussy at Balmoral and I think the King was very open with him. I killed 5 stags and had all the luck, which is a very mixed blessing on these august occasions. Now I am settled here till November 1st, when I go south. Francis Knollys has had a severe shake from his fall. He bears pain badly and he has suffered a good deal.

[*Journals.*]   THE ROMAN CAMP,
                                              OCTOBER 11TH.

Haldane came here to lunch—and we talked Army and Budget. He says there is truth in the idea of H. Gladstone going to S. Africa; and in that case Burns might go to the H. Office and Loulou [Harcourt] to the Local Government Board. I don't think Loulou will like this at all. I showed him my plan for Boy Scouts. He agreed, and I sent it to B. P. [Baden-Powell].

[*From Sir Douglas Haig.*]   SS. "MANTUA,"
    [*Personal.*]   OCTOBER 11TH.

MY DEAR ESHER,

I was very sorry to leave England without seeing you to say good-bye. You were in Scotland when I came away. I saw

Lord Morley and Mr. Haldane. The latter thanked me cordially for the help which I have given him, especially in the T.F. scheme.

Personally I felt that I had done but little and that the thanks were really due to those who were working under me at that time, and to yourself more than to anyone else. I shall never forget the many discussions which we had together and the careful way in which you used to revise our proposals, etc. etc., and helped me also to deal with opposition which existed even in the Gen. Staff. I wish you had been present and heard Haldane's praise, because it was you who suggested my name to him, for the work and I was, consequently, brought back from India.

> Yours ever,
> DOUGLAS HAIG.

[*From His Majesty the King.*]   JOCKEY CLUB, NEWMARKET,
          [*Private.*]   OCTOBER 13TH.

MY DEAR ESHER,

It gives me great pleasure to learn from your letter received to-day that you enjoyed your visit to Balmoral. It always gives me the greatest pleasure to receive you under my roof—and that we were able to have interesting conversations on so many subjects which are congenial to us! . . .

> Yours very sincerely,
> EDWARD R.

[*To Lord Morley.*]   THE ROMAN CAMP,
                    OCTOBER 13TH.

I had a very pleasant time at Balmoral, and shot 5 stags. The King was wonderfully well, and in one of his best moods. The P.M. seemed in good spirits, but not at all clear about the probable trend of events. I do not suppose for a moment that the King's intervention will have any effect.

The Opposition Leaders were rather nervous at the idea of a meeting with the King. They seemed to have forgotten the Queen's attempts in 1869 and 1885 to compose differences. They apparently did not know that in the latter year, when Mr. Gladstone and Harcourt were at Invercauld, the Queen summoned the D. of Richmond and Cairns to Balmoral. Who remembers anything in these days? Ll. George seems to be establishing a firm position for himself at the expense of Winston [Churchill]. He appeals strongly to "the man in the street." It is that dash of Celtic blood, I suppose, which gives him his attractive quality of political "good humour."

Ll. George and Churchill.

It was interesting to see how *The Times* deflected from a wise appreciation of the crisis, under the pressure of the Amalgamated Press. The article written a month ago and those of to-day in parallel columns would be a good object-lesson in high journalism! . . .

[*To the Rt. Hon. J. S. Sandars.*]   THE ROMAN CAMP,
OCTOBER 14TH.

The King Meets Balfour and Lansdowne.

Your letter is most interesting. Of course I see your point of view perfectly, and if there was not a great deal to be said on both sides, how easy it would be to arrive at grave decisions. On the whole, however, I think good, and not harm, can only come out of the King's interview with A. J. B. [Balfour]. Of course, as you say, the Prime Minister had to give his assent to the King's action, and no doubt H.M. told him what took place.

That was the underlying "motive" of the transaction. So often things go wrong because the principal leaders are misled by idle rumours. What can, for instance, be madder than the idea that Asquith ever contemplated a "Referendum"? Yet Buckle, who must have softening of the brain, evidently believed it. Of course, I don't know what took place at the interview, but if the King repeated to A. J. B. what Asquith said to him at Balmoral, then only good, and not harm, can come of the interview.

I see your distinction between "earlier stages of the drama" and a "deadlock." There is force in what you say. But, on the other hand, the circumstances are slightly different from those of the Irish Church Bill and the Reform and Redistribution Bills. There was no question then (whatever its merits or demerits may be) of the House of Lords acting in a manner outside the ordinary understanding between the two Houses.

The King may readily have held that once the Budget is rejected the mischief is done; and he may have thought it his duty to bring A. J. B. and Asquith into touch, *before* any final decision is taken. I am sure that the country will appreciate H.M.'s action, and comprehend it in a degree which politicians, half-blinded by the dust of battle, perhaps cannot realise.

When you say that "no responsible member of the opposition has declared his decision on the question at future issue" that is not the general impression. The speeches made by Walter Long and George Wyndham, Chamberlain's letter read at A. J. B.'s meeting, and A. J. B.'s own speech, all point (to the ordinary man) only to one issue.

And if these indications were rightly interpreted, then it was surely natural and proper that the King should do his utmost to avert a conflict, into which (by having possibly to say Yes or No to a request to use his prerogative) he was almost certain to be drawn.

There would now appear to be every probability that the Constitution, i.e. the relations between the two houses of Parliament and the tenure of a seat in the H. of L.—will be readjusted in the near future. It is not strange if the King may have thought that such changes as are inevitable should, if possible, take place when the Conservative Government was in office, which has the support of the majority of the H. of L. It would not be surprising if he looked with dismay upon a remodelling of the Constitution by a Radical Government, partly by the use

The Crown and the Constitutional Issue.

of threats or even force, in which his own position might be compromised. What, if I may venture to say so, it seemed to me the King intended, was to interpret the wish of the majority of his people, and his view was evidently that they wish for some accommodation between the two parties, if accommodation is possible.

If it is possible I do not think that the result will show that the King will be blamed. My impression is that here and abroad he will be thought to have used his influence in the direction of peace.

That is not a bad halo, even for martyrdom! so surely, in lesser degree, it can only be counted to His Majesty for righteousness. My letter is almost as long as yours.

[*To M. V. B.*]   ORCHARD LEA,
                                                   OCTOBER 18TH.

. . . I finished the *Pluralistic Universe*, which is the last new thing in metaphysics. I dislike that so-called science almost as much as politics, but it is well to be up to date. *Nightingales and Trees* are better, however, than musty philosophers as elixirs of youth.

[*To the Rev. C. D. Williamson.*]   ORCHARD LEA,
                                                   OCTOBER 24TH.

. . . There is no change in the political situation. I still think the H. of L. will be extremely foolish, and deservedly blamed, if they destroy the Budget.

Did you read Lloyd George on Arthur Balfour? It was a pretty speech. . . .[1]

[1] The speech in question was delivered at the Annual Dinner of the Honourable Society of Cymmrodorion, Mr. Balfour being the guest of the evening and Mr. Lloyd George being appointed to propose the toast. The speech, with Mr. Balfour's long and equally pretty reply, is given in *The Times* of Oct. 22, p. 10, col. 3.

[*Journals.*]   WINDSOR CASTLE,
                                         NOVEMBER 17TH.

So much has happened that I do not know where to begin. We left Scotland regretfully at the end of the month. We went by train to Crewe—Nellie, Maurice, and I. We then met the motor, and went home in a day by Worcester and Gloucester. Beautiful weather. Before leaving Scotland, we began the new library, and I arranged to give the rifle club a range.

Then came London, and all the fuss which the certain action of the Lords *re* the Budget was bound to make. I lunched one day with A. J. B. [Balfour] and had a long talk with him. He sees no danger in the position of the King, whatever course he may adopt. "You forget," he said, "the changed circumstances since 1832. During the latter half of Queen Victoria's reign, and more than ever now, Great Britain means the British Empire. Our people oversea do not care a rush for Asquith or me. They hardly know our names. For them the symbol of the Empire is the King. Hands laid on the Sovereign would mean the disruption of the Empire."

Balfour on the Strength of the Crown.

Anyhow, from the opening days of the controversy, certainly from the day of Lloyd George's speech at Limehouse, the fate of the Budget was sealed.

Jackie [Fisher] has got his Peerage, to the great disgust of his foes. Asquith's letter to him was very flattering, and the King's was perfectly charming. It was worth more than the honour....

Fisher's Peerage.

. . . Zena and Phyllis [Dare] came here last Sunday. Barrie was here. He talked to me very freely. . . .

[*Journals.*]   ORCHARD LEA,
                                         NOVEMBER 26TH.

Yesterday morning Maurice left for Ceylon. We had two charming days before he started. He had not been well for a week, and was laid up here for a few days. Then we went to

London and he was with Zena constantly. He gave her a
diamond ring. It engaged him to her; and she knows this.

The night before last I joined them at supper, and we had a
long and serious talk. She came to the station to see him off.
The platform was full of Generals. Nellie and Syv were there.
But Zena was the centre of attraction. I hope she will wait for
him, and love him all his life, since he so wishes it.

We are in the midst of a political crisis. But my heart is too
full of M.'s departure. He telephoned from Marseilles this
morning.

[*To M. V. B.*]   ORCHARD LEA,
                                          NOVEMBER 29TH.

. . . I have bought 80 feet of oak panelling from the Woking-
ham man. It is not much, but the pattern is beautiful. It came
out of Basing House and was bought in a cottage close by. It
can be fitted in with plainer stuff if I can find some. It was
cheap. I gave £10 for the lot.

[*To M. V. B.*]   2, TILNEY STREET,
                                          DECEMBER 1ST.

On Winston   . . . Yesterday I dined with Winston [Churchill] at his home
Churchill.   in Eccleston Square. He has a charming double room on the
first floor, all books. A splendid library. It was a birthday
dinner. Only 6 people. But he had a birthday cake with 35
candles. And *crackers*. He sat all the evening with a paper cap,
from a cracker, on his head. A queer sight, if all the thousands
who go to his meetings could have seen him.

He and she sit on the same sofa, and he holds her hand. I
never saw two people more in love. If he goes out of office, he
has not a penny. He would have to earn his living, but he says it
is well worth it if you live with someone you love. He would

loathe it, but he is ready to live in a *lodging*—just two rooms—with her and the baby! They have a cook now, two maids and a man. *She* ran down to the kitchen before dinner to see that it was all right. And an excellent dinner it was!

I came away early, as they went down to the House of Lords to see the division.[1] In the afternoon I had been to see Millie [Sutherland] for about an hour. She was very sweet, and asked most affectionately after you, and whether you were still madly in love with Zena.

The political atmosphere is very charged with storm. The Government propose to ask the King for authority to use his prerogative to create Peers in the event of their obtaining a majority at the election. But they want him to give his pledge *now*. I most sincerely hope he will refuse. He may have to give way *after* an election. But it is monstrous to ask him to do so now. His action ought to be guided by the state of parties after the appeal to the country. *The Cabinet and the Crown.*

One always knew that he would be placed in a great difficulty, and probably a most humiliating position. I cannot believe that the Tories can win. But one never can tell.

[*To Lord Knollys.*]   2, TILNEY STREET,
DECEMBER 1ST.

I saw Haldane yesterday, and he told me the following very grave facts.

The Cabinet are discussing whether, instead of attempting to alter by Statute the relations between the two Houses of Parliament, they shall advise the King to place permanently in the hands of the Prime Minister of the day H.M.'s prerogative to create Peers. *Cabinet Attempt to Force the Crown—*

The only alternative, according to their views, is a Bill which they would introduce, coupled with a statement that the Ministers had obtained from the Sovereign a promise to create

---

[1] The division in which the Finance Bill was thrown out.

a sufficient number of Peers to pass the measure. Haldane said that he was anxious to know what I thought of these proposals.

I pointed out that the former would be an abdication by the Sovereign of his prerogative not only on his own behalf but on that of his successors, and to my mind was an outrage.

And with regard to the second, that for the King to create the enormous number of Peers required to pass a Bill, opposed by a majority, through the present House of Lords, would also be an outrage on the common sense of the country.

There is only one precedent in England for the creation of Peers for the purpose of obtaining a majority in the House of Lords; when Queen Anne created 12, a small creation compared with that which is now under discussion. The case of 1832 is no precedent, as no Peers were created, and it is by no means certain that the King would in the last resort have made them.

—and Involve it in Politics.

But the graver aspect of the question is, that the Prime Minister wishes to obtain a promise from the King *before* the General Election.

In other words, the Government wish to make the King a party to their dissolution programme. I cannot conceive a more monstrous proposal, and even now I cannot believe that responsible Ministers, anxious as they must be to sustain the Monarchy, will determine to make such a request to the King.

I have no doubt, not a shadow of doubt, that if any of these proposals are made to the King *before* the General Election H.M. should meet them with a firm refusal.

The Sovereign's freedom of action should be unimpaired; and H.M.'s ultimate decision will, of course, be guided largely by the result of the appeal to the country. The situation, and the King's decision, cannot fail to be affected by the balance of parties in the House of Commons in the new Parliament.

If the Government were to resign *before* the General Election, because the King refused assent to their plan, I feel sure that, notwithstanding the very serious crisis which would arise, the King would be supported by this country, and all over the Empire.

I think it would be unwise to breathe a word of this to anyone except the King, as the results might be disastrous, for reasons which you readily understand. It is to be hoped that further reflections on the part of the Cabinet will spare the King from having to discuss either alternative with his Ministers. But I think it of such vital importance that the King should have *ample time* to consider the various dilemma in which he may be placed, that I thought it my duty to write this letter.

[*To M. V. B.*]   2, TILNEY STREET,
                                      DECEMBER 7TH.

Yesterday's rush to Birmingham was not so bad after all. It only took two hours getting there, and I travelled down with little Amery. I stayed with quite a nice man, and a little hostess aged 14. Comfortable bed, but *such* an ugly middle-class house. The audience was fine. 1500 people, and they listened wonderfully. Much more intelligent than the Royal Institution. There was not a sound, except repeated applause at the "purple patches." I must send you my letters to *The Times* on the H. of L. But I shall wait until I have finished the set of three or possibly four.[1]

    . . . I am *furious* about that Aerial League and have resigned on the spot.[2] I have got Lord Morley to telegraph to Minto to warn Creagh and to say I never had any knowledge of this man's trip to India. I never heard such cheek. Anyhow, *that* is over.

    . . . We went to Beethoven last night. It is very lovely—

Birmingham Territorials.

---

[1] Three very long letters written under the pseudonym "Historicus" were published in *The Times* on the 6th, 10th, and 20th December, 1909. The first was a defence of the House of Lords against charges recently made by Mr. Masterman; for it appeared to Historicus that the vices alleged by Mr. Masterman were exactly the virtues that every framer of Constitutions demanded of a second chamber. The second and third were full and documented accounts of the creation of peers by Queen Anne and the threat to create them by William IV.

[2] His name was being used by a man who had gone to India.

because of the music. But a bad play. It is not a play at all. Only a romantic musical dream.

A War Scare.   . . . I enclose the *D. Mail* to-day in order to show you the unscrupulousness of those people. They would be quite ready to get up a war with Germany in order to cover up their probable defeat on the Budget. I don't think political crime can go much lower than that. Blatchford—whom they are exploiting —is a socialist and a self-advertising fellow. I suppose the country and the Germans will see through the dodge.

[To M. V. B.]   ORCHARD LEA,
                                 DECEMBER 11TH.

. . . We came down to-day, as I had to go to a prize-giving last night, and make a speech. It was a Yeomanry affair, and there were some distinguished guests, including Carson—who made a very neat little speech. He has a son in the Regiment. This morning British Museum. I lunched at the Ritz yesterday with Francis [Knollys]. He had J. M. [Morley] to lunch and Mrs. Leo [Rothschild] and Mrs. Arthur [Sassoon]. It was amusing to see J. M.'s futile attempts to get a word in. Francis gave it up. But J. M. fought against it as though it were a wind on the top of Ben Ledi!

[To M. V. B.]   2, TILNEY STREET,
                                 DECEMBER 16TH.

Bouchier and the Shakespeare Memorial.   . . . In the afternoon we had a most heated meeting at the Shakespeare Memorial Committee, with Alfred Lyttleton in the chair. There is a row on between the committee and a group of actors, headed by Bouchier and tailed by Seymour [Hicks]. I said some very tart things about Bouchier, who had written a very impertinent letter from the Garrick Club—evidently at one in the morning.

[*To M. V. B.*]   2, TILNEY STREET,
                                         DECEMBER 17TH.

. . . King Leopold is dead. In the odour of sin, with all his *On King* cruelties unrepented of. I was only reading yesterday the high *Leopold.* hopes of him as a "beautiful child" when the Queen came to the throne. Your grandfather, however, never liked him.

[*To M. V. B.*]   2, TILNEY STREET,
                                         DECEMBER 21ST.

Maggs sent me 5 letters which he had advertised as auto- *The King's* graphs of the King. They were all private letters. Two written *Letters for* to the Duchess d'Avarny, two to the brother of Prince Edward *Sale.* of Saxe-Weimar, and one to the Landgravine of Hesse—a sister of the Red Prince! He wanted £35 for them. I took them to the King, who of course dislikes extremely his letters being hawked about. But, if he buys them, it will evidently lead to a system of organised blackmail. All this would have been prevented if the Lord Chancellor had had the pluck to pass my bill.[1] To *sell* letters is *publication* in law—I am told. But the present law is futile. The King was charming and very uneasy about his future. I think he is going to have a pretty bad time. There was on view in his room a statue of the daughter of Germanicus, in bronze, picked up in Lake Nevi, sent by Spink for him to look at, price £25,000. It will go to America. It was wonderful but not pretty.

[1] See ante, p. 257.

[*To M. V. B.*]   ORCHARD LEA,
DECEMBER 23RD.

. . . Last night we had a box at the Haymarket for the *Blue Bird*. It is *not* good. Maeterlinck has no humour—and very little pathos, and is far too fond of the obvious. The whole thing—play, performance, and setting—is amateurish.

[*To the Rt. Hon. A. J. Balfour.*]   ORCHARD LEA,
DECEMBER 24TH.

The Admiralty Obstructs the Defence Committee.

I told you that we were trying to get a sub-committee of the Committee of Imperial Defence appointed to sit weekly and work out the details of decisions already settled by the full committee. This work is most essential, as the ability to carry out suddenly the settled plans of the executive Government, based upon the Committee of Imperial Defence reports, depends upon the details being understood and jointly worked out by the Navy and Admiralty.

Haldane (who, by the way, is *very* unwell) and the W.O. warmly approve. So does E. Grey—so does Asquith. So *did* McKenna. But Wilson, who is at the Admiralty now every day, has objected and cannot see that the Committee of Imperial Defence has anything to do with the general planning of naval and military operations in certain contingencies. He maintains that these are matters which should be left to the C. of General Staff and the 1st Sea Lord to discuss and arrange between themselves.

This of course is putting the clock back some years. If Asquith acquiesced in this view, it would strike a very severe if not deadly blow at the Committee of Imperial Defence. It would certainly strengthen Haldane's plea for a "Minister of Defence" who should control both services.

For the present, unless we can overcome the difficulty, it postpones the day when, *to quote you*, the Prime Minister can

touch a bell and send for the Secretary of the Defence Committee and obtain from him the conclusions of the Committee
upon any probable offensive or defensive joint naval and
military operation.

There is a great deal of truth in Haldane's contention that the
weak point in our national armour just now is, not the material
or personnel of the Navy, but the Board of Admiralty, its want
of modern ideas and its inefficient organisation. *State of the Admiralty.*

I am annoyed at the stagnation of the Committee of Imperial
Defence. Since August we have done *nothing*. I see no prospect
of getting anything done for months to come.

Yet there is an almost hopeless amount of work to be done.
And plenty of people eager to do it. As you are aware, I am
talking of the spade work: the preparation of material upon
which the whole committee can base, after consideration, its
decision.

I know you like these matters; so I don't mind bothering you
at Xmas time. I shall try to get to you for a night presently.

[*To M. V. B.*]　　　ORCHARD LEA,
　　　　　　　　　　DECEMBER 24TH.

. . . Barrie has given me a Xmas present, the MS. of *What
Every Woman Knows*. A beautiful MS. on notepaper in his
fine small handwriting.

[*To M. V. B.*]　　　ORCHARD LEA,
　　　　　　　　　　DECEMBER 26TH.

This morning I drove to Nuneham. I went alone in my
motor. There was a huge party of children—and *one* interesting
man. Simon, the K.C., of whom you have heard. He is a
widower with 3 small kids; a fellow of All Souls, and a very
attractive and clever man. I should think the future holds *On Sir John Simon.*

something big for him. I got back at 6. Loulou [Harcourt] is confident about winning the General Election, but he is frightened of personal violence from the Suffragettes. They have marked him out for their prey.

[*To M. V. B.*]   ORCHARD LEA,
                                              DECEMBER 28TH.

. . . It has been blowing hard all day, a south-westerly gale— and very enervating. Poor old Haldane seems worse to-day. I am getting really alarmed. His retirement would be a dreadful calamity.

. . . *The Times* has 88 sheets to-day about S. America—a really marvellous account, illustrated, of that marvellous country. I mean to have a dash into the Argentine before very long. These things are beginning to interest me—not only for financial reasons—but political and social. Such momentous changes seem to be ahead. It is impossible yet to measure their dimensions, but our whole system of Government here is about to undergo a sea-change.

[*To M. V. B.*]   2, TILNEY STREET,
                                              DECEMBER 29TH.

. . . I have resigned—as I told you—the Aerial League. I am now having a row about the Defence Committee. There has been no work done here since August; and owing to the Election, and subsequent crises, there will be nothing done. The Admiralty is very obstructive. Unless the P.M. makes some change I shall come off the Committee. I am not anxious to be responsible for disaster. We come to decisions, and they are treated as the amiable aberrations of a few well meaning but harmless amateur strategists. That being the case, I prefer more freedom and more unqualified irresponsibility. I will let you know how the row ends.

[*To M. V. B.*]   2, TILNEY STREET,
DECEMBER 30TH.

I have had a long day. George Murray, who knows a good *Liberal* deal from "whips" etc., thinks that the Tories have been getting *Forecasts.* stronger in the country every day, and the Government weaker. He told me also that, even if Asquith gets a majority, the Government cannot fail to break up over *next* year's Budget. In his view it is impossible for Ll. G. [George] and McKenna to continue to hold the posts they now occupy, as neither can give way over Navy estimates. He says this means reconstruction of the Cabinet, or resignations. The Tories are unlucky, however. So many of their best men ill, and now they lose Percy, one of the most promising of the young ones. He died in 3 days of pneumonia, aged 38.

I was some hours with old Nick [Nicholson]. He is in charge *On Sir W.* of the W.O. now that Haldane is ill. He certainly is an under- *Nicholson.* rated man—and no one will ever know what a large debt of gratitude is due to him for his hard work, patience, and good sense. He is *not* a self-advertiser. He has had bother with the A.G. about the Home Defence Scheme. Johnnie Hamilton has caved in. I think he had something to say for himself! Nick was excellent about the Staff, and Staff College. He spoke with real warmth of the General [French], to whom he is *most grateful.* You might tell the General.

[*To the Rt. Hon. A. J. Balfour.*]   2, TILNEY STREET,
DECEMBER 31ST.

Would next Saturday, 8th Jan., suit you for me to spend at Whittingehame? I have got to be in York on Friday, and would go up to you next day. Then continue my wanderings on Sunday (by motor) to Callander.

Will you read the little book I send? I came across it casually. It is worth looking at.

Privately. Francis [Knollys] said he doesn't know whether it is Fisher who influences Wilson, or Wilson Fisher; but it is evident that they have agreed to shut down as much as possible the work of the Defence Committee. Well, I always remember that you put me on the committee to "hold the fort" for you. So I propose to fight them. When you become P.M. again, I shall be ready to say my *nunc dimittis*.

[*To M. V. B.*]   ORCHARD LEA,
                                   JANUARY 1ST, 1910.

On Lord   . . . This morning I drove up to see little Bobs.[1] He is ageing
Roberts.   a little, but not much. Wonderfully open-minded and virile for so old a man. He is full of modern ultra radical ideas about the army and tactical fighting. Between ourselves (don't tell the General [French]), it is a pity he is not a younger man. I am sure he would realise *facts*—which it is so hard to get soldiers to do.

For example, I think *he* would understand my pet fads about bicycles and motors in war, i.e. means of locomotion and mobility which increase from day to day, versus the horse, which is becoming obsolete.

We talked all about the usual things. Yeomanry and India. He has been swept off his feet by the *Valour of Ignorance*, which has been sent to him from America by the author. He was just as amiable and kindly as he always is.

This afternoon I went to the Castle and muddled with papers.

[*To M. V. B.*]   ORCHARD LEA,
                                   JANUARY 3RD.

. . . This afternoon I went to see Haldane. He is still in the dark, with an electric pad on his eye night and day, warmed by a battery. He will recover all right now, and is very cheerful. But he has had a wonderful escape.

[1] F.M. Lord Roberts.

[*To M. V. B.*]　　　　　　　2, TILNEY STREET,
　　　　　　　　　　　　　　　　JANUARY 4TH.

Your letter from Kandy just arrived. I have been dining at Brooks's with Francis [Knollys], Jackie [Fisher], and McKenna—and found your letter on my return home just now.

It is curious how things always turn out contrariwise. I imagined that Ceylon was really the garden of the world and that you would find it so. Whereas evidently you were left comparatively cold by its far-famed beauties. How dull, however, appears to be the level of that provincial "society" with its dinners and functions all drearily based upon the model banquets at Windsor Castle! And then the planters, too, with their attempts at gaiety founded on buckets of intoxicating drink. Queer people, ours. They rule by sword and "fire water." How long will it last?

. . . Our dinner this evening was interesting, because there was some very outspoken talk, first about McKenna's position, and secondly about the political situation. McKenna finds Sir Arthur Wilson "very difficult." He is high-handed and treats Admiral Bridgeman as if he were a second Lieutenant on board a ship—and he is very obstinate. It is quite possible that if this Government remains in office, Wilson will upset McKenna. It is more probable still that Lloyd George will persist in cutting down the Navy estimates and that McKenna or Lloyd George will have to go. This possible break-up of the Government, even if they get a large majority, is a glimmer of light on the otherwise dark prospect. Dark—because the crisis we always foresaw is rapidly approaching. It is like Halley's comet. About Feb. 10th the Prime Minister will be asking the King for a promise to create Peers. That is *certain*. If the King says yes, he mortally offends the whole Tory party to which he is naturally bound. If he says no, he lets loose all the Radical gutter press at his position as Sovereign and his person as a man. A charming dilemma, full of revolutionary possibilities. We have never

Instability of the Government.

been nearer a revolution since 1688 and probably *never* nearer to a big and sudden European conflict.

The tension between Germany and England is a newspaper tension, but it is severe for all that.

[*To M. V. B.*]   2 TILNEY STREET,
                                                  JANUARY 5TH.

American Wealth. . . . Joe Duveen, who is passing through London on his way to America. This last year was the biggest year in business they have ever had. These immense fortunes are accumulating so quickly that people don't know how to spend their money. The result is that they become reckless of what they spend in *objets d'art*. The highest price ever given for a picture is £120,000 for a Velasquez. In a few years that price will be largely exceeded.

[*To M. V. B.*]   2 TILNEY STREET,
                                                  JANUARY 6TH.

To-day has been very dull and blank, except that I met Seymour Lucas[1] in St. James's St. He has bought a XVth-century house in Suffolk, two miles from Ipswich, on the main line. He is doing it up with old oak. It has the two old circular stairways and a central hall. Five acres of ground. He says it will be lovely. I have got the refusal of it.

. . . To-night we went to *The Importance of Being Earnest*. Very funny, just as funny as ever, which is a great triumph for Oscar Wilde.

[*To M. V. B.*]   STATION HOTEL, YORK,
                                                  JANUARY 7TH.

. . . Zena met us in a riding habit, having been 14 miles at a trot! . . . I can more than understand your loving her so much.

[1] The artist.

I could so easily be in love with her myself. You can imagine what she was in her dressing-room to-night in those pretty clothes. It was Peter Pan all over again, almost. She is quite excellent in the part.[1]

[*To M. V. B.*]   WHITTINGEHAME,
JANUARY 9TH.

There are ten girls staying in this house, and all sit at Arthur [Balfour]'s feet and adore him. All nieces. One dear little nephew—a Westminster boy. One girl is a desperate flirt. *Balfour at Home.*

. . . A lot more children came over for lunch—including a wonderfully clever little Asquith, aged 12 and talking with Margot's brilliance. A freak.

I have talked over the whole political situation with Arthur, and will write to you about it when I get to Pinkie. There has not been for years so dangerous a political crisis. It will be over about February 10th or at latest February 14th. Just before your return.

Repington sent me a letter written by Lonsdale Hale to Moberley Bell, in which he says, "I should like to see my old friends French, Esher, and Repington tied to 3 stakes to which I would gladly set light." Tell the General [French]. It will make him laugh. Rep. writes angrily about the poor old man. Rep. is a great fool sometimes. This patriarchal house is full of charm. We had family prayers to-night, beautifully read by Arthur. But I could not help thinking of Arthur Benson's ludicrous "avalanche of lacqueys" as they all filed in and took their places.

[*Journals.*]   WHITTINGEHAME,
JANUARY 9TH.

Mr. Balfour could not believe that it was really intended to ask the King for a promise to create Peers *before* a Bill was introduced dealing with the H. of L. *Balfour's Opinion on the Constitutional Issue.*

[1] *The Dashing Little Duke.*

He was amazed at the impudence of the thing. He has no shadow of doubt that the K. ought not under any circumstances to agree. His opinion is that first Asquith should be asked to put his request in writing. That a *reasoned* answer should be given, pointing out

(*a*) No crisis necessitating urgency in dealing with H. of L., as Lansdowne pledged the H. of L. to pass the Budget if Liberals returned to power.

(*b*) That it would be a breach of the King's duty, if not of his Coronation oath, to pledge himself to create Peers to pass a Bill which he has never seen.

(*c*) No precedent for asking the Sovereign to use his prerogative to pass through the H. of L. a measure which has not even obtained assent of the H. of C.

(*d*) That though there might be some justification for asking him to use his prerogative to pass a Bill which already had received assent of an overwhelming majority of the H. of C., NONE for asking him to promise to use it for the purpose of passing ultimately through the H. of L. a Bill which the H. of C. has not even seen.

(*e*) As regards principle of the use of prerogative, must refuse to discuss it, as the principle is entirely dependent upon the circumstances. . . .

Asquith may resign. In that case the King will probably send for Mr. Balfour and authorise him to state in Parliament the dilemma in which Ministers had placed the King, and Mr. Balfour feels confident that the King would be supported by the country.

As to the question whether Mr. Balfour would himself form a Government, it depends entirely on the composition of the next H. of C. . . . Premature to discuss it. He, however, feels this, that whatever risk may be run by the Sovereign in refusing such a request as it is assumed Asquith will make next month, there would be greater risk in acceding to it.

[*To M. V. B.*]   2 TILNEY STREET,
                                    JANUARY 14TH.

. . . I saw old Haldane to-day. He is much better, but will
not go out of the house for some time yet. The Elections began
to-day. Here is a poster—"England expects the Foreigner to
pay the Duty." Not so bad!

I have been dining at the Ritz with Hardinge and Francis *European*
[Knollys]. The former says that the Germans are trying to get *Situation.*
us to accept an arrangement as to armaments which will tie our
hands and leave them free. His master is dissatisfied with
Metternich because he has failed to delude us, and he will
probably before long be dismissed.

I have suggested to Repington that he should write an article
proposing to convert our "entente" into *alliance*. I am sure it
would be a great safeguard to the peace of Europe. If he does
this, he will send me the article to look over. J. Morley told
me that he is anxious to get rid of Minto before June, as he has
broken down in health.

Although India is in a very dangerous state, he will not send
K. [Kitchener] out, as he has become hopelessly idle. Sir G.
Clarke wrote to Morley that he had been reading a "very interesting and instructive book, which he *supposed* was familiar
to J. M."—Carlyle's *French Revolution*. Imagine J. M.'s face!

. . . A. J. Balfour has sent me to-day his memo. upon the situation which may occur if Asquith tries to force from the King a
promise to create Peers *before* any Bill dealing with the H. of L.
is through the House of Commons. He is strongly of opinion
that the King should refuse and take all risks. I think he is right.
In fact, there is no doubt on the point—A. J. B. would, if necessary, come to the rescue. All sorts of difficult situations may
arise unless the majority is very large for one party or the other,
which seems impossible. I have a sort of feeling that the Tories
will win 139 seats.

That will leave the Irish the controlling power, and the
Radicals will have to buy them with Home Rule.

I think the "Islanders" will have done marvellously if they can, by moral pressure, get A. J. B. to pronounce in favour of a 2 to 1 naval policy, and I am not sure that he will not do so.

There are 80 new members this morning. It is a growing boom.[1]

[*To M. V. B.*]   2 TILNEY STREET,
                                   JANUARY 20TH.

I went up to Seymour Lucas this morning, and I bought the beautiful piece of oak, of which I send you a picture. It is at the Society of Antiquaries, but will be fetched away to-morrow. You see the account of it printed on the sheet next the engraving. It will form the top of the mantelpiece in the library at Pinkie, and the lower part will just be plain stone. Then I am copying the bookshelves from Hatfield, and the oak panelling I have settled to pick up by small sections. Some, I have already got. I am sure you will love these glorious arms of Leicester. Did you ever see better? They seem to me wonderful.

[*To M. V. B.*]   2 TILNEY STREET,
                                   JANUARY 21ST.

. . . This evening I saw one of the best plays you can imagine. *The House of Temperley.* Two prize fights, and such lovely

---

[1] Lord Knollys wrote:—

                                   SANDRINGHAM,
                                   JANUARY 16TH.
MY DEAR ESHER,

I showed to the King the paper you sent me, and he thinks the "Islanders" is a very good thing, and he wishes it every success.

                                   Yours ever,
                                   KNOLLYS.

dresses and typical pictures of 1812. It ends on the storming of Badajoz. I am going to take the whole theatre on February 11th and send my Terriers, or a section of them!

It will be rather fun. It is a very virile play.

[*To M. V. B.*]   ORCHARD LEA,
                      JANUARY 22ND.

. . . The Elections indicate to-day beyond all doubt a Govern- *Results of* ment majority, *but* dependent on the Irish. Lloyd George's de- *the Election.* nunciations etc. have not weighed with the constituencies much —and Feudalism holds its own. The King is at Windsor. I came down late and didn't see him to-day. But I had a long talk with the Archbishop, who is very reasonable and clear-headed. He sees, I think, that all must end in a compromise. But there will be difficult times intervening.

[*To M. V. B.*]   WINDSOR CASTLE,
                      JANUARY 23RD.

. . . The King is less depressed than he was, because undoubt- *Easier* edly the fix in which the Ministers find themselves makes it *Position of* impossible for them to bully him. On the other hand, I think *the Crown.* circumstances may arise in which his responsibility will be all the greater, as an absolute deadlock is not out of the question. If the Irish turn against Asquith on the Budget (which they have always disliked) he could not pass it without the assistance of his political opponents.

Altogether it is a queer situation, and on the whole not a bad one for the country. The Archbishop was here all day and *The* preached a political sermon in the private chapel. He wrote a *Archbishop* very sensible letter this afternoon to Francis Knollys offering, *as Mediator.* should it become necessary, to act as mediator between the two parties. No one would be more suitable. But my opinion now is, that Asquith will be forced by circumstances to throw in his lot with the Irish, and to commit the Liberal Party to Home Rule.

Barrie is at O'Lea, and I will tell you any news I may pick up from him when I write to-morrow.

[*To the Rt. Hon. A. J. Balfour.*]   WINDSOR CASTLE,
                                          JANUARY 24TH.

The recent elections have caused great relief here. Under no circumstances now can affairs take altogether the turn which we discussed at Whittingehame. There can be no question, with this lowered majority, dependent upon the Irish, of Asquith trying to "bully" the King. So you can imagine that the tension is somewhat relaxed. The Archbishop was here yesterday and talked very sensibly about the situation.

If it becomes necessary at any time to use an intermediary between Asquith and you, I think the King could hardly do better than employ the Archbishop, who is no partisan, and who, although he is not brilliant, has plenty of common sense. It is clear now that the country has refused a "mandate" to the present Government.

There is no majority of the nation either for the Budget or for the destruction of the House of Lords.

Forecast of Liberal Policy.

As for the *immediate* future, judging from Asquith's character (not a strong one), he will probably choose the line of least resistance, which I imagine to be a close alliance with the Irish members; and, having chosen it, he will probably prove exceedingly obstinate and tenacious of the policy which I suppose must form the basis of such an alliance, i.e. an attack on the veto of the H. of L. and a measure of Home Rule for Ireland.

It is *possible* that Asquith may be asked here at the end of the week.

[*To M. V. B.*]   ORCHARD LEA,
                                   JANUARY 24TH.

I have been at the Castle to-day, and only got back late.
Barrie was here yesterday. He read aloud in the green library
two one-act plays which he is producing at the Repertory
Theatre. They are very good. One is gloomy, the other much
lighter in his whimsical vein. You will see them both. They
propose a triple bill. These two plays with a fragment by
George Meredith—which Barrie got from the old poet's
executors.

. . . I wrote a long memo. on the political situation for the
King at H.M.'s request. Not bad. Now I am about to compose
a preface for my volume of essays which is coming out soon.
All these scraps which I glean from old magazines. It will not
be a volume that will take the town by storm!

As I have just finished reading the scene in the *Dynasts* which
describes Godoy dallying with the Queen of Spain, while
Murat and his cavalry were at the gates of Madrid, you must
forgive the levity of these pages.

[*Journals.*]   WINDSOR CASTLE,
                                 JANUARY 24TH.

Barrie read us two new one-act plays last night. Wonderfully
good. Oliver is home, defeated and disappointed, but bearing
defeat well.[1]

The elections leave the Irish in command of the situation so
far. It is perfectly plain that the country has refused a mandate
to the present Government.

There is no majority of the nation either for the Budget or for
the destruction of the H. of L. On the other hand, we must
regretfully admit that there is no clear pronouncement in favour
of an overwhelmingly strong Navy or other measures of

---

[1] He contested Huntingdon as a Liberal.

Imperial Defence, military and commercial, which, if they desire to remain a great nation, the people ought to force their rulers to adopt. . . .

[*To M. V. B.*]   WINDSOR CASTLE,
                                                  JANUARY 25TH.

The King
on the Peers—   I had a talk with the King this morning. It was mainly on the political situation. He is quite clear that he will not assent to any request to make Peers. I told him of my interview with Arthur Balfour, and that *he* was clear also that the King should refuse, and if necessary he would come to the King's assistance. Of course the result of the election makes the position of the King much more secure.

—on
Germany—   Then he began about Germany and lamented Blatchford's violence. He is writing to the Emperor a letter of congratulation on his birthday, and proposes to say that the two countries have no cause for quarrel or jealousy, and that the Press should not be allowed to stir up ill-feeling.

   Prince Henry of Prussia is coming over here on a private visit next week. He is going to stay with Prince Louis of Battenberg, I think. The King says the Crown Prince is a charming boy, and very English in all his sympathies and tastes.

—on
Kitchener—   Then he passed on to Kitchener and is violently in favour of sending him to India. I suggested that he was a bit too old, and told him that Morley disliked the idea very much. I suggested that he should see J. M. about it. He scoffed at the idea of Beauchamp; and rightly. I still think Charles Hardinge would make the best Viceroy.

—and on
Fisher.   Then he said a few words about Jackie Fisher, who retires to-day—his birthday. He laments his loss—and says, "Lady Londonderry and Walter Long think they are going to govern the country, with Charles Beresford in the background, but they will find their mistake." It is quite true.

[*To M. V. B.*]   2, TILNEY STREET,
                                   JANUARY 26TH.

. . . I came up from Windsor to-day, after our dinner at the
Castle last night. Nellie was specially asked to meet the
"Belgian mission," sent over to announce the accession of the
new King. It was a very long affair. We did not get away till
12. The Queen was in tremendous spirits. This evening I dined
at Lincoln's Inn. It was my father's old Inn, so I always go
there when they invite me.

Then I joined the others at *Beethoven*. I got in in time to hear
the lovely music. Old Tree [1] is wonderfully striking in the
part. I must go back to Windsor to-morrow.

The weather has turned very cold. In France, and particularly
along the Seine, there are terrible floods, sweeping away all the
boats and cottages anywhere near the river. Terrible losses
and devastation.

Oliver had an interview with J. Morley to-day, and told
him he was off to America. He goes on the 9th. It is an excellent
thing. I am sending him to see Bryce, our Ambassador at
Washington, to learn the hang of American politics. It gives
him a fresh interest after his disappointment.

[*To the Rt. Hon. A. J. Balfour.*]   WINDSOR CASTLE,
                                       JANUARY 27TH.

You will be amused to hear that after the King—with some
difficulty—screwed himself up to ask Asquith here on Saturday,
A. has refused! You can imagine that this is causing some
annoyance. So Crewe and Grey are coming, and Morley on
Monday. It is plain that so far the Government have not settled
anything, and I should doubt any of them knowing their own
minds.

Cabinet Uncertainty.

Winston Churchill, however, has been telling me that there

---

[1] Afterwards Sir Herbert Beerbohm Tree.

is only one possible policy, which is not to swerve from their original course.

J. Morley told *him* that the idea was preposterous and childish. I am hoping that the next few days will weaken them a bit more.

[*To M. V. B.*]   ORCHARD LEA,
                                             JANUARY 28TH.

. . . Yesterday morning, as I think I told you, I spent talking to the Princess of Wales. She, as usual with me, spoke almost entirely about her family affairs, and I got an opportunity of saying a few things which I hope will be helpful to her in the future.

. . . *This* morning, as a corrective to the Merry Wid.[1] with whom (as I told you) I spent last evening, I was two hours with the *Prince* of Wales. He is pessimistic about his own future, in years to come, and I did not give him much comfort.

The King is much annoyed with Asquith, who was invited to Windsor and has refused. He is going abroad. The Queen would never have stood this, but the King is far too good natured. *So* good natured that the common type of Minister takes liberties. It *is* common for a Prime Minister to refuse the Sovereign, because, unlike a private person, the Sovereign cannot retaliate.

[*To M. V. B.*]   ORCHARD LEA,
                                             JANUARY 30TH.

No agreed   Edward Grey and Crewe were at Windsor to-day. They
Government   both say Asquith is "done up" and requires rest, but they both
Policy.   think it unfortunate that he should have to go abroad at this juncture. As Lord Roberts said to me this afternoon, "Prime

[1] Miss Lily Elsie.

Ministers should not get 'done up.' " It is a quite sound doctrine. Grey says he thinks they will have "trouble among themselves" when the Cabinet meets. Crewe does not agree with him. But I think Grey is right. They both agree that Winston Churchill has shown marked improvement during the elections, in grasp and tone. They both say "the other one" [1] is incorrigible. *Nous verrons!* Twenty years ago, much the same thing could have been said of Chamberlain.

It is plain from the talk of these Ministers that although the session approaches, they have no settled policy. Indeed, they have discussed nothing! They both say that John Burns was not educated enough to be Home Secretary. I suppose Loulou Harcourt will go there. He will not like it—having to forcibly feed Suffragettes, although he hates them. But he hates abuse and unpopularity more.

Voilà, all my news. I wrote an excellent little lecture for the King to-day, urging him not to agree to any reform of the Constitution which did not deprive him of the power of creating more than a fixed number of Peers in any one year. This is to safeguard the Crown and the Constitution!

[*To M. V. B.*]　　　　　　WINDSOR CASTLE,
　　　　　　　　　　　　　　　JANUARY 31ST.

I have been here all day, and am not very well. The King wants me when he gets back from shooting, so I cannot get away until late.

. . . Stanley has just rung up to say that there were over 240 *Growth* "Islanders" in this morning. There are over 3,000 now and they *of the* keep coming by every post. It is a wonderful success, and they *"Islanders."* have done a great deal of work all through the election. It is very curious, because we took no special trouble, and the thing has just burst into flame after smouldering for some time.

[1] Mr. Lloyd George.

Lawrence has been nearly off his head—and they have had to increase their staff by three extra hands!

[*To the Rt. Hon. A. J. Balfour.*]   WINDSOR CASTLE,
                                                     JANUARY 31ST.

One or two things are clear.

Summary of the Political Situation.

(*a*) That so far the Cabinet have no policy and that Asquith left England without giving his colleagues any idea what he proposes to do.

(*b*) That the centre of Cabinet gravity has shifted somewhat towards the so-called moderates.

(*c*) That Spender—representing what section I know not—is urging A. to keep his pledge about the H. of L. and to put the veto bill in the forefront of the battle.

(*d*) That Lloyd George and Winston Churchill are contemplating a Navy Loan!!!

(*e*) That John Morley is very anxious about *India*. The native army is showing signs again of disloyalty.

I told you that he and A. both wished *me* to go to *India*; and I flatly and finally refused. J. M. then thought of Balfour of Burleigh and inclines to him still.

I am sure that there is only one man who—at this juncture—ought to go, and that is Lord Kitchener.

Personally I have an intense disbelief in Press Laws and expedients of that kind in Oriental countries, and I *do* believe in personal prestige.

But J. M. and Asquith dislike the idea of a *soldier*. This seems to me folly. We return to London to-morrow. I hope your dentist was successful. So sorry to hear about it.

[*To M. V. B.*]   2, TILNEY STREET,
                               FEBRUARY 1ST.

The Necessity for Kitchener as Viceroy.

. . . J. Morley came to Windsor, and we had a long discussion about the situation in India. Minto has broken down and will have to come home. There is great nervousness about the Indian Army. Every sort of repressive measure is asked for, and the Council, including O'M. Creagh, asked for "martial law."

If I were J. M. I should send Lord K. out there, on condition that he asked for no fresh "powers," and governed India.

I am sure he would do it, for the prestige of his name is great. Lord Roberts opposes K., but it is a little bit of jealousy in the old man, of a posthumous kind. Morley again asked *me* to go, but I told him I would rather break stones.

I urged the King to press J. M. about K., and I think this made an impression on his republican soul!

[*To M. V. B.*]   2, TILNEY STREET,
                                                FEBRUARY 2ND.

. . . I saw Loulou Harcourt this evening. He is posing as the statesman weary of politics—tired of the H. of C. This is probably preparatory to migrating to the H. of L.—in spite of his professed hostility to that chamber. It will be very amusing to see the extremists gradually making tracks to the red benches and the scarlet robes before they are altogether abolished, or dyed green.

. . . I send you a paper I have just written for the Defence Committee. You can show it to the General [French]. It was written to *try* and interest Asquith, and induce him to appoint the Committee I want. *Nous verrons.* I am not very sanguine.

[*To M. V. B.*]   2, TILNEY STREET,
                                                FEBRUARY 4TH.

. . . I was late, too, last night, dining with Knollys and Jack Sandars. Everyone is absorbed by the doubtfulness of the political future. The Tories are trying to hammer out a new constitution by altering the composition of the H. of L. with

Uncertainty in Political Circles.

fancy qualifications, etc. And the Radicals are bewildered by many counsels and the silence of their chief, who has given no one an idea of his plan. He returns next Monday. If he is a fighter, he will at once approach the King, and, on the latter's refusal to help him, will resign. But he is not a fighter. At least I don't think so. The Government will more likely drift into ineffectiveness and so into contempt with their own people. This will mean another election in the autumn. That is the political outlook to-day.

[*To M. V. B.*]   ORCHARD LEA,
                                       SUNDAY, FEBRUARY 6TH.

. . . I went to see Bobs, poor little man—who is getting smaller—never a good sign in the old. Still, he is boiling over with patriotic fervour, and I urged him to write a *book*, giving a final message to the country on the demands of modern war— if it ever has to be waged in defence of these shores.

[*To M. V. B.*]   2, TILNEY STREET,
                                              FEBRUARY 7TH.

. . . As I was reading your letter for the second time, Zena walked in here. She, too, had got a letter from you. It was a pure fluke, as it was the first time she had been home for weeks. . . . She looked *charming*. And she was very, very sweet.

[*To M. V. B.*]   2, TILNEY STREET,
                                              FEBRUARY 8TH.

. . . I hear that Lord Kitchener will probably *not* take up the Malta Command. He will not sit on the Defence Committee, and if he does not go to India as Viceroy, he wishes to be Secretary of State for War! This is authentic. He *might* hold office under the Tories![1]

[*To M. V. B.*]   2, TILNEY STREET,
FEBRUARY 11TH.

To-day has been rather full of incident. There appeared this morning Redmond's threat that his people would vote against the Budget, when reintroduced in the H. of C.[2] I saw Arthur Balfour, who wanted to see me, and found him enormously interested in the new situation which is thus created, and by no means clear what the attitude of the Tories should be. So much depends upon what effect the Irish threat has upon Asquith, and what occurs at the Cabinet to-day. He is inclined to think that if the Irish move an amendment to the Budget the Tories should walk out of the House.

Redmond's Threat to the Liberals.

That is my opinion. If I were he, I would not follow Redmond! The question is, will Asquith yield to their pressure? ... This evening Haldane and Bron Lucas dined with me and we went off to the Adelphi.[3] It was a really fine sight. 1500 people

Territorials see "The House of Temperley."

[1] Three months later Lord Morley wrote:—

WIMBLEDON,
MAY 3RD.

MY DEAR ESHER,

Lord K. is to dine with me on May 13th. Only 4 of us in all. Will you be kind enough to make one? Pray *do.*

Yours,
J. M.

Private room, Carlton.

[2] Mr. Redmond maintained that the Government was pledged to open at once upon the House of Lords, and that if they broke this pledge by putting the Budget first it would be the duty of the Irish to vote against them.

[3] To see *The House of Temperley.*

all in uniform—no women—*such* an audience. Conan Doyle [1] and Barrie came to our box. I am sending you the account from the *Daily Telegraph* and keeping you the programme. Then Bron and I went and sat at the Carlton for a bit, drinking coffee. The prize fights were better done than ever. Barrie thought it all quite excellent of its kind. I wished so much you had been there. You would have liked the enthusiasm and the pretty sight too.

[*To M. V. B.*]   ORCHARD LEA,
                                   FEBRUARY 12TH.

This morning I was at the British Museum for the Committee of Printed Books, and then the Standing Committee. We had a wonderful lot of large Chinese pictures, XVIth century, submitted—quite wonderful. There is nothing like them in Europe. They are really *beautiful*, which is so odd. I drove home, as usual, with the Prince of Wales, and talked politics most of the time. Haldane told me last night that the Government had decided to *defy* Redmond, to go on with their Budget at once, and not hurry with their veto bill.

Liberals and the Irish Party.

It is most unexpected, and highly creditable to Asquith. He goes to Brighton to-day to see the King. He is *not* going to ask the King for any assurances at this stage, feeling that he is not

---

[1] Sir Arthur Conan Doyle had written:—

                                   WINDLESHAM, SUSSEX,
                                   JANUARY.

DEAR LORD ESHER,

Let me thank you in the first instance for the honour you have done me in choosing my play for a territorial night. I have never had any honour come my way which I appreciated more. Mr. Hardy wrote to me about a speech, but it seems to me the men will enjoy it all the better without me. I hate making—and I fancy most people hate hearing—speeches.

I shall hide in a box, as I shall not be in uniform.

                                   Yours, etc.
                                   ARTHUR CONAN DOYLE.

justified in doing so, with so small a majority. He is merely
going to say that the Budget will be proceeded with, and that
if the Irish defeat the Government they will resign.

Whether the Ministry will contrive to show all this degree
of backbone is doubtful, but at present they are much to be
commended.

[*To M. V. B.*]   ORCHARD LEA,
                                       FEBRUARY 13TH.

I forgot to tell you that Arthur Balfour found Chamberlain
—with whom he lunched on Friday—very unintelligible. It
was altogether painful. Mrs. Chamberlain was there and acted
as interpreter. She seemed so much better able to understand.
The poor man was absolutely paralytic, and it is inconceivable
that his brain power should not correspond in a great degree to
the physical condition in which he finds himself.

[*To M. V. B.*]   2, TILNEY STREET,
                                       FEBRUARY 16TH.

In these stirring times, although I cannot post this letter, you
may like to know the changes in the political kaleidoscope. I
saw Arthur Balfour for about half an hour this morning. He has
quite recovered in health and spirits. His view is, that whatever
the Irish do, it is impossible for the Tory party *not* to vote
against the Budget. They were elected to do so, and would
never be forgiven or understood if they failed.

Balfour and the Irish Party.

There is conquering force in this. We had a good deal of discussion about a Tory socialist policy, which is, I am sure, vital if
headway is to be made in future.

At luncheon with J. Morley I heard that the King's Speech is
moderate and that the Cabinet are united upon a course of
action. They will *not* give way to the Irish. Lloyd George was
to interview Redmond to tell him. Winston Churchill brought

J. M. a letter some time back from Asquith offering him the Irish Office; and his draft refusal, in which he said he preferred remaining where he was.

J. M. advised him to *rewrite* the letter and ask for the Home Office. This he did, and got it.

Loulou Harcourt, they say, behaved well, and showed no pique at being passed over. I fancy he hated the idea of being Home Secretary on account of the hangings and forcible feeding.

[*To the Rt. Hon. J. S. Sandars.*]   ORCHARD LEA,
                                             MARCH 3RD.

The Navy and the Tories.

I am slightly better to-day. So many thanks for your letter.

1. Arthur Lee last night in the H. of C. It is very serious. There are over 10,000 Islanders, all real workers, not nonsense people, who will organise against him and the Unionist candidates in future unless they repudiate him. This is sure to happen unless he can put himself right. Last night he went out of his way to endorse C. Beresford's view that *we* are "wild men." I like Arthur Lee, and am very sorry that he should have said what he did. I am taking the report of *The Times*. I have been flooded with telegrams on the subject.[1]

2. Look at page nine of *The Times*, at a letter signed Z. It may make you laugh. In bed, there is nothing to do but write squibs.[2]

[1] Mr. Lee rejected the two keels to one demanded by "The Islanders" and reverted to the old Two-Power Standard. The inference that he agreed to the term "wild men," however, does not of necessity follow from the debate. The whole discussion was made a little confused by the incoherence of Lord Charles Beresford.

[2] The letter reviews the situation of the House of Lords in the light of the peerages given to Mr. H. Gladstone and Mr. Ivor Guest, and adds: "No one in 1832 would have believed that Lord Grey really intended to pass the Reform Bill by a violent wrench of the Constitution if in 1831 he had preluded his campaign by creating two rotten boroughs."

3. As for your great policy, I am too feeble just now to write
about it. Reasonable reform, based on (*a*) constitutional experience, (*b*) historical sequence, I do not object to. But I am deadly
opposed to the views of those who think the "hereditary principle" defensible in 1900 and indefensible in 1910; who want to
go one better than Lloyd George, and call that statesmanship;
who do not desire to "broaden" the bases of our Institutions but
to tear them up by the roots.

Perhaps if I wrote reams I could not say more. But I will
write again.

[*To Lord Morley.*]   2, TILNEY STREET,
                                            APRIL 9TH.

Hélas! I go to Scotland to-morrow (Sunday night) till
Thursday. But immediately I get back I shall ask to see you.
All the pundits say that the Budget will go through. If that is
so, perhaps the crisis may be postponed until after the holidays!
Personally I dislike the Grey and Haldane policy—intensely.
There is very little "clear thinking" about it, to my mind. How-
ever, these things must wait until I have had a blow in the
northern hills.

[*To H.M. the King.*]   2, TILNEY STREET,
                                            APRIL 10TH.

Viscount Esher, with humble duty, thinks Your Majesty *Liberal*
should know that he had an urgent request from Lord Morley *Manœuvres.*
to call to-day, in view of the fact that Viscount Esher is going
to-night to Scotland for a few days and Lord Morley was most
persistent that he should call before his departure.

Accordingly he motored to Wimbledon on his way to
London from Windsor, and found Lord Morley in much doubt

and hesitation upon the course which he should take at the Cabinet appointed for to-morrow.

The Cabinet are to be asked to adopt the following policy, and to commit themselves to it by an act, which Viscount Esher will describe presently.

After setting forth five different eventualities which might lead to the defeat of the Government upon the "Veto" resolutions or upon a Veto Bill, it is assumed that a moment would come when the Prime Minister would ask Your Majesty to dissolve Parliament. Your Majesty's Ministers would then *warn* Your Majesty, and this is the phrase used, that in the event of a majority being returned in favour of the Government Veto Bill, they would not remain in office, or attempt to pass any measure through the House of Commons, unless they had obtained from Your Majesty an assurance that Your Majesty would create Peers enough to pass the Veto Bill through the House of Lords.

If the Cabinet agree upon this course of procedure, they will proceed to the act of which Viscount Esher spoke earlier in the letter. The act in question is to communicate confidentially their decision to the leaders of the Irish and Labour Parties, and to certain of their own supporters in the House of Commons.

Secondly, that, in the event of a dissolution, the Prime Minister would, prior to the Election, communicate this political procedure to the country. Your Majesty can imagine that a policy of so unprecedented and tortuous a kind, having its origin solely in a desire to buy the vote of the Irish party, is not viewed with favour by Lord Morley.

Morley's Dissent.

Yesterday, he had an interview, of quite a friendly character, with Mr. Churchill, and expressed his unwillingness to sanction the procedure contemplated. Mr. Churchill, without any display of temper, but with great firmness, said that in the event of its rejection by the Cabinet, he and the Chancellor of the Exchequer would resign. As Lord Morley then proceeded to ask Viscount Esher's opinion, he ventured to tell him plainly that it would be a lamentable outcome of Lord Morley's long training and experience in statesmanship, if he were to lend his name and authority to a policy of menace to the Crown, and of parliamentary corruption.

The intention of those advocating this course of action is to purchase the assent of the Irish representatives to a Budget of which they disapprove, and the price given is to threaten Your Majesty, with a view ultimately of inducing Your Majesty to assist in a *coup d'état*.

Viscount Esher urged upon Lord Morley, in view of the high character he bears, and the affectionate regard in which he is held by many who have known him intimately for years, the imperative necessity of retiring from the Cabinet, if the policy in question is adopted.

Viscount Esher has written this hurriedly, as he is leaving almost immediately for Callander, but he is anxious that Your Majesty should know the details of this curious interview. He ventures to beg that Your Majesty will not show this to anyone except to Francis Knollys.

[*To the Rt. Hon. A. J. Balfour.*] 2, TILNEY STREET,
APRIL 10TH.

I am just off to Scotland. J. Morley wired most pressingly for me to see him before I left. It was to consult about his personal position. He is old, and his power of deciding is weak. It is humiliating to be dragged into devious courses by men who are his inferiors in experience and intellect. *On Morley's Position.*

I hope he will come out of the Government. If so, the event must be very near. Probably to-morrow. *Nous verrons.* I shall call and see you when I get back on Friday.

[*To M. V. B.*] 2 TILNEY STREET,
APRIL 21ST.

. . . After that I spent the whole morning with Joe Duveen. We went to Gill and Reigate and afterwards to the Tate Gallery.

The wing added by his father and himself will be lovely. Gorgeous room.

. . . Then had tea with Arthur Balfour. He is more than reasonable and really anxious about the coming crisis, with every desire to come to an arrangement, if possible. Barrie lunched with me. He was in tearing spirits though he had an abominable cold. Possibly he may come to O'Lea on Sunday. It is doubtful, however. . . . Then we went to *Twelfth Night*. That little Terry girl,[1] aged 17, had a stupendous success. Viola could not be better done. She sings charmingly and her speaking voice has been beautifully trained.

[*To the Rt. Hon. A. J. Balfour.*]   2, TILNEY STREET,
APRIL 25TH.

I have just seen Francis Knollys, who tells me that the Archbishop is most anxious that you and I and Francis Knollys should dine with him at Lambeth on Friday.

That I understand is the day, and the hour would be 8.15. They want me to *sound* you, as to whether you would dine? Will you?

[*Memorandum of a Conference at Lambeth.*[2]]   LONDON,
APRIL 27TH.

The Archbishop's Informal Conference.

The Archbishop of Canterbury received Mr. Balfour, Lord Knollys, and Lord Esher at Lambeth to-day at 3 o'clock.

The Archbishop said that he should not have ventured of his own initiative to trouble Mr. Balfour, but that Lord Knollys had made a suggestion which, in view of the grave matters at

---

[1] Miss Phyllis Neilson-Terry.

[2] The phrasing of this memorandum has been corrected in places in the handwriting of the Archbishop.

issue, he could not but adopt. He felt that as the King had already spoken to him upon the subject of the House of Lords, and might do so again, he was anxious to clear his mind and formulate his ideas.

To this end, he had ventured to ask Mr. Balfour to come to Lambeth, in the hope that Mr. Balfour would give him some assistance in unravelling the tangle in which he felt himself involved.

From what had fallen from the Prime Minister lately in Parliament, it seemed plain that the time was not far distant when the King would be asked either to create 500 Peers for the purpose of passing the "Veto" Bill through the present Parliament, or, to grant a dissolution coupled with a promise to create Peers in the event of a Liberal majority being returned after the Election.

The King's course in the former of these contingencies seemed clear, but in the latter it was not so simple to determine, and much would depend—indeed the future of the Monarchy itself might depend—upon the substance and form of the King's reply.

Mr. Balfour thought that the King, should His Majesty determine to refuse, should do so in a carefully worded document —so carefully worded as to show no bias towards either party or policy, and that this document should be read by the Prime Minister in Parliament. The Archbishop observed that the difficulty of formulating such a document lay in the well-nigh impossibility of avoiding the Scylla of appearing to side with the Unionist Party, and not falling into the Charybdis of appearing to dance to the Liberal Pipe, by saying beforehand that he would acquiesce, if a Liberal majority was returned to Parliament. *Balfour on a Policy for the Crown.*

Mr. Balfour said that it would require care, but that in his opinion a satisfactory document could be framed and, if successfully framed, would add much lustre to the position of the Sovereign. He pointed out that if the King refused the Prime Minister's proposal the Government would resign, and that he,

Mr. Balfour, would then form a Government, and immediately ask the King to grant him a dissolution.

He would not attempt to carry on the Government with a minority in the House of Commons, nor would he ask Mr. Asquith for support. His treatment of the whole question of supply would depend on the circumstances, and upon communication with the permanent officials of the Treasury.

He strongly suspected that the Government intend by every means, however unscrupulous and tricky, to prevent a dissolution by their opponents, and this inference is only a natural one from their attitude in Committee of Supply, and the short votes on account. He was not prepared to say that they would succeed and that the position could not be turned.

Lord Esher suggested that there was an alternative before the King, who might follow the example of 1884 and endeavour to arrange a compromise. Mr. Balfour could not see that any compromise was possible in view of the relations between the Government and the Irish, as no compromise could be imagined which would not be fatal to Home Rule.

Possibility of Referendum—

Lord Knollys mentioned the word Referendum, and Mr. Balfour at once said that upon that question he had an open mind, although he gathered that Mr. Asquith had now rejected the idea although he was once favourable to it.

—or Compromise.

Lord Esher then suggested that upon the first portion of the Government Scheme some accommodation might be found were the Government to abandon the plan of making the Speaker the deciding authority in regard to "tacking," and upon the second portion at the instance of the House of Lords, should any bill be rejected twice by that House.

Mr. Balfour agreed that in 1884 compromise appeared impossible because of the unbending attitude of Mr. Gladstone, who insisted upon "Franchise first"; but when Lord Salisbury offered to accept "one member constituencies" on the understanding that a redistribution bill should be passed simultaneously with the Franchise Bill, Mr. Gladstone was constrained by public opinion to give way.

And Lord Esher argued from this illustration that Mr. Asquith would be unable to resist a reasonable compromise, if based on a "Referendum" to the people of questions at issue between the two houses.

Lord Knollys asked whether it would be unconstitutional or in any way improper for the King to propose this or any form of compromise. Mr. Balfour could see no objection, but he was silent upon the specific points alluded to by Lord Esher. *The King's Intended Rôle.*

Lord Knollys said that the King might ask for information as to the meaning of the Preamble of the Bill, and the Archbishop laid great stress upon the right of the Sovereign to ascertain whether the "Veto" Bill was a temporary measure intended to bridge over a period while some undivulged policy was maturing.

Mr. Balfour pointed out the logical absurdity of the supposed plan of the Government, who in the preamble of their Bill indicated the necessity for a second Chamber, and in the body of their Bill proceed to abolish its functions.

Lord Knollys then summed up the discussion by making it clear that Mr. Balfour would come to the King's assistance if His Majesty refused the "advice" of his present Ministers to dissolve Parliament, and that there was no objection to the King proposing a compromise if any reasonable basis could be found.

The Archbishop, who was overdue at St. Paul's, thanked Mr. Balfour for coming to Lambeth, and the Conference ended.

[*Journals.*] LONDON, MAY 3RD.

Interview with Mr. Balfour, the Archbishop of Canterbury, and Francis Knollys at Lambeth on 27th April recorded in a memo.

Yesterday the Archbishop telegraphed to me to go again to see him. We had an hour's talk at Lambeth yesterday evening, accordingly, at 6.30. Also recorded in memo. . . .

[Journals.]   LONDON,
                                              MAY 7TH.

The King is dead. . . .

The King is Dead.

The currents of life are inscrutable, and no one can read the writing on the wall of fate. The loss of the King at this moment seems irreparable. He stands for our country, our Empire, and all our people in the eyes of Europe and of the world. So much did his personality count, that many virtues were attributed to him and many acts which he was the first to laugh at. No man ever knew more truly his strength and weakness.

Experience, knowledge, instinct, not reflection, made him a statesman. I remember Soveral saying to him once, "Vous êtes un grand diplomate, un homme d'état remarquable, et vous l'ignorez." The King looked puzzled for a moment and smiled. He knew himself so well. Soveral was right. He had an instinct for statecraft which carried him straight to the core of a great problem, without deep thought or profound knowledge of the subject. He had one supreme gift, and this was his unerring judgment of men—and women.

With this clear-sightedness he never allowed his likes and dislikes to interfere. He weighed men's capacity for work in hand with almost unfailing skill. He saw through all attempts to cajole or mislead him, and stratagem availed nothing to those who were misguided enough to use it. . . .

Towards politicians, even towards those who worried him, I never knew him to be unjust. He often condemned them, but not unkindly; for his perfect straightforward honesty could not sympathise with the attitude of mind which yields a strong conviction to the exigencies of party—but he never failed to comprehend.

His friends, therefore, were not chosen among political combatants. Single-minded devotion to himself, as man and Sovereign, he never failed to appreciate. Genius he invariably recognised, even though its luckless possessor was as much abused as Mr. G. or Jackie Fisher.

The latter he thoroughly believed in as a great sailor and loved as a man.

To his son he was a charming friend and a generous father. He always wished the Prince to be informed of everything and to keep in touch with public affairs. Jealousy was a word he could not understand—and a thing he could not tolerate in man or woman. . . .

I can only write of him as a master and friend—and the kindest and most considerate that a man could have. If he gave his confidence, it was given absolutely. To me he was never once inconsiderate, and whenever I had from him a word of reproach, I generally deserved it.

I have known all the great men of my time in this land of ours, and many beyond it. He was the most kingly of them all.

END OF VOL. II.

NOTE ON THE INDEX

This index includes a certain number of very broad headings designed to enable a reader to follow a single topic right through the book. They are distinguished typographically, being printed in large capitals.

These are the general heads included:

THE ARMY

BOOKS AND AUTHORS

CAREER

CONSTITUTIONAL ISSUES

THE CROWN

FOREIGN AFFAIRS

THE GOVERNMENT

IMPERIAL DEFENCE
    COMMITTEE

IRELAND AND IRISH
    POLITICS

MEDITATIONS

THE NAVY

THE PARTIES

PERSONALITIES

POLITICAL THEORY

THE PRESS

THE ROYAL FAMILY

SOCIAL EVENTS AND
    CHANGES

Under CROWN are the official acts of the sovereign in political affairs: the entries under ROYAL FAMILY are of a more personal nature. The entries under GOVERNMENT refer to the concerted official acts of both Parties: those under PARTIES to their internal affairs. Under the heading PERSONALITIES are the fuller estimates of a character, the minor references being arranged under the name of the person in the usual way.

(*The letters a, b, etc., refer to the items on each page, whether complete on that page or not.*)

INDEX

CONSTITUTIONAL ISSUES:
ministerial breach of confidence,
2*a*, *also* 103*b–04a*, 105*b–06a*;—
necessity of Cabinet unity, 29*b–
30a*;—constitutional position of
Defence Committee, 37;—responsibility of civil servants, 45*b*;—
procedure on change of government, 56, 77*b*, *also* 119*a*, 272*b*;—
precedents for P.M. defeated in
the house, 91*c*;—the House of
Lords, 92*a*, *also* 153*a*, 154;—necessity of official unanimity, 97*a*, *also*
111*ab*, 113*a*;—the rôle of the
Prince Consort, 99*b*;—relation of
Crown and ministers, 103*b–07*, *et
infra*;—precedents governing resignation of P.M., 119*a*;—undue
influence of Volunteers, 168*d*;—
the coronation oath, 202*a*;—first